**AMSCO**® ADVANCED PLACEMENT®
# HUMAN GEOGRAPHY

**AMSCO**® **SCHOOL PUBLICATIONS, INC. ,**
**a division of Perfection Learning**®

*AMSCO® Advanced Placement® Human Geography:* is one of a series of
Advanced Placement® social studies texts first launched with the book now titled
*AMSCO® Advanced Placement® United States History.*

**© 2019 Perfection Learning®**

Please visit our websites at:
*www.perfectionlearning.com*

When ordering this book, please specify:

Softcover: ISBN 978-1-5311-2920-0 or **R742601**
Hardcover: ISBN 978-1-5311-2921-7 or **R742606**
eBook: ISBN 978-1-5311-2922-4 or **R7426D**

1  2  3  4  5  6  EBM  23  22  21  20  19  18

Printed in the United States of America

# Contributors

## Senior Consultant

**David L. Palmer** is a national consultant for AP® Human Geography, and has served as a reader, lead table leader, and test item creator for the AP® Human Geography Exam. He is a frequent speaker and leader at seminars and conferences across the country, and he has taught social studies at Eaglecrest High School in Centennial, Colorado, for more than 20 years. In 2012, he received the Distinguished Geography Teacher Award from the National Council for Geographic Education.

---

## Writers

**Dan Berry**
Former Member, AP® Human
  Geography Test Development
  Committee
Morgantown High School
*Morgantown, West Virginia*

**Christopher Hall**
Former Member, AP® Human
  Geography Test Development
  Committee
Davis School District
*Farmington, Utah*

**Jane Purcell**
AP® Human Geography Exam
  Table Leader
Norman Public School System
*Norman, Oklahoma*

**Dan Snyder**
AP® Human Geography Exam
  Lead Table Leader
Pine Crest School
*Fort Lauderdale, Florida*

**John Trites**
Former Member, AP® Human
  Geography Test Development
  Committee
Acadia University
*Wolfville, Nova Scotia*

**David Valdez**
AP® Human Geography Exam
  Table Leader
Cherry Creek High School
*Greenwood Village, Colorado*

**Tom Wurst**
AP® Human Geography Exam
  Table Leader
Magnolia West High School
*Magnolia, Texas*

---

## Reviewers

**Kenneth H. Keller**
Former Member, AP® Human
  Geography Test Development
  Committee
George Walton Comprehensive
  High School
*Marietta, Georgia*

**David Lanegran**
Former Chair, AP® Human Geography
  Test Development Committee
*Macalester College*
*St. Paul, Minnesota*

**Sharon Shelerud**
AP® Human Geography Exam
  Table Leader
Retired Teacher, Metcalf Middle School
*Burnsville, Minnesota*

**Pam Wolfe**
AP® Human Geography Teacher
Yeshiva of Greater Washington
Silver Spring, Maryland

# Contents

# Unit 2: Population and Migration

# Unit 3: Cultural Patterns and Processes

# Unit 5: Agriculture, Food Production, and Rural Land Use

# Unit 6: Industrialization and Economic Development

# Unit 7: Cities and Urban Land Use

# Preface

This edition of *AMSCO® Advanced Placement® Human Geography* provides a concise narrative, skills instruction and practice, multiple-choice questions, free-response questions, and essential questions designed to help students understand the signficant content and develop the vital skills needed to master the subject. It can be used in classes as either the core textbook or along with other resources.

For teachers, an answer key is available from the publisher.

As of its publication, *AMSCO® Advanced Placement® Human Geography* was up to date with all standards and guidelines published by the College Board. For the latest information on AP® Human Geography courses and the exam, check the human geography section of apcentral.collegeboard.com and advancesinap.collegeboard.org.

# Introduction

## Studying Advanced Placement® Human Geography

The AP® Human Geography course has grown dramatically since it was first introduced in 2001. These are some of the reasons students give for enrolling in AP® courses:

- Evidence that the student has the ability to succeed as an undergraduate
- Increased eligibility for scholarships
- Evidence that taking AP® courses strengthens a college application
- Opportunity to save on college expenses by earning college credit
- Opportunity to test out of introductory college courses
- Evidence that AP® students have better college graduation rates
- Enrichment of the AP® student's high school experience

Because geography is often taught as part of more general social studies courses rather than as a discrete subject, you might feel you have not had much specific instruction in it. And for many students, AP® Human Geography is their first course at the advanced placement level, so it can appear very challenging. This introduction will help you understand the structure of the exam and the content of the course.

## Overview of the AP® Human Geography Exam

The AP® Human Geography exam assesses understanding of geographic concepts and principles. It also looks at knowledge of foundational geographic facts and domain-specific vocabulary. Questions on the exam check a student's ability to use spatial concepts and landscape analysis. Checking for knowledge of the tools and methods used by geographers is also part of the exam. Importantly, part of the exam will assess your ability to use your understanding of the world's geography to analyze or illustrate geographic concepts in the real world. The exam consists of two parts.

| ORGANIZATION OF THE AP® HUMAN GEOGRAPHY EXAM | | | | |
|---|---|---|---|---|
| Section | Question Type | Number of Questions | Timing | Percentage of Total Exam Score |
| I | Multiple Choice | 75 | 60 minutes | 50% |
| II | Free-Response | 3 | 75 minutes | 50% |

Each of these components will be described in this introduction. AP® Examinations, including the Human Geography exam, score student performance on a five-point scale. The following descriptions are used regarding the College Board's recommendation of a student's performance on the exam:

5 = Extremely well qualified

4 = Well qualified

3 = Qualified

2 = Possibly qualified

1 = No recommendation

Another way to think about exam scores is to compare them to the performance of a college student:

- A score of 5 indicates the equivalent to earning a grade of A in the college Human Geography courses.
- A score of 4 is equivalent to a grade of A-, B+, or B.
- A score of 3 is equivalent to a grade of B-, C+, or C.

An AP® score of 3 or higher is usually considered evidence that a student has demonstrated proficiency with the material covered in an introductory college course in human geography.

## The AP® Exam Compared to Classroom Tests

AP® exams are prepared differently than typical classroom tests prepared by a teacher. Teachers select questions to assess whether you have learned the materials that they have taught you. A teacher knows what you read, heard, practiced, and experienced in your course of study and creates a test that addresses those things specifically. Although you may not always know the answer on a test in your classroom, you most likely realized that it was something that had been covered in the reading or classroom activities.

The AP® test is different. It is prepared by a team of college professors and high school teachers from across the country. Because one single exam cannot assess every aspect of human geography, the team makes decisions about what material will be addressed in the test and how it will be presented. Students often find material on the AP® exam that they are not familiar with.

In addition, the AP® exam is designed to be more difficult than tests used in classrooms. A teacher is pleased to see all students demonstrate understanding by performing well on a test. In contrast, the AP® test is designed so that it can identify students that are better prepared from those who are still attempting to master the material. You should not be surprised if you find that many of the questions seem more difficult than you expected. But you should not necessarily be worried because of this. Many other well-prepared students will be experiencing the same feeling. The test writers do not expect that students will do as well on this exam as they do in their own classrooms.

Finally, the AP® exam is scored differently than a classroom test. The cutoffs for the different scores vary a little each year depending on how well a control group of college students enrolled in introductory Human Geography courses who also took the test did. You may feel like you performed poorly on the exam and still receive a score of 5. Much depends on how your performance on the exam compares to that of others who also take it.

## Organization of This Book

Each chapter of this book contains the following elements:

- *Introduction:* This introduction surveys the type of information covered in an AP® Human Geography course and that is tested on the exam.
- *Unit Introduction:* Each of the seven units in the book begins with a list of the chapters in the unit, an overview of the content, and a list of the essential understandings that are covered in the unit.
- *Chapter Narrative:* The 20 chapters are organized according to major themes of human geography as identified by the College Board. Each will present you with the basic vocabulary, concepts, and geographic models of the theme. Additionally, you will find examples from the real world that illustrate key topics.
- *Geographic Perspectives:* This feature focuses on how geographers approach a topic by highlighting the spatial perspective that is distinctive to the field.
- *Key Terms.* At the end of each chapter is a summative list of the vocabulary terms identified in the chapter narrative. Familiarity with these terms will be an important part of your success in understanding AP® Human Geography.
- *Multiple-Choice Questions:* Each chapter is followed by eight multiple-choice items that you can use to review the chapter and check your understanding of it.

- *Free-Response Question:* A sample free-response question is included with every chapter. These are written to mirror the questions on the AP® exam. You should be able to answer them based on reading this book.
- *Think as a Geographer:* This feature at the end of each chapter builds one of the skills used by geographers, such as interpreting maps, understanding networks, recognizing scales of analysis, and defining regions.
- *Write as a Geographer:* This feature at the end of each unit focuses on one of the writing skills needed to answer a free-response question on the AP® exam.
- *Respond to the Chapter Essential Questions:* Each chapter opens with a broad question that is then addressed by the content in that chapter. These questions are repeated at the end of each unit to provide students an opportunity to answer them.
- *Practice Examination:* Following the final chapter is a complete practice examination modeled on the AP® exam.
- *Index:* The index is useful for locating coverage of key terms and topics for review.

A separate Answer Key is available for teachers and other authorized users of the book, and can be accessed through the publisher's website.

## The Study of AP® Human Geography

Geographers, like historians, economists, sociologists, and others, study human behavior and relationships. What makes geographers distinctive from these other groups is that they use a set of skills that emphasize **spatial thinking**. Spatial thinking is a way of looking at things "in space," which means understanding the location and distribution of things in terms of their relationship to other things.

Location, then, is at the heart of all geographic understanding. The thinking skills used by geographers help them understand why things and people are where they are, and why the location of an item or of people with particular traits is important.

Through the study of human geography, you will develop a set of skills which will enable you to think spatially. The AP® Human Geography test contains questions, in both the multiple-choice and free-response sections, that will attempt to assess how well a student can use these skills to analyze geographic information and think spatially. The skills can be grouped into four categories.

### Interpret Maps and Analyze Geospatial Data

Maps are the signature element of geography. Geographers examine maps to look for clues and patterns, and by using the location and distribution of phenomena portrayed on the map. There are specific terms—density, dispersion, etc.—that geographers employ in order to communicate about locations and distributions. This book will teach you how to use those terms.

Geospatial data is any kind of data that can be tied to locations on the planet. It is data that could be mapped, even if it has not been. For example, a list of cities that are located where rivers enter an ocean, or statistics on the number of Hindus who live in each country, or data on the effectiveness of boundary walls at preventing interaction of people are all types of geospatial data. The data might be from ancient handwritten records or a modern satellite.

The AP® Human Geography exam often provides test takers with a small spatial data set and then asks for some kind of analysis or application of the data. Test takers should be able to create a map in their head of this data. An understanding of location is critical.

### Understand Associations and Networks

The ways that phenomena in particular places are connected to each other, and the implications of these connections, is always important to geographers. Sometimes it is a cause-and-effect connection, such as a study of why people decide to migrate from one country to another. Sometimes the connection between phenomena is one of relatedness, such as when different crops, all of which need a similar type of climate and/or terrain, compete for each other in an agricultural region.

Geographers look at the networks which exist between locations, how they evolve, and what their effects are. Networks can be physical, like roads and undersea communication cables. Or, they can be subtler, such as the network connecting divisions of a transnational corporation. In all cases, it is the spatial perspective of geography which is used to understand, explain, and interpret the connections. This book will describe and explain examples of various types of networks which might be encountered as you study.

### Interpret Patterns at Different Scales

Geographers recognize and interpret the relationships among patterns and processes at different scales of analysis. Examination of things at different scales, from the local to the global, is a fundamental component of geographic analysis. Geographers learn to imagine and investigate differences between how a concept applies in a small town, in a country, or to the entire world. A disease that spreads rapidly in a village could have profound effects, but it might appear to be insignificant when seen in a global scale. When studying AP® Human Geography, be aware of how one concept can appear at many scales.

Dr. Ryan presents his controversial theory
proposing that the cow is not flat.

## Define Regions

A region is to a geographer what a time period is to a historian. Regions are areas over which characteristics are shared. Almost any characteristic can define a region: average rainfall, dominant political views, how often people pronounce a particular word, etc.

Regions are separated by boundaries. Boundaries are a fundamental tool of geographic analysis, and geographers are interested in identifying and describing them, and then understanding how they came to be and how they are changing. This is the regionalization process. Some boundaries are clearer than others.

- Some are distinct: the Mississippi River provides a clear dividing line between Illinois and Missouri.
- Some are blurry and include a large transitional zone: the region where most people are Chicago Cubs fans live and the region where most people are St. Louis Cardinals fans live overlaps in southern Illinois.

To fully understand AP® Human Geography, you should be able to demonstrate your understanding of the world's regions in several ways. You should be able

- to write about a specific region, such as New England or Latin America
- to illustrate a concept with examples from two or more different regions
- to analyze or describe multiple characteristics of a single region

# Course Content

Human geography is one of two broad divisions of geography—the other is physical geography. The AP® Human Geography course is divided into seven broad topics:

- *Geography: Its Nature and Perspectives:* Geographers seek to understand the world through spatial analysis. They use location, distance, scale, pattern, and distance to examine the distributions, what causes them, and what results they have. Students of human geography learn to examine the changing interrelationships between places, human-environment interactions, and the evolution of landscapes. Although geographers often use the information provided by other historians, biologists, and other scholars, the perspective of a geographer is distinctive because it focuses on spatial organization.

- *Population and Migration:* Critical to human geography is the human population. Geographers seek to understand the distribution of people on earth, why people decide to live where they do, why they migrate from one place to another, and the effects of migration. The demographic characteristics of populations, such as their birth rates, death rates, and life expectancy, are key to understanding population change.

- *Cultural Patterns and Processes:* The languages, religions, and ethnicities of people vary tremendously. The regional patterns exhibited by these elements of culture are part of human geography. Geographers study conflict, cooperation, cultural exchange, and cultural evolution. In recent years, gender and the cultural role it plays in the spatial distribution of human activities has become a greater component of human geography.

- *Political Organization of Space:* People divide the world into political units, such as countries, cities, and neighborhoods. Geographers are interested in how units at each scale evolved, and how they function both internally and with each other. Political geography examines the forces that create and strengthen countries as well as those that work to tear them apart.

- *Agriculture, Food Production, and Rural Land Use:* Food is central to all human life. Hence, human geographers examine questions relating to how people grow, process, and consume food. Key issues include how and why the techniques and purposes of farmers vary by region, and why farmers decide to grow certain crops in certain places. Geographers study the impact of modern food production on the population, the environment, rural landscapes, and society in general.

- *Industrialization and Economic Development:* The distribution of manufacturing facilities, the reasons why certain industries locate where they do, and how those reasons evolve are essential to understanding the geography of industry. Geographers analyze where resources are located, how people use them, and the impact of resource use on the environment, as well as how sectors of the economy change over time. Large questions include the methods that countries use to develop their economies, and how people respond to economic inequality and the growing economic interdependence in the world.

- *Cities and Urban Land Use:* Geographers study why cities are where they are and how those reasons continue to evolve. They develop models to explain the spatial organization within cities that determine which regions are business districts, cultural zones, residential areas, and manufacturing zones. These models can help explain how urban areas vary from country to country.

These topics can be learned in any sequence and subdivided in several ways. This book is organized into chapters based on the seven topics in the order above. The first topic is covered in Chapters 1 and 2, and there are three chapters devoted to each of the other topics.

# The AP® Exam Questions

The Course and Exam Description describes both the content of AP® Human Geography and the basic skills you need to develop. You can practice these skills throughout the school year in all subject areas.

## Answering the Multiple-Choice Questions

The AP® Human Geography exam includes 75 multiple-choice questions, which students have 60 minutes to answer. This portion of the exam accounts for 50 percent of a student's score. Each question will consist of a stem that can be either a question or statement and five possible choices. One choice is correct and the others are distractors, or incorrect, but are often plausible.

**Analyzing the Stimulus** Some of the multiple-choice questions will refer you to a graphic stimulus, such as a map, chart, graph, or photograph. Take a moment to read the question, refer to the graphic, and then reread the question. Be careful to look at elements of the graphic that may be important:

- *Maps:* Check the scale of the data being represented. Is it showing a local community? a state or province? a country? Look at all information given to you in the map legend. If the map includes a title, it will probably also give you information you can use in answering the question.

- *Graphs:* Check each axis of any graph. Notice where each begins and ends. For example, does the axis go from 0 to 2,000, or did it begin at 1,200 and then end at 2,000? If an axis denotes a time period using years, notice the time period it covers. How big are the intervals or increments between elements on the axes?
- *Photographs:* Clues to interpreting a photograph might not be obvious, but look closely for them. One strategy is to examine the photograph systematically in quarters—top left, bottom left, bottom right, top right—so that you don't miss anything.
- *Tables and Charts:* As with other types of graphics, note carefully titles and any words on the chart. Details such as the geographic scale, units of measurement, and the regions that are included or excluded can give you clues or information that you can use.

Most multiple-choice questions will not have a graphic stimulus. Read them carefully. If, as you are reading the stem, your eyes glance at the choices, and you see what you believe is the correct answer, finish reading the question before you select it. Information given at the end of the stem may reverse any initial interpretation of the question itself. Always note if specific time periods or geographic regions are a part of the question.

**Tips on Making a Choice** You will often know the right answer to a question quickly and with confidence, but sometimes you will not. Here are a few suggestions to help you when you are uncertain about an answer.

| HOW TO ANSWER CHALLENGING QUESTIONS | |
|---|---|
| **Advice** | **Rationale** |
| **Answer every question.** | Your score will be based on how many correct answers you give. Unlike some standardized tests, AP® Human Geography exam does not penalize people for guessing a wrong answer. |
| **Apply what you know.** | If a question asks about a specific place or situation that you have not studied, focus on the general concept that the question addresses. Use what you know to determine the most reasonable answer. |
| **Move forward.** | Since you have 60 minutes to answer 75 questions, you can spend an average of 48 seconds on each question. If you find a question difficult, guess the answer, note the question's number, and return to it if you have time at the end. |

**Recommended Activities** Answering multiple-choice questions is a powerful way to review content and practice skills. Each chapter in this book presents several multiple-choice items to help you check your understanding of important concepts in AP® Human Geography. Often, the questions include a map, diagram, chart, photo, or other source that you need to analyze in order to determine the best answer to the question.

## Answering the Free-Response Questions

There are three free-response questions on Section II of the AP® Human Geography exam. You are expected to answer all three in 75 minutes. That means you have an average of 25 minutes per answer. However, you can divide this block of time in any way you would like, spending more time on one particular question and less time on another. You will be scored based solely on the quality of the content of your response. Try to use correct grammar so that you make your ideas clear, but you will not be penalized for grammatical errors.

**Composing Your Response** The free-response questions used on the AP® Human Geography exam are sometimes called constructed response. This type of question consists of a stem (usually a statement or short, topical introduction) followed by a series of related questions or response prompts. Each chapter in this book ends with a free-response question.

Your response should be written in prose rather than as an outline or a bulleted list. The format, or construction, of your response should reflect that of the question. One method is to use paragraphing to reflect the different parts of the question. Use separate paragraphs for each part of question. Some parts may require multiple paragraphs. For example, if one part of the question asks you to identify and describe three examples of something, you should use a single paragraph for each of the examples.

Another effective method for answering the questions is to label each part of the question. That is, when you are answering part A of the question, label it "A" in your test book. Then label "B," etc. Within each labeled portion of your response, you may still want to use paragraphing to provide clarity to your writing.

**Analyzing the Question** The stem of the free-response question sets up parameters for your response. You can often think of it as a sort of introduction to your answer. You don't need to restate, rephrase, or incorporate the stem in your answer. You do need to pay attention to any limitations it places on you.

Make note of any dates or time periods indicated in the question. Some questions may require you to consider a specific period, such as "in recent decades" or "after 1950". Evidence in your response which falls out of these historical periods will not be counted, even if it otherwise supports your point.

Notice if you are required to provide evidence or examples from specific world regions. As with time periods, information provided from other regions cannot be counted toward your score. The use of world regions on the AP® Human Geography exam is discussed in Chapter 2 of this book.

Many previous questions have asked for information from one or more specific categories. Generally, these are economic, social, cultural, political, demographic, or environmental. Your response should clearly relate to the category or categories indicated in the question.

**Action Verbs** Action verbs are those words in the question's prompts that indicate what you are to do. In the past, the most common verbs have been: identify, define, describe, explain, and discuss.

| RESPONDING TO VERBS USED IN PROMPTS | | |
|---|---|---|
| **Action Verb** | **Definition** | **Expectation** |
| **Identify** | To state a clear, concise, specific answer | Often, a single, well-written sentence is sufficient, but you can add clarifying details. However, do not contradict or add confusion to your original answer. |
| **Define** | To give the precise meaning or the basic qualities of something | Provide a concrete, real-world example to strengthen a definition. |
| **Describe** | To provide a representation in words | Note the attributes or characteristics of a place, idea, or person. |
| **Explain** | To give an account or add details | Offer reasons or examples to make an idea plainly understood. |
| **Discuss** | To offer a considered review | Give factors, definitions, descriptions, explanations, examples, etc. of something. |

Many questions on the AP® Human Geography exam ask students to "identify and explain," or "identify and describe," or "identify and discuss" a concept or situation. In these cases, you are being asked to do two separate things. In general, the "identify" portion of the prompt can be answered in a single sentence which acts like a topic sentence in a paragraph. The "describe/explain/discuss" portion of the prompt can serve as the body of the paragraph. It should clearly relate to whatever was identified in the topic sentence.

If a prompt asks you to describe, explain, or discuss, you will probably need to write approximately one paragraph for each part of the question. For example, "describe two ways that..." would suggest the need for two paragraphs; one for each "way" you describe. In general, use the first sentence of your paragraph to identify the "way" and the remainder of the paragraph to describe it by adding details. The same is true for prompts that ask you to explain or discuss.

**Questions with Graphic Prompts** Some free-response questions contain a graphic prompt such as a graph, table, photograph, or map. As with the graphics in multiple-choice questions, take time to examine and analyze the prompt carefully. Understand how the graphic relates to the question prompt itself. Some parts of the free-response might relate directly to the graphic, while others might be linked more generally by the concept. You don't need to refer to the graphic in those parts of your response. On the other hand, when you are answering the parts of the question that relate to the graphic, you should clearly link your response to evidence in the graphic.

**Questions About Geographic Models** Free-response questions often ask about one or more geographic models. You should be able to comment on the models in several ways:

- *Analyze the model.* You should be able to identify the various elements of the model, understand the role each plays in the model, and know the model is applied. Most models make certain assumptions in order to reduce the number of variables that they consider. You should be aware of these assumptions and how they simplify the world.

- *Apply the model.* Models enable geographers to compare the real world to a potential reality. To apply a model is to examine an actual situation and identify and describe places in which the model and reality are different. If the model is a mathematical one, it means that you should be able to plug in the numbers and make whatever calculations are required.

- *Evaluate the model.* For several reasons, geographic models rarely describe or predict reality perfectly. Human nature is very hard to predict. Decision-making can be arbitrary. Changes in technology and culture have made some models less useful than they once were. Some models fit the cultures they were created in better than they fit other cultures. Be aware of the times and places in which models were developed so that you can explain why or why not a model might be useful in specific situations.

**Questions Requiring Examples** Many of the free response questions on the AP® Human Geography exam ask you to supply more than one example or reason to illustrate or explain a concept. For example, the question might require "two reasons that globalization of culture is increasing" or "three examples of how gendered space is created." To answer these questions, you might want to begin by brainstorming a list of several ideas and selecting the best ones to include in your answer. Provide exactly the number of examples called for in the prompt. You will not get full credit if you provide too few examples. You will be wasting your time if you provide extra examples.

Some questions require you to examine two sides of an issue. You might be asked to give both positive and negative examples of a certain process or trend. Many of the topics studied in geography are complex and can be understood from multiple perspectives. What one person considers a positive, another might view as a negative. Practice seeing topics from opposing viewpoints.

A question may ask that you provide evidence for a concept from a specific category of information, such as economic, social, cultural, political, demographic, or environmental. For example, you could be asked to describe one social impact and one environmental impact of the rise of industrialization in China and Southeast Asia. A social impact could be the changing roles for women. An environmental impact could be the increasing air pollution.

As you study human geography, you can prepare for questions such as the one above by thinking about content in these categories. The chart below gives you more specific examples to think about in each category.

| ORGANIZING CONTENT TO ANSWER QUESTIONS | |
|---|---|
| **Category** | **Examples** |
| **Economic** | • Levels of development<br>• Wealth and poverty<br>• Employment and types of jobs<br>• Structure and sectors of the economy |
| **Social/Cultural** | • Language, religion, and ethnicity<br>• Gender roles<br>• Cultural perspectives and views<br>• Health and welfare |
| **Political** | • Government structure<br>• International relationships<br>• Laws and legal systems |
| **Environmental** | • The physical environment, such as landforms<br>• The natural environment, such as plants and animals<br>• Climate<br>• Pollution and resources |

You might be asked to identify and explain a certain number of things related to a concept. For example, a question might require you to explain two positive and two negative effects of industrial growth in China and Southeast Asia. Considering each category will help you recall information and organize your answer. From the list you brainstorm, you can choose your best ideas. In the case of the question described above, you might decide that positive effects include increased roles for women (social) and increased trade (economic).

You might decide that negatives include increased pollution (environmental) and a decline in industrial jobs in more developed countries (economic).

**General Writing Advice** The principles of good writing that you have learned in school will help you write a good answer to a free-response question:

- *Plan your time.* Take time to plan your answer before you begin writing. A few minutes taken for brainstorming your ideas, selecting good examples, and organizing your response is time well spent.

- *Consider whether to include introductions and conclusions.* You do not need to restate the prompt or write an introduction to your answer. Conclusions are also not necessary. If you choose to write them, information contained in them that responds correctly to the prompt will be considered as part of your answer.

- *Make changes.* If you think of something you would like to add to part A (or B, or whatever) of your response but you have already moved on to another part, simply add it and indicate which part of your response it belongs in. If you write something that you decide you do not want included in your response, draw a line through it and it will not be scored.

- *Do not let grammar, spelling, and handwriting limit you.* Your answer to a free-response question will not be graded on grammar, spelling, or handwriting. So, think of it as a rough draft. Try to use correct grammar, spell words as best you can, and write legibly so that readers understand what you are saying. But focus on the content, not on these other concerns.

**Evaluation of Your Answer** Your answer to a free-response question will be graded using scoring guidelines that are sometimes called a single-point rubric. Each is designed to relate to a single, specific free-response question on the exam.

This type of rubric identifies what correct responses to the writing prompt include and how many points they are worth. When your response is scored, the scorer will be looking for particular information that has been pre-determined to be correct.

Free-response items on the AP® Human Geography exam are generally worth between 6 and 9 points. The number of points depends on the construction of the writing prompt—on how many action verbs were used. Answers should respond to each task, and the readers will look for each one.

Even though one question might be worth 6 points, another 7 points, and the third question 8 points, they each contribute an equal part of the total score represented by the free-response section of the exam. None of the questions are intended to be easier or harder than the others, and none matter more than any other to the overall score.

**Recommended Activities** As with the multiple-choice questions, you should practice writing answers to free-response items. Each chapter in this book contains one which is clearly related to the material contained within the chapter. Each unit concludes with an activity that draws upon content from that entire unit.

Free-response questions from previous AP® exams are available online. If you choose to practice with these, be aware that many of them are meant to cut across the various major topics in the course. Therefore, you may see parts of questions that you have not studied yet. Using the accompanying online scoring guides as a study and review tool is also very helpful.

## Review Schedule

Set up a review schedule as you prepare for the exam in the weeks prior to the test date. Studying with a group of fellow students can be helpful. Below is a sample of a seven-week review schedule, including information on the chapters in this book that cover the content to review. Because AP® tests are given during the first two full weeks of May, this review schedule assumes you begin your review in mid-March.

| PROPOSED REVIEW SCHEDULE | | |
|---|---|---|
| **Week** | **Content** | **Chapters in This Book** |
| 1 | How to Think Like a Geographer | 1, 2 |
| 2 | Population and Migration | 3, 4, 5 |
| 3 | Cultural Patterns and Processes | 6, 7, 8 |
| 4 | Political Organization of Space | 9, 10, 11 |
| 5 | Agriculture, Food Production, and Rural Land Use | 12, 13, 14 |
| 6 | Industrialization and Economic Development | 15, 16, 17 |
| 7 | Cities and Urban Land Use | 18, 19, 20 |

You should also plan to review the information in this introduction. The suggestions and ideas about answering multiple-choice questions and free-response items will be helpful to you.

# UNIT 1: How to Think Like a Geographer

## Unit Overview

More than others who study people, geographers see the world through a spatial perspective. They focus on where people live and why they behave as they do.

### Concepts, Skills, and Tools

To understand the spatial aspects of phenomena, geographers use a broad set of concepts, skills, and tools. One basic concept is distance. For example, how far apart in space are houses in a community? This distance affects everything from how people relate to their neighbors to where stores will open. A geographic skill is an ability to apply spatial concepts to understand how people live.

The most common tool for geographers is a map. A map can show almost any phenomenon that has a spatial distribution. Maps can help people identify and analyze world patterns and processes. For example, mapping the spread of a disease can help public health officials decide what steps to take to counter the spread.

One systematic way to study geographic phenomena is to use Four-Level Analysis. The four levels are comprehension of the basic information, identification of patterns, explanation of how individual phenomena might form a pattern, and prediction of what the pattern might lead to.

### Gathering Information

Traditionally, geographers gathered data through field experiences. To make maps, they carefully measured distances and drew what they saw. Today, geospatial technologies make gathering information far simpler.

---

### Enduring Understandings

I. Geography: Its Nature and Perspectives

    A. Geography, as a field of inquiry, looks at the world from a spatial perspective.

    B. Geography offers a set of concepts, skills, and tools that facilitate critical thinking and problem solving.

    C. Geographical skills provide a foundation for analyzing world patterns and processes.

    D. Geospatial technologies increase the capability for gathering and analyzing geographic information with applications to everyday life.

    E. Field experiences continue to be important means of gathering geographic information and data.

**Source:** *CollegeBoard AP®. Human Geography Course Description. 2015.*

---

# The Spatial Perspective

*Geography is the "WHY of WHERE."*

—National Geographic Society

**Essential Question:** How does the way geographers look at the world differ from that of other scientists?

Geography shares content with many other sciences. Geographers are interested in the phenomena studied by climatologists, botanists, economists, sociologists, and demographers, for example. These scientists study the weather, plants, business, human society, and the characteristics of populations. In this sense, geography is a science of synthesis, a field that integrates the learning of many others. What distinguishes geography from all other fields is that it focuses on a particular perspective, or way of looking at things. That distinctive perspective is spatial.

A **spatial approach** considers the arrangement of the phenomena being studied across the surface of the earth. Important considerations of this approach are things such as location, distance, direction, orientation, pattern, and interconnection. A spatial approach also looks at elements such as the movements of people and things, changes in places over time, and even human perceptions of space and place. Geographers ask questions about spatial distributions such as these:

- Why are things where they are?
- How did things become distributed as they are?
- What is changing the pattern of distribution?
- What are the implications of the spatial distribution for people?

## Geography as a Field of Study

Geography has been called the "mother of all sciences." This is partly because it is one of the oldest fields of study. In addition, it is because geographers are interested in the content of so many other sciences. The word *geography* comes from Greek and combines the idea of studying, or writing about (*-graphy*), with the idea of the earth (*geo-*). So the word *geography* means "earth writing."

## Subfields of Geography

Geography is commonly divided into two major branches:

- **Physical geography** is the study of spatial characteristics of various elements of the physical environment. Physical geographers, like physical scientists, study topics such as weather and climate, ecosystems and biomes, and volcanism and erosion.
- **Human geography** is the study of the spatial characteristics of humans and human activities.

Human geographers share a spatial approach with physical geographers and often rely on information from physical geography and other physical sciences. The concern of human geographers, however, is the human population and the spatial characteristics associated with people. Human geographers specialize in subfields. These subfields include geographers who study the following:

- population (health, births, migrations, etc.)
- culture (language, religion, popular music, etc.)
- economics (agriculture, level of development, wealth distribution, etc.)
- urban areas (cities, suburbs, challenges from growth, etc.)
- politics (local government, nations, distribution of power, etc.)

The degree of specialization in human geography reflects the wide interests of geographers: there is medical geography, environmental geography, social geography, and even the geography of sports. However, all subfields share a spatial perspective and their interest in human populations.

Since geography studies spatial information, maps are one of the most important tools for geographers. Cartography, the art and science of mapmaking, is closely associated with geography. Many geographers are also cartographers and vice versa. Geospatial technologies, such as satellite imagery and remotely sensed data, geographic information systems (GIS), and global positioning systems (GPS) can require technical skill on the part of their scientists. Geographers rely on cartographers to help them organize spatial information.

## The Early History of Geography

For as long as humans have been able to write, they have written "geographies" in their descriptions of place and observations of phenomena on earth. The first maps were probably simply scratched in the soil with sticks by early humans. In the river valleys of the Huang He in China, the Tigris-Euphrates valley in Mesopotamia (modern-day Iraq), and Egypt, ancient people studied geography and made maps.

The Greeks and Romans were the first people in western Eurasia to formalize a study of geography:

- Homer's *Iliad* and *Odyssey* are geographic in nature and point to Greek interest in descriptions of the world.

- Aristotle was a keen observer of the earth and its features and how they influence human behavior.
- Using geometry, Eratosthenes calculated the circumference of Earth from Alexandria in Egypt during the 3rd century B.C.E., and he was very nearly correct. He coined the term *geography*.
- Ptolemy, a Greek who lived about 500 years after Eratosthenes, wrote a summary of Greek knowledge about geography, including the location and size of continents, that dominated European thought for 1,000 years.
- Strabo wrote descriptions of various areas of the Roman Empire and proposed theories about how geography influenced history.

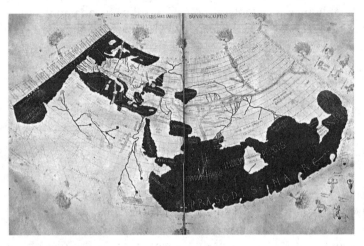

A map based on Ptolemy's view of the world

During the European Middle Ages (about 500 C.E. to 1450 C.E.), Europeans rarely ventured outside their region. But the Muslim culture that flourished in the Middle East and North Africa built strong trading ties with Africa and East Asia. As people traveled, they collected information about new places, created maps, and wrote books about geography. Scholars such as Muhammad al-Idrisi (12th century) and Ibn Battuta (14th century) advanced the study of geography.

### The Modern History of Geography

Starting with the historic voyage of Christopher Columbus in 1492, Europeans launched a new era in exploration, description, and mapping. One important geographer of the early modern period was a Dutch scholar, Gerardus Mercator. He created a world map that was very useful for sailors and is still widely used today. In the late 18th century, a German, Alexander von Humboldt, traveled extensively through South America. His study of the continent's wealth in plants and his detailed, accurate maps combined to spur European interest in the Americas. But most importantly, Humboldt saw the world as a connected whole, in which all types of knowledge contributed to each other. It is this approach that has inspired geographers ever since.

In the early 19th century, European geographers established geographical societies, marking the birth of the formal academic discipline of geography. Early efforts remained focused on the great themes of the discipline that had emerged up to that point: exploring, mapping, gathering data about physical and human geography, and seeking to analyze and understand the diversity of the world's regions.

In the past century, geographers such as Carl Sauer (1889–1975) expanded the focus of geography beyond physical traits of the earth to include human activity. Since then, geography has become increasingly diverse and specialized. Geographers study the spatial distribution of nearly everything to explain what people eat to why they migrate to how they vote.

## Concepts Underlying the Geographic Perspective

Historians look through the lens of time to understand the past. Similarly, geographers look through the lens of space to understand place.

### *Location*

Locations may be absolute or relative. **Absolute location** is the precise spot where something is according to some system. The most widely used system is the global grid of lines known as latitude and longitude. **Latitude** is the distance north or south of the **equator**, an imaginary line that circles the globe exactly halfway between the North and South Poles. The equator is designated as 0° and the poles as 90° north and 90° south.

**Longitude** is the distance east or west of the **prime meridian**, an imaginary line that runs from pole to pole through Greenwich, England. It is designated as 0°. On the opposite side of the globe from the prime meridian is 180° longitude. The **International Date Line** roughly follows this line but makes deviations to accommodate international boundaries. Thus, on this system, the absolute location of Mexico City is 19° north latitude and 99° west longitude.

## THE GLOBAL GRID

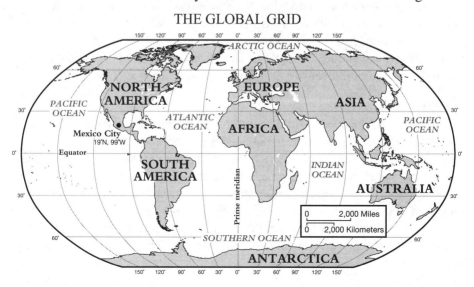

**Relative location** is a description of where something is in relation to other things. To describe Salt Lake City, Utah, as being "just south of the Great Salt Lake and just west of the Rocky Mountains, on Interstate 15 about halfway between Las Vegas, Nevada, and Butte, Montana," is one way (of many) to describe its relative location. Relative location is often described in terms of **connectivity**, how well two locations are tied together by roads or other links, and **accessibility**, how quickly and easily people in one location can interact with people in another location.

THE RELATIVE LOCATION OF SALT LAKE CITY

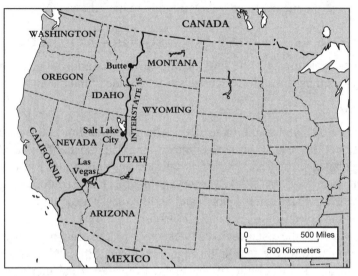

Relative locations can change over time and as accessibility changes. For example, the many **ghost towns** (abandoned settlements) of the western United States once had relative locations near water sources (which dried up), along trade routes (which changed), or near mines (which closed). Their good relative locations lost the advantages—access to resources or trade—that they once had. However, their absolute locations, as described by the global grid of latitude and longitude, remain the same.

## Place

**Place** refers to the specific human and physical characteristics of a location. A group of places in the same area that share a characteristic form a **region**.

Two ways to refer to place are its site and situation. **Site** can be described as the characteristics at the immediate location—for example, the soil type, climate, labor force, and human structures. In contrast, **situation** refers to the location of a place relative to its surroundings and other places.

The situation of Riyadh, Saudi Arabia, is roughly in the center of the Arabian Peninsula; the situation of the Arabian Peninsula is between the continents of Africa and Asia. When the interstate highway system was created in the United States in the 1950s, the situation of many small towns changed dramatically. Towns along old railroad lines became less important as centers of trade while towns along the new interstate suddenly became more important.

Related to the concept of place is a **sense of place**. Humans tend to perceive the characteristics of places in different ways based on their personal beliefs. For example, the characteristics of Rome, Italy, might be described differently by a local resident than by an outsider or by a Catholic than by a Hindu. If a place inspires no strong emotional ties in people, it has placelessness.

Finally, locations can also be designated using **toponyms**, or place names. Some toponyms provide insights into the physical geography, the history, or the culture of the location. The entire coast of Florida is dotted with communities with "beach" in the name—Fernandina Beach, Miami Beach, Pensacola Beach—all of which are on beaches. Salt Lake City is named for a lake with unusually salty water. Iowa is named for a Native American tribe. Pikes Peak is named for an explorer, Zebulon Pike. Sometimes toponyms get confusing. Greenland is icier than Iceland; Iceland is greener than Greenland. And some toponyms are deceiving. Lake City, Iowa, is not on a lake, and few people consider Mount Prospect, Illinois, at an elevation of 665 feet above sea level, on a mountain.

# The Importance of Distance

A consideration of **distance** is an important part of the geographic perspective and spatial approach. Distance is a measurement of how far or how near things are to one another. The term **proximity** indicates the degree of nearness. Distance can be measured in terms of geography and is given in a type of measurement, such as meters, miles, or kilometers. It may be straight-line distance ("as the crow flies") or travel distance using a route that turns and twists. Milwaukee to Kalamazoo is 130 miles by air but 250 miles by car because the normal route goes around the southern tip of Lake Michigan.

## Distance and Time

Distance can be measured in terms of time: one place might be "a two-hour drive" from another place. **Time-space compression** is the shrinking "time distance" between locations because of improved methods of transportation and communication. New York City and London are separated by an ocean, but the development of air travel greatly reduced travel time between them. As a result, they feel much closer today than they did in the 19th century.

One result of time-space compression is that global forces are influencing culture everywhere and reducing local diversity more than ever before. In the 19th century, the mountainous regions of southeastern Europe were famous for the local variations in their music. Today, because of radio, the Internet, and other changes, people in southeastern Europe listen to the same music as everyone else in the world.

### Distance and Connection

The increasing connection between places is reflected in the growth of **spatial interaction**. Spatial interaction refers to the contact, movement, and flow of things between locations. Connections might be physical, such as through roads. Or they can be through information, such as through radios or Internet service. Places with more connections will have increased spatial interaction.

The **friction of distance** indicates that when things are farther apart, they tend to be less well connected. This inverse relationship between distance and connection is a concept called **distance-decay**. A clear illustration of this concept is the weakening of a radio signal as it travels across space away from a radio tower. Friction of distance causes the decay, or weakening, of the signal. Natural characteristics like waves, earthquakes, and storm systems exhibit the distance-decay function. Human characteristics also exhibit distance-decay, although the key issue is more accurately described as connectedness than distance. When a new pet store opens, its influence is strongest in the area closest to the store but only among the pet owners who have a connection to the store. Improvements in transportation, communication, and infrastructure have reduced the friction of distance between places as they have increased the spatial interaction.

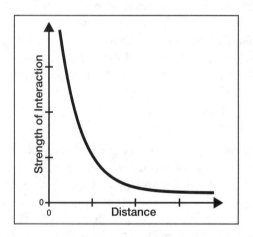

Concepts such as accessibility and remoteness are changing. The world is more spatially connected than ever before in history. The Internet can be used to illustrate several of these concepts. It allows a person living in El Paso, Texas, to shop at a store in New York City (via its website) and receive a product shipped from a warehouse in Atlanta, Georgia. Distance-decay is less influential than it once was.

## Density and Distribution

**Density** is the number of something in a specifically defined area. Population density is the number of people per square mile. Densities are often compared to one another as "higher" or "lower." The population density in a ten-acre city block of tall apartment buildings is likely higher than the population density of a ten-acre block filled with single-family homes. A simple population density for an area can be calculated by counting the people and dividing by the area.

Besides describing density using numbers, density can be described in psychological terms. In a full elevator, one person might feel that the density is fine. Another might feel it is uncomfortably dense.

Geographers are also interested in **distribution**, the way a phenomenon is spread out over an area. Some areas might have a cluster or concentration of something that is sparse in other areas. For example, two city blocks with the same density might have very different distributions. In one, people might be spread evenly throughout the block. The other might consist of a large building where everyone lives and a large park where no one lives. Geographers look for patterns in the distribution of phenomena across space that give clues about causes or effects of the distribution. Common patterns include the following:

- Linear phenomena are arranged in a straight line, such as the distribution of towns along a railroad line.
- Circular phenomena are equally spaced from a central point, forming a circle, such as the distribution of the homes of people who shop at a particular store.
- Geometric phenomena are in a regular arrangement, such as the squares formed by roads in the Midwest.
- Random phenomena appear to have no order to their position, such as the distribution of pet owners in a city.

Matching patterns of distribution is called **spatial association** and indicates that two (or more) phenomena may be related, or associated with one another. For example, the distribution of malaria matches the distribution of the mosquito that carries it. However, just because two distributions have a similar pattern does not mean one is necessarily the cause of the other. The distribution of bicycle shops in a large city might be similar to the distribution of athletic wear stores—but one probably does not cause the other. They both might reflect the distribution of active people.

## Human-Environment Interaction

The dual relationship between humans and the natural world are at the heart of human geography. The connection and exchange between them is referred to as **human-environment interaction**. Geographers who focus on how humans influence the physical world often specialize in studying sustainability, pollution, and environmental issues.

The study of how humans adapt to the environment is known as **cultural ecology**. The belief that landforms and climate are the most powerful forces shaping human behavior and societal development is called **environmental determinism**. In the 19th and early 20th centuries, some people used environmental determinism to argue that people in some climates were superior to those of other climates.

In reaction came the view known as **possibilism**, a view that acknowledges limits on the effects of the natural environment and focuses more on the role that human culture plays. Different cultures may respond to the same natural environment in diverse ways, depending on their beliefs, goals, and available technologies.

# Landscape Analysis

The word *landscape* comes from older Germanic words that refer to the condition, the "shape," of the land. The term can also imply a specific area, as in a "desert landscape" or the "landscape of Tuscany." The task of defining and describing landscapes is called **landscape analysis**.

## *Observation and Interpretation*

The first part of landscape analysis is careful observation. Geographers are keen observers of phenomena and collect data about what they see. The term **field observation** is used to refer to the act of physically visiting a location, place, or region and recording, firsthand, information there. Geographers can often be found taking notes, sketching maps, counting and measuring things, and interviewing people as they walk through an area that they are interested in studying. For most of the history of geography, this was the only way to gather data about places. All of the information that can be tied to specific locations is called **spatial data**.

Modern technology has increased the ways in which geographers can obtain spatial data. Remotely sensed information from satellites that orbit the earth above the atmosphere and **aerial photography** (professional images captured from planes within the atmosphere) are important sources of observed data available today. Ground-level photography has replaced sketching as a tool for capturing information about landscapes. Sound recordings and the ability to get chemical analyses of air, water, and soil have also changed the way geographers observe a landscape.

Once data has been gathered, it must be interpreted. Geographers depend on their skills of synthesizing and integrating, or putting together, all of the collected information to better understand the place, area, or landscape being studied. A common example clearly observable today is the changes that occur in the landscapes of rural and urban areas over time. A geographer may be interested in understanding what changes are likely to occur as people move into or out of an area:

- Who are the people migrating into this area? Who is leaving?
- What are the cultures of these groups of people?
- What effects will the changes have on the local economy?
- What are the causes of people moving?
- What types of human-environment interaction are occurring?

## *The Built Environment*

When we use the word *environment*, we usually think of nature and natural things. Plants, the air, water, and animals are all part of the natural environment. Human geographers often refer to the **built environment**, by which they mean the physical artifacts that humans have created and that form part of the landscape. Buildings, roads, signs, and fences are examples of the built environment.

The architectural style of buildings varies from place to place. Think of typical homes and buildings in China, and then think of homes and buildings in Germany. These differences occur because people with different cultures living in different physical landscapes construct buildings, roads, and other elements to create a unique built environment. Anything built by humans is part of the **cultural landscape**.

## Four-Level Analysis

One systematic way to study geographic phenomena is to use Four-Level Analysis. This method is summarized in the chart below.

| FOUR-LEVEL ANALYSIS | | |
|---|---|---|
| **Level** | **Description** | **Key Questions** |
| **1. Comprehension** | Establish the basic information clearly | • What?<br>• Where?<br>• When?<br>• Scale? |
| **2. Identification** | Identify and describe patterns in phenomena | • Are phenomena connected? |
| **3. Explanation** | Explain how individual phenomena might form a pattern | • Why is something where it is?<br>• How did something get where it is? |
| **4. Prediction** | Explain why a pattern is important, and predict what it might lead to | • So what?<br>• What if?<br>• What are the effects? |

**GEOGRAPHIC PERSPECTIVES:** THINKING ABOUT DISTANCE

Geographers use the concept of distance to study the spatial distribution of phenomena. The perception of distance reflects context. Neighboring families in a small town in Iowa might live 50 feet apart. To a family in a high-rise apartment in Manhattan, 50 feet might seem like a long distance. To a family living on a ranch in Wyoming, miles from their nearest neighbor, 50 feet might feel uncomfortably close.

**Time and Distance**

In addition, what people consider a long distance changes over time. In the mid-1800s, Irish families held funeral-like ceremonies for emigrants leaving for the United States, Australia, and elsewhere. Trips by ship to these other lands were so long, expensive, and dangerous that families expected they would never see the departing person again. And they often didn't. But what seemed far away in the 1800s seems much closer today. A flight by jet from Dublin to Boston takes about seven hours, costs only two days' pay for many people, and is remarkably safe.

## Scale and Distance
A third factor shaping the perception of distance is scale. At a personal level, eight people crowded into an elevator, separated by inches, probably feel close together. At the community level, Tampa and Orlando seem close together, even though they are about 85 miles apart. At the global level, the countries of Mali and Chad seem close together, separated by only 1,500 miles.

## Other Disciplines and Distance
Geographers are not alone in studying distance. Historians might research the change over time in how immigrants viewed distance. Sociologists might focus on how distance affects how neighbors interact. However, unlike others who study human actions, geographers emphasize the role of distance and other concepts that describe spatial distribution.

| KEY TERMS | | |
|---|---|---|
| spatial approach | region | spatial association |
| physical geography | site | human-environment interaction |
| human geography | situation | |
| absolute location | sense of place | cultural ecology |
| latitude | toponyms | environmental determinism |
| equator | distance | |
| longitude | proximity | possibilism |
| prime meridian | time-space compression | landscape analysis |
| International Date Line | spatial interaction | field observation |
| relative location | friction of distance | spatial data |
| connectivity | distance-decay | aerial photography |
| accessibility | spatial association | built environment |
| ghost towns | density | cultural landscape |
| place | distribution | |

## MULTIPLE-CHOICE QUESTIONS

**Questions 1 to 3 refer to the map below.**

1. Which statement best describes the absolute location of Paris, France?
   (A) 127 miles away from the English Channel
   (B) in the Northern Hemisphere and Eastern Hemisphere
   (C) 49° N, 2° E
   (D) the capital of France
   (E) in the heart of France

2. Which statement describes the relative location of Barcelona, Spain?
   (A) 386 miles west of Madrid and 644 miles south of Paris
   (B) in the Northern Hemisphere and Eastern Hemisphere
   (C) 41° N, 2° E
   (D) the capital of the Catalonia region
   (E) one of the largest cities in Spain

3. The word *Madrid* is a toponym because it designates
   (A) a center of political power
   (B) the name of a specific location
   (C) a community in a plains region
   (D) the largest city in a country
   (E) that it is part of a region called the Iberian Peninsula

**Question 4 refers to the following image.**

4. Which best describes the effect on time-space compression of the technology shown above?

   (A) It decreased it by using less space than older machines.

   (B) It decreased it by shortening the time writing took.

   (C) It decreased it by making communication easier.

   (D) It increased it by making writing more efficient.

   (E) It increased it by speeding up communications.

**Question 5 refers to the following image.**

5. Which best explains why the above image is considered part of the built environment?

   (A) It is found primarily in rural areas.

   (B) It is often used as part of boundaries.

   (C) It is designed to regulate the movement of animals.

   (D) It is part of the landscape made by humans.

   (E) It is a product that was invented to solve a problem.

**6.** Which technology had the greatest effect on the application of the distance-decay function?

(A) food preservatives because they reduce decay

(B) cars because they weakened family connections

(C) barbed wire because it stretches for long distances

(D) new medicines because they keep people healthier

(E) a jet, because it strengthens the connections between distant places

**7.** The frequency of occurrence of something within a specifically defined area is the

(A) density

(B) distribution

(C) incidence

(D) interconnection

(E) pattern

**8.** One way that possibilism differs from environmental determinism is that it emphasizes

(A) culture

(B) climate

(C) history

(D) regions

(E) trade

## FREE-RESPONSE QUESTION

**1.** The geographic perspective consists, in part, of concepts relating to place, or location, and distance.

A. Identify and describe a similarity between the absolute location and the site of a city.

B. Identify and describe a similarity between the relative location and the situation of a large sports stadium.

C. Explain the concept of distance-decay, and describe an example of it from the real world.

How people group information can emphasize certain patterns in the data. In turn, this can influence how readers interpret it. Imagine you are creating a map based on the data in the table.

| POPULATION CHANGE FOR THE LARGEST CITIES IN 1900 | | | | |
|---|---|---|---|---|
| City | Population in 1900 | Population in 2015 (estimate) | Total Change | Percentage Change |
| New York | 3,437,202 | 8,550,405 | +5,113,203 | +149% |
| Chicago | 1,698,575 | 2,720,546 | +1,021,971 | +60% |
| Philadelphia | 1,293,697 | 1,567,442 | +273,745 | +21% |
| St. Louis | 575,238 | 315,685 | −259,553 | −45% |
| Boston | 560,892 | 667,137 | +106,245 | +19% |
| Baltimore | 508,957 | 621,849 | +112,892 | +22% |
| Cleveland | 381,768 | 388,072 | +6,304 | +2% |
| Buffalo | 352,387 | 258,071 | −94,316 | −27% |
| San Francisco | 342,782 | 864,816 | +522,034 | +152% |
| Cincinnati | 325,902 | 298,550 | −27,352 | −8% |

1. If you use large dots to show cities of three million or more people in 1900 and small dots for the other cities, what impression would the map give readers about the relative size of cities?

2. If you use large dots to show cities of 600,000 or more people in 1900 and small dots for the other cities, what impression would the map give readers about the relative size of cities?

3. If you use an upward-pointing arrowhead for cities that increased in population and a downward-pointing arrowhead for cities that decreased in population, what would you be emphasizing?

4. If you use large, medium, and small dots, into what three classes would you divide the cities based on their population in 2015?

5. If you divided the cities into three categories by percentage of change, what classes would you use? Explain.

**2**

# Patterns and Processes

*The map—what a great idea!—is also one of the oldest and perhaps the most powerful and constant of geographic ideas. . . . Although they may be as beautiful as any work of art, we distinguish maps from art in the way we look at them. . . . The map's message does not lie in its overall effect but in the locational information it carries.*

—Anne Godlewska, *Ten Geographic Ideas That Changed the World*

**Essential Question:** What tools and techniques do geographers use to analyze the world?

Geographers emphasize spatial **patterns**, general arrangements of things being studied, and the **processes**, the repeated sequences of events, that create them. Learning to recognize and use geographical patterns is a fundamental skill in understanding the discipline.

## Maps

Maps are the most important tool of a geographer. No tool communicates spatial information more effectively than a map. They are essential in highlighting and analyzing patterns.

### Scale

Nearly every map is a smaller version of a larger portion of the earth's surface. In other words, a map is a reduction of the actual land area it represents. **Scale** is the ratio between the size of things in the real world and the size of those same things on the map. A map has three types of scale: cartographic scale, geographic scale, and the scale of the data represented on the map.

**Cartographic scale** refers to the way the map communicates the ratio of its size to the size of what it represents:

- Words: for example, "one inch equals ten miles." In this case, two and a half inches on the map would be 25 miles on the surface of the earth.
- A ratio: for example, 1/200,000 or 1:200,000. This means that 1 unit of measurement on the map is equal to 200,000 of the same unit in reality. For example, 1 inch (or centimeter or millimeter) on the map represents 200,000 inches (or centimeters or millimeters) on the ground.

- A line: for example, the map may show a line and indicate that its distance on the map represents ten miles in reality. This is sometimes called a linear, or graphic, scale.

**Geographic scale,** sometimes called **relative scale,** refers to the amount of territory that the map represents. For example, global scale means a map of the entire planet, and it is used to show data that covers the entire world. In contrast, local scale means a map of a city. It might be used to show finer details, such as school attendance boundaries. Geographers often zoom in and out of maps that use different scales in order to see the patterns that exist at each scale. In addition, the reasons patterns exist can often be explained differently depending on the scale of analysis. A rise in unemployment might be shaped by global forces at a global scale or by local forces at a local scale.

The **scale of the data** differs from cartographic or geographic scale. Compare the maps showing the population density of Australia. The scale of both maps is the same, but the scale of the data differs. One map shows the scale of data at the country level; the other, at the state and territory level. One map shows Australia as moderately populated throughout. The other shows that the country consists of large, sparsely populated areas and a few small, densely populated areas.

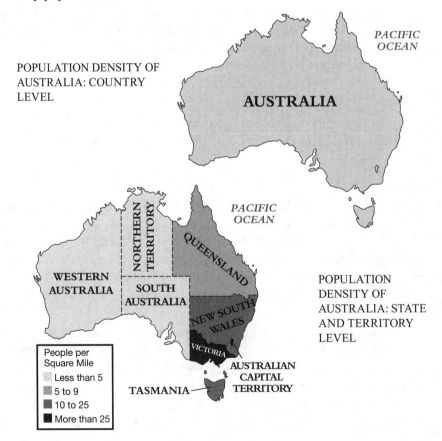

## Reference Maps

There are two broad categories of maps: reference maps and thematic maps. **Reference maps** are aptly named because they are designed for people to refer to for general information about places:

- **Political maps** show and label human-created boundaries and designations, such as countries, states, cities, and capitals.

- **Physical maps** show and label natural features, such as mountains, rivers, and deserts.

- **Road maps** show and label highways, streets, and alleys.

- **Plat maps** show and label property lines and details of land ownership.

- **Locator maps** are illustrations used in books and advertisements to show specific locations mentioned in the text.

MEXICO

## Thematic Maps

**Thematic maps** show spatial aspects of information or of a phenomenon. Following are descriptions of four common types of thematic maps.

**Choropleth maps** use various colors, shades of one color, or patterns to show the location and distribution of spatial data. They often show rates or other quantitative data in defined areas, such as the percentage of people in a country who speak English. The maps showing the population density of Australia are choropleth maps. As they demonstrated, the scale of data influences how the map looks.

**Dot distribution maps** are used to show the specific location and distribution of something across the territory of the map. Each dot represents a specified quantity. One dot might stand for one school building—or for millions of people who own dogs. While these maps are known as dot distribution maps, any kind of symbol—a triangle, the outline of a house, a cow—can be used instead of dots.

**Graduated symbol maps** use symbols of different sizes to indicate different amounts of something. Larger sizes indicate more of something, and smaller sizes indicate less. These maps make it easy to see where the largest and smallest of some phenomena are by simply comparing the symbols to each other. The map key is used to determine the exact amount. The symbols themselves are arranged on the map centered over the location represented by the data, so they may overlap. Graduated symbol maps are also called proportional symbol maps.

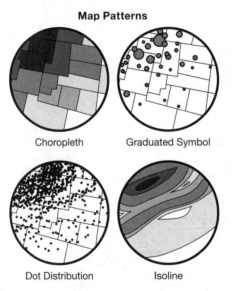

**Map Patterns**

Choropleth

Graduated Symbol

Dot Distribution

Isoline

**Isoline maps,** also called isometric maps, use lines that connect points of equal value to depict variations in the data across space. Where lines are close together, whatever the map depicts is changing rapidly; where the lines are farther apart, the phenomenon is relatively the same. The most common type of isoline maps are **topographic maps**, which are popular among hikers. Points of equal elevation are connected on these maps, creating contours that depict surface features. Other examples of isoline maps are weather maps showing changes in barometric pressure, temperature, or precipitation across space.

## Cartograms

In a **cartogram**, the sizes of countries (or states, counties, or another areal unit) are shown according to some specific statistic. In the example on the next page, the cartogram of world population shows Canada and Morocco as roughly the same size because they have similar populations (about 35 million people), even though Canada is more than 20 times larger in area. Any variable for which there are statistics can be substituted for the size of the country and mapped in the same way. Cartograms are useful because they allow for data to be compared, much like a graph, and distance and distribution are also visible, like on a traditional map.

WORLD POPULATION CARTOGRAM

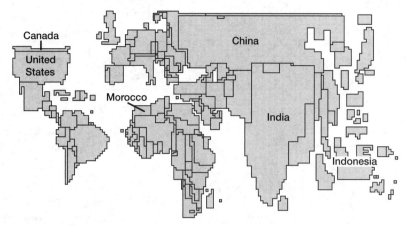

## Projections

Because the earth is a sphere and maps are flat, all maps distort some aspect of reality. The process of showing a curved surface on a flat surface is done using a **map projection**. Cartographers decide whether they want to preserve area, shape, distance, or direction on their map accurately, knowing that other elements will have to be less accurate as the earth is "flattened" on their map.

| COMPARING MAP PROJECTIONS | | | |
|---|---|---|---|
| **Purpose** | **Strengths** | **Distortion** | **Projection** |
| **Navigation** | • Directions are shown accurately<br>• Lines of latitude and longitude meet at right angles | • Distance between lines of longitude appears constant<br>• Land masses near the poles appear large | Mercator |
| **Spatial Distributions Related to Area** | • Sizes of land masses are accurate | • Shapes are inaccurate, especially near the poles | Peters |
| **General Use in Midlatitude Countries** | • Lines of longitude converge<br>• Lines of latitude are curved<br>• Size and shape are both close to reality | • Direction is not constant<br>• On a world map, longitude lines converge at only one pole | Conic |
| **General Use** | • No major distortion<br>• Oval shape appears more like a globe than does a rectangle | • Area, shape, size, and direction are all slightly distorted | Robinson |

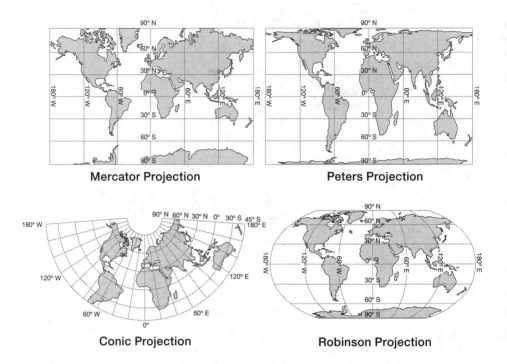

Mercator Projection

Peters Projection

Conic Projection

Robinson Projection

# Models in Geography

Geographers, similar to biologists, meteorologists, and others dealing with complex reality, create **geographic models**, representations of reality or theories about reality, to help them see general spatial patterns, focus on the influence of specific factors, and understand variations from place to place. Models help explain, describe, and sometimes even predict spatial activity and phenomena. There are two basic types of geographic models: spatial and nonspatial:

- **Spatial models** look like stylized maps, and they illustrate theories about spatial distributions. Spatial models have been developed for agricultural land use (the von Thünen model, Chapter 14), industrial location (least cost theory, Chapter 15), the distribution of cities (central place theory, Chapter 18), and the structure of urban areas (Chapter 19).

- **Nonspatial models** illustrate theories and concepts using words, graphs, or tables. They often depict changes over time rather than across space. Examples are the demographic transition model (Chapter 4) and Rostow's modernization model (Chapter 17). Wallerstein's world-systems theory combines elements of both spatial and nonspatial models (Chapter 17).

## Formulas and Graphs

Geographers use mathematic formulas to help them understand how the world works. These formulas function much like models. Some formulas, such as those that determine crude birth and death rates, doubling times for populations, and population densities, are mathematical calculations that are used to produce a statistic. Other formulas, such as the one used in the rank-size rule (Chapter 18), produce results that are more theoretical, as is typical in a model. Graphs are used to illustrate population structures (population pyramids, Chapter 3), geographic concepts (distance-decay, Chapter 1), and even models (the demographic transition model, Chapter 4).

## Use of Models

One of the most famous geographic models is von Thünen's model of land use. It was developed by a German farmer and economist, Johann Heinrich von Thünen, in the first half of the 1800s. The chart below shows how von Thünen's model, like all models, is a generalization, a simplification, and a theory.

| RELATIONSHIP OF VON THÜNEN'S MODEL TO REALITY | |
|---|---|
| **Model Attribute** | **Application** |
| **Generalization from Reality** | Von Thünen studied how farmers decided to use their land. For example, should they grow vegetables or raise cattle or plant fruit trees? Based on what people did, he developed a general model about agricultural land use. |
| **Simplification of Reality** | Von Thünen focused on two variables—transportation and distance—even though a farmer might be influenced by several other variables, such as the location of mountains and the fertility of the soil. |
| **Theoretical Description of Reality** | Von Thünen's model could be applied around the world. But since no other set of circumstances exactly matched the one he studied, his model would never exactly match reality. However, the differences between the model and reality can help geographers understand the reality more accurately. |

Models are often mathematical formulas based on data, and people use them to make predictions. When reality varies from a prediction, geographers rethink the model. They ask: Why are things the way they are here and now? Why does this real situation differ from the situation that the model was based on? Models are never "wrong" or "right," but they can be more or less useful in understanding the world.

# Regionalization and Regions

**Regionalization** is the process geographers use to divide and categorize space into smaller areal units. This is much like how a writer divides a book into chapters and then names (or classifies) them.

## Types of Regions

Geographers classify regions into one of three basic types: formal, functional, or perceptual. **Formal regions**, sometimes called **uniform regions** or **homogeneous regions**, are united by one or more traits:

- physical, such as the Sahara, a vast desert in northern Africa
- cultural, such as southwestern Nigeria, an area where most people speak Yoruba
- economic, such as the Gold Coast of Africa (Ghana), which exports gold

**Functional regions** are organized around a focal point and are defined by an activity that occurs across the region. These regions are often united by networks of communication and transportation that are centered on a node. For this reason, they are also known as **nodal regions**:

- Pizza delivery areas are functional regions; the pizza shop is the node.
- A country is a functional region; the capital city is the political node.

A necessary part of any functional region is the flow of some phenomenon across the networks that unite the region, whether the flow is visible (cars delivering pizza using roads) or invisible (political and legal authority from the capital city).

**Perceptual regions** differ from formal and functional regions in that they are defined by the informal sense of place that people ascribe to them. The boundaries of perceptual regions vary widely because people have a different sense of what defines and unites these regions. The American "South," the Middle East, and "Upstate" New York are examples. While all of these regions exist, their exact boundaries depend upon the person who is defining them. Perceptual regions are also known as **vernacular regions**.

Similar to perceptual maps are **mental maps**, or the maps that people create in their minds based on their own experience and knowledge. Mental maps evolve over time. The mental map of a child entering kindergarten for the first day of class might be just a door, a classroom, and a playground. After a month, or a year, or several years in the building, the child will have a much fuller mental map.

## World Regions

In the same way that historians divide history into eras and periods, geographers divide the world into regions and subregions. One type of large region is a continent. However, dividing the world into continents is not simple. Are Europe and Asia two continents or one? Where is the dividing line between North and South America? Is Greenland its own continent?

## Large Regions

The following map shows the ten large regions used in AP® Human Geography. It includes the seven continents that are based on physical features. It also includes three cultural regions that are based on shared languages and histories:

- Central America is part of North America but with a culture more influenced by Spain and Portugal than by Great Britain and France.
- Sub-Saharan Africa is distinguished from the rest of Africa.
- The Russian Federation spans eastern Europe and northern Asia.

WORLD REGIONS: A BIG PICTURE VIEW

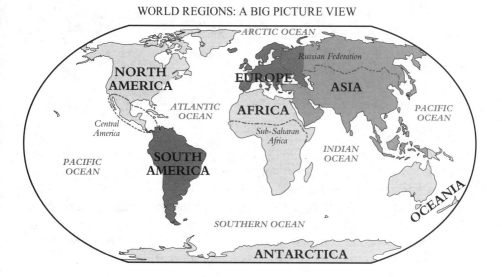

## Subregions

Geographers divide regions into smaller areas, or **subregions**. A subregion shares some characteristics with the rest of the larger region but is distinctive in some ways. For example, the region of Latin America covers parts of North and South America, from Mexico to Chile. Within it is the subregion of Brazil. As in other Latin American countries, most people in Brazil are Roman Catholics. However, Brazil's primary language is Portuguese, which makes it unlike any other country in the mostly Spanish-speaking Latin America. Because of its language, Brazil is a distinct subregion.

The map below shows the standard subregions used in AP® Human Geography. For example, Sub-Saharan Africa is subdivided into West, Central, East, and Southern Africa. Asia is divided into five subregions: Middle East, Central Asia, South Asia, East Asia, and Southeast Asia.

WORLD REGIONS: A CLOSER LOOK

## Smaller Regions

By changing the scale and zooming in, subregions can be even further divided. The further subdivisions can be based on elements of physical geography, such as climate and landform, or human geography, such as culture, politics, or economics. Western Europe can be divided into Northwestern Europe and Southern Europe, each unified by more specific traits.

Since many kinds of regions exist, any one place is part of many regions or subregions at the same time. For example, Florida is part of

- a climate region based on its warm weather
- a cultural region known as the South
- an economic region known as the Sun Belt

# Geospatial Data

Geospatial data includes all information that can be tied to a specific place. Besides locations of things, such as mountains or roads or boundaries, it includes human activities and traits. Where do speakers of Mandarin live? How common is poverty in each U.S. county? Where is the dividing line in a city between students who attend one high school and those who attend another?

## Obtaining Geospatial Data

Much geospatial data is gathered in the field. This means that the data was observed and recorded on location, and the act of collecting it is known as

**fieldwork**. Important sources of this type of data can come from a census of the population, from interviews, or even from informal observations made by geographers. Land surveys, photographs, and sketches are also important ways in which this data is obtained. Technology is making the collection, accuracy, storage, analysis, and display of geospatial data easier than at any time in the past. The following chart illustrates three technologies that have revolutionized the importance of geospatial data.

| GEOSPATIAL TECHNOLOGIES | | |
|---|---|---|
| **Type** | **Description** | **Uses** |
| **GPS: Global Positioning System** | GPS receivers on the earth's surface use the locations of multiple satellites to determine and record a receiver's exact location | • Precisely locating borders<br>• Navigating ships, aircraft, cars<br>• Mapping lines (trails) or points (fire hydrants) |
| **Remote Sensing** | The use of cameras or other sensors mounted on aircraft or satellites to collect digital images of the earth's surface | • Determining land cover and use<br>• Monitoring environmental changes<br>• Assessing spread of spatial phenomena<br>• Monitoring the weather |
| **GIS: Geographic Information Systems** | Computer system that can store, analyze, and display information from multiple digital maps or geospatial data sets | • Analysis of crime data<br>• Effects of pollution<br>• Transportation/travel time analysis<br>• Urban planning |

## Quantitative and Qualitative Data

Geospatial data can be quantitative or qualitative. **Quantitative data** is information that can be measured and recorded using numbers. Some examples are the distribution of people by income or age group. Quantitative data is often used with geographic information systems because it lends itself to analysis using formulas and computers.

In contrast, **qualitative data** is not usually represented by numbers. This data is collected as interviews, document archives, descriptions, and visual observations. For example, asking people whether they feel that an intersection is dangerous is qualitative. Qualitative data is harder to analyze than quantitative data. People's perceptions, opinions, and reasons for doing things are important parts of human geography. This qualitative data contributes greatly to geographic understanding of places and the people who use them.

One of the most useful maps in history is also one of the most inaccurate. And its inaccuracies are what make it so useful. The map of the London subway system, known as the Underground, demonstrates the value of the concept of relative location. A portion of this map is shown below.

### Beck's Map

By 1931, the Underground had become so complex that an accurate but conveniently small map was hard to read. Harry Beck, an Underground employee, realized that a simpler map would be more useful. Passengers did not need to know every twist and turn in the routes, so he created a map with straight lines. And passengers were not particularly concerned with distances, so he adjusted the space between stops on the map. He spread out the ones in the congested central city and reduced space between the outlying stops so they fit on the map easily.

The result was a map based on relative location that was easy to read and convenient to use. Passengers knew where to get on, where to get off, and at which stops they could transfer from one line to another.

### Popular Demand

When the first version of the map was distributed to a few passengers in 1933, people demanded more. Since then, the map has been revised regularly to add new subway lines, more information about which lines have limited service, which stations are accessible to people using wheelchairs, and other improvements. Other transit systems have adopted a similar approach.

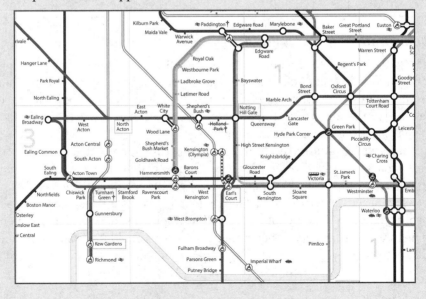

## KEY TERMS

patterns

processes

scale

cartographic scale

geographic scale

relative scale

scale of data

reference maps

political maps

physical map

road maps

plat maps

locator maps

thematic map

choropleth maps

dot distribution maps

graduated symbol maps

isoline maps

topographic maps

cartogram

map projection

Mercator map projection

Peters projection

conic projection

Robinson projection

geographic models

spatial models

nonspatial models

regionalization

formal regions

uniform regions

homogeneous
  regions

functional regions

nodal regions

perceptual regions

vernacular regions

mental maps

subregions

fieldwork

quantitative data

qualitative data

**Questions 1 and 2 refer to the map below.**

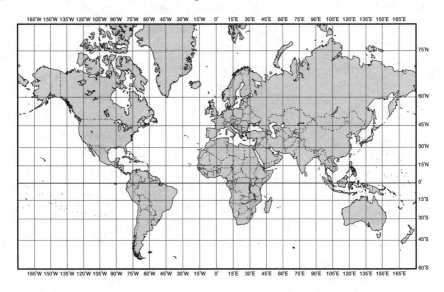

1. Why is the map projection shown here especially useful for navigation on the surface of the earth?

    (A) Distortion of shape is minimized.

    (B) Direction is constant across the map.

    (C) Distances are correctly portrayed.

    (D) Area of land masses is shown accurately.

    (E) It shows the sizes of bodies of water realistically.

2. Like the map above, all maps have some kind of distortion. Why?

    (A) The earth's surface is curved and a map is flat.

    (B) All maps are smaller than the areas they actually represent.

    (C) Human error is always present when a map is made.

    (D) Maps can depict only a small number of the many details of the earth's surface.

    (E) The world constantly changes so maps are never current.

**3.** How are a cartogram and a graduated symbol map similar?

    (A) Both indicate exact locations of specific data precisely.

    (B) Both portray numerical data for comparison between places.

    (C) Both provide a good compromise among distortions of shape, size, direction, and distance.

    (D) Both display latitude and longitude accurately.

    (E) Both are useful for comparing the physical area of a country.

**4.** Which term most closely describes a model in geography?

    (A) replica

    (B) guess

    (C) theory

    (D) map

    (E) proportion

**5.** Which phrase refers to the collection of geospatial data through the use of satellite imagery?

    (A) using remote sensing

    (B) gathering information through fieldwork

    (C) using a global positioning system

    (D) forming a mental map

    (E) creating a projection

**6.** Which is the best example of qualitative data used by geographers?

    (A) personal descriptions of processes and events

    (B) surveys about how often people visit other places

    (C) census counts such as population statistics

    (D) measurements of distance made using GPS receivers

    (E) tables showing the age distribution of people in a community

**Questions 7 and 8 refer to the passage below.**

Smartphones, each one with a tiny GPS pinging, have revolutionized cartography. Matthew Zook, a geographer at the University of Kentucky, has partnered with data scientists there to create what they call the DOLLY Project (Digital OnLine Life and You)—it's a searchable repository of *every* geotagged tweet since December 2011, meaning Zook and his team have compiled billions of interrelated sentiments, each with a latitude and longitude attached.

—Christian Rudder, "The United States of Reddit," *Slate*, 2014.

7. Why are geographers interested in the information in DOLLY?

   (A) It provides information about spatial distribution of people's reactions to events.

   (B) It provides an opportunity for geographers to work with data scientists.

   (C) Geographers focus on the sentiments of people more than do other scientists.

   (D) Geographers are more likely to use new technology than are other scientists.

   (E) The data is searchable, and most geographic information is hard to organize.

8. Which issue would a geographer research using DOLLY?

   (A) how people in different areas reacted to results of a presidential election

   (B) why people consider themselves either conservative or liberal

   (C) at what temperature people begin to describe the day as "cold"

   (D) how the weather affects the number of people who feel sick

   (E) why some people are more likely than others to use new technology

## FREE-RESPONSE QUESTION

1. Elements of both culture and the environment can be used by geographers to define regions.

   A. Define the term *built environment* as it is used by geographers.

   B. Discuss the concept of *region* and how geographers use the term to make sense of locations.

   C. Discuss how changing the scale of analysis can help geographers develop a deeper understanding of a region.

An area of Earth defined by one or more distinctive characteristics is a region. People, activities, and environment exhibit similarities within a region and differ in some way from other regions.

| SOUTH CENTRAL PLAINS STATES | | | | | |
|---|---|---|---|---|---|
| **State** | **Adult Population Whose Primary Language is English** | **Corn Production (tons)** | **Largest Religious Denomination** | **Annual Precipitation (inches)** | **Athletic Conference of the Largest State University** |
| **New Mexico** | 64% | 2,075,000 | Catholic (34%) | 14.6 | Mountain West |
| **Texas** | 65% | 5,250,000 | Catholic (23%) | 28.9 | Big 12 (Big 12 headquarters are in Irvine, Texas) |
| **Oklahoma** | 90% | 255,000 | Baptist (28%) | 36.5 | Big 12 |
| **Kansas** | 89% | 3,145,000 | Catholic (18%) | 28.9 | Big 12 |
| **Arkansas** | 93% | 30,000 | Baptist (27%) | 50.6 | Southeastern |
| **Louisiana** | 91% | 14,000 | Catholic (26%) | 60.1 | Southeastern |

1. What characteristics could you use to create a formal region from these six states? Explain your answer.

2. What characteristics could you use to create a functional/nodal region? Explain your answer.

3. What characteristics could be used to create a vernacular (perceptual) region? Explain your answer.

4. What problems are inherent in trying to classify places into regions?

# UNIT 1: Review

## WRITE AS A GEOGRAPHER: COMPREHEND THE PROMPT

The first step in writing a good answer to a free-response question is to understand the question. First, note the topic: if the prompt asks about "squatter settlements," then your answer should as well. Second, note the type or types of thinking to use: if the prompt says to "identify and explain," then the answer should do both. Only after understanding the prompt fully can you write an answer that includes relevant claims.

*In the following questions, identify the content and the type or types of thinking to use.*

1. Identify and explain two consequences of rapid urbanization on the transportation system of a region.

2. Give a specific example of how the concept of distance-decay applies to the customer base for a retail store.

3. With reference to a specific city, explain the difference between absolute location and relative location.

4. Describe the distribution pattern of main highways in Florida.

5. Using Weber's theory of industrial location, explain how the discovery of a new, inexpensive raw material used in an industry will affect location of factories in that industry.

## REFLECT ON THE CHAPTER ESSENTIAL QUESTIONS

*Write a one- to three-paragraph answer to each question.*

1. How does the way geographers look at the world differ from that of other scientists?

2. What tools and techniques do geographers use to analyze the world?

# UNIT 2: Population and Migration

## Unit Overview

The distribution of people influences all other elements of human geography. Where people live, whether spread out in small communities or concentrated in large cities, affects how they relate to each other, what demands they place on the environment, and what decisions they make as a community. For example, the spatial distribution of children will influence where a community will build a new school.

People decide where to live based on many factors. Some are physical: people want to be near sources of food and water, and where the climate is not too extreme. Some factors are human: people might move to take a job or to be close to family.

### Changes in Populations

For most of human history, women typically gave birth to many children, but so few children survived to adulthood that the total human population grew slowly. However, in the past two centuries, advances in public health, medical care, and the economy have enabled people to live longer. The number of births per woman has decreased, but children are more likely to survive to adulthood. As a result of these new patterns, the global population has exploded. However, in recent decades, population growth has leveled off in the prosperous countries.

### Why People Move

People have always been on the move. Usually, they migrated by choice, wanting to leave a place of poverty or persecution or warfare in order to live in a place with economic opportunity, religious liberty, political freedom, and peace. In some cases, people had no choice. For example, for nearly four centuries, Africans were enslaved and brought to the Americas.

---

### Enduring Understandings

**II.** Population and Migration

    **A.** Knowledge of the geographic patterns and characteristics of human populations facilitates understanding of cultural, political, economic, and urban systems.

    **B.** Populations grow and decline over time and space.

    **C.** Causes and consequences of migration are influenced by cultural, demographic, economic, environmental, and political factors.

**Source:** *CollegeBoard AP®. Human Geography Course Description. 2015.*

---

# 3

# Population Distribution

*Half the world's population lives in just 1 percent of the land.*
—Max Galka, *Metrocosm*, January 4, 2016

**Essential Question:** How does understanding where people live help to explain how they live?

Human geography tries to explain why people live where they do. It includes the study of two distinct but related concepts:

- **Population distribution** is the pattern of human settlement—the spread of people across the earth. Representing it on a map highlights places that are crowded, or sparsely settled, or even empty.
- **Population density** is a measure of the average population per square mile or kilometer of an area. It measures how crowded a place is.

Understanding both population distribution and density helps people make important decisions on issues such as where to set the boundaries of an electoral district or where to develop new housing. These are among the many issues influenced by the number, distribution, and density of current and projected population.

Humans live on a small percentage of the planet. The world contains seven times as many people as it did two centuries ago. Population density has increased significantly. However, population distribution has not. The vast majority of growth has been in areas already settled. For example, eastern China was one of the most populated parts of the world in 1800—and it still is today. Why have people chosen to live in such crowded places?

## Where People Live

People want to live in places where they can survive with relative ease and comfort—places where they can raise or obtain food and live in moderate climates. Even when there were only 1 billion people on Earth, they were dispersed throughout such desirable lands. As population increased, the amount of suitable land stayed about the same, so people chose to live in greater densities on that same land.

## *Physical Factors Influencing Population Distribution*

Survival for the earliest humans depended on food, water, and shelter. Thus, these hunter-gatherers settled where these features were most readily available. Similarly, people today have the same basic needs, which helps explain why the population distribution has remained so similar over time. The map below of Earth's population distribution today shows where people live—where they consider the most suitable land for human habitation.

**Midlatitudes**  Most people live in the **midlatitudes**, the regions between 30° N and 60° N, and between 30° S and 60° S. These areas have more moderate climates and better soils than do regions at higher or lower latitudes. This pattern is particularly noticeable in the northern hemisphere because it includes more land than the southern hemisphere.

**Low-Lying Areas**  Most people live in low-lying areas rather than high in mountains. Low-lying areas typically have better soils for raising crops than do upland or high altitude areas. In addition, these areas are often close to oceans, which facilitate transportation, provide a source of food, and have a moderating effect on temperature. Oceans keep the land warmer in the winter and cooler in the summer.

**Fresh Water**  Most people live near lakes or rivers. People need fresh water to drink, and they can use it for irrigation, transportation, and to provide food.

**Other Resources**  People also desire natural resources, such as forest products and minerals. These can influence where people live.

WORLD POPULATION DISTRIBUTION, C. 2015

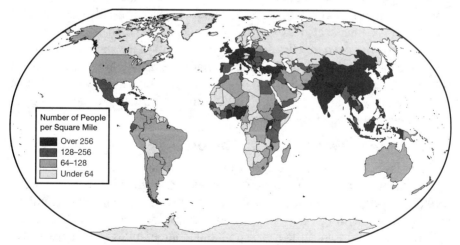

## Human Factors Influencing Population Distribution

In places where humans first settled, people did so because a place's natural features attracted them. However, then the people themselves became an attraction. Newcomers moved in for safety, or to find a job, or to be with friends or relatives. The populations and densities of urban areas have continued to grow, often to extreme levels.

Where people decide to place transportation networks also has a significant impact on population distribution. People prefer to live close to trade routes. Roads, train lines, and rivers often produce a linear settlement pattern in which houses and communities stretch out in a line.

Political decisions sometimes bring clusters of populations to isolated locations where physical attributes would not normally attract settlement. For example, a Canadian military base named Alert is the most northerly community in the world. It was situated where it was because it was close to what was the Soviet Union, and it allowed the Canadian military to monitor possibly hostile Soviet military activities.

Cultural and political situations often result in new distributions of particular groups of people. Religious groups such as the Amish and the Mormons, who were persecuted for their beliefs, resettled thousands of miles from their homelands to protect themselves and preserve their beliefs.

## Scale of Analysis and Physical Factors

The basic principle that people want to live on the most desirable land applies at any scale, or level of analysis by size. As the scale of inquiry changes, the relevance of certain factors such as climate, elevation, and industrialization changes as well.

On the global scale, high-altitude areas, such as in the Himalayas and the Rocky Mountains, have cold climates, so such places usually have limited populations. Climate also explains population distribution of a large state such as California, where climate varies greatly within the state. On a smaller scale, such as a city, the spatial climate variation is usually too small to affect settlement. However, elevation is sometimes important at the city level. People might prefer living at the highest elevations in a city because these spots offer safety from floods and inspiring views of the landscape.

## Scale of Analysis and Human Factors

Polluted air is a health hazard, yet it may signal industrialization, economic development, and employment opportunities. On a global or national scale, millions of people are often attracted to areas of such economic opportunities, and they might willingly move to the polluted area. At a city scale, few people intentionally choose to settle near a pollution source, unless they have to live there because of lower property values.

Governments also have a significant influence on population distribution at different scales. A national government might increase the population of an area by building a new military base. A state might reduce population in an area by creating a new state park. A city government might affect population distribution by allowing high-rise apartment buildings in some areas and reserving other areas for single-family homes.

Factors influencing a city's population distribution such as elevation, proximity to desirable land uses, and land use laws commonly result in a population distribution that reflects **social stratification**—the hierarchical division of people into groups based on factors such as economic status, power, ethnicity, or religion.

## Population Density

Population density measures the average number of people in an area. It is calculated by comparing the area's population to its size, and it is usually expressed in the number of people per square mile or square kilometer. Demographers study three types of population density.

### *Arithmetic Population Density*

The most commonly used population density is the **arithmetic population density**, calculated by dividing a region's population by its total area. In July 2015, the United States had a population of approximately 321,368,864 in a total area of 3,841,999 square miles, so its arithmetic population density was 83.6 people per square mile, or 32.7 people per square kilometer. These figures are given in various styles. Two common ones are as 83.6/sq. mi. and $83.6/mi^2$.

But arithmetic density says little about population distribution. Population density is simply an average number of people overall in an area. It does not indicate where in the area they live. The diagram below shows three areas with 10 people per square mile, but with different distributions:

- In A, people are evenly dispersed throughout the area. This pattern is common in areas where each person or household lives on a large plot of land. At different scales and with different numbers, this basic pattern appears in many suburbs and many farming and ranching areas.
- In B, people are clustered, or nucleated, in one part of an area. This is a common pattern when people live near a central feature, such as a church, or are concerned about defense.
- In C, people are spread out in a line, known as a linear pattern. This pattern is common for people who live along a river or transit route.

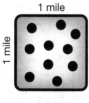

A  Even Distribution  B  Cluster Distribution  C  Linear Distribution

## Physiological Population Density

Another measure is **physiological population density**, calculated by dividing population by the amount of **arable** land, or land suitable for growing crops. For example, in a recent year, the physiological density for Egypt (with 2.8 percent arable land) was 8,078/sq. mile (3,156/sq. kilometer) compared to an arithmetic density of 226/sq. mile (88/sq. kilometer).

Such a large difference between the arithmetic and physiological densities indicates that a small percentage of a region's land is capable of growing crops. Egypt's high physiological density suggests a need for greater crop yields or for other food sources. The physiological population density is a much more useful measure than the arithmetic density when trying to determine a region's **carrying capacity**—the population it can support without significant environmental deterioration.

A country with a high physiological density indicates that it needs high crop yields, but higher yields are not always possible. Many regions rely on imported food. Egypt and Japan both have physiological densities greater than 8,000 people/sq. mile of arable land. In both countries, growing enough food to feed everyone is not practical with current technology. Both supplement crops through the fishing industry and with imported food. Paying for imported food is easier for a developed country such as Japan than it is for a less developed country such as Egypt.

Examine the table below. Notice the relationship between the percent of arable land in a country and the difference between the arithmetic and physiological densities. Countries with high physiological densities face extra challenges feeding their populations.

| ARITHMETIC AND PHYSIOLOGICAL POPULATION DENSITIES | | | |
|---|---|---|---|
| Country | Arithmetic Density (people/sq. mi.) | Physiological Density (people/sq. mi.) | Arable Land |
| Iceland | 8 | 687 | 1.2% |
| Australia | 8 | 125 | 6.0% |
| Canada | 9 | 192 | 4.7% |
| United States | 84 | 498 | 16.8% |
| Egypt | 226 | 8,078 | 2.8% |
| Japan | 962 | 8,218 | 11.7% |
| Netherlands | 1,044 | 3,505 | 31.0% |
| Bangladesh | 2,914 | 4,938 | 59.0% |
| Singapore | 19,982 | 2,498,197 | 0.8% |

### Agricultural Population Density

The third type of population density, **agricultural population density**, compares the number of farmers to the area of arable land. This value gives an indication of the efficiency of the region's farmers. Developed countries have lower agricultural densities because farmers have resources to use technology to produce large quantities of food with few workers. The agricultural densities in less developed countries are higher because farmers often cannot afford modern technology, so they depend more upon labor. As a result, they are not able to produce as much food per farm worker.

For example, compare all three types of population density for Bangladesh and the Netherlands. Both had high arithmetic densities. Bangladesh had 2,914/sq. mi. For the Netherlands the figure was 1,044/sq. mi. Both also had high physiological densities, with Bangladesh at 4,938/sq. mi. and the Netherlands at 3,505/sq. mi. Yet the countries' agricultural densities were drastically different, as might be expected because of their different levels of economic development. The more economically developed Netherlands had a low agricultural density of 31/sq. mi., indicating that Dutch farmers could afford technology and produce food more efficiently than farmers in Bangladesh, which had an agricultural population density of 431/sq. mi.

### Population Density and Time

Density also varies by time of year. Warm-weather states such as Arizona and Florida become more dense each winter as "snowbirds" from northern states flee the cold weather.

Time of day also influences population density. About 1.5 million people reside in the New York City borough of Manhattan. But each weekday, when commuters enter the city to work, the population rises to about 3 million. Such variation is a challenge for Manhattan, which provides water, sewer, fire protection, and other services for 3 million people—even though most return home elsewhere.

## The Implications of Distribution and Density

The distribution of a region's population and its density reflect choices people make. These choices, in turn, reflect their values, such as whether they prefer rural or urban areas.

### Economic, Political, and Social Processes

Most economic decisions are based at least partly on population distribution and density. Businesses are more likely to earn profits when they are near a large customer base. For manufacturing plants, being close to a large labor force is important. Towns and cities have large concentrated populations that provide customers and workers for businesses so that is where most businesses locate.

Rulings by the Supreme Court require state legislatures to create electoral districts of reasonably equal population sizes so each representative serves approximately the same number of people. Since population distribution and densities continually change, legislators have to adjust boundaries every ten years to maintain similar numbers of voters per district. Because urban areas are continuing to increase in population and the population of rural areas is usually shrinking, these **redistricting** situations usually result in physically smaller urban districts and larger rural districts.

The population characteristics of a region can also affect the number of government and private services and the location of these services. Facilities such as schools, police stations, fire stations, social assistance offices, and hospitals are usually positioned close to concentrations of population. Since towns and cities have greater populations and more concentrated populations than rural areas, these urban areas have many more such facilities much closer together than in rural areas.

## Environment and Natural Resources

Whether a region experiences **overpopulation**—having more people than it can support—is partially dependent on its population distribution and density. Another factor is the region's carrying capacity, the number of people it can support without damaging the environment. The higher the population density, usually the greater the strain on the environment. A region with good soil, climate, and other resources might support many people. Another with less favorable attributes will be unable to support as many people.

Cities could be built on land with low carrying capacity, such as where the soil is not ideal for farming. However, for historical reasons, many are located on land with the greatest carrying capacity. Towns and cities started to grow on land that could support a large population and they have remained there.

In addition to agriculture, many other aspects of the environment are affected as population density increases. High population density can result in environmental problems such as pollution or depletion of resources. Because of factors such as sewage and industrial wastes, many lakes and rivers no longer provide drinkable water. In some areas water must be purified or piped in from hundreds of miles away.

## Infrastructure and Urban Services

When people want to live in a particular region—from a country to a neighborhood—they can drive up the population density. They can live in high-density housing units rather than single-family homes. Since many people enjoy living in the centers of big cities, these neighborhoods usually feature apartment and condominium buildings that house many households. In Chicago, the population of the central part of downtown, known as the Loop, is about 21,000 people/sq. mi., more than double what it is for many neighborhoods.

Providing services such as sewer, water, snowplowing, and policing is more cost-effective in high-density areas. The cost of installing a mile of sewer pipe is mostly based on the labor in digging up the land and connecting the pipe. Whether it is a large pipe to serve tens of thousands of people in high-rise buildings or a small pipe to several dozen people in single-family houses is not that significant.

However, high-density areas have challenges. For example the contamination of the water supply for a downtown area can make thousands of people ill, and a disease that spreads through casual contact is much harder to manage in crowded settings. Similar problems in a rural or suburban area with lower population density would be much less severe.

## Population Composition

Identifying the composition of a region's population is crucial to understanding that region's past, present, and future. Population composition involves demographic characteristics such as language, religion, ethnicity, age, and sex.

### Ethnicity

Frequently, members of a particular ethnic group cluster in particular regions. Group members might choose to live close together for cultural regions. This is often true of immigrants or some religious groups. Or, discrimination may limit the housing choices for members of a particular group. The most notable example of this were the practices in many cities that limited the neighborhoods where African Americans could live.

As the maps below show, the distribution of African Americans varies based on scale. At the scale of the country, African Americans are concentrated in the Southeast. At the scale of states, they are often clustered in large cities. And at the scale of cities, they are often clustered in particular neighborhoods.

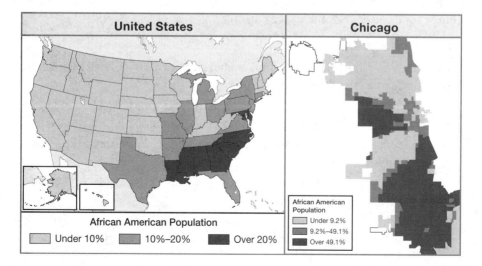

Many cities have neighborhoods named for ethnic clusters such as Little Italy or Chinatown. Recognizing ethnic clustering is important for political leaders. Some ethnic clusters have specific needs requiring special funding, such as funds to help preserve distinctive architecture or to provide English language training.

### Age and Sex

There may also be distribution patterns related to age and sex. Some regions of a country may have a younger or older average population than others. In 2013, Utah had the youngest average age in the United States at 29.9, while the oldest average age was in Maine at 43.5. This difference is so significant that it shapes public policy. Officials in Utah have a higher percentage of school age children to provide for. Officials in Maine might be more concerned with the need for services for seniors. Similar distinctive patterns and resulting issues also exist at the scale of cities and communities.

Differences in the gender balance can result from wars, migrations, and government policies. At the level of entire communities, mining towns and military training bases often have significantly more males than females. Within a city, a gender imbalance might appear if one neighborhood has a post-secondary institution offering courses that tend to attract mostly students of one gender.

## Population Pyramids

One of the most useful tools to study population is the **age-sex composition graph**, which is commonly called a **population pyramid**. Although this tool is based only on age and gender data, it can provide information on birth rates, death rates, how long people live on average, and economic development. It can also give evidence of past events such as natural disasters, wars, political changes, and epidemics. (To understand the use of population pyramids to study economic development, see Chapter 4.)

### Reading a Pyramid

Most pyramids follow the same fundamental structure. However, as with most types of graphics, the format can vary.

- The vertical axis shows age groups, known as **cohorts**. They are often listed in the middle, but are sometimes shown on the left or right side.
- Pyramids usually show the male population on the left and the female population on the right.
- The values on the horizontal axis may be percentages or absolute numbers of males and females.
- Pyramids are most commonly constructed at a country scale, but they can also be constructed for cities, states, or multi-country regions.

### Determining Population Trends

If a population pyramid has a wide base and tapers upward, the region's population is growing. The population pyramid for the African nation of Niger is an example. Notice that the three longest bars are at the bottom of the pyramid and represent ages 0 to 14. As these children age, there will be more people in the older categories. There will also likely be a greater number of children born as these people reach childbearing age.

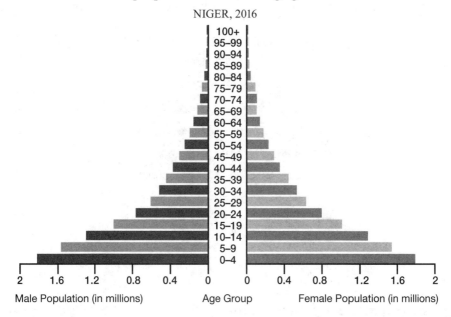

NIGER, 2016

Male Population (in millions) — Age Group — Female Population (in millions)

### Common Patterns

The Niger pyramid is nearly symmetrical, or balanced, left to right, indicating a balance of males and females until approximately age 65. Since women as a group live longer than men, the lack of symmetry in the upper part of the pyramid is typical of many countries.

Another notable trait on the Niger pyramid is that the changes in the size of the bars from one cohort to the next are gradual. There are no sudden indentations or bulges. Assuming there have been no circumstances such as war, natural disaster, epidemics, or government interference, a population pyramid will be symmetrical and show gradual change between cohorts.

### The Impact of War

The clearest effect of war on population is that people are killed. Often, half or more of deaths in wartime are civilians, and the deaths affect people of all ages. However, the loss of fighting-age people, traditionally males between the ages of 18 and 40, is often noticeable.

During war men and women are often separated. Even if they remain together, they may decide to delay a family until the war ends. The bars of the pyramid representing children born during the conflict are often significantly shorter than the bars immediately above and below them. This slowdown of births is called a **birth deficit**.

The post-World War II 1946 graph of Germany shows the loss of life of both males and females in the 20 to 40 age cohorts, with a greater loss of men than women. The birth deficit during war is evident in the 0–4 cohort.

THE GERMAN POPULATION, 1946

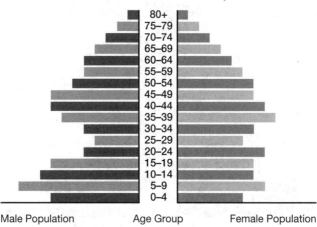

Male Population      Age Group      Female Population

## Baby Booms, Busts, and Echoes

Once hostilities end and peace continues, the birth rate often spikes, an increase known as a **baby boom**. This increase might last a few years or many years. After World War II, the United States baby boom lasted from 1946 to 1965. Baby booms are usually associated with the end of a war, but booms also occur for other reasons, such as times of economic abundance.

Once the boom ends, births are lower for a number of years. This is a **baby bust**, which continues until the boomers reach child-bearing age. With a high number of boomers in the population having children, there can be a significant increase in births that shows up as a bulge on a pyramid. Since this increase reflects an earlier baby boom, it is called an **echo**. As of 2015, children in high school were the last of the echo cohorts, and their parents were the last baby boomers.

Once any anomaly, or unexpected occurrence, appears in a pyramid, it will remain there moving upward until the affected cohort or cohorts disappear from the graph due to death. Notice the upward movement of the baby boom and the echo resulting from World War II in the two U.S. pyramids.

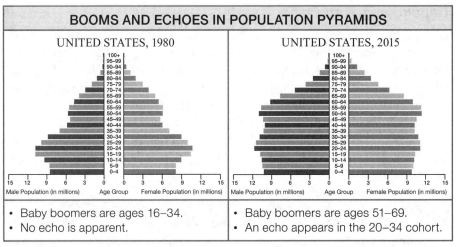

**BOOMS AND ECHOES IN POPULATION PYRAMIDS**

| UNITED STATES, 1980 | UNITED STATES, 2015 |
|---|---|
| • Baby boomers are ages 16–34.<br>• No echo is apparent. | • Baby boomers are ages 51–69.<br>• An echo appears in the 20–34 cohort. |

**Source:** U.S. Census Bureau.

## Migration and Other Anomalies

Many factors can affect a population pyramid. An asymmetrical pyramid, one with significant differences between cohorts, suggests that something notable happened in the population. The viewer of the pyramid will need to determine what historical event caused the irregularity. Several anomalies are described in the table below, along with possible explanations.

| ANOMALIES IN POPULATION PYRAMIDS ||
|---|---|
| **Pyramid Feature** | **Possible Reason** |
| **Bars are longer for people ages 18 to 25 than for people younger or older.** | • A small city includes a large university.<br>• A shortage of school funding causes families to move away when they have children. |
| **Bars are longer for people ages 25 to 50 than for children.** | • An economic crisis causes people to decide to have fewer children.<br>• A government policy to slow population growth discourages births.<br>• An epidemic causes many infants to die. |
| **Bars are longer for people over the age of 65.** | • A community in a warm climate attracts retirees.<br>• A lack of jobs causes young people to move away. |
| **Bars are longer for males than females.** | • An oil boom attracts people for jobs that are traditionally done by men. |

## Dependency Ratio

Population pyramid data is frequently used to estimate the **dependency ratio** (DR), a value comparing the working to the nonworking parts of a population. Demographers consider people ages 15–64 the **potential workforce**, the group expected to be the society's labor force. Everyone else—people under 15 or over 64—are the **dependent population**, because they are considered too young or too old to work full-time. Dividing the potential workforce by the dependent population results in the dependency ratio. Since many people who are 15 to 64 do not work for pay, and since many people under 15 and over 64 do, this number is only a rough estimate.

| CALCULATING DEPENDENCY RATIO | | | |
|---|---|---|---|
| **Country** | **Population by Age Group** | **Calculation** | **Dependency Ratio** |
| **United States** | • under 15: 18.8%<br>• 15 to 64: 65.9%<br>• over 64: 15.3% | $\dfrac{18.8 + 15.3}{65.9} = 0.52$ | 1 : 0.52 |
| **Niger** | • under 15: 49.3%<br>• 15 to 64: 48.1%<br>• over 64: 2.6% | $\dfrac{49.3 + 2.6}{48.1} = 1.08$ | 1 : 1.08 |

**GEOGRAPHIC PERSPECTIVES:** INTERPRETING DEPENDENCY NUMBERS

Comparing the dependency ratios of any two countries or regions suggests differences in how people live in each place. For example, the United States and Niger have very different dependency ratios:

- Each person in the U.S. Potential Labor Force supported himself or herself plus an average of 0.52 additional people.
- In Niger, each member of the Potential Labor Force supported 1.08 additional people.

A map showing dependency ratios of countries around the world would show that Japan, Australia, and most of the countries in Europe have dependency ratios similar to the one for the United States. In contrast, countries throughout Africa and parts of South America and Asia have dependency ratios more like the one for Niger.

## Composition of Dependent Groups

A closer look at the distribution of the dependency ratios could focus in on the composition of the dependent groups and spatial distributions they influence. The United States includes more seniors than children. This composition reflects that families have relatively few children and that people live relatively long lives. Compared to the United States, families in Niger have more children and people live shorter lives. As a result, Niger has more children than senior citizens. When thinking about dependency, geographers specify whether the dependents are younger or older than the working age population.

## Spatial Distribution

The distinctive composition of the dependency ratio in the United States and Niger shapes the spatial distribution of the population in each country. In the United States, senior citizens who have retired often choose to move to warm climates, so the populations of Arizona and Florida and other warm-weather states have grown rapidly. In Niger, the high ratio of children means that school density should be high to provide education for them. However, Niger's poverty makes that difficult to achieve.

| KEY TERMS | | |
|---|---|---|
| population distribution | carrying capacity | birth deficit |
| population density | agricultural population density | baby boom |
| midlatitudes | | baby bust |
| social stratification | redistricting | echo |
| arithmetic population density | overpopulation | dependency ratio |
| physiological population density | age-sex composition graph | potential workforce |
| | | dependent population |
| arable | population pyramid | |
| | cohort | |

**Questions 1 and 2 refer to the map below.**

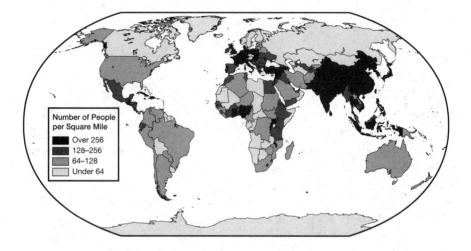

1. Which generalization is best illustrated by the world map above?

    (A) Climate is the primary factor influencing population distribution.

    (B) People are spread out evenly throughout the world.

    (C) The majority of the world's population lives between 20° N and 60° N latitude.

    (D) More people live in the Western Hemisphere than in the Eastern Hemisphere.

    (E) People have preserved fertile land for farming by choosing to settle heavily in areas with poor farmland.

2. Based on the map, which area is most densely populated?

    (A) eastern Asia

    (B) northern Europe

    (C) western North America

    (D) central South America

    (E) southern Africa

**Question 3 refers to the table below.**

|  | Arithmetic Density | Physiological Density | Arable Land Percentage |
|---|---|---|---|
| **Country A** | 226 people/sq. mi. | 8,078 people/sq. mi. | 2.8% |
| **Country B** | 84 people/sq. mi. | 498 people/sq. mi. | 16.8% |

3. According to the table, which country has a greater need for increased crop yields and imported foods and why?

(A) Country A: Its physiological density indicates that its farmers do not have the technological resources to grow crops efficiently.

(B) Country A: The large difference between its arithmetic and physiological densities indicates that it has only a little good farmland.

(C) Country A: Its high arithmetic and physiological densities indicate that it needs to use a high percentage of its land to grow crops.

(D) Country B: It has an arable land percentage of 16.8, which is not sufficient for growing enough food to feed everyone.

(E) Country B: The small difference between its arithmetic and physiological densities indicates it has ample good farmland.

4. Which country has the lowest arithmetic population density?

(A) Egypt

(B) United States

(C) Australia

(D) India

(E) France

5. The Nile River Valley has the greatest concentration of population in Egypt because of its

(A) alpine climate

(B) tourist attractions

(C) extensive in-migration from nearby areas

(D) many sacred sites

(E) high-quality agricultural land

**Questions 6 to 8 refer to the population pyramid below.**

UNITED ARAB EMIRATES, 2016

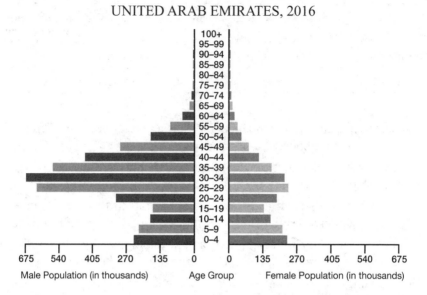

6. Which might explain the asymmetrical part of the population pyramid?

   (A) a high death rate among men ages 25–50

   (B) a large guest-worker population

   (C) an overcounting of children during the census

   (D) an epidemic with a high rate of mortality among the elderly

   (E) a major war fought in the years 2006 to 2010

7. Which statement about birth is best supported by the pyramid?

   (A) More births occurred in 1956 than in 1966.

   (B) More births occurred in 1986 than in 2006.

   (C) The number steadily increased between 1956 and 2016.

   (D) The number steadily decreased between 1956 and 2016.

   (E) Fewer births occurred in 2016 than in 2011.

8. A more-developed country with the same total population as the United Arab Emirates would most likely have shorter bars for

   (A) both males and females at ages 70 and above

   (B) both males and females at ages 9 and below

   (C) both males and females at all ages

   (D) females only at ages 25 to 34

   (E) males only at ages 10 to 19

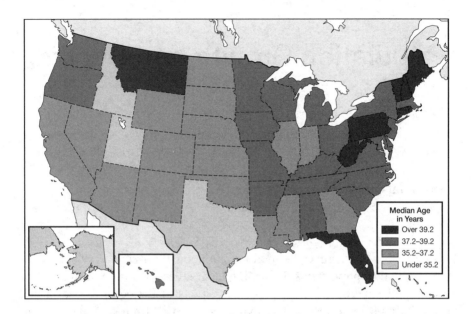

**1.** The median age is the age at which half of all people are older and half of all people are younger.

A. Briefly describe and explain the regional distribution of people in the United States by median age.

B. Explain why Florida has a relatively high median age compared to other states and its economic impact on the state of Florida.

C. Explain TWO age-related issues that are more important in Texas than in Florida.

---

**THINK AS A GEOGRAPHER:** ONE PLACE, MANY DENSITIES

Geographers apply the concept of population density at many scales. A resident of Salt Lake City lives in areas with these numbers of people per square mile: Salt Lake City—1,387; Utah—34; United States—87; the world—130.

**1.** Explain why Salt Lake City might be considered overpopulated.

**2.** What does the difference in density between the United States and the world suggest about the United States?

**3.** Explain why a Salt Lake City resident could claim to live in a place of both high and low population density.

# 4

# Population Growth and Decline

*A finite world can support only a finite population; therefore, population growth must eventually equal zero.*

—Garrett Hardin, "The Tragedy of the Commons," 1968

**Essential Question:** What are the political, social, and economic consequences of the rapid population growth of the past 200 years?

**B**efore the 19th century, the total human population grew very slowly. By making small improvements in farming techniques, clearing forested land to expand land for crops, and finding new regions of the ocean dense in fish, people became more efficient at extracting energy from the environment. Around 1800, the population reached 1 billion. In the 200-plus years since then, world population has exploded: it is around 7.4 billion today. The United Nations predicts it will reach nearly 11 billion by 2100. What problems—and what opportunities—will this growth present? No one knows for sure.

WORLD POPULATION GROWTH SINCE 1760

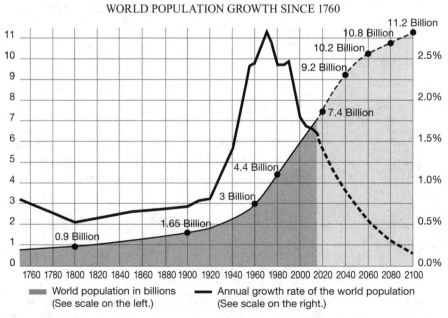

World population in billions
(See scale on the left.)

Annual growth rate of the world population
(See scale on the right.)

**Source:** Population projections come from "World Population Prospects: The 2015 Revision," UN Department of Economic and Social Affairs, 2015.

## Measuring the Number of Births

Geographers commonly use two different statistics to describe the rate at which children are born:

- The **crude birth rate (CBR)** is the number of live births per year for each 1,000 people.

- In contrast, the **total fertility rate (TFR)** focuses on women in their childbearing of ages 15 to 49. TFR is the average number of children who would be born per woman of that group in a country, assuming every woman lived through her childbearing years.

Compared to the CBR, the TFR more accurately reflects cultural norms—such as how people weigh the costs and benefits of having a child and how people perceive the role of women in society.

TOTAL FERTILITY RATES

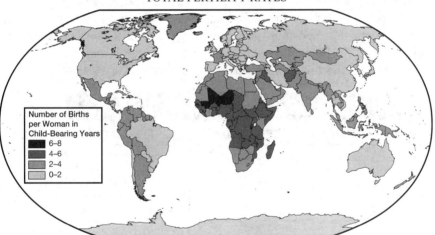

Total fertility rates (TFRs) generally decline as countries become wealthier.

In most of the world, the TFR was higher in the past than it is today. In parts of Europe before 1800, it averaged 6.2 children. In those days, most people lived on farms, and having more children meant more people to work the land. However, so many children died as infants that people lived, on average, only about 40 years. Despite the high TFR, population growth was slow.

## Changes in Fertility

Beginning in the mid-18th century, Europeans began having fewer children. Part of this was unintentional. During this time, countries began keeping larger standing armies, so more men were away from home for longer periods. But most of it was intentional. With the Industrial Revolution, (For a definition of the Industrial Revolution, see Chapter 15.) when people began to rely more on machines than on muscle power to produce goods, couples decided they needed fewer children. But industrialization also enabled people to live longer. So even though TFR declined, population growth increased.

## Role of Women in Society

Cultural, economic, political, and environmental realities have always shaped decisions about whether to have children. Since these conditions have varied across time and cultures, so have birth rates. How people viewed the role of women in a society has been a particularly important factor influencing TFR. Over the past 250 years, as countries industrialized, people moved from rural areas to urban areas and found work in factories. Many women became factory workers or domestic help. They lived in small apartments or small houses in cities, and families became smaller. Urban families did not need children to work their farmland—and they were living in already crowded spaces.

When factories became common in the early 19th century, children worked in them alongside adults. But in the later part of the century, governments passed laws prohibiting child labor and began opening public schools. As young women obtained more schooling, they began to expand their work opportunities. The longer they stayed in school, the fewer children they had, a trend that continues to the present day, as the chart on Ghana shows.

| TFR AND SCHOOLING FOR GIRLS IN GHANA | | |
|:---:|:---:|:---:|
| **Years of Schooling** | **TFR, 1990** | **TFR, 2007** |
| 0 | 7.0 | 6.1 |
| 4 | 6.4 | 5.0 |
| 8 | 5.6 | 3.7 |
| 12 | 2.7 | 2.0 |

Source: worldbank.org.

In Ghana between 1990 and 2007, as young women gained more education, the number of children they had decreased. This suggests that young women who spent more time in school chose to delay marriage.

The United States showed a similar pattern of delayed marriage. As educational opportunities increased for women between 1950 and 2010, the median marriage age of women increased from just over 20 years of age to nearly 27. The average age at which women gave birth to their first child increased as well.

## Family Planning

Throughout the 20th century, the spread of family planning information and changes in technology aided people who wanted to choose the number of children they had. In countries with wide access to family planning methods, including the United States and many countries in Europe, couples gave birth to their first child later in life, had fewer children, had fewer unintended pregnancies, and had larger intervals between having children. In these places, the total fertility rate continued a decline that began with the Industrial Revolution.

Religious values also shape attitudes toward having children. Some religious traditions oppose certain forms of family planning. Women who follow traditional religious beliefs, regardless of their particular religion, have higher fertility rates than those who do not. These women are less likely to use birth control and less likely to be employed outside the home.

## Government Programs to Reduce Births

Governments also influence the TFR. Concerns about **overpopulation**, the growth of population beyond what an area can support, have led to **anti-natalist policies**, programs to decrease the number of births.

The Chinese government introduced two different anti-natalist policies in the 1970s. The first, known as "later, longer, fewer", was introduced in 1972. It encouraged parents to get married later in life, wait longer between children, and as a result have fewer children.

The impact of the "later, longer, fewer" policy can be seen in China's pyramid in the relatively shorter bars for the 40–44 and 35–39 cohorts. The expansion in births in the 25–29 and 30–34 cohorts is the result of the large number of women who entered childbearing age in the mid-1980s.

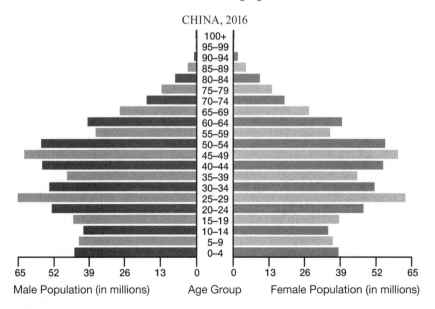

CHINA, 2016

"Later, longer, fewer" did result in reduced fertility but not as quickly as officials wanted. In response, China instituted its One Child Policy in 1979. Parents who had more than one child were subject to fines, although the law made exceptions for rural couples and ethnic minorities. The policy remained in effect until 2016. During that period, China's fertility rate decreased. However, researchers disagree on how much of the decline resulted from the policy and how much from other factors, such as increased education for women.

One effect of China's One Child Policy was that it reduced the number of adult workers in the country. Concerns that a smaller workforce would reduce economic growth and would lead to a shortage of workers to support the elderly led the government to reevaluate the policy.

In addition, the policy contributed to unbalanced gender ratio. Chinese culture has long preferred male children over females. So, when some couples learned that their one child would be a girl, they chose to have an abortion or to immediately give the infant to an orphanage and not register the birth with the government. By doing this, they could have another child, who might be male. By 2010, China had 118 males born for every 100 females. The gender imbalance was so great that Chinese leaders feared it would lead to greater crime and civil unrest among young men who felt they had no prospects to get married and have children.

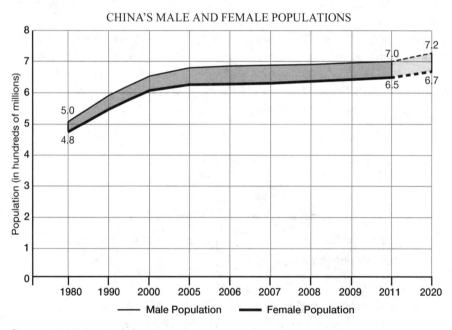

CHINA'S MALE AND FEMALE POPULATIONS

Source: United Nations Development Programme.

Males outnumber females in the total world population. China accounts for roughly half of the gap.

In 2016, the Chinese government modified the controversial program and now allows families to have two children.

While China's One Child Policy was the most comprehensive population-control plan, other countries have used more targeted programs. In European nations, birth control education decreased teenage pregnancy. In Africa and

South Asia, laws banning child marriage raised the average marriage age and the age that a woman had her first child.

### Government Policies to Encourage Births

Throughout history, some governments have encouraged large families. Governments have believed that a growing population stimulated economic growth and increased military power.

In recent decades, a variation of this reasoning has emerged in some highly developed countries. As fertility rates dropped but people lived longer, the percentage of elderly people increased. To keep the economy vibrant, countries such as France, Sweden, and Japan instituted **pro-natalist policies**, or programs designed to increase the fertility rate. For example, they have provided paid time off from jobs held by mothers, free child care, and family discounts on government services.

# Life Expectancy

Even though the total fertility rate worldwide has been decreasing, the world's population continues to grow. This growth reflects a decrease in the death rate and an increase in how long people live.

### Global Population Increase

The most important factor in the increase in global population is the rise in **life expectancy**, the number of years the average person will live. It is commonly expressed from the time of a person's birth, but it can be calculated at any point in his or her lifetime. A century ago, the global life expectancy was about 34 years at birth; today it is nearly 70. In most of Europe, life expectancy at birth is more than 80 years. However, in less-developed areas, such as many sub-Saharan African countries, life expectancy at birth is less than 50 years.

LIFE EXPECTANCY BY COUNTRY

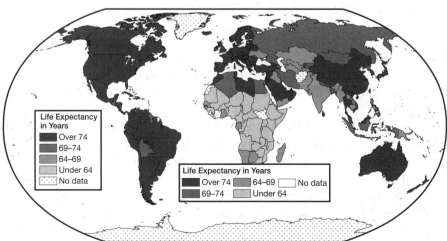

One of the most important factors increasing life expectancy is the drop in the **infant mortality rate**, the number of children who die before their first birthday. For example, in the state of Massachusetts, the infant mortality rate decreased from 130 out of each 1,000 live births in the 1850s to about 4 today.

## Better Food Production and Nutrition

Over the past 250 years, several advances in agriculture have helped increase life expectancy:

- mechanizing food production, such as replacing horses with tractors
- improving seeds, fertilizers, and farming techniques through research by state universities and private companies
- transporting products more efficiently in trucks, trains, and ships, often on roads, rail lines, or canals built with government support

In the United States in 1800, almost everyone farmed. Today farmers make up less than 3 percent of the population, yet they produce enough food to feed everyone in the country and export vast quantities. Advances in agriculture such as the following had effects that rippled through society:

- Greater farming efficiency freed people to work in nonfarm industries, easing the transition to industrialization.
- Food security improved around the world. Hunger and famines still occurred because people were too poor to purchase food or because of political or distribution problems, not because of an actual food shortage.
- As farms depended less on manual labor, farm families became smaller.
- The use of machinery meant that one person could farm more acres. Many small farms were consolidated into larger farms and the owners of those consolidated farms moved to urban areas.
- As the population of rural areas decreased, and cars and better roads allowed people to travel farther and more easily, many small towns that had served farmers disappeared.

## Advances in Public Sanitation

As early industrial cities grew, so did the problems of large concentrated populations, such as the spread of cholera and other diseases through water contaminated by human waste, as well as plague, which is carried by fleas that live on rodents.

One of the most important advances in reducing mortality was the creation of public sewer systems. Before the Industrial Revolution and in its early years, people in cities dumped human waste into streets and rivers. The waste often reached the water supply, contaminating the water and making people sick. Especially vulnerable to disease were children and the elderly. Then cities began to install sewer systems, protecting water supplies from contamination and thus increasing life expectancy.

People also learned that boiling water before they used it could prevent transmission of waterborne illnesses. That worked before citizens decided to pay for clean water through taxes. Communities began to install water treatment plants that transported clean water to the homes in the cities. Cities also created departments of public sanitation and started to collect garbage and other waste produced by city residents. By doing this, cities reduced the number of rodents that fed on the waste and often carried disease.

### Improvements in Healthcare

Improved medical care coincided with improvements in food production and sanitation. The development of vaccines to prevent disease, antibiotics to cure diseases, and improved medical procedures boosted life expectancy.

Prior to the 1800s, smallpox killed as many as 400,000 people each year. However, in the 1700s, Dr. Edward Jenner figured out that if he infected people with cowpox, a much milder disease related to smallpox, those people would be immune to smallpox. Jenner's work led to a smallpox vaccine. Today, efforts by the United Nations, national governments, and private organizations to vaccinate people around the world have been so successful that no case of smallpox has been reported since 1977. Jenner's work was also the basis for vaccines against other serious diseases, such as polio, tuberculosis, and rabies.

While vaccines helped prevent people from getting ill, antibiotics helped cure people who had bacterial infections. The first widely used antibiotic was penicillin, which came into use in the mid-1900s. Before penicillin, deadly bacterial infections killed many people. The deadliest epidemic in history was the plague, which was spread by flea bites. During the mid-1300s, the plague killed about 20 million people in Europe alone. Other common bacterial infections include staph, which commonly killed people who got wounded in battle or suffered a deep cut, strep, and parasitic infections.

Improved medical procedures have also extended life expectancy. Among these procedures was the development and improvement of surgery, which was often deadly before antibiotics. Now surgery is safe enough that it can help an individual suffering from a heart attack, stroke, cancer, or other ailments. Doctors have also saved the lives of pregnant women and their newborn children through the use of caesarean section surgeries.

# The Demographic Transition Model

Changes in the birth rate and death rate in a country are shaped by how a country changes from an agrarian to an industrial society. The **Demographic Transition Model** shows five typical stages of population change that countries pass through as they modernize. Each stage lasts for a period of indeterminate length. The developed countries of the world passed through these stages first, while the underdeveloped areas of the world are still passing through the early and middle stages.

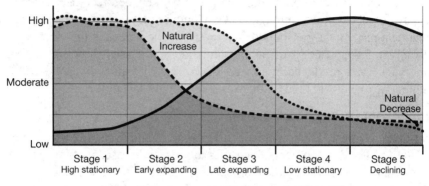

STAGES OF THE DEMOGRAPHIC TRANSITION MODEL

High

Moderate

Low

Natural Increase

Natural Decrease

| Stage 1 | Stage 2 | Stage 3 | Stage 4 | Stage 5 |
| High stationary | Early expanding | Late expanding | Low stationary | Declining |

•••• Birth rate ▪ ▪ ▪ Death rate ▬▬ Total Population

| CHARACTERISTICS OF THE DTM STAGES | | | | | |
|---|---|---|---|---|---|
| Factor | 1. High Stationary | 2. Early Expanding | 3. Late Expanding | 4. Low Stationary | 5. Declining |
| **Birth Rate** | High, but fluctuating as need for farm labor changes | High, but fluctuating to reflect desires for big families | Declining as urbanization decreases the need for child labor | Low, but enough to keep the population stable | So low it falls below the death rate |
| **Death Rate** | High, but fluctuating to reflect diseases and poor sanitation | Rapidly declining as nutrition, sanitation, and medicine improve | Declining, but not as fast as in previous stage | Low and stable | Low, sometimes increasing as the population ages |
| **Population Change** | Very low growth because births and deaths are both high | Rapid growth as death rates fall faster than birth rates | Rapid but slowing growth as birth rates decline | Very low growth because births and deaths are both low | Very low decline as births fall below deaths |
| **Examples Today** | Scattered isolated groups | • Mali<br>• South Sudan | • Mexico<br>• Turkey<br>• Indonesia | • United States<br>• China | • Japan<br>• Germany |
| **Population Structure** | Very young | Very young | Young, with rising life expectancy | Balanced, with more aging | Very old |

## *Demographic Transition and Population Pyramids*

Stages 2 to 5 of the Demographic Transition Model each tend to produce a different-shaped population pyramid. (Stage 1 includes only few isolated groups, which would not be reflected in population pyramids.)

**Stage 2:** Niger represents a Stage 2 country with an **expansive population pyramid**, one with a high birth rate (which produces a wide base) and a low life expectancy (which leads to narrowing in the upper years). Because the younger generations are larger than the older ones, the result is rapid population growth. This is typical of a less developed region.

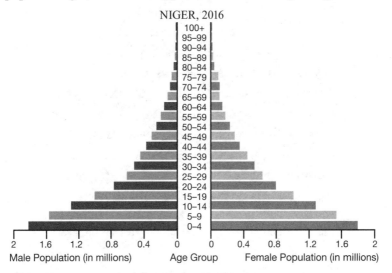

NIGER, 2016

**Stage 3:** Turkey represents an urbanizing Stage 3 nation, with a declining birth rate and a more slowly declining death rate. Notice that the majority of the population is under the age of 34. The society is still young, but the percentage of elderly is increasing as life expectancy goes up.

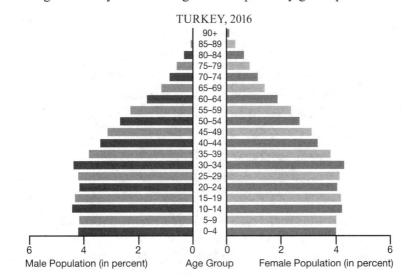

TURKEY, 2016

**Stage 4:** France's pyramid, representing Stage 4, is typical of the shape known as a **stationary population pyramid**. It indicates a population that is not significantly growing or shrinking. The birth rate is low but steady. The death rate is also low, indicating a high life expectancy and increased percentage of older people. This graph shape is usually associated with more developed countries.

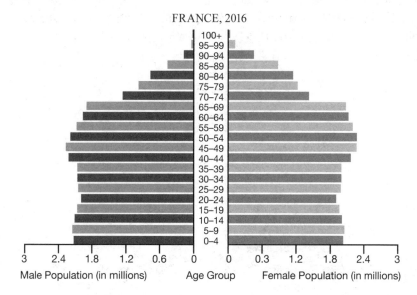

FRANCE, 2016

**Stage 5:** Japan's pyramid represents Stage 5. The narrow base reflects a decreasing birth rate. The population is aging and declining slightly overall. The largest age group is 65–69.

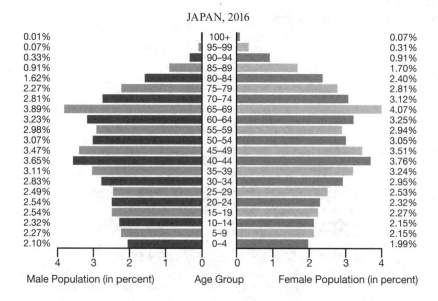

JAPAN, 2016

## Policy Implications

As countries move from stage to stage, they face different challenges. A country in Stage 2 or 3, with a relatively high percentage of young people, often lacks the resources to educate all children. A country in Stage 4 or 5, with a relatively high percentage of old people, often faces problems funding healthcare. However, since the elderly can vote while children cannot, the elderly often have more influence on governmental policy than do children.

## Rate of Population Increase

The natural increase or decrease in a population is measured by subtracting the number of deaths from the number of births. To compare countries of different sizes, demographers use rates rather than total numbers. The crude birth rate (CBR) and the **crude death rate** (CDR) of an area are measured per 1,000 population. The percentage at which a country's population is growing or declining, without the impact of migration, is the **rate of natural increase** (RNI). Calculate it with this formula: RNI = (CBR−CDR) ÷ 10, and then add a percent sign. For the entire world, the CBR is about 20 and the CDR is about 8. Since (20−8) ÷ 10 equals 1.2, the RNI for the world is about 1.2 percent. RNI tends to be less than 1 percent in higher developed countries and greater than 1 percent in lesser developed countries.

## Demographic Balancing Equation

Natural increase is only part of a country's total population change. Migration also plays a part. To calculate a country's total population change, the number of **immigrants**, people who moved into the country, and the number of **emigrants**, people who moved out of the country, must be added to the equation. This is known as the **Demographic Balancing Equation**:

Total Population Change = Births − Deaths + Immigrants − Emigrants

## Population Doubling Time

Demographers describe population growth in two ways:

- Arithmetic growth is when the increase is a constant number each period. Arithmetic growth by the addition of 1 would be 1, 2, 3, 4, etc. Arithmetic growth by 5 would be 1, 6, 11, 16, etc.

- Exponential growth is when the increase is a constant factor each period. If the factor is 2, then the number doubles each period: 1, 2, 4, 8, etc. Exponential growth by 5 would be 1, 5, 25, 125, etc.

Since the early 1800s, global population has been growing exponentially. For any quantity growing exponentially, the time it takes to double in size can be estimated using an equation known as the Rule of 70 (some people use the Rule of 72). Assuming the growth rate remains steady, the approximate doubling time in years will be 70 divided by the growth rate per year.

For example, in 2014, the West African country of Ivory Coast had a population growth rate of about 2.0. Since 70 divided by 2 equals 35, if the growth rate remains about 2.0, the population of Ivory Coast will double in 35 years. The United States had a much lower growth rate: 0.77. If the U.S. growth rate remains at 0.77, the U.S. population will double in about 91 years.

## Epidemiological Transition Model

Because the world did not develop industrially and economically at the same pace in all areas, there is a large discrepancy in the types of diseases found across the world. In the early 1970s, epidemiologist Abdel Omran identified predictable stages in disease and life expectancy that countries experience as they develop. Omran's work is known as the **Epidemiological Transition Model**. The stages of the Epidemiological Transition Model correspond with the stages of the Demographic Transition Model.

| EPIDEMIOLOGICAL TRANSITION MODEL STAGES | | |
|---|---|---|
| **Stage** | **Description** | **Effects on Population** |
| **1. Pestilence and Famine** | Parasitic or infectious diseases, accidents, animal attacks, or human conflicts cause most deaths. | A high death rate and low life expectancy |
| **2. Receding Pandemics** | The number of pandemics (widespread diseases that affect large populations) declines as a result of improved sanitation, nutrition, and medicine. | A decreasing death rate and increasing life expectancy |
| **3. Degenerative and Human-Created Diseases** | Infectious and parasitic diseases continue to decrease, but diseases associated with aging, such as heart disease and types of cancer—increase as people live. | Death rate stabilizes at a low level and life expectancy increases |
| **4. Delayed Degenerative Diseases** | Stage 4 is an extension of Stage 3, but the age-related diseases are put off as medical procedures delay the onset of these diseases through advanced procedures. Diseases such as Alzheimer's and dementia increase. | Death rate reaches its lowest level and life expectancy reaches a peak |
| **5. Reemerging of Infectious and Parasitic Diseases** | Infectious and parasitic diseases increase as some bacteria and parasites become resistant to antibiotics and vaccines. | Life expectancy decreases |

Eating healthier food, drinking less alcohol, and exercising more have enabled many people, particularly those in developed countries, to live longer, more active lives. One of the biggest lifestyle changes has been in smoking. In the United States, the percentage of adults who smoke has declined in the last five decades from around 40 percent to around 15 percent. The change varies by region, with adults in the Midwest and Southeast more likely to smoke than are adults in the West and Northeast. Thus, another important factor in the reduction of mortality rates are changes in lifestyle that keep people healthier and living longer.

## GEOGRAPHIC PERSPECTIVES: THE IDEAS OF THOMAS MALTHUS

In 1798, Thomas Malthus published one of the most provocative books on population growth ever written, *An Essay on the Principles of Population.* Malthus, a member of the clergy and an early economist, focused on one of the underlying concerns of geography: the relationship between people and the earth.

### Malthus in His Time

Malthus lived during a period when people were optimistic that new technology would make life better—but Malthus feared it would not. He analyzed the relationship between agricultural output and the growing number of people, and concluded that society was on a path toward massive starvation.

He believed that food production would increase arithmetically, growing steadily, but by the same amount each generation. In contrast, he believed that people would not limit the number of children they had, so the population would increase exponentially, multiplying by the same amount each generation. Since population would grow faster than food production, the world's population would soon be unsupportable. If people could not limit population growth voluntarily, widespread and massive starvation would.

### Malthus Today

Geographers and other social scientists have debated the usefulness of Malthus's ideas about population growth, known as **Malthusian theory**, since he first published them. Food production grew more quickly than Malthus predicted, so famine did not reach the scale he feared. People today who have adapted his basic ideas to modern conditions are known as **Neo-Malthusians**. They argue that global overpopulation is a serious problem and an even greater threat for the future. They point out continued population growth will lead to the depletion of nonrenewable resources such as petroleum and metals, pollution of air and water, and shortages of food, all of which could bring social, political, economic, and environmental catastrophe.

| KEY TERMS | |
|---|---|
| crude birth rate | Epidemiological Transition Model |
| total fertility rate | stationary population pyramid |
| overpopulation | crude death rate |
| anti-natalist policies | rate of natural increase |
| pro-natalist policies | immigrants |
| life expectancy | emigrants |
| infant mortality rate | Demographic Balancing Equation |
| Demographic Transition Model | Malthusian theory |
| expansive population pyramid | Neo-Malthusians |

**Questions 1 and 2 refer to the population pyramid below.**

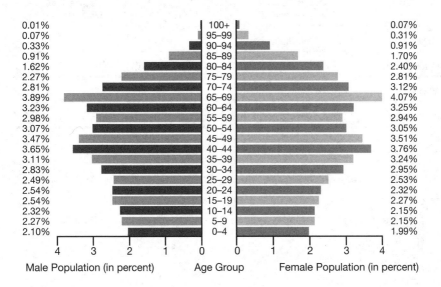

| 0.01% | 100+ | 0.07% |
| 0.07% | 95–99 | 0.31% |
| 0.33% | 90–94 | 0.91% |
| 0.91% | 85–89 | 1.70% |
| 1.62% | 80–84 | 2.40% |
| 2.27% | 75–79 | 2.81% |
| 2.81% | 70–74 | 3.12% |
| 3.89% | 65–69 | 4.07% |
| 3.23% | 60–64 | 3.25% |
| 2.98% | 55–59 | 2.94% |
| 3.07% | 50–54 | 3.05% |
| 3.47% | 45–49 | 3.51% |
| 3.65% | 40–44 | 3.76% |
| 3.11% | 35–39 | 3.24% |
| 2.83% | 30–34 | 2.95% |
| 2.49% | 25–29 | 2.53% |
| 2.54% | 20–24 | 2.32% |
| 2.54% | 15–19 | 2.27% |
| 2.32% | 10–14 | 2.15% |
| 2.27% | 5–9 | 2.15% |
| 2.10% | 0–4 | 1.99% |

Male Population (in percent)　　　Age Group　　　Female Population (in percent)

1. Which stage of the Demographic Transition Model does the population pyramid represent?

   (A) Stage 1

   (B) Stage 2

   (C) Stage 3

   (D) Stage 4

   (E) Stage 5

2. Which is most likely a bigger concern for the country represented in the pyramid than for countries in other DTM stages?

   (A) a greater demand for government spending on pensions and health-care for the elderly

   (B) a greater demand for government spending on education and day-care for children

   (C) a higher rate of unemployment among people of working age

   (D) a higher rate of emigration by people in search of jobs

   (E) a faster overall population growth than in previous decades

| BIRTH RATES AND DEATH RATES BY LEVEL OF DEVELOPMENT | | | |
|---|---|---|---|
| Country | Level of Development | Crude Birth Rate/ 1,000 People | Crude Death Rate/1,000 People |
| Niger | Less Developed | 45.5 | 12.4 |
| Bangladesh | Less Developed | 20.0 | 5.7 |
| Mexico | Developing | 18.8 | 5.3 |
| Australia | More Developed | 13.2 | 6.4 |
| France | More Developed | 12.4 | 9.2 |

3. Which country's population has the highest rate of natural increase?

(A) Niger

(B) Bangladesh

(C) Mexico

(D) Australia

(E) France

4. France's crude death rate is probably higher than Bangladesh's because

(A) France is involved in more wars

(B) France has more natural disasters

(C) France has a higher percentage of elderly people

(D) Bangladesh has a better healthcare system

(E) Bangladesh has a higher life expectancy

5. Which ideas predicted greater famines from overpopulation than occurred?

(A) the Demographic Transition

(B) the Epidemiological Transition Model

(C) Malthusian theory

(D) Neo-Malthusian theory

(E) China's "One Child" policy

6. Which change most reduced fertility rates in less developed countries?

(A) building hospitals and healthcare facilities

(B) providing more education for girls

(C) implementing pro-natalist policies

(D) discouraging the use of birth control

(E) promoting fundamentalist religious values

**7.** Over the past century, the population of the world has been

    (A) growing even though the fertility rate is decreasing

    (B) growing even though life expectancy is decreasing

    (C) growing because the fertility rate is increasing

    (D) declining because life expectancy is decreasing

    (E) declining even though the fertility rate is increasing

**8.** According to the Epidemiological Transition Model, when do vaccines and improved sanitation cause the death rate to decrease?

    (A) Stage 1

    (B) Stage 2

    (C) Stage 3

    (D) Stage 4

    (E) Stage 5

## FREE-RESPONSE QUESTION

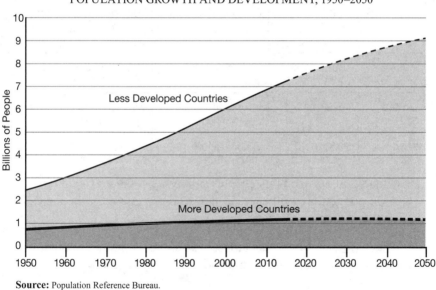

POPULATION GROWTH AND DEVELOPMENT, 1950–2050

**Source:** Population Reference Bureau.

**1.** Since 1950, population has grown fastest in less developed countries.

    A. Identify and explain two reasons for the gap in population growth between the two groups of countries shown on the graph.

    B. Identify and explain two consequences of uneven population growth between less and more developed countries.

Geographers study patterns and trends to help them make predictions about the future. This often has very practical uses. For example, knowing where people will be living in 30 years helps communities plan their investments in roads and schools. But making predictions is very difficult because they are always based on assumptions about how much the future will look like the past.

Use data from the chapter and from this chart to answer the questions that follow about how much the world population will grow.

| EXAMPLES OF POPULATION GROWTH AND DECLINE | | | |
|---|---|---|---|
| **Region** | **Time Period** | **Important Event or Trend** | **Population Change** |
| **World** | 1800 to 2000 | Industrialization | Total increase of about 600 percent |
| **Europe** | Late 14th century | Disease epidemic | Total decrease of about 25 percent |
| **Americas** | 1492 to late 1800s | Disease epidemic | Total decrease among indigenous population of 70 to 90 percent |
| **Russia** | 1987 to 1999 | Political turmoil | Birthrate decrease of about 45 percent |
| **United States** | 1929 to 1941 | Economic depression | Birthrate decrease of about 30 percent |
| **World** | 2000 to 2016 | Globalization | Birthrate decrease |

1. What evidence from this chapter supports a prediction that the world population will increase at a decreasing rate for the next 100 years and then level out?

2. What evidence from the chart above supports a prediction that the growth of the world population will slow in the future?

# 5

# Causes and Consequences
# of Migration

*More than any other nation on Earth, America has constantly drawn strength
and spirit from wave after wave of immigrants. In each generation, they have
proved to be the most restless, the most adventurous, the most innovative,
the most industrious of people.*

—President Bill Clinton, speech at Portland State University, 1998

**Essential Question:** How does migration impact society?

In his 1998 commencement address at Portland State University, President
Bill Clinton highlighted the ongoing impact of immigrants coming to the
United States. The United States is the most populous immigrant country in the
world. Like many countries in the Americas and Australia, most residents are
either immigrants or descendants of immigrants. The United States" culture,
institutions, and population are the products of five centuries of immigration.

## Migration's Push and Pull Factors

The history of the world is a story of constant movement. **Migration** is the
permanent or semipermanent relocation of people from one place to another.
Since the first humans lived in eastern Africa, people have been on the move.
Early humans were very mobile, searching for nuts, seeds, and fruits to eat, and
for animals to hunt. As agriculture and urban settlements developed, people
began to settle down. However, they continued to move, from rural to urban
areas, and from settlement to settlement.

Most people who move do so in search of a better life. They are part of a
**voluntary migration, a movement made by choice**. The choice usually
combines a decision to move away from someplace with a decision to move
toward someplace else:

- People generally decide to move because of **push factors, which are**
  negative circumstances, events, or conditions present where they live.
- Once migrants decide to leave, they usually choose a destination based
  on its positive conditions and circumstances, or **pull factors.**

## Economic Push and Pull Factors

The most common reason people migrate is that they lack jobs and economic opportunities. These migrants go to areas offering greater economic opportunities.

| EXAMPLES OF ECONOMIC PUSH AND PULL FACTORS | | |
| --- | --- | --- |
| **Group and Place of Origin** | **Push Factors** | **Pull Factors** |
| **Factory workers in the U.S. Rust Belt states, beginning in the 1970s** | Unemployment rose among factory workers, particularly in traditional manufacturing states such as Michigan and Pennsylvania. | Many factory workers moved to southern states such as Kentucky and Tennessee, as manufacturers opened new factories there. |
| **Farmers in rural China, beginning around 1950** | Increased use of machines and consolidation of small farms into fewer large farms reduced the number of farmers needed to raise crops. | Farmers moved to China's large cities, increasing the urban population from 64 million in 1950 to 636 million by 2010. |

## Social Push and Pull Factors

People will often migrate when they experience discrimination and persecution because of their ethnicity, race, gender, or religion. They move to locations where they can practice their culture safely. People are often influenced by kinship links, or ties with relatives who have already settled in a place.

| EXAMPLES OF SOCIAL PUSH AND PULL FACTORS | | |
| --- | --- | --- |
| **Group and Place of Origin** | **Push Factors** | **Pull Factors** |
| **Mormon migration, 1845–1857** | Anti-Mormon violence in Illinois and Missouri resulted in dozens of deaths, including that of leader Joseph Smith. | Approximately 70,000 Mormons migrated to the Great Salt Lake area, a place chosen for its isolation and agricultural opportunities. |
| **Hindus and Muslims during and after the partition of India, 1947–1957** | Violence resulted in more than 200,000 deaths. | More than 14 million people migrated in hopes of finding safety in a new country. |

## Political Push and Pull Factors

People who oppose the policies of a government often migrate because they face persecution, arrest, and discrimination. Such political migrants move to countries that support their political views or will offer them **asylum,** or protection from the danger they faced in their home country.

| EXAMPLES OF POLITICAL PUSH AND PULL FACTORS | | |
|---|---|---|
| **Group and Place of Origin** | **Push Factors** | **Pull Factors** |
| **Anti-communist Cubans after Fidel Castro's communist takeover in 1959** | Opponents of Castro were jailed or killed if they spoke out against Castro's government. | Opponents of Castro fled to the United States, where they received asylum. |
| **The Dalai Lama and Tibetan government officials, after China's takeover of Tibet in 1950** | The Chinese persecuted, arrested, and killed many Tibetans who opposed the takeover. | The Dalai Lama and his supporters fled Tibet in 1959 to India, which allowed them to set up a government in exile. |

## Environmental Push and Pull Factors

People often migrate to escape harm from natural disasters, drought, and other unfavorable environmental conditions. Such migrants move to areas that are not under the same environmental stresses.

| EXAMPLES OF ENVIRONMENTAL PUSH AND PULL FACTORS | | |
|---|---|---|
| **Group and Place of Origin** | **Push Factors** | **Pull Factors** |
| **Farmers from Colorado, Kansas, Oklahoma, and Texas, 1930s** | A severe drought caused thousands to lose their farms. | Farmers moved to California hoping to find work. |
| **Residents living near the Fukushima Nuclear Power Plant in Japan, 2011** | An earthquake and tsunami damaged nuclear reactors, releasing radioactive materials. | Residents near the power plant were resettled to cities around Japan. |

## Demographic Push and Pull Factors

Some countries are unbalanced demographically. For example, in the case of a gender imbalance, young adults may not find someone to marry. If the population is too young, the country may eventually become overpopulated.

Geographer Wilbur Zelinsky made a connection between migration patterns and the Demographic Transition Model (see Chapter 4). His model explains that countries in Stages 2 and 3 of the Demographic Transition Model experience rapid population growth and overcrowding. This overcrowding limits the economic opportunities of the people and acts as a push factor. Thus they migrate to less crowded Stage 4 or 5 countries, which offer greater economic opportunities with growing economies and aging populations.

| EXAMPLES OF DEMOGRAPHIC PUSH AND PULL FACTORS | | |
|---|---|---|
| **Group and Place of Origin** | **Push Factors** | **Pull Factors** |
| **Farmers in Europe, 1800s** | The population of industrial countries increased, while land became scarce. | European migrants came to the United States, in part because the Homestead Act gave them plots of land. |
| **Young educated people in less developed countries in Latin America, North Africa, the Middle East, and Asia** | Many people in less developed countries live in areas where population is growing very quickly and unemployment and underemployment is high. | Developed countries in North America and Europe with aging populations need workers for difficult jobs, so they attract immigrants from less developed countries. |

### Intervening Obstacles

Migration consists of more than just push and pull factors. Migrants often encounter **intervening obstacles,** barriers that make reaching their desired destination more difficult. These obstacles might be economic, social, political, or environmental.

PUSH, PULL, AND INTERVENING OBSTACLES

Lee's Model of Migration

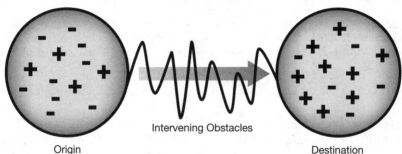

Intervening Obstacles

Origin

Destination

| INTERVENING OBSTACLES | |
|---|---|
| Type of Obstacle | Examples |
| Economic | A migrant lacks enough money to reach a destination. |
| Social | A migrant gets married to someone who lives along the migration route and settles in that person's community. |
| Political | A migrant cannot get a visa needed to enter a country. |
| Environmental | A migrant cannot cross sea, desert, or mountain range. |

# Ravenstein's Laws of Migration

In the 1880s German geographer E.G. Ravenstein noted eight patterns, or "laws," about migration tendencies, patterns, and demographics. Some have been modified, but they still form the basis for migration theory.

**Short Distances** Most migrants travel only a short distance. The further apart two places are, the less likely it is that people will migrate between those places. Ravenstein called this phenomenon **distance decay.** In the 1960s, geographers expanded this to time-distance decay, the idea that things near each other are more closely connected than things that are far apart.

**Urban Areas** Migrants traveling long distances usually settle in large urban areas. This is mainly because migrants believe that a larger city will have more opportunities than a smaller city.

Combining the concept of distance decay, the belief in the greater pull in larger communities, and the assumption that more people are likely to migrate from a large community than a small one, geographers developed the **gravity model of migration.** One demonstration of the model is the Cuban migration to the United States following Fidel Castro's successful overthrow of the government in 1959. Most people settled in the state closest to Cuba: Florida. And most settled in large cities, such as Miami. Today, more than two-thirds of Cuban-Americans in the United States live in Florida. More than half of all Cuban-Americans live in Miami.

**Multiple Steps** Most migration occurs through **step migration,** a process in which migrants reach their eventual destination through a series of smaller moves. For example, in a common pattern in rural-to-urban migration, a migrant from a small town is most likely to move first to a larger town, later to a small city, and finally to a large city.

**Rural to Urban** Most migration in history has been from rural to urban areas. Because of the Industrial Revolution, rural areas needed fewer laborers on farms, and cities needed more people to work, first in factories, and then in offices. This rural-to-urban movement remains common today. It includes migrations both within countries (rural residents of India moving to Indian cities such as Mumbai) and between countries (rural residents of Syria moving to cities in Germany).

**Counter Migration** Each migration flow produces a movement in the opposite direction, called **counter migration.** For example, in the 1990s and early 2000s, as many Mexican migrants were moving to the United States, a counter migration of people moved from the United States to Mexico. Some were part of a **return migration,** immigrants moving back to their former home. Others were retirees from the United States who had never lived in Mexico, but were attracted by its warm weather and lower cost of living. One result of counter migration are neighborhoods of former U.S.-residents now living scattered throughout Mexico. Today, about 1 million retired U.S. citizens live in Mexico.

**Youth** Most migrants are younger adults, between ages 20 and 45. People in that age group are usually not as established with jobs, homes, and families as older groups, so they are more likely to move to improve their fortunes.

**Gender Patterns** Most international migrants are young males, while more internal migrants are female. Men are more likely to move outside of the country looking for work. For example, several countries in the Middle East have guest worker programs where they recruit young men from South and Southeast Asia to work in the oil and construction industries. Women are more likely to move within a country. One reason is that many women living in traditional societies move in with their husbands and husbands' families.

## Global Migration Through History

The rate and breadth of migration increased in the 15th century with the European Age of Exploration. As Spain, Portugal, Great Britain, France, and other countries sought resources and markets around the world, they spread their cultural influences. By the early 20th century, most of the world had at times been colonized by Europeans.

### Effects of Colonization

As a result of colonization, European languages, religion, and culture spread across the globe. Throughout the Western Hemisphere, indigenous populations and their cultures were nearly wiped out by European diseases and replaced by European cultures. As a result, European languages and Christianity dominated the hemisphere.

In contrast, in Africa and Asia, people shared the same diseases carried by Europeans. Hence, European cultures mixed with the existing cultures. Many people largely kept their traditional languages and religions, but some learned to speak European languages and converted to European religions.

The diffusion of goods and ideas went both ways between Europeans and their colonies. Goods such as cotton, tea, coffee, sugar, silver, and diamonds poured into Europe from around the world. Europeans absorbed new words from other languages (from South Asia, English added words as diverse as *pajamas, avatar,* and *bungalow*) and practices such as yoga.

EUROPEAN COLONIZATION OF THE WORLD

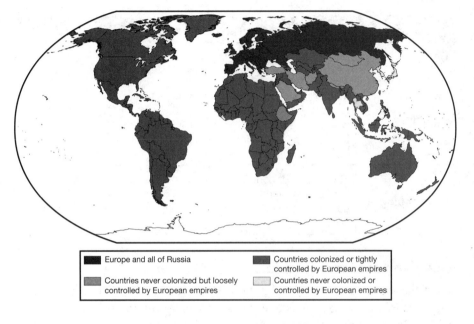

Europe and all of Russia

Countries colonized or tightly controlled by European empires

Countries never colonized but loosely controlled by European empires

Countries never colonized or controlled by European empires

## Forced Migration

One of the most important results of European expansion was the Atlantic slave trade. This was the largest example in history of **forced migration,** a type of movement in which people do not choose to relocate, but do so under threat of violence. In the 15th through the 19th centuries, about 12.5 million Africans were captured, enslaved, and forcibly moved from their homes in Africa to North America, the Caribbean, and South America.

### Slavery Today

While the Atlantic slave trade ended in the 19th century, slavery still exists today. The United Nations estimates that around 21 million people worldwide are victimized by forced labor—five times the number of African Americans enslaved in the United States in 1860.

### Displaced Persons and Refugees

Forced migration can result from political and environmental crises that threaten peoples' lives. Since such migrants must usually flee quickly in order to stay alive, they cannot bring many items with them. Most intend to return to their homes once the danger has passed. If these migrants move to another

part of the same country, they are classified as **internally displaced persons.**
If they cross international borders, and they have a well-founded fear that they
will be harmed if they return home, they are **refugees.** The Syrian Civil War
that began in 2011 forced half the population to flee, resulting in over 6 million
internally displaced persons and over 4 million refugees.

| EXAMPLES OF DISPLACED PERSONS AND REFUGEES | | |
|---|---|---|
| Category | Internally Displaced Persons | Refugees |
| Political | Many Afghan people moved to safer areas during the war between the U.S. and the Taliban, which began in 2001. | Jews fled Nazi Germany in the 1930s and 1940s, hoping to find safety in other countries. |
| Environmental | Thousands of Louisianans fled to neighboring states after Hurricane Katrina in 2005. | Thousands of Haitians relocated to neighboring countries after earthquakes in 2010. |

### Reversing Historical Trends

Since the mid-20th century, migration flows have changed. Europe, once a
region people were leaving, is now a destination for migrants from around the
world. Many come from former European colonies in the Middle East, South
Asia, and West Africa. These immigrants are usually seeking jobs as guest
workers or to unify with family members.

The migration to Europe is one example of a global pattern known as
**chain migration,** which is when people move to communities where relatives
or friends migrated previously. Chain migration increases migrant streams
from one area to another as a result of kinship links, or other social and
political connections. It also results in the formation of **ethnic enclaves,** or
neighborhoods filled primarily with people of the same ethnic group.

### Historical Trends in the United States

The United States has experienced several trends in immigration and forced
migration from other countries. Between 1500 and 1700, European countries
raced to colonize North America. By 1700, North America had been claimed
primarily by England, France, and Spain. However, major sources of migrants
entering the United States have shifted over time:

- 1600s to 1808: enslaved Africans
- 1808 to around 1890: northern and western Europe
- Around 1890 to 1914: southern and eastern Europe
- 1945 to the present: Latin America and Asia

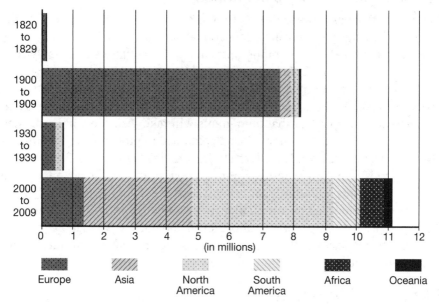

## Migration Policies and Their Consequences

While some countries around the world have encouraged immigrants, others have actively restricted the flow of migration into their countries. Many countries have largely relied on immigrants to improve their economies. However, many people have cultural and political biases against immigrants and try to keep them out.

### *Policies Encouraging Immigration*

Until the 1880s, the United States government placed few restrictions on immigration. The ratio of farmland to the number of people to work it was high, so immigrants were often welcomed. In addition, most people recalled with pride their own immigrant ancestors.

One policy that attracted immigrants was the Homestead Act (1862), a program in which the U.S. government gave land to settlers willing to stay and farm it for five years. After that time, the land became the property of the settler. Currently, the U.S. government offers visas to migrants who are well educated, hoping to get them to remain in the country.

Many countries have guest worker programs to attract immigrants to do hard, unpleasant work. These programs allow the immigrants to improve their fortunes in their new countries. Most countries also have family reunification policies allowing the migrants to sponsor family members to migrate to the country. Other policies include allowing refugees to migrate quickly in emergency situations and allowing foreign college students an easy pathway to becoming permanent residents after they graduate.

### Policies Discouraging Immigration

Countries often pass laws to restrict immigration. They can make entering the country difficult by establishing educational standards for immigrants or by restricting the type of work immigrants can do. Or, countries can simply set a quota to limit the number of people allowed to enter the country legally.

Some policies to restrict immigration reflect **xenophobia**, a strong dislike of people who practice another culture. Other restrictions are based in economics: people fear that immigrants will take their jobs. In the United States, xenophobia and economic fears combined to prompt Congress to pass laws that banned nearly all immigration from China between 1882 and 1943.

Countries sometimes restrict immigration primarily in an attempt to preserve their own cultural homogeneity. For example, the people of Japan form one of the most ethnically similar countries in the world. Japan maintains this by sharply limiting immigration, even though its population pyramid indicates that it faces a shortage of working-age people and would benefit from immigration.

## Effects of Migration

There are several effects, both positive and negative, that migration has on the countries of origin as well as on the destination countries. Effects include ones that are demographic, economic, cultural, and political.

### Effects on Countries of Origin

One positive effect on the countries of origin is relief from overcrowding. When countries have too many people, opportunities are scarce. As migrants leave in search of better lives, overcrowding problems are lessened. Zelinsky's Migration Transition Model helps explain this effect. Because of high population growth in Stage 2 and 3 countries, people will migrate to countries in Stage 4 or 5.

Migration can also have negative effects on the places people are leaving. If the working-age people leave, the area of migration is left with a population skewed toward the elderly and children. Economically, this creates a dependency ratio problem. Culturally, it can undercut the traditional family structure. Both of these have occurred during China's rural-to-urban migration, which is the largest migration within a country in history.

When migration out of a country is made up of many highly skilled people, it is called a **brain drain.** Today, students from around the world enter the United States or Great Britain to study medicine, engineering, or other fields and decide to stay rather than return to the land of their birth. This creates a brain drain on their countries of origin. A recent United Nations report found that about 11 percent of Africans with graduate or professional degrees were living in the United States, Europe, or other developed countries.

## Effects on Receiving Countries

Countries receiving immigrants usually benefit greatly. Immigrants make cultural contributions to their new countries, including new foods, new words and languages, diverse forms of entertainment, and a variety of religious traditions.

In addition, because most immigrants want to better their economic situations, they are highly motivated to get an education, work hard, and succeed. Many start businesses. Immigrants often start small, labor-intensive businesses such as restaurants, nail salons, and other service-oriented enterprises. But not all of these businesses stay small. Nearly 200 of the 500 largest businesses in the world were started by immigrants or their children.

Since immigrants generally move from poorer regions to wealthier ones, they often can afford to make **remittances,** money they send to their family and friends in the country they left. Remittances help the individuals receiving them, and account for nearly 40 percent of the income of some small countries, such as the Central Asian countries of Tajikistan and Kyrgyzstan. According to the World Bank, the United States and Saudi Arabia are among the leading countries as origins of remittance. India and China are often the leading countries as recipients of remittances.

Conflicts sometimes arise between immigrants and native-born citizens. The two groups might clash over religious beliefs, cultural practices, or access to jobs. Countries sometimes pass laws and businesses follow practices that discriminate against immigrants. In the early 1900s, signs such as the one shown below appeared in U.S. cities with large numbers of Irish immigrants.

Americans have a reputation as a restless people. In part, this comes from a history of migrations. The first people to arrive in the Americas were hunters from Asia, who were pulled across the land bridge then connecting Asia and America in search of animals. People have been moving to the Americas ever since, often in search of employment that would provide them food. Most came willingly—except for the millions of enslaved Africans who were transported against their will.

## The Great Migration from the South

Starting with the entry of the United States into World War I in 1917, millions of African Americans migrated from the South to cities in the rest of the country. This movement is known as the Great Migration. The major push factor was to escape severe racial discrimination and violence; the major pull factor was employment. Factory jobs were growing in cities. With reduced immigration from Europe because of World War I, opportunity for black laborers increased.

## The Migration to the South

A second large migration still shaping the modern United States is from the Northeast and Midwest to the South and Southwest. After World War II, government policies—the construction of a fast-moving national highway system and tax subsidies for buying new homes— made moving anywhere easier. But the development of air conditioning made life in hot climates more pleasant, and the expansion of defense industry jobs in the South and Southwest pulled many people to the band of states from southern California to Florida. These migrants felt pushed out of the North and Northwest by harsh winters and the decline in job opportunities because of factory automation. Between 1950 and 2016, Arizona's population grew from 750,000 to over 6 million.

| KEY TERMS | | |
|---|---|---|
| migration | distance decay | internally displaced person |
| voluntary migration | gravity model of migration | |
| push factors | | refugees |
| pull factors | step migration | chain migration |
| asylum | counter migration | ethnic enclaves |
| intervening obstacles | return migration | xenophobia |
| Ravenstein's Laws of Migration | forced migration | brain drain |
| | | remittances |

**Question 1 refers to the diagram below.**

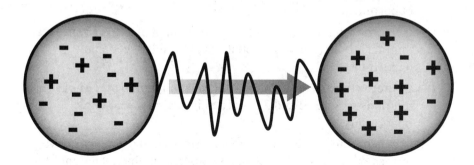

1. Which best summarizes the migration process represented by the diagram?

   (A) With European colonization and migration, positive aspects of European culture spread across the globe in spite of obstacles.

   (B) In the process known as step migration, migrants move from rural to urban areas through a series of smaller moves, or steps.

   (C) Each migration produces a counter migration of people returning to their country of origin.

   (D) The gravity model predicts that most migrants will move to the closest large metropolitan area in search of economic opportunities.

   (E) Migrants leave their homelands because of push factors and move to places with pull factors, but they often face barriers as they migrate.

2. Which statement best summarizes Zelinsky's model of migration in relation to the Demographic Transition Model (DTM)?

(A) High unemployment in countries in Stages 4 and 5 of the DTM pushes migrants to Stage 2 and 3 countries in search of economic opportunity.

(B) Overcrowding in countries in Stages 2 and 3 of the DTM pushes migrants to Stage 4 and 5 countries in search of economic opportunity.

(C) Overcrowding in countries in Stages 4 and 5 of the DTM pushes migrants to Stage 2 and 3 countries in search of economic opportunity.

(D) A gender imbalance in countries in Stages 4 and 5 of the DTM pushes migrants to Stage 2 and 3 countries to find mates and start families.

(E) Overcrowding in countries in Stages 4 and 5 of the DTM pushes migrants to Stage 2 countries in a counter migration as large as the original migration.

3. Which statement best summarizes the difference between immigrants to the United States before and after 1930?

(A) Between 1830 and 1930 most U.S. immigrants were slaves; between 1930 and the present most were free persons.

(B) Between 1830 and 1930 most U.S. immigrants were wealthy; between 1930 and the present most were poor.

(C) Between 1830 and 1930 most U.S. immigrants were English speakers; between 1930 and the present most immigrants were non-English speakers.

(D) Between 1830 and 1930 most U.S. immigrants were from the Americas and Asia; between 1930 and the present most were from Europe.

(E) Between 1830 and 1930 most U.S. immigrants were Europeans; between 1930 and the present most were from the Americas and Asia.

4. According to the gravity model of migration, in which state and city of the United States would Mexican migrants be most likely to live?

(A) Florida and Philadelphia

(B) Texas and Los Angeles

(C) North Carolina and Chicago

(D) Georgia and Memphis

(E) Alabama and Washington, D.C.

**5.** Which is the most common negative impact of emigration on the country of origin?

(A) an increase in unemployment rates

(B) a decline in the crowded conditions of urban areas

(C) loss of farmers resulting in smaller food supply

(D) loss of working age population to another country

(E) an increase in the number of abandoned and homeless children

**Question 6 refers to the diagram below.**

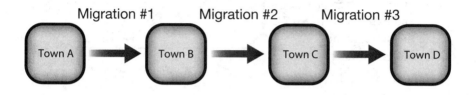

**6.** A person living in Town A moves three times, as shown in the diagram, and settles in Town D. This is an example of

(A) chain migration

(B) step migration

(C) distance decay

(D) intervening obstacle

(E) intervening opportunity

**7.** Which best illustrates counter migration?

(A) Chinese farmers migrating from a village to a small city and then to Beijing

(B) Ethiopians migrating to Turkey and then to Germany

(C) Italians migrating to France at the same time some French are migrating to Italy

(D) Nigerians migrating to Ghana and then migrating back to Nigeria

(E) Enslaved Africans being taken by force to Brazil and then voluntarily migrating to Argentina

**8.** The clearest example of an ethnic enclave is a neighborhood where

(A) many Korean immigrants live and practice Korean culture

(B) the city provides special services to help immigrants learn English

(C) immigrants from several different countries live

(D) most businesses are owned by the children of immigrants

(E) the population is extremely diverse and multicultural

1. The graph shows the relationship between the number of moves a migrant makes and the distance from the place of origin.

A. Identify and explain the concept shown in the graph.

B. Identify TWO different global migration trends and explain how those trends fit the graph.

C. Identify ONE global migration trend and explain how that trend does NOT fit the graph.

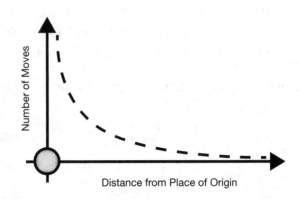

Distance from Place of Origin

---

**THINK AS A GEOGRAPHER:** INFLUENCES ON MIGRATION

Geographers study the push and pull factors that influence migration. Use the information in the chart to help answer the questions.

| Year or Period | Event or Trend |
|---|---|
| **INFLUENCES ON MEXICAN MIGRATION TO THE UNITED STATES** | |
| 1970 to 2010 | The TFR for women in Mexico falls from 7 to 2. |
| 1979 to 1982 | Worldwide oil demand creates a boom in Mexico. |
| 1982 | An economic crisis hits Mexico. |
| 2000 | Election of a new leader in Mexico creates hope. |
| 2000 to 2010 | The United States increases the number of agricultural work visas from 29,000 to 52,000. |

1. List one statement from the chart that increased the push for Mexicans to migrate. List one that reduced the push.

2. List one statement from the chart that increased the pull of the United States for Mexican immigrants.

3. Explain how one statement reflects the global influence on Mexico.

# UNIT 2: Review

## WRITE AS A GEOGRAPHER: PLAN THE ANSWER

Before writing an answer to a free-response question, plan what claims you want to make and can support. Think about what you want to say, the order you want to say it in, and how your points fit together.

Students often begin to plan by making notes about what they know: concepts, facts, and examples. And if the question includes an exhibit, they add information from the map, diagram, chart, or other type of source.

Next, students plan how to transform this list of content into a coherent answer. A good answer is a narrative—not simply a list of points. It states a clear response to the question rather than simply stating information that might be related to the question.

The response does not need to begin with an introductory paragraph, and answers are not graded on grammar or style. And no extra points are given for extraneous information. One challenge many students face is to keep their answer focused. They tend to wander off, inserting interesting facts they know that are not relevant to the question.

*For each part of the following free-response question, plan a possible answer. Describe the type of information you would use and how you would organize it.*

1. People migrate as a result of push and pull factors, and their movement affects both the places they leave and the places they arrive.

   A. Describe TWO pull factors that might cause someone to migrate to the United States.

   B. Describe TWO push factors that might cause someone to migrate away from the United States.

   C. Give a detailed account of THREE consequences of migration to or from the United States.

## REFLECT ON THE CHAPTER ESSENTIAL QUESTIONS

*Write a one- to three-paragraph answer to each question.*

1. How does understanding the population distribution, density, and composition of the world help to understand cultural, political, economic, rural, and urban systems?

2. What are the political, social, and economic consequences of the rapid population growth of the past 200 years?

3. How does migration affect society?

# UNIT 3: Cultural Patterns and Processes

## Unit Overview

While some human attributes, such as hair color, are heavily influenced by biological inheritance, most are not. In general, how people think and act is shaped, formally and informally, by what they learn from other people. All of the practices, technologies, attitudes, and behaviors that people learn from others are part of their culture.

### Behaviors People Share

Areas where many people share an element of culture—such as speaking a particular language—form cultural regions. Geographers use maps, from small to large scale—to show the boundaries of these regions.

When people of different cultures meet, they sometimes have conflicts, but they always adjust to each other. For example, if they speak different languages, one group might learn the other's language. Or people might blend the two languages to create a new one. Improvements in transportation and communication have increased the interaction of cultures throughout history. Culture spreads as people move from one place to another and as people interact and learn from each other. In 1500, the region where most people spoke English was a small area on the northwest corner of Europe. Today, English is the dominant language in countries scattered around the world and widely spoken in many others.

### Variations in Culture

Geographers uses maps to show regions, and they use various types of charts and diagrams to show relationships among the elements of culture. For example, a tree diagram can show how several languages, including French and Spanish, are branches that diverge from a common ancestor, Latin.

---

### Enduring Understandings

**III.** Cultural Patterns and Processes

   **A.** Concepts of culture frame the shared behaviors of a society.

   **B.** Culture varies by place and region.

**Source:** *CollegeBoard AP®. Human Geography Course Description. 2015.*

---

# Concepts of Culture and Diffusion

*The Buffalo was part of us, his flesh and blood being absorbed by us until it became our own flesh and blood. Our clothing, our tipis, everything we needed for life came from the buffalo's body. It was hard to say where the animals ended and the human began.*

— John (Fire) Lame Deer, *Lame Deer, Seeker of Visions*, 1972

**Essential Question:** How do folk and popular cultures differ in the ways they help form a society's overall culture?

To the Lakota, and other indigenous people on North America's Great Plains, the bison was an essential part of their culture. The bison provided meat for nutrition, a hide for clothing and shelter, bones for tools, and fat for soap. The bison was also central to their religious beliefs. So, when European settlers hunted the bison nearly to extinction, Lakota culture suffered.

Culture is central to a society and to its continued existence. Geographers thus study culture as a way to understand similarities and differences among societies across the world, and in some cases, to help preserve these societies.

## Analyzing Culture

All of a group's learned behaviors, actions, beliefs, and objects are a part of **culture**. It is a *visible* force seen in a group's actions, possessions, and influence on the landscape. For example, in a large city you can see people working in offices, factories, and stores, and living in high-rise apartments or suburban homes. You might observe them attending movies, concerts, or sports events.

Culture is also an *invisible* force guiding people through shared belief systems, customs, and traditions. All these elements, visible and invisible, make up the **cultural traits** that are the building blocks of a culture. A single cultural artifact, such as an automobile, may represent many different values, beliefs, and traditions. These interrelated traits make up a **cultural complex**.

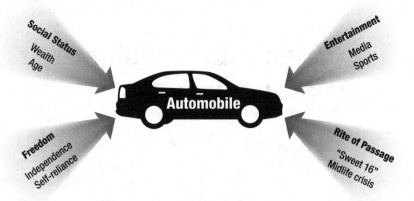

The automobile provides much more than just transportation, as it reflects many values that are central to American culture.

One generation passes its culture to the next in many ways. Children learn in three basic ways:

- by imitation, as when a child learns a language by repeating sounds
- by informal instruction, as when a parent reminds a child to say "please"
- by formal instruction, as when a school teaches students history

# Origins of Cultures

The area in which a unique culture or a specific trait develops is a **culture hearth**, also known as a cultural hearth. Classical Greece was a culture hearth for democracy more than 2,000 years ago. New York City was a culture hearth for rap music in the 1970s. Geographers study how cultures develop in hearths and diffuse to other places.

Geographers also study **taboos**, behaviors heavily discouraged by a culture. Many cultures have taboos against eating certain foods, such as pork or insects. What is taboo changes over time. In the United States, marriages between Protestants and Catholics were once taboo, but they are not widely opposed now.

## Folk Cultures

The beliefs and practices of small, homogenous groups of people, often living in rural areas that are relatively isolated and slow to change, are known as **folk cultures.** Like all cultures, they demonstrate the diverse ways that people have adapted to a physical environment. For example, people learned to make shelters out of available resources, whether it was snow or mud bricks or wood. However, people used similar resources such as wood differently. In

Scandinavia, people used entire logs to build cabins. In the American Midwest, people processed trees into boards, built a frame, and attached the boards to it.

Sometimes, people independently developed similar responses to similar environments. Long ago, Mongols in Central Asia and Plains Indians in North America, both living in flat, open land with extreme weather, developed similar types of housing: portable, round shelters made of frames and animals skins.

Many traits of folk culture continue today. Corn was first grown in Mexico around 10,000 years ago, and it is still grown there today.

### The Spread of Cultures

Folk cultures provide a unique **sense of place** and belonging. These long-established culture hearths are very important to the inhabitants. Their shared cultural traits bring homogeneity to the culture, which gives the people a sense of place. This, in turn, also gives the inhabitants a tie to the area where they live and gives them a sense of ownership.

However, because people, goods, and ideas move throughout the world, cultures spread spatially, well beyond their hearths. Prior to the mid-20th century, kiwi were part of the food culture of people only from China to New Zealand. Today, kiwi have diffused throughout the world.

## The Spatial Dimensions of Culture

**Cultural regions** are broad areas where groups share similar but not identical cultural traits. For example, geographer Wilbur Zilensky divided the United States into 12 major culture regions, yet people in these regions still consider themselves part of a larger American culture that shares a common heritage. Cultural regions are one of three types:

- **Formal regions**, such as states, are clearly defined by government or experts.
- **Functional regions**, such as the city of Miami and the communities around it, are based on interaction and are usually centered on a node or focus point.
- **Perceptual** (or vernacular) **regions** are based on how people think about particular places. The boundaries are often blurred. Zilensky's 12 regions are this type. People might agree that the Midwest stretches from somewhere in Nebraska to somewhere in Ohio. But they might not agree on where in Ohio the Midwest ends and other regions, such as the East and Appalachia, begin.

### Cultural Landscapes

The boundaries of a region reflect the human imprint on the environment. This is called the **cultural landscape** or the visible reflection of a culture, or the built environment. Some are described in the following chart.

| CULTURAL LANDSCAPES | | |
|---|---|---|
| **Element** | **Area** | **Significance** |
| **National Park** | United States | Land set aside from development reflects the desire to preserve unique environments |
| **Signage** | Quebec | Bilingual signs in French and English reflect the desire of French Canadians to retain their heritage |
| **Schools** | Pakistan | Gender-segregated schools reflect attitudes toward male and female roles |
| **Office Buildings** | Shanghai | Massive skyscrapers reflect economic power and a desire to have businesses in a central, well-known location |

An observant traveler can observe changes in the cultural landscape while driving along a highway. For example, travelers on Interstate 25 going from Wyoming to New Mexico see a definite change, both in toponyms (place names) and in the built environment. Names change from Anglo words to Spanish names. Wooden buildings are replaced by adobe buildings. Architectural styles shift from looking like ones in England to looking like ones in Spain.

## CULTURAL CHANGE ALONG INTERSTATE 25

Buildings in Santa Fe, New Mexico, reflect a blend of the styles of Native American pueblos and Spanish missions.

## *Ethnic Enclaves*

The neighborhood level of the cultural landscape might include **ethnic enclaves**, clusters of people of the same culture, but surrounded by people of a culture that is dominant in the region. Ethnic enclaves sometimes reflect the desire of people to remain apart from the larger society. Other times, they reflect a dominant culture's desire to segregate a minority culture. Inside these enclaves are often stores and religious institutions that are supported by the ethnic group, signs in their traditional language, and architecture that reflects the group's place of origin. These enclaves can provide a buffer against discrimination by the dominant culture.

### Borders and Barriers

Unless regions are defined by clear features, such as a mountain range, identifying cultural borders can be hard. Often a transition zone exists where cultures mix and people exhibit traits of both cultures. The border between the United States and Mexico clearly illustrates this pattern. People who live in border communities such as El Paso, Texas, are often fluent in both Spanish and English, and they have cultural ties to both Mexico and the United States.

### Realms

Geographers also identify larger areas, **culture realms**, that include several regions. Cultures within a cultural realm have a few traits that they all share, such as language families, religious traditions, food preferences, architecture, or a shared history.

TEN MAJOR CULTURE REALMS

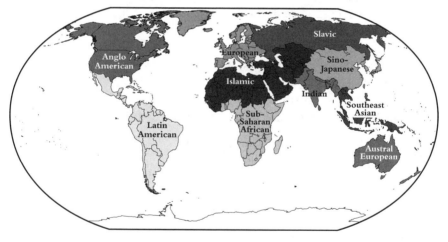

## Globalization and Cultural Change

As a result of the Industrial Revolution, improvements in transportation and communication have shortened the time required for movement, trade, or other forms of interaction between two places. This development, known as **space-time compression**, has accelerated culture change around the world. In 1817, a freight shipment from Cincinnati needed 52 days to reach New York City. By 1850, because of canals and railroads, it took half that long. And by 1852, it took only seven days. Today, an airplane flight takes only a few hours, and digital information takes seconds or less.

Similar change has occurred on the global scale. People travel freely across the world in a matter of hours, and communication has advanced to a point where people share information instantaneously across the globe. The increased interaction has had a profound impact on cultures, spreading English across the world.

**Globalization** is the process of intensified interaction among peoples, governments, and companies of different countries around the globe. More specifically, globalization usually refers to the increased integration of the world economy since the 1970s.

### Globalization and Popular Culture

When cultural traits such as clothing, music, movies, types of businesses, and the built landscape spread quickly over a large area and are adopted by various groups, they become part of **popular culture**. Elements of popular culture often begin in urban areas and diffuse quickly through the media, particularly the Internet. They can quickly be adopted globally. People around the world follow European soccer, Indian Bollywood movies, and Japanese animation known as *anime*. With people around the world wearing similar clothes, listening to similar music, and eating similar food, popular cultural traits often promote uniformity in beliefs, values, and the cultural landscape across many cultures.

The culture of the United States is intertwined with globalization. Through the influence of its corporations, Hollywood movies, and government, the United States exerts widespread influence in other countries. But other countries also shape American culture. For example, in 2014, the National Basketball Association included players from 30 countries or territories.

### Popular Culture Versus Folk Culture

Popular culture emphasizes trying what is new rather than preserving what is traditional. Many people, especially those in the older generation or who follow a folk culture, openly resist the adoption of popular cultural traits. They do this by preserving traditional languages, religions, values, and foods. While they often slow down the adoption of popular culture, they seldom are successful in keeping their traditional cultures from changing, especially among the young people of their society.

One clash between popular and folk culture is occurring in Brazil. As the population expands to the interior of the rain forest, many indigenous folk cultures are having greater contact with outside groups. Remaining isolated by the forest is becoming increasingly difficult and many young people become exposed to popular culture and are beginning to integrate into the larger Brazilian society. As the young people leave their communities, they are more likely to accept popular culture at the expense of their indigenous cultural heritage, which threatens the very existence of their folk culture.

| COMPARING FOLK AND POPULAR CULTURE | | |
|---|---|---|
| Trait | Folk Culture | Popular Culture |
| Society | • Rural and isolated location<br>• Homogeneous and indigenous population<br>• Most people speak an indigenous or ethnic local language | • Urban and connected location<br>• Diverse and multiethnic population<br>• Many people speak a global language such as English or Arabic |
| Social Structure | • Emphasis on community and conformity<br>• Families live close to each other<br>• Well-defined gender roles | • Emphasis on individualism and making choices<br>• Dispersed families<br>• Weakly defined gender roles |
| Diffusion | • Relatively slow and limited<br>• Primarily through relocation<br>• Oral traditions and stories | • Relatively rapid and extensive<br>• Often hierarchical<br>• Social media and mass media |
| Buildings and Housing | • Materials produced locally, such as stone or grass<br>• Built by community or owner<br>• Similar style for community<br>• Different between cultures | • Materials produced in distant factories, such as steel or glass<br>• Built by a business<br>• Variety of architectural styles<br>• Similar between cities |
| Food | • Locally produced<br>• Choices limited by tradition<br>• Prepared by the family or community | • Often imported<br>• Wide range of choice<br>• Purchased in restaurants |
| Spatial Focus | • Local and regional | • National and global |

## Geography of Gender

The geography of gender has become an increasingly important topic for geographers in recent decades. In folk cultures, people often have clearly defined gender-specific roles. Often women take care of the household while men work outside the house to earn money and serve as leaders in religion and politics. In popular culture, gender-specific roles are diminishing. Women have more access to economic resources, more opportunity to work outside the home, and more chances to serve as leaders.

The concept of gendered spaces or gendered landscapes clarifies the importance of cultural values on the distribution of power in societies. Throughout history, in many cultures, certain behaviors have been acceptable for only one gender, and often only in certain spaces. Often, men have operated more freely than women in public spaces, while certain private spaces have been reserved for women. These differences might appear in the etiquette of visiting someone's home. The host might welcome men in the public areas on the main level, but feel comfortable only with women visiting the more private rooms on the upper level.

### Resistance to Globalization

The spread of popular culture creates tensions around the world between globalization and local diversity. Followers of traditional cultures that define gender roles strictly resent the relatively greater gender equality often portrayed in Hollywood movies. Workers in the United States resist the transfer of their jobs to overseas locations. Speakers of endangered languages struggle to preserve their language in the face of the spread of English.

## Diffusion of Culture

Culture hearths are the original sources of culture. Yet many cultures have spread far beyond their hearths. The spreading of information, ideas, behaviors, and other aspects of culture over wider areas is known as **diffusion**. The two major forms of cultural diffusion come through cultural exchanges both by migration and by more indirect means.

### Relocation Diffusion

One main type of diffusion is **relocation diffusion**, the spread of a cultural trait by people who migrate and carry their cultural traits with them. A small-scale example is the spread of pizza, which Italian immigrants brought to the United States in the late 19th century. A larger-scale example is the spread of European culture around the world starting in the 1500s. At times, the areas where migrants settle continue a trait after it has lost its influence in its hearth. The people in the modern world who pronounce English most like Shakespeare live, not in England, but in Appalachia. Disco music evolved in the United States in the 1970s, but remained popular in Egypt long after it faded in the United States.

### Expansion Diffusion

The spread of cultural traits through direct or indirect exchange without migration is called **expansion diffusion**. It occurs in many ways.

**Contagious diffusion** occurs when a cultural trait spreads continuously outward from its hearth through contact among people. For example, the hearth for blues music is the southern United States. As musicians outside the hearth heard the music, they began to play it themselves. Blues slowly spread northward and eventually reached major cities such as Saint Louis, Chicago, and New York.

**Hierarchical diffusion** is the spread of culture outward from the most interconnected places or from centers of wealth and importance. Cultural traits spread first from one important person, city, or powerful class to another important person, city, or social class. Eventually the trait could be shared with other people, smaller cities, social classes, or less developed countries. Unlike contagious diffusion, hierarchical diffusion may skip some places while moving on to others. Most popular culture, such as music, fashion, and fads, follows the hierarchical diffusion path.

Cell phone technology demonstrates how hierarchical diffusion works. When cellular phones first appeared on the market in the 1980s, they were expensive and were most commonly owned by wealthy people in large cities in more developed countries. As cell phone networks grew and cell phones became mass-produced, they eventually spread to a wider market. Today, cell phones have diffused throughout the world.

At times, a trait diffuses from a lower class to a higher class, in a process called **reverse hierarchical diffusion**. For example, in the United States in the 1940s through the 1960s, people commonly considered tattoos to be a symbol of low social status. Tattoos were associated with three types of places: seaport towns (among dockworkers and sailors), military bases, and prisons. Since the 1970s, the custom of getting tattoos has diffused throughout many segments of society and geographic areas.

Some reverse hierarchical diffusion goes from small, rural communities to larger urban areas. Walmart stores diffused from rural Arkansas to nearly every city in the United States.

**Stimulus diffusion** occurs when people in a culture adopt an underlying idea or process from another culture, but modify it because they reject one trait of it. For example, Hindus in India adopted the practice of eating fast food, but they rejected eating beef because doing so would violate their Hindu beliefs. So, they adapted the custom by making vegetarian and other nonbeef types of burgers. Five centuries ago, Europeans adopted the use of lightweight, beautifully decorated porcelain dishes that they obtained from China, but they rejected the high cost of importing the dishes. So, when people in Germany found deposits of the right type of clay to make their own porcelain, they modified the process of obtaining porcelain by making it in Europe.

## Contact Between Cultures

Diffusion describes the ways cultures spread. As they spread, they come into contact with other cultures. The interaction of cultures is one of the driving forces in human history, and it can have several types of results.

## Acculturation

Often, an ethnic or immigrant group moving to a new area adopts the values and practices of the larger group that has received them, while still maintaining major elements of their own culture. This is called **acculturation**. For example, in the 1880s, the Syndergaard family migrated from Denmark to the United States, settling in a Danish enclave in Iowa. The mother and father gave most of their ten children common Danish names, such as Inger and Niels. They commonly ate Danish foods, including spherical pancakes called *abelskivver*. Within three generations, their descendants still ate abelskivver, but they had names common in U.S. culture, such as Susan, Jim, and Dave.

## Assimilation

Unlike acculturation, **assimilation** happens when an ethnic group can no longer be distinguished from the receiving group. This often occurs as ethnic groups become more affluent and leave their ethnic areas. Complete assimilation rarely happens though. Often, the one trait that is retained the longest is religion. For example, the grandchildren of immigrants from India might no longer speak Hindi or other Indian languages or eat traditional Indian cuisine daily, but they might still practice their Hindu faith. Often, the third and fourth generations of an ethnic group display a resurgence in ethnic pride by organizing festivals, learning the ethnic language, and revitalizing ethnic neighborhoods.

## Multiculturalism

Without full assimilation, most receiving societies such as the United States are characterized by **multiculturalism**, the coexistence of several cultures in one society, with the ideal of all cultures being valued and worthy of study. A major idea of multiculturalism is that the interaction of cultures enriches the lives of all.

However, coexistence of cultures can also bring conflicts, as people and groups with different values, beliefs, and customs often clash. Minority groups often face prejudice and discrimination. Refugees fleeing the civil war that began in Syria in 2011 who hoped to settle in the United States often faced opposition from Americans who feared that some refugees would be terrorists.

## Nativism

In some cases, the conflict between two cultures becomes harsh. **Nativist,** or anti-immigrant, attitudes may form among the cultural majority, sometimes bringing violence or government actions against the immigrant or minority group. Often, nativist attitudes are directed toward one particular group, such as opposition in the United States to Roman Catholic immigrants in the 1800s and early 1900s. Other times, nativism reflects a general dislike of people from other countries, or xenophobia.

## GEOGRAPHIC PERSPECTIVES: THE DIFFUSION OF DEADLY DISEASES

Many people study deadly diseases. Doctors might focus on how to treat patients. Economists might focus on how a disease affects the demand for medicines. Geographers focus on spatial distribution, including how a disease diffuses across space, outward from its hearth.

### The 1918 Influenza Epidemic

The influenza outbreak of 1918–1919, immediately after the end of World War I, was an example of contagious diffusion. The outbreak was devastating, killing three times as many people as World War I had. The source of the outbreak is not clear. It might have been located in Kansas, Great Britain, or France. Some scholars believe laborers from China who were traveling across Canada to Europe to work on the war front carried it with them.

In the United States, American cities on the East Coast quickly emerged as hubs of diffusion. Troops returning home after the war either carried the virus, or contracted it in the port. Then, as they traveled home by train, they spread the disease throughout the country.

### Recent Epidemics

More recently, outbreaks of Ebola in West Africa in 2013 and the Zika virus in South America in 2015 threatened death and serious illness. Zika particularly attacked fetuses. But using information about how diseases diffuse, coordinated global public health efforts prevented devastation on the scale of the 1918–1919 flu outbreak.

| KEY TERMS | | |
|---|---|---|
| culture | ethnic enclave | hierarchical diffusion |
| cultural trait | culture realm | reverse hierarchical diffusion |
| cultural complex | globalization | stimulus diffusion |
| folk culture | space-time compression | acculturation |
| culture hearth | popular culture | assimilation |
| cultural region | diffusion | multiculturalism |
| formal region | relocation diffusion | nativist |
| functional region | expansion diffusion | sense of place |
| perceptual region | contagious diffusion | taboos |
| cultural landscape | | |

**Question 1 refers to the diagram below.**

CULTURAL COMPLEX OF THE AUTOMOBILE IN THE UNITED STATES

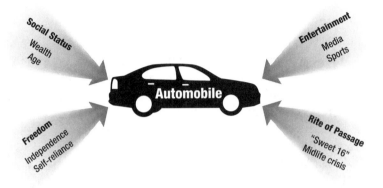

1. According to the cultural complex described in the diagram, auto ownership provides transportation but also

    (A) represents a set of American cultural traits, such as self-reliance and independence

    (B) provides greater likelihood that its owner will attain American values such as wealth

    (C) represents one American cultural trait, depending on the values of the auto's owner

    (D) comes about as a result of possession of a particular American trait, such as wealth

    (E) helps identify the owner's cultural landscape, region, realm, and level of freedom

2. Which of the following best demonstrates the concept of a culture hearth?

    (A) the Middle East, where many cultures share the religion of Islam

    (B) Latin America, which consists of several distinct but related cultures

    (C) the places in the world where material and nonmaterial traits emerged

    (D) the buildings, roads, and other elements built by humans

    (E) an area within a city where people share a common culture distinct from the surrounding culture

**3.** Which pattern is more typical of folk cultures than other types of cultures?

(A) welcoming in new practices from other cultures

(B) promoting a high level of religious diversity

(C) taking steps to transform rural areas into urban areas

(D) emphasizing the value of tradition

(E) establishing flexible gender roles

**4.** The various cultural regions that compose the United States demonstrate how

(A) various cultural regions share some values and yet remain distinct

(B) culture hearths spread their values through diffusion

(C) clear lines divide cultural regions distinctly

(D) cultural boundaries match political boundaries

(E) each cultural region is composed of a variety of cultural realms

**5.** The onion-domed churches in Moscow are most clearly examples of that city's cultural

(A) barriers

(B) enclaves

(C) realm

(D) landscape

(E) borders

**6.** A family that immigrates from China to the United States and chooses to live in an ethnic enclave is probably hoping to

(A) expose their children to people of many other cultures

(B) assimilate their family into American culture as quickly as possible

(C) find a buffer against discrimination while they seek new opportunities

(D) find more religious and language diversity than in most communities

(E) separate itself from its Chinese culture rapidly and completely

7. Which information would be most useful to a geographer trying to identify the borders of cultural regions that each cover hundreds of square miles within a large country?

(A) the locations of urban ethnic enclaves with businesses that cater primarily to one ethnic group

(B) the locations of geographic features, particularly rivers, streams, and lakes

(C) the locations of major and minor airports across the country

(D) the sights travelers see as they travel along major highways across the country

(E) how well the average person in the entire country is connected to Internet and other media

8. One effect of the spread of popular culture through globalization is that

(A) cultural realms have become more diverse

(B) several traits have become part of a worldwide culture

(C) traditional cultural values have spread to developed countries

(D) less-developed countries have adopted stricter gender roles

(E) the primary impact has been to change American culture

## FREE-RESPONSE QUESTION

1. Cultural values and traditions help people develop a sense of place in the area where they live.

A. Define cultural landscape.

B. Identify and explain two specific cultural trait differences between popular culture and folk culture.

C. Discuss the tension that exists between popular and folk culture.

Innovation and diffusion are essential to human progress. People in one place figure out something—how to grow crops or make a steam engine or form a stable government—and then their knowledge spreads to others. Use the information in the chart below to help you practice using the concept of diffusion.

| EXAMPLES OF DIFFUSION | | | |
|---|---|---|---|
| **Example** | **Hearth** | **Receiving** | **How** |
| **Rice** | China, about 10,000 years ago | Spread to Southeast Asia by 4,000 years ago | Knowledge of how to grow rice spread from one to community to its neighbor |
| **Baseball** | Developed in the United States in the middle of the 19th century | Spread to Japan in the late 19th century | American teachers and missionaries taught the game to individuals of influence in Japan, who then taught it to others |
| **Soccer** | The modern form developed in Europe in the 19th century | Spread to the United States | Immigrants brought the game with them and native-born people joined in playing |
| **Woke** (to be aware of social injustice) | First used in predominantly black, urban communities in the early 2000s | Spread to young people of all ethnic and racial groups | The term was popularized when it was used in a song in 2008 |

1. Which type of diffusion does the spread of rice cultivation represent?

2. How did the spread of baseball and soccer differ?

3. Explain why the spread of "woke" is an example of reverse hierarchical diffusion.

**7**

# Language and Culture

*In 1979, [schools on the Navajo reservation had about] 80 percent of students speaking Navajo – ten years later, 5 percent. There's just too much English influence to really be effective in keeping our language. [If the Navajo language is lost] we will not be a unique people. We will have no culture; we will have no prayers.*

— Marilyn Begay, 5th grade teacher, The Navajo Language Immersion School, Navajo Nation reservation, Arizona

**Essential Question:** What do the spread of and changes in languages tell about the cultures of the world?

The Navajo, a Native American group of the United States Southwest, face many of the same problems as indigenous people across the world—the loss of their native language and culture in the context of globalization. Currently there are approximately 7,000 languages that people speak around the world; but by the end of the century, about half of those languages will be gone. Most of the languages are spoken by small, isolated groups. As these groups become integrated into the larger society, the people often learn the language of the majority. The traditional language falls into disuse and becomes extinct. Since language is the key element in communication, with this loss of the language comes a loss of a central part of a group's history and cultural identity.

## Relationships Among Languages

As the Navajo example illustrates, language is essential to a group's culture. It creates a sense of place and a cultural landscape. The Navajo experience shows that today's communication technologies are reshaping cultures and bringing drastic change to, and even destroying, age-old practices and languages.

Yet language, like all elements of culture, has long been changing. The earliest languages spread from their culture hearths and faced a multitude of local, international, and global forces, including conquest, colonialism, imperialism, and trade, up to the globalization and widespread instant communication of the present day.

### Origins of Language

Currently, **linguists**, scientists who study languages, think that humans first began communicating through spoken sounds as recently as tens of thousands of years ago, or as long as a few hundred thousand years ago. They are not sure how language diffused. Was it through the dispersion of people, who carried language with them as they dispersed across the planet? Or was it through transmission, as people learned language from their neighbors? Or was it through conquest, with one people imposing language on others?

### Language Families

Linguists also are not sure whether all languages descended from one original language. They do believe that nearly all of the languages spoken today can be grouped into about 15 families of languages. The relationship among these language families is often shown on a **language tree** because it suggests how several languages are related to each other, as well as how one language grows out of another.

The distribution of languages reflects human migrations. The migration of Huns from central Asia to central Europe around 1,500 years ago explains why the languages most like Hungarian are found nearly 3,000 miles east of it.

### Indo-European Languages

One of the 15 major language families is the **Indo-European language family**, a large group of languages that might all have descended from a language spoken around 6,000 years ago. Nearly half of the world's population speaks one of the languages of the Indo-European language family. This family includes about 2.8 billion native speakers of between 400 and 500 languages.

EXAMPLES OF INDO-EUROPEAN LANGUAGES

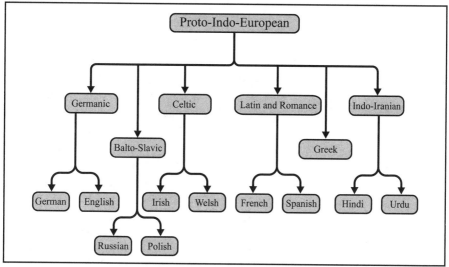

English evolved out of a combination of a Latin language (French) and a Germanic language (Anglo-Frisian) beginning about 1,000 years ago.

Within Indo-European, one of the branches is Latin. The history of Latin shows how difficult the study of language is: languages constantly evolve as people move away from the languages' cultural hearths, because of contact with other languages or isolation from other languages.

Two thousand years ago, when the Roman Empire dominated much of what is today Europe, people in the empire spoke Latin. However, as the empire dissolved starting in the 5th century, transportation became more dangerous and trade declined. As a result, Latin speakers became geographically isolated from each other. The unifying language of Latin diverged into distinct regional languages, known as **Romance languages**. Most of these later vanished, but Portuguese, Spanish, French, Italian, and Romansch survived and grew. The historical connection among these languages is evident in their similar words.

| LATIN WORDS RELATED TO WORDS IN OTHER LANGUAGES | | | | | |
|---|---|---|---|---|---|
| **Latin** (meaning in English) | **Pater** (father ) | **Mater** (mother) | **Panis** (bread) | **Lupus** (wolf) | **Die** (day) |
| **Portuguese** | Pai | Mae | Pao | Lobo | Dia |
| **Spanish** | Padre | Madre | Pan | Lobo | Dia |
| **French** | Pere | Mere | Pain | Loup | Jour |
| **Italian** | Padre | Madre | Pane | Lupo | Giorno |
| **Romansch** | Tata | Mama | Paine | Lup | Zi |

Note that English words such as *father* and *mother* are similar to Latin words, but words such as *bread* and *wolf* are not. This suggests that English is not a direct descendant of Latin—it evolved from a Germanic language—but it has been heavily influenced by Romance languages such as French.

### Accents and Dialects

Languages can be further divided into smaller categories by other traits. One is by accent, how words sound when pronounced. Accents often reflect social class or geographic region. The boundaries between variations in pronunciations or word usage are called **isoglosses**.

Variations in accent, grammar, usage, and spelling create **dialects**, or regional variations of a language. Variations between dialects are large enough that most speakers notice them, but small enough that speakers can understand each other easily. Often, the dialect spoken by the most influential group in a country is considered the standard, and others are modifications of it. "Hello, everyone" is standard. "Hi, y'all" and "Hi, yous guys" are dialectical variations. Dialects often include distinct **adages**, or sayings that attempt to express a truth about life, such as "The early bird gets the worm." The following chart shows differences between two dialects of English: American and British.

| DIALECTS OF AMERICAN ENGLISH AND BRITISH ENGLISH | | |
|---|---|---|
| **Category** | **American English** | **British English** |
| **Vocabulary** | • Elevator<br>• Apartment<br>• Parking lot<br>• Trunk (of a car)<br>• Gas (for a car) | • Lift<br>• Flat<br>• Car park<br>• Boot<br>• Petrol |
| **Pronunciation** | • Lieutenant (loo-TEN-uhnt)<br>• Schedule (SKED-juhl) | • Lieutenant (lef-TEN-uhnt)<br>• Schedule (SCHEDZH-uhl) |
| **Spelling** | • Meter<br>• Color<br>• Tire<br>• Center<br>• Theater | • Metre<br>• Colour<br>• Tyre<br>• Centre<br>• Theatre |
| **Common Phrases** | • "I'm tired."<br>• "I'll call you." | • "I'm knackered."<br>• "I'll ring you." |

Within dialects are subdialects. For example, in the United States, a native of Texas is likely to speak a different dialect than a native of New York City.

Often, dialects are the legacy of differences in the past, but they can also be a first step in the evolution of a new language. Just as the Romance languages emerged as regional variations of Latin, new languages are developing today. For example, if the differences between British English and American English increased so much that speakers could not easily communicate with each other, the two would be classified as different languages instead of dialects of one.

## Diffusion of Languages

Languages often spread through diffusion—the spread of culture over wide areas through migration as well as by more indirect means. The major globalized languages of the world—English, French, Spanish, and Arabic—spread from their hearths largely because of conquest and colonialism. In the case of Arabic, its use as a standard religious language in Islam contributed to its success.

Some languages never diffuse widely. Mandarin Chinese, though the second most commonly spoken language in the world, did not. Though China was the most powerful and innovative country in the world for much of the past 2,000 years, and its merchants settled in various parts of Asia and Oceania, China never established colonies outside of Asia. As a result, Chinese speakers have always been concentrated in China.

### English as a Lingua Franca

Unlike Chinese, English has a wide spatial distribution. English is the most widely used language in the world, with nearly 1.5 billion speakers. Native speakers are concentrated in lands colonized by Great Britain such as the United States, Canada, South Africa, India, and Australia.

However, most speakers of English do not use it as their primary language. Rather, they use it as a **lingua franca**, a common language used by people who do not share the same native language. For example, Nigerians commonly speak one of 500 indigenous languages at home, but they learn English to communicate with everyone who does not speak their language. Globalization and new technology explain why English is a common lingua franca:

- Multinational corporations based in the United States and Great Britain made English the common language for international business.
- Scientists and other scholars, airline pilots throughout the world, and many journalists began to use English to communicate across the globe.
- English evolved as the lingua franca of the Internet and is widely used in social media.
- Television shows and movies are often in English and they are shown around the world.

The wide use of English has made communication among people around the world easier. However, it has also sparked resentment in some who feel that the intrusion of American language and culture dilutes their own unique linguistic and cultural practices.

### Other Lingua Francas

Other major lingua francas are Arabic, Spanish, French, Swahili, and Russian. Each has a wide distribution and is often learned as a second language.

## Creating New Words and Languages

Many new words begin as **slang**, informal usage by a segment of the population. For example, the word brunch was slang before it became standard.

### Pidgin Languages

When speakers of two different languages have extensive contact with each other—often because of trade—they sometimes develop a **pidgin language**, a simplified mixture of two languages that has fewer grammar rules and a smaller vocabulary, but is not the native language of either group. In Papua New Guinea, the pidgin combines English and Papuan languages.

### Creole Languages

Over time, two or more separate languages can mix and develop a more formal structure and vocabulary so that they are no longer a pidgin language. They create a new combined language known as a **creole language**. Afrikaans is a creole language spoken in South Africa that combines Dutch with several European and African languages.

On the islands of the Caribbean, creole languages are common. Africans captured and brought to enslavement in the Americas between the 1500s and the 1800s were unable to transplant their languages. Stolen from their communities, they were forced onto ships with captives from various regions in Africa. With no common language among the groups of captives, communication was difficult. Because of this linguistic isolation, most lost their languages after a generation in the Americas. Yet they were able to create creole languages by combining parts of their African languages with the European colonizers' languages of English, Spanish, French, or Portuguese.

The most widely used creole language in the Americas is found in Haiti. Haitian Creole is derived mostly from French with influences from numerous languages of West Africa. It has become an official language of Haiti and a source of national pride and cultural identity.

The United States included a smaller percentage of enslaved Africans than did many Caribbean islands, so it had fewer creole languages. One exception is the *Gullah* or *Geechee* language of South Carolina and Georgia, in places where enslaved Africans once made up about three-quarters of the population.

### Swahili in East Africa

Another example of language mixing occurred in East Africa. As early as the 8th century, trade between Arab-speaking merchants and Bantu-speaking residents resulted in the development of **Swahili**. Swahili is still spoken by some groups in Africa and is an official language of four African nations: Kenya, Uganda, Tanzania, and the Democratic Republic of the Congo.

## Language Policies and the Cultural Landscape

Language is important to a group's cultural identity. Because a culture occupies a certain spatial area, its language becomes intertwined with that place and its landscape. For example, native Hawaiians, whose economy relies on fishing, have five dozen words for fishing nets. In addition, signs in some places create a cultural landscape as they reflect the people's linguistic heritage and tie them to that place—from the single-language signs in France to bilingual signs in places such as Belgium or Quebec.

### Toponyms

Toponyms, the names of places, reflect culture. For example, in 657 B.C.E., the Greeks founded a colony that they named Byzantium, probably after a leader named Byzas. After the city fell under Roman control, the Romans renamed it Constantinople, after one of their emperors. When the Turks seized the city in 1453, they started to call it Istanbul, which means "to the city."

### Official Languages

While the United States does not have an **official language**, one designated by law to be the language of government, some countries do. These countries can be grouped into three categories:

- Some countries are **homogeneous**, or made up largely of ethnically similar people, such as in Iceland, Japan, or Slovenia.

- Some countries use language to discourage people from maintaining a traditional culture. English colonizers did this in Ireland, Scotland, and Wales to promote quick assimilation.

- Some countries include several large ethnic groups. These countries want to honor all groups equally. For example, Zimbabwe is home to several large ethnic groups, so it has 16 official languages. People use English as a lingua franca to make communication easier.

EXAMPLES OF OFFICIAL LANGUAGES IN AFRICA

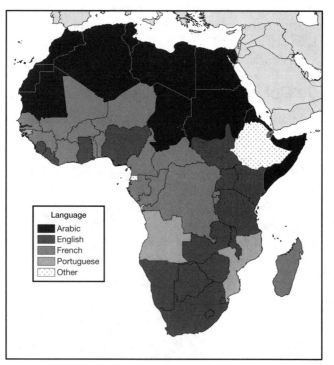

What defines the region of the United States where Spanish is widely spoken? Geographers answer this question using various tools, such as census data, surveys, and the cultural landscape. They have found that the Spanish-speaking region changes depending on the level of analysis.

**Spanish at the Country and State Levels**

At the global level, the answer is the entire country. The United States includes more than 41 million people who grew up speaking primarily Spanish, and another 11 million people who are bilingual. On a cartogram showing the total number of Spanish-speakers in a country, the United States would be the second largest country in the world; only Mexico would be larger.

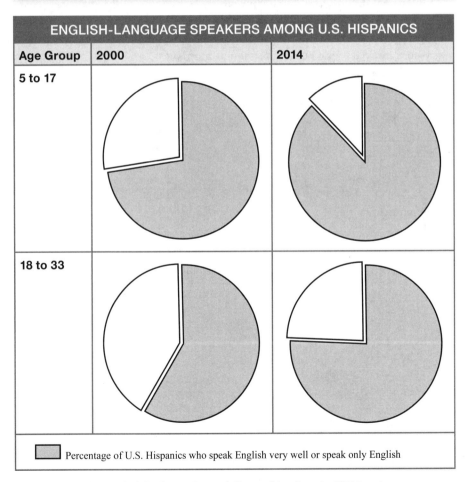

| ENGLISH-LANGUAGE SPEAKERS AMONG U.S. HISPANICS | | |
|---|---|---|
| **Age Group** | **2000** | **2014** |
| **5 to 17** | | |
| **18 to 33** | | |

Percentage of U.S. Hispanics who speak English very well or speak only English

Source: Based on analysis by the Pew Research Center of data from the 2014 American Community Survey and the 2000 Census (IPUMS).

At the state level, the answer is slightly more complex. States vary, generally according to history and relative location. The states with the highest percentages of Spanish-speaking Americans were all once colonies of Spain and are located relatively close to Latin America: California, Nevada, Arizona, New Mexico, Texas, and Florida.

### Spanish at the Lower Levels

At the county level, the issue becomes even more complex. Large cities throughout the country have large populations of residents who speak Spanish as either a first or second language. The Chicago metropolitan area has more Spanish speakers than the entire populations of either New Mexico or Arizona. In addition, scattered counties around the country, from southern Idaho to eastern North Carolina, each have at least 7 percent of their population who speak Spanish.

New technology might make possible the mapping of language regions on an individual level. Analyzing Twitter or other social media could allow geographers to create an ever-changing map of where people are speaking any particular language at any particular moment.

| KEY TERMS | |
|---|---|
| linguist | lingua franca |
| Romance language | slang |
| Indo-European language family | creole language |
| language tree | pidgin language |
| dialect | Swahili |
| isogloss | official language |
| adage | homogeneous |

**Questions 1 and 2 refer to the language tree below.**

EXAMPLES OF INDO-EUROPEAN LANGUAGES

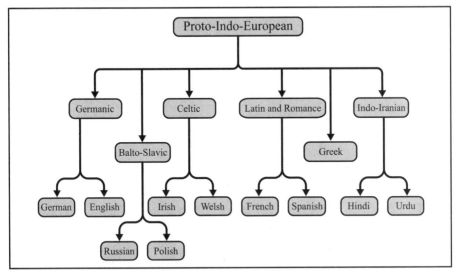

1. Which most accurately describes a relationship shown on the language tree above?

   (A) Polish grew out of Balto-Slavic.

   (B) Celtic is based on Welsh.

   (C) Greek is a Romance language.

   (D) French and Spanish are creole languages.

   (E) Hindi is an older language than Indo-Iranian.

2. One distinctive feature of the Indo-European family is that it

   (A) has a smaller spatial distribution than other language families

   (B) is the only language family with just one major lingua franca

   (C) includes most of the world's oldest languages

   (D) is spoken by nearly half the world's population

   (E) is the only one that is spoken in Europe today

**3.** Some countries have several official languages because they want to

(A) make international diplomacy easier

(B) foster political cooperation with neighboring countries

(C) make government operate more efficiently

(D) prepare students to participate in the global economy

(E) give recognition to different groups within the country

**4.** Which statement best describes the most common reason groups wish to preserve their traditional languages?

(A) Language is central to cultural identity, so preserving a language helps preserve a culture.

(B) Language is used in religious services, so preserving a language is primarily a religious obligation.

(C) Language is used for trade, so preserving language is one way to keep a group economically prosperous.

(D) Language change is a politically disruptive force, so preserving a language is one way to keep stability.

(E) Language preservation passes on a group's history, so preserving a language is the only way to record history accurately.

**5.** The Arabic language spread from its hearth and became one of the major global languages mainly through

(A) increased use of communication technology in Arab nations

(B) spread of Middle Eastern multinational oil corporations

(C) worldwide colonization beginning around 600 C.E.

(D) conquest and its use as a standard religious language

(E) resisting colonization by European nations and the United States

**Question 6 refers to the map below.**

COUNTRIES WHERE ENGLISH IS USED EXTENSIVELY

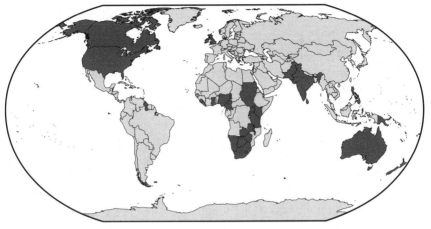

6. Which phrase does NOT help explain the language distribution shown on the map?

   (A) the ease of trade between Great Britain and the United States

   (B) the widespread use of the Internet

   (C) the differences between American and British English

   (D) the impact of British colonization in Africa and Asia

   (E) the increase in the power of U.S.-based corporations

7. Which resulted from the mixing of two languages to create a new one so that people who spoke different languages could trade more easily?

   (A) Indo-European

   (B) Amerindian

   (C) American English

   (D) Arabic

   (E) Swahili

8. Which is the best example of the diffusion of a language?

   (A) the decline in use of the Navajo language

   (B) the spread of English via the Internet

   (C) the creation of a new language in Haiti

   (D) the designation of one official language for a country

   (E) the use of bilingual signs in a country with two official languages

**The free-response question refers to the excerpt below.**

1. "Many of the 113 languages spoken in the Andes Mountains and Amazon basin are poorly known and are rapidly giving way to Spanish or Portuguese, or in a few cases, to a more dominant indigenous language. In this region, for example, a group known as the Kallawaya use Spanish or Quechua in daily life, but also have their own secret tongue, used mainly for preserving knowledge of medicinal plants, some of which were previously unknown to science.

—John Noble Wilford, *New York Times*, September 18, 2007

A. Identify ONE cultural trait that the groups with endangered languages have in common.

B. Explain TWO reasons why languages such as the Kallawaya's are dying out.

C. Write a brief general statement explaining what is lost and what is gained as languages such as the Kallawaya's die out.

| PRIMARY LANGUAGES OF PEOPLE IN PERU | |
|---|---|
| **Language** | **Percentage of Population** |
| **Spanish** | 84.1% |
| **Quechua** | 13.0% |
| **Aymara** | 1.7% |
| **Ashaninka** | 0.3% |
| **Other Native Languages** | 0.7% |
| **Other Nonnative Langauges** | 0.2% |

**Source:** *The World Factbook.*

The connection between language and culture is often very close. However, it is often not identical. When immigrants come to the United States, they often lose their ancestral language but keep elements of their ancestral culture. The reverse can also occur: people might continue to worship in their traditional language, such as Arabic, Hebrew, or Greek, but also speak English, watch baseball, and eat apple pie.

New York City, a magnet for immigrants from around the world, includes native speakers of every major language. These speakers form networks—among each other and with overseas communities. English and Spanish are widely spoken, but neighborhoods are often pockets of speakers of other languages. Look at the data in the chart below.

| NEW YORK CITY LANGUAGES | |
|---|---|
| Language | Number of Speakers in New York City |
| English | 3,700,000 |
| Spanish | 1,870,000 |
| Chinese | 419,000 |
| South Asian Languages (Hindi, Urdu, and others) | 200,000 |
| Russian | 186,000 |
| French Creole | 106,000 |
| Yiddish | 85,000 |
| French | 81,000 |

1. Based on the languages spoken in other parts of the world, with which parts would New York have the strongest network?

2. Explain how English creates a network in New York City by serving as a lingua franca.

3. What evidence would you look for in the cultural landscape to see whether you were in a neighborhood where a language other than English was widely used?

# 8

# Religious and Ethnic Landscapes

*Cultural values are, in themselves, neutral as well as universal, and so much depends on how individuals or ethnic groups use them. Values are influenced by so many factors such as geography, climate, religion, the economy and technology.*

—F. Sionil Jose, Filipino novelist

**Essential Question:** How do religious and ethnic groups both reflect and influence the geography of places at different scales?

Religion is intertwined with all other aspects of history and geography because, compared to other aspects of culture, it is relatively resistant to decay over time and distance. For example, descendants of immigrants often adopt a new language but continue to practice the faith of their ancestors. Developing strong mental maps of the origins, diffusion, and distribution of major religions and their divisions is one of the most valuable ways to understand culture.

## Religion, Ethnicity, and Nationality

Religion is often closely linked to **ethnicity**, or membership in a group of people who share characteristics such as ancestry, language, customs, history, and common experiences. Most geographers distinguish between **nationality**, which describes people's connection to a particular country, and ethnicity, which is based upon group cultural traits. For example, Russian Jews make up a different ethnicity than Russians in general. Geographers often study ethnic groups as minorities within a greater population. To do so, they focus on mapping and analysis, as they trace the movement of ethnic groups and investigate their spatial dimensions and cultural landscapes.

### Spatial Dimensions of Religious and Ethnic Groups

To analyze religious and ethnic groups, geographers try to define, locate, and study them. Religion and ethnicity are easier to define than is the process of examining each group's space, place, identity, and movement. One way to see the relationship among all of these aspects of culture is to focus on historical connections. Geographers start by mapping a **culture hearth**, the source, or origin, where a religion or ethnicity began, and then track its movement and predict its future direction.

## Cultural Variation by Place and Region

Patterns and landscapes of religious and ethnic groups vary by place and region at various scales. For example, at the regional level, Baptists are the most common religious group in the southeastern United States. Zooming in to the state level, the same is true for most states, including South Carolina. However, at the county level, many individual counties in South Carolina have more Methodists or Lutherans than any other group. And at the census tract level, the state appears even more diverse.

The degree of adherence to tradition varies within each religion. Every religion includes followers who practice **fundamentalism**, an attempt to follow a literal interpretation of a religious faith. Fundamentalists believe that people should live traditional lifestyles similar to those prescribed in the faith's holy writings. In some traditions, this means that women are likely to leave school at a young age, to live in an arranged marriage, and to avoid working outside the home. Fundamentalists are more likely than others in their faith to enforce strict standards of dress and personal behavior, often through laws.

The strength of fundamentalism often diminishes with greater distance from the religious hearth. For example, the hearth of Islam is the Arabian Peninsula, and that is where fundamentalism has long been strongest. Fundamentalism is less prevalent in Muslim-majority countries farther from the hearth, such as Malaysia and Indonesia. One way to measure fundamentalism in Islam is by the role of **sharia**, the Islamic legal framework for a country. Sharia is strongest in countries of the Arabian Peninsula such as Saudi Arabia and Yemen.

Some fundamentalist countries, such as Iran, are **theocracies**, countries whose governments are run by religious leaders through the use of religious laws. Fundamentalists often clash, sometimes violently, with those who wish to follow religious traditions more loosely or to live a more secular lifestyle.

## Regional Patterns in U.S. Religion

The distribution of ethnic and religious groups in the United States reflects historical patterns. Congregationalists are still strong in New England, where their English ancestors settled in the 1600s. Baptists and Methodists are most common in the Southeast, where these denominations were spread by traveling preachers in the 1800s. Lutherans live mostly in the Midwest, where their German or Scandinavian forbears who immigrated in the late 1800s could find good farmland. Many Mormons live in or near Utah, where Mormons settled in the mid-1800s after religious persecution drove them out of Missouri and Illinois. Roman Catholics are most common in urban areas in the Northeast and throughout the Southwest. Jews, Muslims, and Hindus live most often in urban areas, the traditional home to immigrants.

## Globalization and Religion

Advances in communication, such as printing, television, and the Internet, have had contradictory effects on the distinctive traits of many religious communities. In 1850, a farmer in western Ireland lived in a community where nearly everyone was Roman Catholic and so had little contact with other traditions. Today, no one is isolated. Exposure to other ideas can erode traditions. However, if that Irish farmer immigrated to the United States, he was nearly cut off from the community of his birth. Today, an Irish immigrant can keep in close touch with friends and family.

And sometimes people respond to globalization with **neolocalism**, the process of re-embracing the uniqueness and authenticity of a place. For example, a neighborhood in a large city might hold a festival to honor the religion, cuisine, and history of the migrants who settled the community.

### Religious Patterns and Distributions

Religions, like other elements of culture, diffuse outward from their hearths in various ways. The spread of religious settlements, both locally and globally, contributes to the sense of place and of belonging for each religious group and greatly shapes the cultural landscape. Geographers analyze maps, charts, and other data to understand the growth, decline, movement, and cultural landscapes of the world's religions. They have traced the geographic patterns of each major world religion, including the religion's hearth, or place of origin, the geographic spread of the religion, and practices that can influence both the culture and the cultural landscape.

LARGEST RELIGION BY COUNTRY

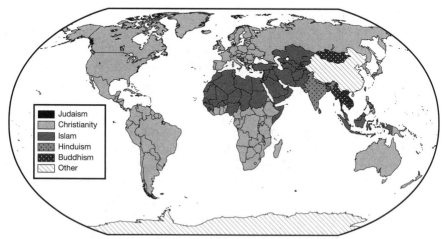

Judaism is the largest religion in Israel. In China, most people identify no religious affiliation.

## Two Major Eastern Religions

Several belief systems have developed in Asia. Of these, two developed in India and have diffused to other places from there.

**Hinduism** Hinduism includes the worship of many deities, so some people consider it **polytheistic**, which means having many gods. However, Hindus consider all deities as manifestations of one god, so it can be considered **monotheistic**, which means having one god. Hindus believe in **karma**, the idea that behaviors have consequences in the present life or a future life, and in dharma, which means the righteous path. For part of its history, Hinduism worked closely with a **caste system**, a rigid class structure, that shaped Indian society.

**Buddhism** Buddhism grew out of the teachings of a prince named Siddhartha who lived about 600 years B.C.E. Accepting many beliefs of Hinduism, Siddhartha (who became known as the Buddha, or "enlightened one") advised followers to escape the cycle of suffering through "right" views, hopes, speech, conduct, livelihood, effort, and mindful meditation.

## Three Major Middle Eastern Religions

Three major religions trace their history to Abraham. He was a religious leader who lived in the Middle East around 1800 B.C.E.

**Judaism** Judaism was among the first monotheistic faiths. Jews believe that the writing known as the Torah expresses divine will. It is supplemented by other writings as well as unwritten laws and customs. For the past 2,000 years, most Jews lived in Europe and North Africa. Always a small minority, they often suffered persecution. In the late 1800s, Jews in search of religious liberty began efforts to establish a homeland in the Middle East and began migrating to the United States. During World War II, the systematic murder of six million Jews by Nazi Germany, an event known as the Holocaust, strengthened the movement to create a predominantly Jewish state in the Middle East. In 1948, the country of Israel was formed. Jews from around the world migrated there.

**Christianity** Christianity began when followers of a Jewish teacher, Jesus (c. 4 B.C.E. to c. 30 C.E.), evolved into their own religion based on the belief that Jesus was the son of God and the savior of humans. He emphasized the importance of faith, love, and peace. Christianity spread outward from the Middle East to become the dominant religion in Europe, and then to America and other parts of the world.

**Islam** Islam is the religion followed by Muslims. Muslims believe that Allah (the Arabic word for God) revealed his teachings to humans through a series of prophets. The last of these was Muhammad, who lived in what is now Saudi Arabia in the sixth and seventh centuries C.E. Muslims believe that Allah communicated his teachings to Muhammad, who shared them with people in the book of holy writings known as the Koran.

## RELIGIOUS HEARTHS AND DIFFUSION

| Religion | Hearth | Type of Diffusion |
|---|---|---|
| **Hinduism** | Along Indus River in present-day Pakistan | • Contagious diffusion across Indian subcontinent<br>• Relocation diffusion in recent decades to Europe and the United States |
| **Buddhism** | South Asia in present-day Nepal | • Contagious diffusion as teachings spread throughout East and Southeast Asia<br>• Relocation diffusion throughout the world |
| **Judaism** | Eastern Mediterranean and southwestern Asia | • Relocation diffusion throughout North Africa and Europe forced by the Romans beginning around 70 C.E.<br>• Relocation diffusion to the United States and other countries |
| **Christianity** | Eastern Mediterranean and southwestern Asia | • Contagious diffusion through the Middle East, Europe, and Central Asia<br>• Hierarchical diffusion through conversion of rulers, who then forced their followers to adopt the faith<br>• Relocation diffusion throughout the world |
| **Islam** | Southwest Asia | • Contagious diffusion by trade and conquest to Spain, Africa, and much of Asia<br>• Relocation diffusion throughout the world |

## Ethnic and Universal Religions

**Ethnic religions** are belief traditions that emphasize strong cultural characteristics among their followers. In most cases, members of an ethnic religion are born or adopted into it. Members have a shared historical experience or struggle that creates strong bonds. Ethnic religions rarely recruit new followers actively. Rather, they spread as a result of relocation diffusion. Hinduism and Judaism are the world's two most widespread ethnic religions. The Jewish **Diaspora** and global migration of Hindus from India are examples of such relocation diffusion.

In contrast to an ethnic religion, a **universal religion** actively seeks converts to its faith regardless of their ethnic backgrounds. Universalizing religions have spread far from their original hearths because existing members feel a mandate to spread their beliefs to others. To carry out this mandate, members of universalizing religions often serve as missionaries who both perform charitable works and convert non-believers.

The two largest universalizing religions, Christianity and Islam, also spread from their hearths through conquest and colonization. Christianity, which was found mostly in Europe in the fifteenth century, added millions of followers when Christian missionaries accompanied the European explorers and conquerors to the Western Hemisphere, southern Africa, and Australia. As Europeans expanded their empires, they converted people to Christianity, sometimes violently. Islam spread in much the same way, through the Middle East, North Africa, and Asia.

In many faith traditions, followers feel called to go on a **pilgrimage**, a religious journey taken by a person to a sacred place of his or her religion. Each year, over 20 million Hindus journey to the Ganges River, millions of Muslims travel to Mecca (a pilgrimage known as a *hajj*), and many Muslims, Jews, and Christians visit Jerusalem's many holy sites.

### Influences of Colonialism, Imperialism, and Trade

Colonialism, imperialism, and trade have played a powerful role in spreading religion and culture. Historians often divide European colonialism into two separate waves. From the 1500s to about 1800, Europeans colonized the Americas and South Asia. Then, during the late 1800s to the mid-1900s, European powers colonized most of Africa and Southwest Asia.

The European colonizers imposed their cultural traits on the local populations. For example, before European colonization, most religions practiced by the native people of Africa and North America were forms of **animism**, the belief that non-living objects, such as rivers or mountains, have a spirit. Europeans forced many of their colonial subjects to adopt the Christian faith of their colonizers. The Spanish and French spread Roman Catholicism throughout Latin America, North America, and Quebec. The English, Belgians, and Dutch spread forms of Protestantism in their colonies.

Today, few formal colonies remain in the world, but the practices left behind by the European powers are present in their former colonies. The afternoon break for tea, a British tradition, is still practiced in Kenya and India. The Christianity that was brought by the European colonizers is widespread in many former colonies.

# Religion's Impact on Laws and Customs

Since religious traditions predate current governments, they are often the source for many present-day laws and punishments by the government. Some religions have strict systems of laws that have been adopted fully by some governments. An example of this is sharia, or Islamic law, which is based entirely on the teachings of Islam and has been adopted by some fundamentalist religious groups, such as the Taliban in Afghanistan, as the law of the land.

While no highly industrialized countries have fully adopted religious laws, their legal codes often show clear influence of religion. In the United States, many communities have blue laws, laws that restrict certain activities, such as the sale of alcohol, on Sundays. In Colorado and some other states, all car dealerships must be closed on Sundays as well.

In most countries, religious beliefs are more influential as guides to personal behavior than as state-sponsored laws. For example, many faiths include guidelines on the choices people make about what clothes they wear and how they cut their hair. Most faiths include some food taboos, prohibitions against eating and drinking certain items. For example, many Hindus do not eat beef, and many Jews and Muslims do not eat pork.

Religion is also the source of many daily, weekly, or annual practices for adherents:

- Many Muslims pray five times a day, and many Buddhists and Hindus engage in daily meditation.
- Most religions have weekly religious services for worship or instruction. For example, Muslims usually gather on Fridays, Jews on Friday evenings or Saturday mornings, and Christians on Sundays.
- Many people celebrate important religious holy days, such as Holi, a festival of light, for Hindus, and Vesak, which commemorates the birth of Buddha.

In addition, many days that people now commonly treat as secularized holidays have their roots in religious practices. Valentine's Day, St. Patrick's Day, and Mardi Gras all originated as Christian holy days.

# Religion and the Landscape

Like all human activities, religion influences the organization and use of space. This appears in both how people think about natural features and what people build.

### The Physical Landscape

Many specific places and natural features have religious significance. Some sites are sacred spaces where deities dwell: followers of Shinto view certain mountains and rocks as the homes of spirits. Other sites are not sacred but are important for what occurred at them: Mt. Sinai is honored by Jews, Christians, and Muslims because they believe it is where God handed the Ten Commandments to Moses. Some entire cities, such as Jerusalem (Israel), Mecca (Saudi Arabia), and Lhasa (Tibet), have special religious meanings.

### The Cultural Landscape

Sacred physical features are important, but rare. More commonly, people express their beliefs through the cultural landscapes that they create:

- Memorial spaces to the dead, such as cemeteries, are traditionally located close to worship spaces.
- Restaurants and food markets often cater to particular religious groups by offering religiously approved food.
- Signs often are written in the language and sometimes the alphabet that reflects the ethnic heritage of the group.

The most obvious example of the cultural landscape shaped by religion is in architecture. Each major faith provides examples of this.

**Christianity** Christian churches often feature a tall steeple topped by a cross. Churches also demonstrate how the origin of the architectural style was often influenced by the environment, such as the climate and the available building materials. The hearths of that faith are more likely to resemble the original architecture. Christian churches closer to the eastern Mediterranean tend to have dome-shaped roofs that reflect the traditional style of architecture popular with the Romans, while churches in northern Europe have steep-pitched roofs designed for snow to slide off in the winter, because the build-up of snow on a flatter roof can cause the roof to cave in. Cultural influences similarly shape the preferred and available materials to build such structures.

One similarity among Christians is in treatment of the deceased. In most parts of the world, Christians bury the dead in cemeteries. However, cemeteries vary greatly. Most are underground, but in New Orleans, where the water table is very high, they are above ground.

The Orthodox Christian church on the left, in Greece, illustrates the dome-shaped roofs of the eastern Mediterranean region. The Protestant Christian church on the right, in Norway, shows the style of churches farther from the hearth.

**Hinduism** Hindu temples often have elaborately carved exteriors. Thousands of shrines and temples dot the landscape in India. Sacred sites, such as the Ganges River, provide pilgrims a place to bathe for the purpose of purification. Many Hindu shrines and temples are located near rivers and streams for this very purpose.

Hindus practice cremation of the dead as an act of purification as well—although a shortage of wood has made cremation very expensive. The ashes of the deceased are often spread in the Ganges River. As the population of India has increased, so has the amount of ashes in the river, which has raised concerns about pollution.

**Buddhism** The practice of Buddhism differs widely from place to place, from ethnic group to ethnic group. However, most Buddhists emphasize meditating and living in harmony with nature. These features of Buddhism are represented in stupas, structures built to symbolize five aspects of nature—earth, water, fire, air, and space—where people can meditate. Among Buddhists, the decision to cremate or to bury the dead is a personal choice.

**Judaism** Jews worship in synagogues or temples. Once concentrated in the Middle East, Jews spread throughout the world because of exile or persecution, or though voluntary migration. This scattering is known as the **Diaspora** (a diaspora occurs when one group of people is dispersed to various locations). Temples vary in size based on the number of Jews in an area. Burial of the dead customarily occurs before sundown on the day following the death.

**Islam** In places where Islam is widely practiced, the mosque is the most prominent structure on the landscape and is usually located in the center of town. Mosques have domes surrounded by a few minarets (Arabic for *beacon*) from which daily prayer is called. Burial of the dead is to be done as soon as possible, and burials are in cemeteries.

**Shinto** Shinto, whose cultural hearth is Japan, emphasizes honoring one's ancestors and the relationship between people and nature. One common landscape feature of Shinto shrines is an impressive gateway, or torii (see below), to mark the transition from the outside world to a sacred space.

# How Religion and Ethnicity Shape Space

The first group to establish cultural and religious customs in a space is known as the **charter group**. Native Americans were the original charter group in the Americas. Their influence appears in many places, such as in place names from Mt. Denali in Alaska to Miami, Florida. Often, charter groups show their heritage. For example, English settlements in colonial America resembled the settlements they migrated away from in England, and names such as Plymouth and Jamestown reflect this heritage.

### Ethnic Symbolic Landscapes

Ethnic groups that arrive after the charter group may choose to bypass the particular location and establish their space with their own customs. In urban areas, these enclaves become ethnic neighborhoods.

In rural areas, ethnic concentrations form **ethnic islands**. Their cultural imprints revolve around housing types and agricultural dwellings that reflect their heritage. Because ethnic islands are in rural areas and have less interaction with other groups than do groups in cities, they maintain a strong and long-lasting sense of cohesion. Today, Germanic ethnic islands of people who fled religious persecution in the past continue to exist in the United States (the Pennsylvania Dutch and the Amish), Canada (Mennonites in Alberta), and in scattered locations in the Balkan region of southeastern Europe.

### Urban Ethnic Neighborhoods

Ethnic neighborhoods in urban settings are often occupied by migrants who settle in a charter group's former space. The charter group has already shaped much of the landscape, but new arrivals create their own influence as well. Dozens of cities around the world—Melbourne, Australia; Gachsaren, Iran; Liverpool, England; San Francisco—have neighborhoods known as "Chinatown." Often, the name lives on even if the new arrivals have moved out or assimilated, and the neighborhood primarily caters to tourists.

### New Cultural Influences

Ethnic groups move in and out of neighborhoods and create new cultural imprints on the landscape in a process geographers call **sequent occupance**. In Chicago, the Pilsen neighborhood is heavily Hispanic today, but its name recalls its history as a home for German and Czech immigrants. In New York City, the neighborhood of Harlem has been home to many ethnic groups: Jews from Eastern Europe starting in the late 1800s, African Americans from the southern United States starting in the 1910s, and Puerto Ricans starting in the late 20th century. As result of sequent occupance, Harlem's cultural landscape includes former Jewish synagogues, public spaces named for African American leaders such as Marcus Garvey Park, and street names honoring Puerto Rican leaders such as Luis Muñoz Marin Boulevard.

## GEOGRAPHIC PERSPECTIVES: MUSLIMS IN THE UNITED STATES

Muslims have been living in the Americas since the days of Columbus. Geographers have studied the patterns in the diffusion of Muslims in the Americas, including the reasons behind their involuntary or voluntary migrations and where they they have been concentrated.

### Muslims Among Enslaved Africans

The first concentration of Muslims was in what is now the southeastern United States. Maybe 15 percent of the enslaved Africans brought to the Americas were followers of Islam.

### Migrants to Industrial Cities

Then, between 1890 and 1917, a new wave of Muslim immigrants entered the United States. Most came from Bosnia, Turkey, Syria, and other lands in the Middle East. Pulled by the lure of industrial jobs, most settled in the growing cities of the North and Midwest. However, some of the first mosques were founded in small communities in Iowa, Maine, and North Dakota.

Industrial cities in the 1920s and 1930s also attracted millions of African Americans from the rural South. Some African Americans joined a distinctive movement within Islam, known as the Black Muslims. They were concentrated in New York, Detroit, and Chicago. Today, about one-quarter of American Muslims are African Americans.

### Diverse Immigrants

In recent decades, Muslim immigrants have come from around the world. While many come from the Middle East and South Asia, others migrate from Nigeria, Indonesia, and other countries. Again, the primary places of settlement have been large urban areas, but increasingly in suburban communities, such as Dearborn, Michigan. Today, Muslims constitute about 1 percent of the total population.

| KEY TERMS | | |
|---|---|---|
| ethnicity | monotheistic | charter group |
| nationality | caste system | ethnic island |
| culture hearth | karma | sequent occupance |
| fundamentalism | ethnic religion | polytheistic |
| theocracies | universal religion | animism |
| sharia | pilgrimage | |
| neolocalism | Diaspora | |

**Questions 1 and 2 refer to the map below.**

DIFFUSION OF BUDDHISM OUT OF INDIA

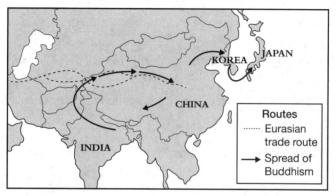

1. The map shows the spread of
   (A) Hinduism
   (B) Buddhism
   (C) Islam
   (D) Judaism
   (E) Christianity

2. Which general conclusion about the expansion diffusion of the religion does the map most strongly support?
   (A) It requires mass migrations of people over long distances.
   (B) It usually moves in an eastward direction.
   (C) It is aided by the presence of a major trade route.
   (D) It occurs more in Asia than on other continents.
   (E) It experiences strong fundamentalism at its hearth.

3. Judaism, Christianity, and Islam are alike in that they all
   (A) began as universal religions
   (B) are examples of ethnic religions
   (C) evolved into polytheistic religions
   (D) trace their heritage to Abraham
   (E) started in a region that is now part of Europe

4. Which best describes the main difference between ethnicity and nationality?
   (A) Nationality is connected to a state while ethnicity is connected to culture.
   (B) Nationality is connected to culture while ethnicity is connected to a state.
   (C) Nationality is connected to a language while ethnicity is connected to a religion.
   (D) Nationality is connected to cities while ethnicity is connected to rural areas.
   (E) Nationality is connected to religion while ethnicity is connected to urban enclaves.

**Question 5 refers to the picture below.**

5. Based on its architecture, the worship site in the picture is probably used by people of which religious tradition?
   (A) Christianity
   (B) Judaism
   (C) Islam
   (D) Hinduism
   (E) Buddhism

6. Which was the most common religious change among Africans as a result of contact with people from Europe and the Middle East?

(A) from animism to a universalizing religion

(B) from an ethnic religion to animism

(C) from a universalizing religion to an ethnic religion

(D) from monotheism to polytheism

(E) from polytheism to an ethnic religion

7. Which type of influence has been most significant in shaping the distribution of religious groups in the United States?

(A) climate and landforms

(B) immigration patterns

(C) federal government policies

(D) economic development

(E) shifts in agriculture

8. Which is an example of sequent occupance?

(A) the forced movement of Native Americans from their homelands to reservations

(B) the Diaspora of the Jews after being banished from their homeland by the Romans

(C) the decision by Amish immigrants to settle in rural areas rather than in urban enclaves

(D) an ethnic group that is completely surrounded by another ethnic group

(E) the shift in a neighborhood population from Germans to Poles to Koreans

## FREE-RESPONSE QUESTION

1. The two major religion hearths in the world are the Middle East and South Asia.

   A. Identify ONE religion that originated in each region and a country today in which the religion is dominant.

   B. For each religion identified in Part A, discuss a significant person, event, or idea that shaped the religion's origin, and explain how the religion diffused over time to other countries or regions.

**THINK AS A GEOGRAPHER:** RELIGIOUS SPACES AT DIFFERENT SCALES

The distribution of religious elements on the landscape reflects the importance of religion in society's values. How each religion distributes its elements across the landscape depends on its beliefs. The impact of religion is clearly seen on the landscape at several scales from small areas within homes to entire communities.

Explain how the concept of scale applies to the three following religious landscapes.

1. How does the location of the Hindu shrine reflect the religious traditions in Hinduism?

2. What scale of analysis does the photograph of Vatican City represent?

3. How does the photograph of the pagoda suggest a regional scale of analysis?

1. Hindu home shrine in India

3. Buddhist five-story pagoda, Japan

2. Vatican City, Italy

# UNIT 3: Review

## WRITE AS A GEOGRAPHER: WRITE IN COMPLETE THOUGHTS

A response to a free-response question should be more than just a list of unrelated points. Each point should be stated clearly in one or more sentences that each express a complete thought. Related sentences should be linked with words such as "for example," "as a result," and "in the next stage" that make the relationship between ideas clear. Together, all of the sentences should work together to form a larger complete thought that answers the question.

*For each word, write one or two sentences that demonstrate how that word might be used in answering a free-response question about categories of religion.*

**1.** monotheistic

**2.** polytheistic

**3.** fundamentalism

**4.** ethnic

**5.** universal

**6.** animism

**7.** theocracies

*Write a sentence that includes each pair of words or phrases and states a clear relationship between the concepts.*

**8.** Jewish Diaspora; relocation diffusion

**9.** sharia; religious law

**10.** universalizing religions; members feel a mandate

**11.** Mecca, Jerusalem, Lhasa; sacred space

## REFLECT ON THE CHAPTER ESSENTIAL QUESTIONS

*Write a one- to three-paragraph answer to each question.*

**1.** How do folk and popular cultures differ in the ways they help form a society's overall culture?

**2.** What can geographers learn about cultures of the world by studying the spread and the changes of their diverse languages?

**3.** How do religious and ethnic groups both reflect and influence the geography of places at different scales?

# UNIT 4: Political Organization of Space

*Chapter 9* The Shape of the Political Map

*Chapter 10* Territory, Power, and Boundaries

*Chapter 11* Globalization

## Unit Overview

Today's political map consists mostly of independent states in which all territory is connected, and most people share a language and other cultural traits. This was not true in the past. Many states were sprawling, diverse empires, such as the Ottoman Empire in the Middle East or the British Empire that included people of many cultures. At the same time, many cultural groups were divided into several political groups, such as the hundreds of small German states in central Europe or the various groups of nomads in central Asia.

### Political Power Over a Territory

A government demonstrates its power over a geographic area by enforcing laws that govern individual behavior and affect how resources are used. Boundaries separate territories at various scales, from those that divide the world into countries to those that determine where students attend school.

Political power can be divided in several ways. In a country, it can be centralized in one national government or divided between the national government and several local governments. In the United States, local power can be centralized under regional or county governments, or it can be divided into a patchwork of cities, school districts, and other types of districts.

### Impact of Globalization

Independent states face challenges from globalization. Transnational corporations, international organizations, and global environmental problems all make the boundaries around a state less important than they once were.

Another challenge to independent states comes from within. Regions with distinctive cultural groups, such as Catalonia in Spain and Quebec in Canada, have successfully argued for more autonomy.

---

**Enduring Understandings**

IV. Political Organization of Space

    A. The contemporary political map has been shaped by events of the past.

    B. Spatial political patterns reflect ideas of territoriality and power at a variety of levels.

    C. The forces of globalization challenge contemporary political-territorial arrangements.

**Source:** *CollegeBoard AP®. Human Geography Course Description. 2015.*

---

# 9

# The Shape of the Political Map

*[Soviet] General Secretary Gorbachev, if you seek peace, if you seek prosperity for the Soviet Union and Eastern Europe, if you seek liberalization, come here to this gate. Mr. Gorbachev, open this gate. Mr. Gorbachev, tear down this wall!*

—President Ronald Reagan, speech, 1987

**Essential Question:** What social, historical, and economic factors have influenced modern political maps at various scales?

Empires and kingdoms were common in most of the world for the past two thousand years. However, global forces, wars, and changing ideas about political power, economics, and self-rule have reshaped the world map over the last 400 years.

## The Structure of the Contemporary Political Map

People often use the words *country, state,* and *nation* to mean the same thing. But they have different meanings. *Country* is the most general term. It is often used to describe any political entity that is independent from the control of any other entity. *State* and *nation* have more precise meanings.

### Independent States as Building Blocks

Political units exist at various scales. In the United States, for example, a person resides in several political units at once: maybe a town or city, a county, a state, and finally, in the country as a whole. Note that the term *state* can be confusing because it can be used in two different ways. In this example, it refers to one of the 50 states that make up the United States. But in the area of international relations, a **state** is the largest political unit, the formal term for a country. It meets the following criteria:

- has a defined boundary
- contains a permanent population
- maintains sovereignty over its domestic and international affairs
- is recognized by other states

The United States recognizes 195 states based on these criteria, but the number can vary depending on which government or international organization is making the list. These four requirements are easily defined, but in the geopolitical arena, they can be difficult to recognize.

Consider the complicated relationship between the People's Republic of China and the nearby island of Taiwan. In 1949, China ended a long civil war. The victorious communist forces led by Mao Zedong established their capital in Beijing. About two million supporters of the losing side, known as the nationalists, retreated to Taiwan. China was divided between two governments, one on the mainland and one in Taiwan, that each considered itself China's legitimate ruler. The government on the mainland never gave up its claim on Taiwan, and Taiwan never declared independence. Today, Beijing rules more than 1 billion residents. Taiwan rules about 24 million, but it manages its own affairs and has diplomatic relations with about 20 countries.

**Sovereignty**, the power of a political unit to rule over its own affairs, is a key principle in understanding how these units function. In order for a political unit to have legitimacy, it must have sovereignty. Sovereignty may be challenged on the global or local scale. China's claim that Taiwan is nothing more than a renegade province is a direct challenge to Taiwan's sovereignty. And since Taiwan is recognized by so few other states, it seems to be an effective challenge. (Largely because of China's opposition, Taiwan is not a member of the UN.) So, the case can be made that Taiwan does not fully meet the third and fourth criteria listed above.

## Types of Political Entities

Often the term *nation* is interchangeably used with *country*; however, the terms are not identical. In general, a nation is a group of people who have certain things in common:

- share a common cultural heritage
- have beliefs and values that help unify them
- claim a particular space based on tradition as their homeland
- desire to establish their own state or express self-determination in another way

Depending on how tightly one applies these standards, the number of nations ranges from a few hundred to several thousand. Many political entities combine aspects of nationhood and statehood.

**Nation-States** A singular nation of people who fulfill the qualifications of a state form a **nation-state**. Among the best examples of nation-states are Iceland and Japan. Icelanders make up 94 percent of its total population of 300,000. Scandinavian settlers founded Iceland on an island that had no indigenous population. Japanese account for 99 percent of the total population of its 128 million permanent residents. A strong national identity coupled with strict immigration policies have maintained Japan as a nation-state.

## DISTINGUISHING NATIONS AND STATES

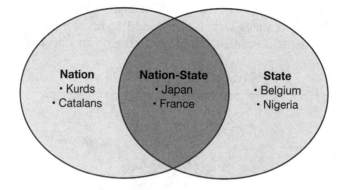

**Multinational States** A **multinational state** is a country that contains more than one nation. Most multinational states consist of one dominant nation that controls most of the political power. Numerous multinational states fit these criteria, including Canada. While the English-language culture dominates, about 25 percent of Canadians speak French primarily. Most live in the province of Quebec. In an effort to prevent Quebec from demanding independence, the national government passed legislation making Canada a bilingual state and gave the province increased local autonomy in government and education.

Similarly, the Canadian government granted more autonomy over local affairs and natural resources to the indigenous nations. As part of this effort, it created the territory of Nunavut in 1999. Nunavut is in the far north of Canada. Over 80 percent of the population consider themselves Inuit.

**Autonomous Regions** A defined area within a state that has a high degree of self-government and freedom from its parent state is sometimes known as an **autonomous region**. States often grant this authority to geographically, ethnically, or culturally distinct areas. For example, Åland is a group of islands in the Baltic Sea. It is part of Finland but lies near Sweden. Most residents are ethnically Swedish and speak that language. A desire to join Sweden after World War I was submitted to the League of Nations. The League ruled that Åland should remain part of Finland, but as a nonmilitarized, largely self-governing entity, which it still is today.

**Stateless Nations** Since the world consists of far more nations than states, many nations do not have a state of their own, although they often have a political organization. These cultural groups that have no independent political entity are called **stateless nations**. Stateless nations seeking to become independent states include the Palestinians (Gaza Strip and Occupied West Bank) and the Basque (northeastern Spain and southwestern France).

The largest stateless nation belongs to the Kurdish people. Spread among six states in southwest Asia (Turkey, Armenia, Iraq, Iran, Azerbaijan, and Syria), the Kurds number between 25 million and 30 million people in an area called Kurdistan. As states such as Syria and Iraq became destabilized in the 2000s, ethnic Kurds intensified their push for their own independent country.

THE KURDISTAN REGION

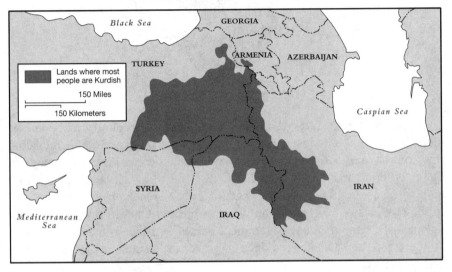

**Multistate Nations** A **multistate nation** occurs when a nation has a state of its own but stretches across borders of other states. For example, most Hungarians live in Hungary, but many live in the Transylvania region of Romania. The Korean nation is divided primarily between two states—the Democratic People's Republic of Korea (North Korea) and the Republic of Korea (South Korea)—but with large numbers in China and the United States.

# Evolution of the Contemporary Political Map

Today's world map includes nations without states, nations in multiple states, and states containing multiple nations. This mixture of situations reflects the evolution of politics, economics, and warfare over the last roughly 600 years.

## The Modern Nation-State Concept

For most of European history, no relation existed between the language people spoke and the state to which they belonged. For example, most people who paid allegiance to the king of France in the 1500s did not speak French. Rather, they spoke a regional language. And people who spoke various forms of Italian in the 1600s did not assume that they should all be part of the same state. By the 1700s, the idea that people should live in nation-states had caught hold in some areas, beginning in France and England. However, the map of Europe was still a patchwork of tiny states and a few large multi-ethnic empires (Russian Empire, Ottoman Empire, etc.). The 1800s saw an explosion of nationalism in Europe. On the one hand, groups rebelled against being part of large empires that were controlled by another culture. On the other hand, divided groups, such as Germans and Italians, wanted to consolidate into unified countries.

THE EIGHT INDEPENDENT ITALIAN STATES IN 1858

## Forces Unifying and Breaking Apart Countries

One definition of **nationalism** is a nation's desire to create and maintain a state of its own. Since nationalism unifies people, it is an example of a **centripetal force**. Other centripetal forces include:

- a shared religion—Roman Catholicism unites Mexicans
- external threats—Estonians are united by fear of Russia
- a common language—Japanese share the same language

A counter to centripetal forces would be **centrifugal forces**. These are forces that "pull away from the center," or ones that tend to break apart states or keep one from forming. Religion and language divide the people of Belgium. Most people in the north speak a Dutch language called Flemish and are historically Protestants, while people in the south speak French and tend to be of Roman Catholic descent.

## Imperialism and Colonialism

Imperialism and colonialism are related ideas, but they are not the same. **Imperialism** is a broader concept: it includes a variety of ways of influencing another country or group of people, by direct conquest, by economic control, or by cultural dominance. **Colonialism** is a particular type of imperialism in which people move into and settle on the land of another country. Examples of imperialism and colonialism can be found throughout history and all over the world, but modern European imperialism and colonialism are the most relevant to the current political map. They occurred in two distinct waves.

**Early Colonialism** The first wave of European colonialism was led by Spain and Portugal, and then by France and Britain. These countries established large empires in the Americas, and they were motivated by "God, gold, and glory." They wanted:

- religious influence by spreading their form of Christianity
- economic wealth from exploiting land, labor, and capital to enrich the home country
- political power by expanding their influence throughout the world

The European powers justified their conquests through the legal concept of *Terra Nullius,* a Latin phrase meaning "land belonging to no one." According to this concept, they could legitimately seize "uncivilized land." The result was the dispossession of indigenous people. The impact of this concept is still being redressed throughout parts of the world today.

Wars among empires influenced colonial claims. In the Seven Years' War (1756–1763), known in North America as the French and Indian War, the British won control of Canada from France. However, the strain of paying for the war led to conflicts between Britain and its colonies, soon resulting in the American Revolution. U.S. independence then inspired similar movements in other colonies. By 1833, most of Latin America was free from European rule, and nationalism was spreading through the region.

**Later Colonialism** During the nineteenth century, the Spanish and the Portuguese empires declined, but other European countries launched a second wave of colonization. Led by Great Britain, France, the Netherlands, Belgium, Italy, and Germany, this wave focused on controlling lands in Africa and Asia.

In 1884 and 1885, representatives from the major empires of Europe met in the German capital of Berlin to lay out claims made on the continent of Africa. The **Berlin Conference** (or sometimes known as the Congo Conference) used these claims to form state boundaries in Africa. These boundaries showed little regard to the existing ethno-linguistic, cultural, and political boundaries in place. As a result, one colony might include a patchwork of rival cultural groups, and one cultural group might be divided among multiple colonies.

# Geopolitical Forces Influencing Today's Map

While the European colonies in Africa and Asia did not last long, their legacy was strong. It can be seen in contemporary maps and the links among countries.

## Modern Colonial Independence Movements

Colonists, inspired by nationalism, resisted the rule of Europeans, sometimes with violence. People in colonies wanted economic control over natural resources (petroleum, precious metals, and so on), free elections, and changes in society such as racial equality and religious freedom. The United Nations, created in 1945, supported the demands of subject people in colonies for self-determination. Within a century of the Berlin Conference, almost all European colonial territories had won independence, a process known as **decolonization**.

Many colonies gained independence politically, but not economically. Transnational corporations based in the former colonial powers continued to control the extraction of natural resources through mining and the cultivation of coffee, cacao, bananas, and other crops on plantations. A new form of colonization, called **neocolonialism**, emerged in which control over developing countries was exerted through indirect means, whether economic, political, or even cultural power.

## Civil Wars in the Developing World

From 1960 through 1970, 32 colonial territories in Africa gained independence. However, since independence was won by colonies rather than by cultural groups, the boundaries imposed by Europe remained in the newly independent states. As a result, cultural boundaries and political boundaries did not match. Cultural conflicts within countries led to many civil wars. Then, because cultural groups spanned political borders, conflicts in one country often spilled over into other countries.

Among the worst of these wars was in Rwanda in 1994, which led to charges of genocide. Before colonization by Belgium, two rival ethnic groups, the Hutu and Tutsi, had competed for control of territory and resources. In 1961, Rwanda won independence. The Hutu majority won elections to govern the country, but the rivalry with the Tutsi continued. In April 1994, the Rwandan president, a Hutu, died when his plane was shot down. Although no one knew then who was responsible, Hutus exacted revenge by killing Tutsis and moderate Hutus on a vast scale. This type of mass, organized killing, in which people are targeted because of their race, religion, ethnicity, or nationality, is called **genocide**. Within just a few months, close to one million Rwandans were killed with many more migrating as refugees to neighboring countries.

This pattern of independence followed by civil wars and regional conflicts is nothing new to the political landscape. Serious problems result when national and ethnic rivals are forced to share political space because of boundaries drawn by outside powers. And in many cases, one ethnicity may be spread over several states, so a conflict in one state quickly escalates into a regional one. Today, many of the geopolitical "hotspots" in Africa and the Middle East are difficult to solve because of borders established long ago.

## THE SPREAD OF INDEPENDENCE, 1945 TO 2015

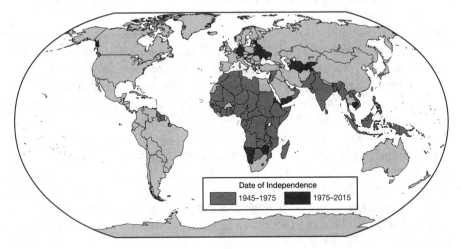

Date of Independence
1945–1975      1975–2015

### The Cold War

The **Cold War** was a period of diplomatic, political, and military rivalry between the United States and the Union of Soviet Socialist Republics (Soviet Union). It started at the end of World War II (1945), continued through the collapse of the Berlin Wall (1989), and ended with the breakup of the Soviet Union (1991).

Although the United States and the Soviet Union did not fight a direct war against each other, they fought several proxy wars (a proxy is a representative) in Africa, Latin America, and Asia. For the United States, the largest of these conflicts were in Korea, Vietnam, and Afghanistan. The superpowers wanted to extend their spheres of influence, the areas over which they had some degree of control. This meant winning allies in other countries and thwarting their rival from doing so. The American-Soviet contest often influenced the newly independent states emerging out of colonialism.

The frontline for the Cold War was in Europe. After the defeat of Nazi Germany, a tenuous peace divided Europe between East and West. The Eastern European countries liberated and occupied by the Soviet army became Soviet **satellite states**. This type of state is dominated by another state politically and economically. Attempts by Hungary in 1956 and Czechoslovakia in 1968 to break away from Soviet domination were put down with overwhelming force.

Germany's status was complicated. In 1945, it was divided into four zones of occupation among the victorious powers: the United States, United Kingdom, France, and the Soviet Union. The first three of these zones united to form the Federal Republic of Germany (West Germany), which allied with the United States. The Soviet zone became the German Democratic Republic and allied itself with the Soviet Union.

The split in the country was repeated on a smaller scale in the city of Berlin. The city itself was located inside of the Soviet zone, but it was divided into four parts. The Soviet part became East Berlin. But the other three parts merged into West Berlin, which was part of West Germany, even though it was surrounded by East Germany.

COLD WAR BLOCS, C. 1960

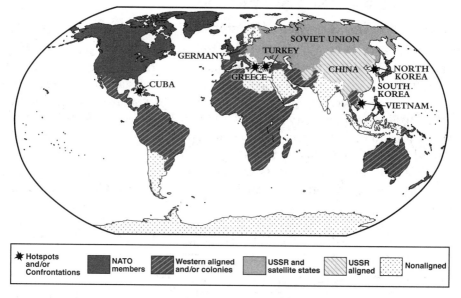

## The Collapse of Communism

In the late 1980s, new leadership in the Soviet Union began to relax its grip over its satellite states in Eastern Europe. Finally, in November 1989, citizens of both Germanys brought down the wall that had divided the city of Berlin since 1961. In fact, within the next year and a half, Germany had reunited, and former satellite states of Eastern Europe were holding free elections without influence from the Soviet Union. But change in Europe did not end there.

The Union of Soviet Socialist Republics (USSR or Soviet Union), a confederation of 15 republics, began to collapse as well. Eventually these 15 republics would become independent countries.

### Newly Independent States

After 1990, the political boundaries were once again altered. The collapse of communism and the Soviet Union created an enormous power vacuum not only in Europe but also throughout the world. Most of Europe made a peaceful transition into the post-communist world. For example, in 1993, Czechoslovakia smoothly divided into the Czech Republic and the Republic of Slovakia, an event known as the "Velvet Divorce."

However, the breakup of Yugoslavia in 1991 was complicated and violent. Long-standing ethnic tensions erupted. Hundreds of thousands died in clashes between Serbs, Bosnians, and others before a handful of independent countries emerged. Many died because of **ethnic cleansing**, the forced removal of a minority ethnic group from a territory. (The breakup of Yugoslavia as an example of balkanization is described in Chapter 11.)

### Changes in the Balance of Power

The collapse of communism and the Soviet Union drastically changed the balance of power in Europe and throughout the world. Some former communist countries of Eastern Europe as well as some of the independent states have joined the European Union (see map below) and the North Atlantic Treaty Organization (NATO), the western military alliance formed in 1949 to oppose Soviet military power in Europe. The balance of economic, political, and military power tilted toward Western Europe and the United States.

This shift frightened the Russians. They reacted by intervening militarily to support pro-Russian groups in the Republic of Georgia (2008) and Ukraine (2014).

## THE GROWTH OF NATO, 1945 TO 2015

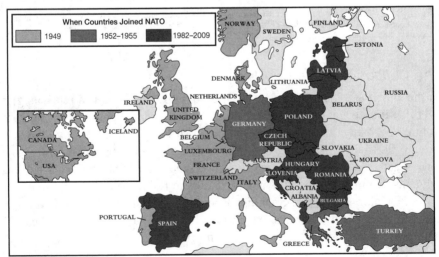

The United States has been roughly the same size since 1867, when the country purchased Alaska. Since then, the United States has added important islands, including Hawaii and Puerto Rico, but all additions have been small in size. However, there is no guarantee that this stability will continue into the future.

**Better Communication**

One of the forces that might reshape the political map of the United States is technology. Computers, the Internet, and cell phones have increased the connections among people across space. Technology could be a centripetal force. As people communicate more closely across long distances, variations from region to region might diminish. The United States might become a more tightly united country, with less cultural variation than in the past.

Or the technology could be a centrifugal force. As Americans find people with whom they share interests and values in other places in the country, they could relate more to them than to the neighbors in their community. Place might become less important.

**Movement of People**

Migrations of people could also have mixed results for American political unity. The migration of people from one region to another could reduce regional variation in politics. For example, in most presidential elections in the past century, states in the Northeast and the Southeast have voted for opposing candidates. Will continued migration from the Northeast to the Southeast change this? Will the two regions become more similar politically, either because the migrants take their voting behavior with them or because the migrants adapt to the behavior of their new neighbors?

| KEY TERMS | | |
|---|---|---|
| state | nationalism | decolonization |
| sovereignty | centripetal forces | neocolonialism |
| nation | centrifugal forces | genocide |
| nation-state | imperialism | Cold War |
| multinational state | colonialism | satellite state |
| autonomous region | Berlin Conference (Congo Conference), 1884 | ethnic cleansing |
| stateless nation | | |
| multistate nation | | |

1. Which of the following is NOT a necessary criterion for a state?

 (A) sovereignty

 (B) defined boundary

 (C) common culture and identity

 (D) recognition by other states

 (E) a permanent population

**Question 2 refers to the map below.**

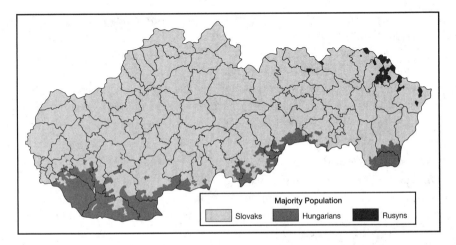

2. Which term best describes Slovakia?

 (A) stateless nation

 (B) multinational state

 (C) empire

 (D) dependent territory

 (E) autonomous region

**3.** Which event symbolically marked the end of the Cold War?

(A) the election of President Ronald Reagan in 1980

(B) the end of World War II, 1945

(C) the end of the Vietnam War, 1975

(D) the Soviet invasion of Hungary, 1956

(E) the collapse of the Berlin Wall, 1989

**Question 4 refers to the map below.**

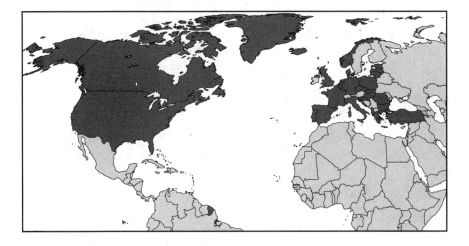

**4.** Countries highlighted in the darker shade in the map above represent which of the following organizations?

(A) North Atlantic Treaty Organization

(B) Warsaw Pact

(C) United Nations

(D) League of Nations

(E) European Union

| ETHNIC GROUPS IN MYANMAR (BURMA) | | |
|---|---|---|
| Group | Percentage of the Population | Traits |
| Burmans | 68 | • Spread throughout the center of the country<br>• Speak the dominant language of the country |
| Shan | 9 | • Concentrated in eastern region<br>• Speak their own language |
| Kachin | 7 | • Concentrated in northeast region<br>• Speak their own language<br>• Desire for independence |
| Other | 16 | • Government recognizes more than 130 ethnic groups<br>• Many desire independence |

5. Based on the information in the chart, Myanmar is a
   (A) nation
   (B) nation-state
   (C) multinational state
   (D) stateless nation
   (E) multistate nation

6. Based on the information in the chart, the lands of the Kachin can be considered
   (A) a multistate nation
   (B) an autonomous region
   (C) a nation-state
   (D) a stateless nation
   (E) a newly independent state

7. Which group represents the largest stateless nation in the world?
   (A) Basque
   (B) Palestinians
   (C) Kurds
   (D) Abkhazians
   (E) Roma

8. People who all consider themselves part of a stateless nation share all of the following characteristics EXCEPT

(A) a history that people remember

(B) a widely spoken language

(C) a formal government recognized by other countries

(D) a religion that most people practice

(E) a similar ethnic identity

## FREE-RESPONSE QUESTION

1. Since 1989, the fall of communism has altered the political landscape by increasing the number of countries in Europe.

   A. Identify and explain two effects on boundaries that resulted from the fall of communism in Europe.

   B. Identify and explain two types of conflicts that emerged after the fall of communism in Europe.

**THINK AS A GEOGRAPHER:** LABELING A BOUNDARY DISPUTE

Various titles of a single map can reflect competing perspectives on geographic relationships. In 1947 the British ended colonial rule in the Indian subcontinent. They divided the colony into two countries, India and Pakistan. (In 1971, the eastern part of Pakistan became the independent country of Bangladesh.) The basis for the separation was religion. Regions where nearly everyone was a Muslim became Pakistan. The rest of the region, with a Hindu majority, became India.

However, people disputed control over the region of Kashmir, in the northern tip of the subcontinent. Most people were Muslims, but the rulers were Hindus, so both Pakistan and India felt a strong claim on it. People failed to agree on a formal boundary. Instead, they accepted a "line of control." Pakistan controls the territory northwest of this line, while India controls the territory southeast of the line. To make the issue more complicated, China claims part of eastern Kashmir.

Evaluate how two titles for this map, "Religious Differences in South Asia" and "Indo-Pakistani Boundary" emphasize different points of view.

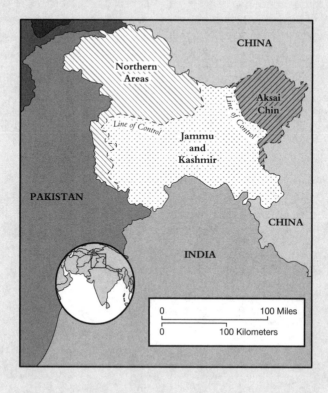

# 10

# Territory, Power, and Boundaries

*Who rules East Europe commands the Heartland*
*Who rules the Heartland commands the World Island*
*Who rules the World Island commands the world.*

—Sir Halford John Mackinder
*British geographer*, 1919

**Essential Question:** How do boundaries reflect ideas of territoriality and political power on various scales?

The concepts of power, territoriality, and boundaries are often intertwined and dependent on one another. Economic systems, cultural patterns and processes, and political systems have shaped various theories of how power is distributed on the political landscape. Physical geography and the natural landscape impact the distribution of power, the form and function of boundaries, and the morphology of political units. The forms of governance on international, national, regional, and local scales are products of both the human and physical landscapes.

## Concepts of Political Power and Territoriality

**Geopolitics** is the study of the effects of geography on politics and relations among states. More than just political power, geopolitics also relates to trade, resource management, and the environment on a global scale. A key concept in geopolitics is **territoriality**, a willingness by one person or a group of people to defend space they claim. People express their territoriality when they influence others or shape events by asserting control over a space. Geographers use three theories to explain the distribution of power in the world.

### Organic Theory

Among the first Europeans to systematically study why some states grew powerful while others were weak was Friedrich Ratzel (1844–1904). He was trained as a biologist and influenced by the ideas of his contemporary, Charles Darwin. Ratzel viewed states as similar to living organisms, and believed that the forces of natural selection applied to relationships among them. Ratzel's **Organic Theory** argues that states are born and that they need nourishment and living space to survive. They obtain this living space, or *lebensraum,* usually by annexing territory from weaker states. But if a state stayed weak, other states, stronger and more vigorous, would seize its land. According to Ratzel, a state either had to grow or it would cease to exist.

Ratzel could support his Organic Theory by pointing to the westward expansion of the United States and the overseas colonization by Europeans. After Ratzel's death, German Nazis used the idea of *lebensraum* to justify their plans to expand eastward into the farmland of Poland. These moves, along with efforts to annex parts of Austria and Czechoslovakia where many German-speaking people lived, led to World War II.

## Heartland Theory

In the late nineteenth century, many Europeans saw the success of colonial acquisitions and concluded that countries derived power from controlling water routes in the ocean. A British geographer, Sir Halford Mackinder (1861–1947), dissented. He developed the **Heartland Theory**, which argued that land-based power was essential in achieving global domination. Mackinder believed that establishing Eastern Europe led to control of the heartland (Eastern Europe plus Russia and Central Asia), which would lead to domination of the "world island" (Eurasia plus Africa), thus resulting in command of the world. He based his theory on a combination of beliefs and geographic facts:

- Improvements in land transportation—roads and railroads—enabled military forces to move as fast or faster on land as on water.
- Control over land was therefore much more important than maritime power.
- The heartland has large coal deposits and a wealth of other resources.
- The heartland is mostly landlocked, so it is well protected from naval attack.
- The only land route to invade the heartland is through Eastern Europe.
- The "world island" includes the majority of Earth's land and population.

MacKinder's theory factored into policy decisions of world powers for both world wars and the numerous Cold War conflicts.

## Rimland Theory

Dutch-American Nicholas Spykman (1893–1943) created the **Rimland Theory**, which argued that power is derived from controlling strategic maritime areas of the world. The rimland comprises densely populated coastal areas that reside outside of the heartland. Spykman thought these areas were more crucial to worldwide power because they had more and more varied resources than the heartland—including people and access to the sea. He valued sea power more than did Mackinder.

Although Spykman died before the end of World War II, his writings influenced western policymakers throughout the Cold War. The creation of the North Atlantic Treaty Organization (NATO) in 1949 and President Harry Truman's policy of containing Communist expansion reflected Spykman's beliefs. The Rimland Theory may best be described as the following:

"Who rules the rimland rules Eurasia;

Who rules Eurasia controls the destinies of the World."

THE WORLD ISLAND

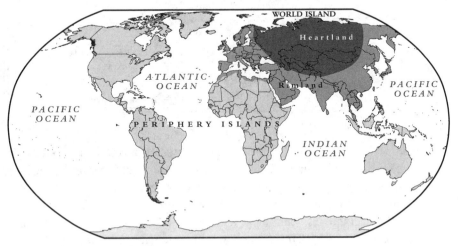

## *Territoriality Connects Culture and Economy*

Defining territoriality may be easy, but applying it is complex. Under the influence of cultural forces and economic interests, people often disagree on how to allocate control of territories. Maps that show the boundaries of a state as clear, precise lines might suggest those boundaries are well-defined. However, people might hotly disagree over the boundaries, or simply ignore them in reality. Similarly, a state's sovereignty might be well-established on paper, but people might not fully accept it.

One example of the connection of territoriality to culture is the relationship between Sunni and Shia Muslims. These two branches of Islam divided on the question of who should succeed Muhammad after his death in 632. They have remained divided ever since, a division that has sometimes contributed to violence. (See the map on the next page.)

In recent years, the conflict within Islam has been clearest in the rivalry between Sunni-dominated Saudi Arabia and Shia-dominated Iran. Adding to the religious conflict between the countries is an ethnic difference: the Saudis are Arabs and the Iranians are Persians. Each country has tried to expand its power over territory, which has led to tension and instability.

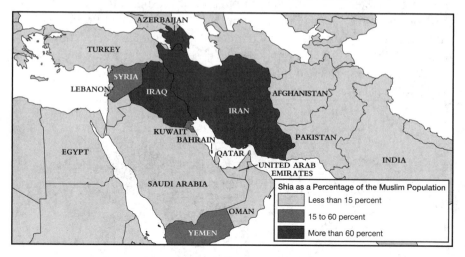

Territoriality has always been closely connected to economic issues. In recent years, the Philippines, Malaysia, Brunei, Vietnam, Taiwan, and China have claimed sovereignty over the Spratly Islands, an isolated group of islands in the South China Sea. Tensions run high on the subject in the region. But why are these countries seemingly willing to risk conflict over a group of islands, islets, and reefs? The answers are, in large part, economic:

- Experts believe that significant, but unconfirmed, petroleum reserves exist in the area.
- The region's fishing grounds supply work and food for many in the entire region.
- Major international shipping lanes pass through the area.

As of 2016, each of the countries involved (except Brunei) occupied at least part of the island group. China was attempting to expand the size of its holdings through dredging and land reclamation, building up small reefs into full-fledged islands, from which, conceivably, to better push and/or enforce its claims of sovereignty.

## International and Internal Boundaries

In theory, boundaries of all kinds exist to add clarity. They signal where people agree that one political entity ends or begins, helping people within them know what territory is theirs to administer and what is not. But when neighbors disagree on where the line separating them should be, boundaries become the subject of uncertainty. Throughout history, uncertain boundaries have been a frequent cause of bloodshed and war.

## Categories of Boundaries

Boundaries represent changes in the use of space as one crosses from one side to the other. Crossing a boundary implies that some rules, expectations, or behaviors change. When moving across a formal international, national, or local boundary, these rules are referred to as laws.

Some very influential boundaries are not set formally. Informal boundaries include ones marking the spheres of influence of powerful countries in the world, and ones reflecting neighborhoods controlled by street gangs in a city.

Boundaries can be identified in various ways:

- A **defined boundary** is one established by a legal document such as a treaty that divides one entity from another (invisible line). The entity could range from a country to a single plot of real estate.
- A **delimited boundary** is a line drawn on a map to show the limits of a space.
- A **demarcated boundary** is one identifed by physical objects placed on the landscape. The demarcation may be as simple as a sign or as complex as a set of fences and walls.

Political boundaries can be natural or geometric. A **natural boundary** is based on physical features to separate entities. For example, the Missouri River divides Iowa and Nebraska, and the Himalayan Mountains separate India and China.

In contrast to a natural boundary, a **geometric boundary** is a straight line drawn by people that does not follow any physical feature closely. On a large scale, a geometric boundary divides the countries of Libya and Egypt. On a small scale, a geometric boundary might divide two suburbs of a city.

Political boundaries are often precise. However, a **cultural boundary** is one based on human traits or behavior, so it often exists in the midst of a gradual change over space. For example, in China cuisine was once divided into two regions: wheat-based in the north and rice-based in the south. But no exact line ever divided the two regions sharply.

## Limited Sovereignty and International Boundary Disputes

As the number of states has increased over the last century, so too have international boundary disputes. There are four main categories of boundary disputes: definitional (position), locational (territorial), operational (function), and allocational (resource).

**Definitional boundary disputes** occur when two or more parties disagree over how to interpret the legal documents or maps that identify the boundary. These types of disputes often occur with antecedent boundaries. One example is the boundary between Chile and Argentina. The elevated crests of the Andes Mountains serve as the boundary, but since most of the southern lands were neither settled nor accurately mapped, this territory lies in dispute.

Boundary disputes that center on where a boundary should be are known as **locational boundary disputes**. The post-World War I boundary between Germany and Poland was set by treaty. However, Germans disputed the location because many people who considered themselves ethnically German lived on the Polish side of the border. This led to a type of expansionism, **irredentism**, that occurs when one country seeks to annex territory in another because it has ties to part of the population that lives there.

An **operational boundary dispute** centers not on where a boundary is, but how it functions. As refugees fled the civil war in Syria that began in 2011, Europeans viewed their national boundaries differently. Some viewed the boundaries as lines where responsibility for helping refugees shifted from one country to another. Others viewed boundaries as barriers to keep refugees out.

When a boundary separates natural resources that may be used by both countries, it is referred to as an **allocational boundary dispute**. When it comes to natural resources, boundaries serve as vertical planes that extend both up into the sky and down into the earth. The extraction of subterranean resources extending on both sides of the boundary may become complicated and lead to conflict. In 1990, Iraq invaded Kuwait because it claimed that the Kuwaitis were drilling too many wells and using oblique boreholes, thus breaking the vertical plane and extracting oil on the Iraqi side of the boundary.

| CLASSIFICATIONS OF BOUNDARIES | | |
|---|---|---|
| **Type** | **Definition** | **Example** |
| **Antecedent** | A boundary drawn before a large population was present | The boundary between the United States and Canada along the 49th parallel |
| **Subsequent (Ethnographic)** | A boundary drawn to accommodate religious, ethnic, linguistic, or economic differences | The boundary between Northern Ireland (part of the United Kingdom) and the Republic of Ireland |
| **Relic** | A boundary that no longer exists, but evidence of it still exists on the landscape | The boundary between East and West Germany (states that are now combined) |
| **Superimposed** | A boundary drawn by outside powers | The boundary between Mali and Mauritania (very common throughout Africa and Southwest Asia) |
| **Militarized** | A boundary that is heavily guarded and discourages crossing and movement | The boundary between North Korea and South Korea |
| **Open** | A boundary where crossing is unimpeded | The boundaries between countries in Europe that signed the Schengen Agreement |

## Boundaries Influence Identity, Interaction, and Exchange

Boundaries, regardless of the type, can influence a state's identity, interaction with neighboring countries and the international community as a whole, and the exchange of resources, goods and services, and people. These can result in positive or negative effects.

Extending a state's boundaries or reacting to aggressive forces on a state's boundaries can stir strong feelings of nationalism. Boundaries help establish a country's reason for existence. Therefore, national identity can play an important role in how boundaries function.

Boundaries influence how people interact. Following the end of World War II in 1945, Europe had its most peaceful seven decades in the past seven centuries. One reason for this is that agreements among EU member states (and further agreements with non-EU states) made most of the continent effectively borderless. With goods and people flowing freely from one country to another, people seemed less willing to turn to violence to settle disputes.

In contrast to Europe, the Korean Peninsula has become sharply divided. In 1953, a truce ended combat in the Korean War. The two sides accepted a temporary military boundary that divided the Democratic People's Republic of Korea (North Korea) and the Republic of Korea (South Korea). Though called the Demilitarized Zone (DMZ), the boundary became heavily militarized, and it now almost completely blocks the flow of trade and people (see photo below). Since the early 1960s, South Korea, using strong government support of its industries to produce goods for export, has transformed itself into a prosperous, democratic country. However, North Korea has become mired in poverty under an authoritarian government and isolated from most of the world.

## The Law of the Sea

As earlier stated, a vertical plane extends above and below ground along a state's boundary. Widely accepted by countries throughout the world, this principle defines airspace and subterranean space. However, how far horizontally out into the ocean should a country's influence spread? Conflicts over the use of the ocean have been common in modern history. Only in the last half of the twentieth century were water boundaries addressed systematically. Between 1973 and 1982, the **United Nations Convention of the Law of the Sea** was signed by over 150 countries. It defined four zones as follows:

1. **Territorial Sea**: Up to 12 nautical miles of sovereignty; commercial vessels may pass, but non-commercial vessels may be challenged.

2. **Contiguous Zone**: Coastal states have limited sovereignty for up to 24 nautical miles, where they can enforce laws on customs, immigration, and sanitation.

3. **Exclusive Economic Zone (EEZ)**: Coastal states can explore, extract minerals, and manage up to 200 nautical miles.

4. **High Seas**: Water beyond the EEZ is open to all states.

If two coastal states share a waterway and are less than 24 nautical miles apart, then the distance between the two coasts is divided by half. For example, if only 20 miles of water separated two countries, then each would be entitled to 10 miles of territorial sea.

States that have islands have been granted vast areas of space. For example, if a country's farthest island extends several hundred miles from the mainland, then the EEZ of that outward island extends that country's claims by another 200 miles. For example, around Alaska, where islands extend far out in the Bering Sea, the EEZ of the United States is huge.

Disputes over territorial control in coastal waters can turn violent. In 1973, Libyan dictator Muammar Gaddafi extended his 12-mile territorial sea to include the entire Gulf of Sidra. He created a "line of death" that was not to be crossed. U.S. leaders considered the line a violation of the Law of the Sea, and U.S. Navy ships challenged the line by sailing through the gulf. In August 1981, while flying inside the line of death but outside the 12-mile limit, U.S. F-14 fighter jets engaged and shot down two Libyan fighter jets. Similar incidents between the United States and Libya occurred in 1986 and 1989.

## Voting Districts, Redistricting, and Gerrymandering

International boundaries are important, but countries' internal boundaries are as well. In representative democracies, citizens vote for leaders to govern on their behalf. At the national, state/provincial, and local levels, these elected officials represent citizens, known as the **electorate**, and are designated to defined districts with distinct boundaries.

In the United States, to ensure the districts have close to the same number of people, the Constitution requires the federal government to take a **census**, a count of the population, every 10 years. After the results of the census have been calculated, the national government determines each state's number of representatives through **reapportionment**, changing the number of representatives granted each state so it reflects the state's population. State legislatures then redraw district boundaries so that each district contains roughly the same number of people. This process is known as **redistricting**. The total number of representatives in the U.S. House of Representatives has been fixed at 435 since 1912. Regardless of reapportionment results, each state is guaranteed at least one representative.

This process often becomes filled with political maneuvering. **Gerrymandering** is the drawing of boundaries for political districts by the party or group in power to extend or cement their advantage. The term is derived in part from Massachusetts Governor Elbridge Gerry (1744–1814). He influenced the drawing of districts in Massachusetts to benefit his own political party. A newspaper editor noted that an oddly shaped district resembled a salamander, and coined the term *gerrymander*. The process of gerrymandering has been used from the national scale, to influence Congressional districts (see map of Louisiana below), to the local scale, to influence city council districts.

LOUISIANA CONGRESSIONAL DISTRICTS

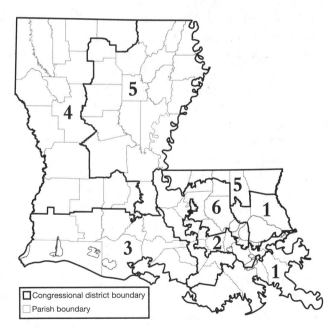

## TYPES OF GERRYMANDERING

| Type | Definition |
|------|------------|
| Cracking | Dispersing a group into several districts to prevent a majority |
| Packing | Combining like-minded voters into one district to prevent them from affecting elections in other districts |
| Stacking | Diluting a minority populated district with majority populations |
| Hijacking | Redrawing two districts in order to force two elected representatives of the same party to run against each other |
| Kidnapping | Moving an area where an elected representative has support to an area where he or she does not have support |

# The Effects of Boundaries

A boundary is more than a line between two political entities. It has effects that stretch well beyond simple questions of space and into political, cultural, and economic regions that affect various populations in various ways.

## Language and Religion

Political boundaries often do not follow cultural and economic landscapes. Sometimes boundaries separate people who speak the same language, practice the same religion, or share other traits.

Other times, a region becomes a **shatterbelt**, one that suffers instability because it is located between two very different regions. Eastern Europe has historically been a shatterbelt between Western Europe and Russia. While Western Europe has historically been Roman Catholic or Protestant, Russia has been Orthodox. For most of the 20th century, Western Europe was generally capitalist, and Russia was communist. Other shatterbelts include the Caucasus mountain region and the Sudan.

As people move and boundaries change, so too does language. The language often changes because people separated by boundaries develop distinct dialects. When boundaries are placed in an attempt to unite people who have distinct dialects, the unification process proves to be difficult, as was the case with Italy. Italy did not become a unified state until the 1860s. Before unification, people spoke a variety of languages depending on where they lived. From the Alps in the north to Sicily in the south, no single language united everyone. Despite over 150 years as a single state, people in Italy remain only loosely bound together.

Religion and boundaries can make for a volatile mixture. Within the boundaries of India, most people are Hindus, but a large minority are Muslims. This division creates tension that sometimes leads to violence. However, countries such as the United States and South Korea demonstrate that people of different faiths can live in harmony.

The division of Ireland demonstrates how complicated religion and boundaries can become. In the mid-twentieth century, most of Ireland won its independence from the United Kingdom and formed the Republic of Ireland, which was 95 percent Roman Catholic. However, a small area in the north, known as Northern Ireland, remained part of the United Kingdom. This area was only 35 percent Catholic—it was mostly Protestant.

The boundary between the Republic and Northern Ireland created two problems. On one hand, it divided the Catholics in the Republic and Northern Ireland who wanted to be together in one country. On the other hand, it united Catholics and Protestants into one political entity, Northern Ireland. There, Catholic-Protestant tensions—which included economic and political conflicts as well as religious ones—led to three decades of violence starting in 1968. Before peace was restored, about 3,000 people were killed in bombings and shootings.

### Ethnicity, Nationality, and Economy

Boundaries, often ones that are superimposed or enforced by a dominant nation or ethnic group, can create conflict for nations occupying the same space. Sri Lanka, a large island off the southern tip of India, is home to two groups that see themselves as ethnically distinct from the other: the Sinhalese and the Tamils. The Sinhalese are the majority. They are mostly Buddhist and they live in the southern part of the country. The Tamil minority are mostly Hindus, and they live in the northern and eastern parts of the island.

The Tamils long felt they were treated as second-class citizens by the Sinhalese. Hoping to win an independent homeland, Tamil rebels began fighting in the 1980s. They were defeated in 2009, but around 75,000 Sri Lankans had died in the fighting. It is not clear whether cultural differences between the two groups will lead to more violence, or whether advances in communication, travel, and trade will reduce the tension between them.

## Different Forms of Governance

Countries are governed on more than one level. But different forms of governance allocate power in different ways, affecting how much authority is available at both the national and local levels.

### Federal and Unitary States

Two main types of political spatial organizations are federal and unitary systems of governance. Both systems administer the day-to-day operations of governance with sovereignty, and the national government is the final authority. The differences between each are outlined in the chart that follows.

| FEDERAL VS. UNITARY STATES | | |
|---|---|---|
| **Trait** | **Federal** | **Unitary** |
| **Authority of the Government** | Shared between the central government and provincial, state, and local governments | Held primarily by the central government with very little power given to local governments |
| **Hierarchy of Power** | Multiple levels of power; power diffused throughout the hierarchy | No hierarchy of sovereign powers |
| **Type of Country Where Commonly Used** | Multiple ethnic groups with significant minorities | Few cultural differences and small minorities |

## Local Powers Vary by Government Type

In both federal and unitary states, local divisions of governance have some degree of power. But the amount of that power depends on the level of power exercised by the national government. Large landmass countries, such as the United States, Canada, and Russia, tend to be federal states. In contrast, smaller landmass countries, such as Japan, Egypt, and Spain, tend to be unitary states. These patterns have many exceptions. China is a large country with a unitary, very centralized government. Belgium is a small country that is a federal state, which reflects the ethnic divide between its Walloon and Flemish citizens.

FEDERAL AND UNITARY STATE SYSTEMS

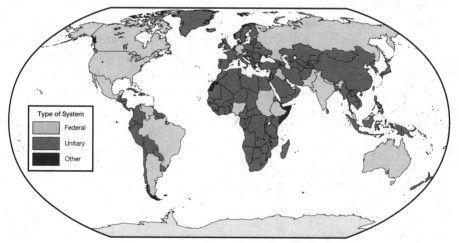

States that use federal governance often do so to placate various cultural differences. Allowing local governments to manage their own affairs, such as education, helps keep the peace and maintain a sense of unity. Provinces in northern Nigeria have enacted sharia to accommodate the growing Muslim majority in that part of the country.

Unitary states have strong centralized governments that control almost all matters of governance. Provincial and local governments, in most cases, are simply extensions of the national government. Unitary states can be either undemocratic, such as China and Saudi Arabia, or fairly democratic, such as France and Indonesia.

## The Effects of State Morphology

A state's shape, or **morphology**, can influence how people in the state interact. In particular, if a country's morphology includes a highly populated central region and outlying areas far from its center, then people in the outlying areas may face the following issues:

- might have difficulty receiving goods and services, especially if the infrastructure is inadequate
- might feel underrepresented in the government or more closely tied to neighboring countries
- might feel isolated from family members or ethnic groups who live far away
- might demand strong local control over natural resources in their region, which could lead to internal political conflict

EXAMPLES OF STATE MORPHOLOGY

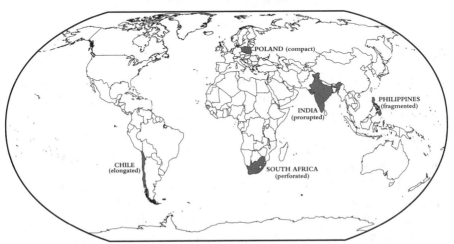

| TYPES OF STATE MORPHOLOGY | | |
|---|---|---|
| **Morphology Type** | **Characteristics** | **Examples** |
| **Compact State** | • Distance from center does not significantly vary<br>• Efficient in trade, travel, and communication from the center | • Poland<br>• Romania<br>• Zimbabwe |
| **Elongated State** | • Potential isolation at the periphery<br>• Difficult communication and travel<br>• Challenging to govern and defend | • Chile<br>• Malawi<br>• Norway |
| **Prorupted State** | • Compact area with an extension<br>• Limited access<br>• Proruption may cause disruption | • India<br>• Thailand<br>• Democratic Republic of Congo |
| **Perforated State** | • State that completely surrounds another state<br>• Surrounded state dependent on perforated state for travel and trade | • South Africa<br>• Italy |
| **Fragmented State** | • Scattered (islands) from the core<br>• Problems with trade, communication, travel, and distribution of power | • Philippines<br>• Indonesia<br>• United States |

# Patterns of Local and Metropolitan Governance

Local and metropolitan forms of governance—things such as municipalities, school districts, and regional planning commissions—are subnational political units that have varying degrees of local control.

Most people in the world are under the rule of overlapping levels of government. In the United States, there is one federal government, over 50 state, commonwealth, and territorial governments, and over 87,000 local governments. This last category includes roughly 3,000 counties, 20,000 cities, 16,000 townships, 13,000 school districts, and 35,000 special purpose districts such as police districts.

The number of units of government changes from year to year. One way this happens is that a city, to increase its individual and commercial tax bases, might seek to add outlying territory to its domain. **Annexation** is the process of legally adding territory to a city. However, residents of a new residential development on what had been farmland might prefer to create their own town rather than being annexed by an existing city. This leads to a new city government—and increased competition for services, business, and taxes.

**GEOGRAPHIC PERSPECTIVES:** UNITS OF GOVERNMENT

Geographers study how political power is distributed across space at different scales:

- At the global scale, power is distributed among countries.
- At the national scale, power is distributed among units such as provinces or states.
- At the local scale, power can be distributed among several types of units: counties, cities, school districts, and others.

**Diverse Local Districts**

Some local districts have very specialized functions. They might fund fire protection or a public library. Illinois includes several mosquito abatement districts. The Des Plaines Valley Mosquito Abatement District includes 77 square miles in the western suburbs of Chicago. It has about five full-time employees and hires another two dozen or so workers seasonally.

Mosquito abatement districts are one reason that Illinois leads all other states in the number of units of local government. In 2013, Illinois had 6,963 units of government. A typical resident lived with six or more layers of local government. In second place was Texas, with 5,147 units. However, the population of Texas is more than double that of Illinois.

**How to Distribute Power**

Mosquito abatement districts highlight the issue of the best way to distribute power spatially. Many problems, such as mosquitoes and the diseases they spread, drug trafficking, and pollution, pay no attention to political boundaries. One response to these types of problems is to create special districts to address these problems. Another is to build cooperation among existing units of government. A third is to refer the problem to a higher level of government such as a state or national agency. Deciding where to locate the power to respond to these problems is a constant issue for debate.

# KEY TERMS

| | | |
|---|---|---|
| geopolitics | open boundary | gerrymandering |
| territoriality | definitional boundary | cracking |
| Organic Theory | locational boundary | packing |
| Heartland Theory | irredentism | stacking |
| Rimland Theory | operational boundary | hijacking |
| defined boundary | allocational boundary | kidnapping |
| delimited boundary | The United Nations Convention of the Law of the Sea | shatterbelt |
| demarcated boundary | | unitary state |
| natural boundary | territorial sea | federal state |
| geometric boundary | contiguous zone | compact state |
| cultural boundary | Exclusive Economic Zone | elongated state |
| antecedent boundary | high seas | prorupted state |
| subsequent boundary | electorate | perforated state |
| relic boundary | census | fragmented state |
| superimposed boundary | reapportionment | annexation |
| militarized boundary | redistricting | |

**Question 1 refers to the following photograph.**

1. Which boundary concept is most clearly shown in the image above?

   (A) defined boundary

   (B) delimited boundary

   (C) natural boundary

   (D) open boundary

   (E) demarcated boundary

2. When Germany invaded Poland in 1939, it said it wanted to reunite the German minority living in Poland with Germany. This is an example of

   (A) nationalism

   (B) irredentism

   (C) supranationalism

   (D) allocation dispute

   (E) operational dispute

**Question 3 refers to the following map.**

THE U.S.-CANADA BOUNDARY

3. The 49th parallel separating the United States and Canada (shown above) is an example of

(A) a relic boundary

(B) a superimposed boundary

(C) an antecedent boundary

(D) a subsequent/ethnographic boundary

(E) an open boundary

4. The United Nations Convention on the Law of the Sea allows naval ships that are 100 miles off the coast of their country to

(A) turn away another country's naval vessel sailing through the area

(B) check a freighter for customs violations

(C) board a ship looking for possible illegal immigrants

(D) aid a scientific expedition from the same country that is exploring the ocean floor

(E) enforce all of the laws of its country within this sovereign area

**Question 5 refers to the following map.**

THE MORPHOLOGY OF INDONESIA

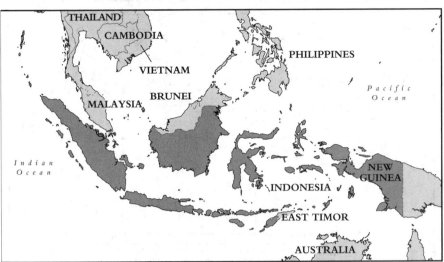

5. In the map above, Indonesia best fits what type of state morphology?

   (A) compact

   (B) elongated

   (C) perforated

   (D) fragmented

   (E) prorupted

6. Argentina has both a national legislature and 23 provincial legislatures, which exercise power separately from the national legislature. Which term best describes the country's government?

   (A) federal

   (B) municipal

   (C) confederate

   (D) autocratic

   (E) unitary

7. Uruguay's national government sets policies that are administered by local governments. This system is best described by the term

   (A) federal government

   (B) unitary government

   (C) reapportioned government

   (D) communist government

   (E) compact government

**Question 8 refers to the following map.**

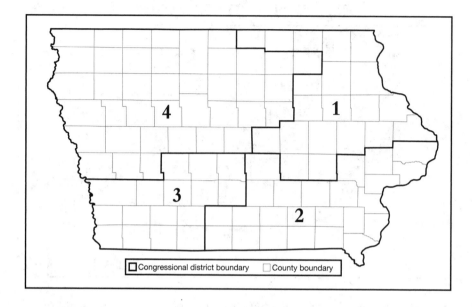

8. Which statement best describes the map of Congressional districts in Iowa?

(A) It shows why the Constitution requires redistricting after each census.

(B) It demonstrates how reapportionment can favor one party.

(C) It suggests strong support for irrendentism.

(D) It provides little evidence of gerrymandering.

(E) It reflects the idea of open boundaries.

1. The morphology of a state influences its economic, political, and social systems.

### THE SHAPE OF THAILAND

A. Using the map at right, identify the morphology type of Thailand.

B. Explain how Thailand's morphology could benefit its economy.

C. Explain how Thailand's morphology might cause a challenge for the country's social system.

D. Explain how Thailand's morphology might cause a challenge for the country's political system.

---

**THINK AS A GEOGRAPHER:** PLACE NAMES AND POWER

Naming a human or physical feature on the landscape reflects a particular set of cultural values. As values change, so do names of features.

Identify the cultural or political reason behind each name change.

1. Leningrad (USSR) to St. Petersburg (Russia)

2. Mt. Denali to Mt. McKinley (Alaska, U.S.)

3. New Amsterdam to New York (U.S.)

4. Peking to Beijing (China)

5. Southern Rhodesia to Zimbabwe (Africa)

6. Sylvan Street to Martin Luther King, Jr. Street (Selma, AL; U.S.)

# 11

# Globalization

*Globalization has produced a new level of interdependence among us.
The economy and multinational supply chains do not abide by
political boundaries. A computer ordered in Brazil is designed
in California and assembled in several other countries.
Economic integration was the first strong evidence
of a new era.*

—Eduardo Paes, Mayor of Rio de Janeiro, Brazil

**Essential Question:** How has globalization changed the way people live?

An athletic conference is a good example of a **network**, a set of interconnected entities, sometimes called nodes, without a center or a hierarchy. The world is full of networks in transportation, communication, trade, social media, beliefs and values, and politics.

In the late twentieth and early twenty-first centuries, advances in communication, trade, and travel created networks around the world. One significant result is increased interactions on an international scale. **Globalization** is the integration of markets, states, communication, and trade on a worldwide scale. While these forces have brought people and systems closer, they have also put a strain on the sovereignty of states. This in turn has led to a race in the creation of special alliances. Globalization has created the necessity for alliances for collective benefits on a global scale. In addition, economic networks between consumers and producers have changed dramatically as a result of globalization.

## Globalization Challenges State Sovereignty

The sovereignty of states in the modern age of globalization has been challenged in many ways. Political borders have become less significant as ideas flow more rapidly among most countries, trade in goods is freer than in the past, and even people can travel easily in areas such as Europe. The state system has attempted to adapt to these changes, but the speed at which these changes occur often outpaces states' attempts to keep up. Similarly, social, economic, and environmental forces have had difficulty in maintaining pace with the forces of globalization.

The Arab Spring, a movement of pro-democracy demonstrations and rebellions that began in late 2010, provides a good example of how rapidly ideas can spread. It began with antigovernment demonstrations in Tunisia. But, aided by social media, protests spread quickly throughout North Africa and the Middle East, leading to turmoil throughout the region.

## Supranationalism

**Supranationalism** occurs when multiple countries form an organization to collectively achieve greater benefits for all members. Sometimes, countries sacrifice a degree of sovereignty by accepting the regulations or decisions of the supranationalist organization. These organizations are often formed to create a military alliance, promote trade, or combat an environmental problem.

Among the first modern supranational organizations was the League of Nations, founded after World War I. Without the United States as a member, and without strong support from other large countries, the League failed. However, it provided the inspiration for a more effective organization, the United Nations, which was founded after World War II.

| SUPRANATIONAL ORGANIZATIONS | | | |
|---|---|---|---|
| Organization | Members | Mission | Headquarters |
| **United Nations (UN), 1945** | 193 countries | Taking on issues facing humanity such as peace and security | New York City, United States |
| **North Atlantic Treaty Organization (NATO), 1949** | United States, Canada, Iceland, Western and Central Europe, and Turkey | The mutual defense of member states | Brussels, Belgium |
| **European Union (EU), 1993** | 28 members mostly in Western and Central Europe | The political and economic integration of member states | Brussels, Belgium |
| **North American Free Trade Agreement (NAFTA), 1994** | United States, Canada, and Mexico | Free trade among members | Washington, DC; Ottawa; and Mexico City |

## Economic Supranationalism

The most common reason for multiple states to participate in a collective cause is economics. Among the supranational economic organizations are the World Trade Organization (WTO), the Association of Southeast Asian Nations (ASEAN), and the Organization of the Petroleum Exporting Countries (OPEC).

Seeking mutually beneficial trade agreements has fostered economic growth for member states of such economic supranationals. Together, the nations of ASEAN, for example, had the second-fastest growing economy in Asia—well ahead of regional powerhouses such as Japan, South Korea, India, and Australia.

The rise of **transnational corporations**, companies that conduct business on a global scale, has dramatically weakened state sovereignty. In contrast to corporations based in a single country, transnationals have no strong connection to any one place. As a result, they can move jobs from one country to another in order to take advantage of lower wages, lower taxes, or weaker laws on worker safety and environmental protection. Their ability to move operations around the world makes them less influenced by any single country.

The cost advantages of conducting economic activity on such a large scale, known as the **economy of scale**, affects trade just as it does other economic activity. As a result of the unprecedented competition for trade at a global scale, more and more transnational corporations have merged with other transnational corporations to create larger businesses and also fewer competitors. The two most common types of mergers (or integrations) are horizontal integration and vertical integration:

- A **horizontal integration** occurs when a corporation merges with another corporation that produces similar products or services. An example would be the merger in 2016 of Abbott Laboratories and St. Jude Medical. This merger expanded the new corporation's control over a broader segment of the medical devices market.

- A **vertical integration** occurs when a corporation merges with another corporation involved in different steps of production. An example of vertical integration is the Spanish clothing company Zara. Zara owns companies that manufacture the clothes as well as the retail chains that sell the clothes to consumers. Zara thus owns its **supply chain**, a network of companies around the world that produce, transport, and distribute a final product. This gives the corporation greater control over more steps in the production process, which increases its ability to make profits.

In the years following World War II, European countries began to eliminate national barriers to trade and travel on the continent. They reduced tariffs (taxes on trade), established one common set of regulations on products to replace individual national regulations, and coordinated labor policies. Leaders hoped that closer economic and cultural ties would bring peace to a region ravaged by war for centuries. The two major steps to overcome nationalism were the formation of the European Union (EU) in 1993, and establishment of a common currency (the euro) in 1999.

The result of these changes provided European corporations with easy access to a large market—one that included far more people than the U.S. market—in which to sell their products. Success in Europe helped EU-based companies compete in the global marketplace.

## THE EUROPEAN UNION, 2016

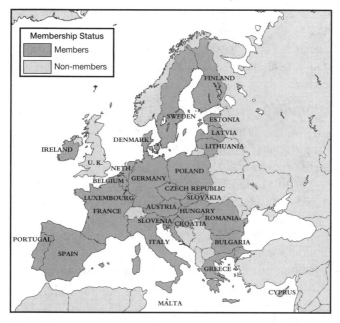

The success of the European Union inspired the creation of other regional, economic supranational organizations such as the aforementioned **North American Free Trade Agreement (NAFTA)**. In 1993, the governments of the United States, Canada, and Mexico signed this economic treaty in order to compete in a rapidly changing and extremely competitive global market.

However, economic supranationalism leads to problems as well as benefits. The transfer of jobs to inexpensive labor markets, the possibility of questionable quality of production, and the skirting of some members' safety and environmental regulations are primary concerns for member states.

While the EU and NAFTA are regional trading blocs, the **Organization of the Petroleum Exporting Countries (OPEC)** focuses on the production of petroleum. Its mission is to coordinate and unify its members' petroleum policies in order to stabilize oil markets. Membership spans three continents, including countries such as Saudi Arabia, Kuwait, Indonesia, Venezuela, Nigeria, and Iran. Ensuring a steady income for its members influences the quantity of oil supplied to the global market. Sometimes conflicts arise between the members. For example, one country may want to curtail production in order to generate more revenue, while another member may want to increase production to generate more jobs.

### Military and Strategic Supranationalism

Another example of supranationalism is military cooperation through mutual defense alliances. One such alliance, the **North Atlantic Treaty Organization (NATO)**, was created in 1949 in response to tensions between the United States and its allies and the Soviet Union. NATO is the largest military alliance in the world. While NATO has never confronted the Soviet military directly, it did use its power to stabilize conflicts in the Balkans during the 1990s.

After the Cold War ended, several former allies of the Soviet Union in Central and Eastern Europe joined NATO. The first were the Czech Republic, Hungary, and Poland in 1999. Their strategic shift angered Russia, and renewed tension between NATO and Russia.

### Supranationalism and the Environment

As the world progresses through the 21st century, the environment has become one of the biggest challenges facing states, supranational organizations, and transnational corporations. Most transnational corporations are based in the economic core—the countries of the developed world. However, much of the production and manufacturing occurs in the economic periphery—countries of the developing world—in order to minimize labor, land, and resource costs. This creates tension. In wealthy countries such as the United States, workers resent seeing their jobs sent overseas.

In poorer countries, people have different concerns. Countries make different economic decisions based on the options they have. A wealthy country may reject an environmentally damaging facility, but a poorer country, more in need of jobs and development, might be willing to accept the costs to its environment and the health of its people.

As a result of lax environmental regulations in periphery countries, transnational corporations often pollute the air, water, and soil. To further exacerbate this problem, neighboring states are subject to this pollution as well. The largest supranational organization, the United Nations, has attempted to resolve some of these issues through the Food and Agriculture Organization, the United Nations Convention of the Law of the Sea, and the World Meteorological Organization.

# Forces Leading to Devolution

**Devolution**, the transfer of political power from the central government to subnational levels of government, mostly follows regional lines. The division of powers (administrative, judicial, and legislative) are divided among the national government and subnational levels such as provincial, regional, and local governments. This division varies among countries and is influenced by whether the state has a unitary or federal system (see Chapter 10). Forces that lead to or accelerate devolution are physical geography, ethno-linguistic divisions, terrorism, economic factors, and social conditions.

### Physical Geography

While globalization promotes connections, the physical geography of a region can cause isolation and increase the likelihood of devolution. The Kashmir region of northern India and northern Pakistan has been and still is a region of conflict. The Pir Panjal and Himalayan mountain ranges can cause people in these regions to feel isolated. Areas claimed by India, China, and Pakistan have had some local autonomy because of the geographical isolation caused by these mountain ranges. Other physical features that have reduced contact among groups of people include deserts, plateaus, and large bodies of water.

## Ethnic Separatism

Many ethnic separatist movements throughout the world take place within specific regional lines within states. Ethnic groups and minorities are often concentrated in specific regions, which can lead to independence movements. In order to maintain unity, the central government will grant more authority to these ethnic regions.

Such has been the case in Spain with the Basques and Catalans, two culturally and linguistically distinct groups within Spain. The intensity of their separatism is tied to actions by the central government of Spain. For example, if the national government imposes more restrictions throughout the country, then the Basques and Catalans may intensify their desire for independence. If the national government allows more local autonomy, it hopes that the desire for independence for the Basques and Catalans will subside.

## Terrorism

**Terrorism** is organized violence aimed at government and civilian targets that is intended to create fear in furtherance of political aims. It is most commonly used by non-governmental groups that do not have an army.

Ethnic separatists sometimes employ terrorist tactics in hopes of achieving devolution. Since its inception in 1959, the Basque nationalist/separatist group Euskadi Ta Askatasuna (ETA) has fought for independence from Spain. Increased repression and frustration spurred the ETA to wage a campaign of violence beginning in 1968. After more than 820 deaths, the ETA declared a permanent cessation of armed activities in 2011. The ETA still seeks the Basque area's independence from Spain.

On a global scale, terrorism often has its roots in specific regions or countries. Terrorist groups seeking power and recognition within a country can expand their operations across international borders and even on a global scale. Al Qaeda has its roots among Sunni Muslims fighting against Soviet occupation of Afghanistan in the 1980s. However, in 1996, Al Qaeda directed its aggression towards the United States to protest U.S. support of Saudi Arabia and Israel. A series of attacks in eastern Africa and the Arabian Peninsula in the 1990s culminated in the attacks on the World Trade Center and Pentagon on September 11, 2001.

## Economics

Control of natural resources such as mineral deposits can prompt regions of countries to advocate for devolution. People in one region might want to use locally produced wealth for local benefits, such as better schools, infrastructure, and healthcare—or simply to lower taxes. The central government might argue that these resources should benefit the entire country.

Many tribal groups in the Amazon River basin of Brazil object to the extraction of resources and the development of the rainforest without local communities benefiting and being a part of the decision-making process. In Scotland, revenues from North Sea oil helped to fuel talk of independence from the United Kingdom. In 2014, Scotland narrowly voted to remain part of the United Kingdom.

### Social Issues

Social devolutions often follow geographic divisions between religious, linguistic, and historical regions. Countries experiencing social devolution usually have concentrated pockets of a specific religion or distinct spoken language by the local inhabitants. Federal systems, as in the United States and Canada, allow local governments to maintain their distinct languages and religions.

The situation in Belgium, in northwestern Europe, is quite different. As the bilingual sign below reflects, the country is split into the Flemish-speaking north (Flemish is similar to Dutch), called Flanders, and the French-speaking south, called Wallonia. As a result of linguistic, cultural, and economic differences, the country is sharply divided. Each region has its own institutions and many people identify themselves as Flemish or Walloon, rather than Belgian. The future of Belgium as a single country is in doubt.

### Irredentism

As mentioned in Chapter 10, irredentism is a movement to unite by people who share a language or other cultural elements but are divided by a national boundary. One example of irredentism comes from the Caucasus Mountains region. Under the Soviet Union, Nagorno-Karabakh was an Armenian-majority region within Azerbaijan. However, when the Soviet Union collapsed in 1991, Armenians in Nagorno-Karabakh demanded that they be allowed to join the country of Armenia (which supported their demands). Azerbaijan refused, and war broke out. It is estimated that 30,000 people died before a cease-fire took hold in 1994. In theory, a new state was created, the Nagorno-Karabakh Republic. In practice, the new state became part of the country of Armenia.

# Devolution and Fragmentation

As previously stated, devolution is the transfer of power from the central government to lower levels of government. However, when devolved powers lead to more autonomy, regions may seek independence, thus causing fragmentation of the state. When this fragmentation occurs, the state fractures along regional lines.

## *Autonomous Regions*

**Autonomous regions** have their own local and legislative bodies to govern a region with a population that is an ethnic minority within the entire country. Though these regions handle their own day-to-day governance, they are not fully independent from the state in which they are located. Many of these regions, such as the Navajo Nation in the United States, reflect the heritage of an indigenous population. Some, such as the Jewish Autonomous Oblast in far eastern Russia are based on religion. Jews began settling in the area in the 1920s. Both federal states, such as India, and unitary states, such as China, include autonomous regions.

## *Subnationalism*

People in autonomous regions usually have a great deal of local power, but give their primary allegiance to the national state. In contrast, **subnationalism** describes people who have a primary allegiance to a traditional group or ethnicity. Many French-speaking people in the province of Quebec, Canada, are subnationalists. They feel a stronger loyalty to Quebec than to Canada. In 1995, advocates of independence for Quebec narrowly lost a popular vote on the issue. Quebec remained part of Canada.

Many countries include several subnational groups as a result of wars, shifting borders, and movement of people. These groups have had various types of goals:

- Equality: In France, citizens of North African ancestry have fought for changes in the law that they argue discriminate against them.
- Independence: In far western China, some members of the Uyghur ethnic group have advocated seceding from China to form a new country, East Turkestan.
- Changing Countries: In eastern Ukraine, many Russian-speaking citizens felt closer ties to Russia than to the rest of Ukraine. Russia invaded and claimed control of this region in 2014. Several thousand people died in the fighting.

### Balkanization

Sometimes an entire country or region explodes in ethnic conflict, as the Balkan Mountains region in southeastern Europe did in the early 1900s and again in the 1990s. The rugged mountains of the area made communication difficult, so the region developed a high density of distinct cultural groups: Serbs, Croats, Slovenes, Bulgars, Romanians, and others. In the early 1900s, several of these groups demanded independence from the Austrian and Ottoman empires that controlled the region. In the 1990s, following the fall of communism, conflicts resumed. Today, **balkanization** means the fragmentation of a state or region into smaller, often hostile, units along ethno-linguistic lines.

## Impact of Technology

The Internet, social media, and the ease of jet travel have had varied effects on how people relate to each other around the world. They have:

- promoted globalization by connecting people across boundaries
- weakened globalization by helping subnational groups to organize
- supported **democratization**, the transition from autocratic to more representative forms of politics, by helping reform movements to communicate in China, Iran, Egypt, and other countries where the government has tried to limit the spread of information
- created a digital divide between countries with and without access to information for either political or infrastructure reasons
- increased **time-space compression**, the social and psychological effects of faster movement of information over space in a shorter period of time

## Centrifugal and Centripetal Forces

As defined in Chapter 9, centrifugal forces divide the citizenry in a country while centripetal forces unite a country's population. Often, an action has potential to be both types of forces at once. For example, a political election can unite people behind a leader—or divide people bitterly.

### Centrifugal Forces

**Regionalism**, the belief or practice of regional administrative systems rather than central systems, is a political factor that plays a role in creating centrifugal forces. Often a minority population is concentrated in various pockets of a state, thus resulting in minority self-awareness.

When a segment of a state's minority population feels underrepresented and lacking political power, it might pursue a path of separation from the larger state. Again, Canada provides a good example. The country's French-speaking population, concentrated in southern Quebec, has pursued more empowerment over local governance such as education and administrative governance, including its judicial system. However, for some French-speaking Canadians in Quebec, this is not enough; therefore political centrifugal forces still exist.

On the economic side, globalization has widened the gap between the rich and poor within a state. For example, India is an emerging economic power, but it is not a strongly united country. Uneven development within a country may lead to divisions between the "haves" and the "have-nots." Uneven development results in uneven benefits, which may result in the separation and fragmentation of a state. Despite rapid economic growth on a global scale, India still has large segments of its population living in abject poverty. This poverty is divided along regional lines.

REGIONAL DISTRIBUTION OF POVERTY IN INDIA

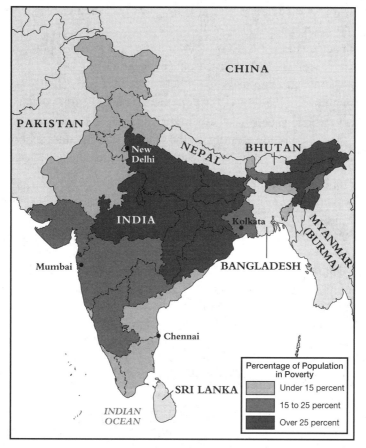

Centrifugal cultural forces have intensified as a result of globalization. Declining state sovereignty and economic advances have empowered ethno-national groups to demand more autonomy. For example, fragmentation within Syria and Iraq gave rise to Kurdish independence movements in those countries.

## Centripetal Forces

Governments, religious groups, and other institutions use a combination of methods to promote unity in a society. Some focus on political identity, others on economic development, and still others on cultural practices.

**Political Identity** Governments attempt to build political unity in several ways:

- Unifying institutions, such as schools, promote social cohesion by educating students on the historical accomplishments of the state. Unifying institutions may also promote holidays that are historically significant, such as an independence day or a day to honor veterans.
- **Nationalism**, the strong feelings of patriotism and loyalty one feels towards one's country, promotes a sense of belonging, even if a country's population is an ethnically diverse one.
- The acceptance of rules or laws and the promotion of political equality help to reinforce political centripetal forces. Examples of this are governmental administration practices such as a fair legal and judicial system and protection of the populace by the government.
- Customs and rituals based on citizenship are a common way to promote a sense of common identity. In the United States, public school students throughout the country recite the Pledge of Allegiance each day.

**Economic Development** One of the most effective centripetal forces used by governments throughout history has been building infrastructure. Efficient transportation systems and well-constructed roads and railways increase and promote trade, communications, dependence, and other forms of connections among the population within a state. These can increase the overall wealth of the country. However, since they commonly help one region or one group of people more than others, they can also lead to greater conflict.

Improvements in transportation are one way to promote unity by increasing interaction among different ethno-linguistic groups. In addition, advances in communication and trade help to eliminate social barriers within a country, thus encouraging solidarity among the citizens of the state. An example of this concept would be how goods, workers, and students flow freely across the borders of European Union member states.

**Cultural Practices** States with a population that is **homogeneous**, one that shares a common trait, likely have cultural practices that function as centripetal forces. For example, in heavily Islamic countries such as Saudi Arabia and Pakistan, Ramadan is a month-long religious observation that helps to unite the overall population. Japan, which has preserved a homogeneous culture by maintaining restrictive immigration policies, has strong cultural centripetal forces such as a common language and a shared sense of history.

In an age of globalization, every problem has ripple effects in other countries. In particular, the policies of the financially powerful core states about money have large spillover effects on the semiperiphery and periphery economies of the world. Geographers study how these effects diffuse from one place to another, and how globalization can make them more or less damaging.

### Thailand's Fragile Prosperity

In 1997, a crisis in one country in the periphery, Thailand, threatened first that country, then its neighbors, and eventually the rest of the world. Thailand's economy had been growing an impressive 10 percent per year for over a decade. However, it relied heavily on foreign investments, particularly from the United States and Japan, and high exports. When investors began to fear that the economy was not as strong in reality as it looked on paper, they began to pull back. When the Thai economy started to slow, concern quickly spread. The Thai stock market crashed, and the currency lost its value.

### Diffusion and Distance Decay

What followed was the runaway hierarchical and contagious diffusion of market disturbances from one country to another. In line with the concept of distance decay, the ripple effect of Thailand's financial crisis hit its neighbors the hardest—Indonesia, Malaysia, Singapore, the Philippines, and South Korea. The interdependent economies of these countries then faced similar financial woes. This crisis threatened to spread beyond the Asian markets and create a global economic panic.

### The Role of Globalization

This crisis—made worse by globalization—stopped when an institution of globalization stepped in. The International Monetary Fund (IMF), a global non-governmental organization, offered loans to the weakening economies. With these loans, confidence was restored and the economies began to grow again.

| KEY TERMS | | |
|---|---|---|
| networks | devolution | democratization |
| globalization | terrorism | time-space compression |
| supranationalism | autonomous regions | regionalism |
| horizontal integration | subnationalism | nationalism |
| vertical integration | balkanization | homogeneous |
| | | transnational corporation |

**Question 1 refers to the following diagram.**

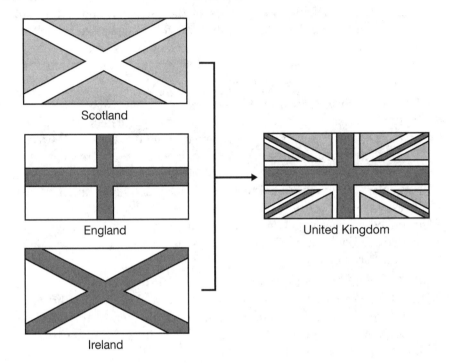

Scotland

England

United Kingdom

Ireland

1. Notice how the crosses in the flags of Scotland, England, and Ireland are combined in the flag of the United Kingdom. Which process does this represent?

(A) the balkanization of the British Isles

(B) the formation of autonomous regions within a state

(C) the process of irredentism in uniting people with the same culture

(D) the creation of a single state out of separate nations

(E) the centrifugal forces pulling a country apart

2. Advances in communication have facilitated all of the following EXCEPT

(A) supranationalism

(B) autocratic states

(C) social media networks

(D) investment

(E) devolution

3. Which provides the strongest support for the conclusion that Japan has few centrifugal forces?

   (A) Japan is an island located off the east coast of China.

   (B) Japan is part of the United Nations.

   (C) Japan has never colonized another country.

   (D) Japan has a high degree of ethnic and linguistic homogeneity.

   (E) Japan has one of the largest economies in the world.

4. Which is NOT an example of a centripetal force?

   (A) About 90 percent of Swedes speak the Swedish language as their first language.

   (B) Officially, about 95 percent of Iranians belong to the Shia Muslim faith.

   (C) The Mindanao region of the Philippines has poor infrastructure and inadequate basic services.

   (D) Since the end of World War II, Europe has worked to remove trade and political barriers between countries.

   (E) Ninety-six out of every one hundred persons in Thailand identify as part of the Thai ethnic group.

5. Which supranational organization focuses on the production of oil?

   (A) ASEAN

   (B) OPEC

   (C) EU

   (D) NAFTA

   (E) NATO

6. Globalization includes all of the following EXCEPT

   (A) stronger transnational corporations

   (B) more isolated states

   (C) weaker state sovereignty

   (D) more powerful financial markets

   (E) stronger forces pushing for devolution

7. Which groups have been gaining more local power around the world as a result of devolution?

   (A) indigenous people

   (B) French-speaking people

   (C) Spanish-speaking people

   (D) recent immigrants from East Asia

   (E) recent immigrants from Syria

8. Which group's desire for an independent state is a devolutionary force in both Turkey and Iraq?

   (A) Chechnyans

   (B) Iranians

   (C) Kurds

   (D) Syrians

   (E) Palestinians

## FREE-RESPONSE QUESTION

1. Globalization has been viewed as a mixed blessing for most states throughout the world.

   A. Define globalization.

   B. Identify and explain two benefits of globalization.

   C. Identify and explain two costs of globalization.

**THINK AS A GEOGRAPHER:** BASEBALL AND GLOBALIZATION

Geographers use data to help them see patterns and trends. One trend in recent decades has been the increasing diversity of baseball players in the major leagues. When the season opened in 2015, more than one-quarter of the players were born outside of the 50 states. Like every other aspect of life, baseball shows the impact of globalization.

Use the data in the chart to answer the questions that follow it.

| BIRTHPLACE OF MAJOR LEAGUE BASEBALL PLAYERS | | |
|---|---|---|
| | **1960** | **2015** |
| **Players Born in Latin America (including Puerto Rico)** | 52 | 365 |
| **Players Born in Asia** | 0 | 22 |
| **Players Born Outside of Latin America, Asia, and the 50 States** | 11 | 24 |
| **Total Number of Players** | 63 | 411 |
| **Total Number of Countries and Territories Where Players Were Born** | 14 | 22 |
| **Total Number of Major League Teams** | 16 | 30 |

1. Which world region outside of the United States has produced the most Major League baseball players?

2. How does the change in the number of teams provide context for understanding the numbers of players?

3. Explain whether baseball was part of a global network in either 1960 or 2015, or both. Support your argument with evidence from the data.

# UNIT 4: Review

## WRITE AS A GEOGRAPHER: USE EXAMPLES

Strong answers to free-response questions usually include specific examples. These examples are one way to show that the writer understands a concept well enough to apply it. They also show that the writer can make distinctions between related concepts such as nation and state, or centripetal and centrifugal.

*For each term, list the letter of the example below that best demonstrates it.*

**1.** terrorism

**2.** subnationalism

**3.** irredentism

**4.** supranationalism

**5.** balkanization

**6.** devolution

  A. Several dozen countries in Africa form an organization to promote security and economic development throughout the continent.

  B. The national government of France transfers decision-making on building roads and bridges to local and regional governments.

  C. In 1881, a group of Russians attempt to overthrow the government by assassinating the country's leader, Tsar Alexander II.

  D. In early 1861, Robert E. Lee felt more loyalty to his state of Virginia than to his country, the United States.

  E. When the French empire in West Africa collapsed, the region split into eight different countries.

  F. Some Norwegians argue that Norway is the rightful ruler of parts of Sweden that were once part of Norway.

## REFLECT ON THE CHAPTER ESSENTIAL QUESTIONS

*Write a one- to three-paragraph answer to each question.*

**1.** What social, historical, and economic factors have influenced modern political maps at various scales?

**2.** How do boundaries reflect ideas of territoriality and political power on various scales?

**3.** How has globalization changed the way people live?

# UNIT 5: Agriculture, Food Production, and Rural Land Use

**Chapter 12** *The Development of Agriculture*

**Chapter 13** *Agricultural Regions*

**Chapter 14** *Rural Land Use Patterns*

## Unit Overview

About 12,000 years ago, people living in Southwest Asia began to grow crops and raise animals intentionally. From the beginning of agriculture in that region, and later in a few other regions, agriculture diffused throughout the world. Since 1750, mechanization, the use of chemicals, and research have dramatically increased agricultural productivity. This increase has allowed more people to work outside of agriculture, but has increased stress on the environment.

### Physical Geography, Economics, and Settlement Patterns

What people have grown and raised has always been shaped by the climate, soils, and landforms of a place. In addition, the types of agricultural products that farmers produce, whether dairy or vegetables or grain, is heavily influenced by the nearness of the market. Farmers have also shaped the landscape by cutting down trees and draining wetlands, etc. Improvements in technology have shifted the industry towards larger enterprises and greater interdependence.

### Changes and Opportunities

Changes in technology and society influence how people produce and consume food. Since women were often in charge of cooking, and food is increasingly prepared outside the home, women now have more flexibility.

---

### Enduring Understandings

V. Agriculture, Food Production, and Rural Land Use

   **A.** The development of agriculture led to widespread alteration of the natural environment.

   **B.** Major agricultural regions reflect physical geography and economic forces.

   **C.** Settlement patterns and rural land use are reflected in the cultural landscape.

   **D.** Changes in food production and consumption present challenges and opportunities.

**Source:** *CollegeBoard AP®. Human Geography Course Description. 2015.*

---

# 12

# The Development of Agriculture

*Twelve thousand years ago, everybody on earth was a hunter-gatherer;
now almost all of us are farmers or else are fed by farmers. . . .
Farming spread mainly through farmers' outbreeding hunters,
developing more potent technology, and then killing the
hunters or driving them off of all lands suitable
for agriculture.*

—Jared Diamond, Guns, Germs, and Steel:
The Fates of Human Societies

**Essential Question:** How has the development of agriculture affected the spatial distribution of people?

**H**unting and gathering are the earliest known ways that people obtained food to eat. They relied on these methods until about 12,000 years ago, around 10,000 B.C.E., when they began to use **agriculture**, the process by which humans alter the landscape in order to raise crops and livestock for consumption and trade. The evolution of agriculture has been punctuated by three great leaps:

- The **First (Neolithic) Agricultural Revolution** was the origin of farming. It was marked by the first domestications of plants and animals. Much of the farming that took place during this time was **subsistence farming**, which is when farmers consume the crops that they grow and raise, usually using simple tools and manual labor.

- The **Second Agricultural Revolution**, which began in the 1700s, used the advances of the Industrial Revolution to increase food supplies and support population growth. Both revolutions benefited from the seemingly continuous innovations in mechanization. In addition, agriculture benefited from improved knowledge of fertilizers, soils, and selective breeding practices for plants and animals.

- The **Third Agricultural Revolution**, which began in the 1960s, included the Green Revolution as well as an agribusiness model of companies controlling the development, planting, processing, and selling of food products to the consumer.

# Centers of Plant and Animal Domestication

The First Agricultural Revolution began in five centers, or hearths. The first hearths were in Southwest Asia, East Asia, South Asia, Africa, and the Americas.

## Agricultural Hearths

Geographer Carl Sauer, writing in the mid-20th century, was one of the first to argue that agricultural hearths were independently established at various times and locations. He thought that the first hearths were located in areas with high biodiversity on the edge of forests:

- **Animal domestication**, raising and caring for animals by humans for protection or food, probably began when Central Asian hunters domesticated dogs. Later, agriculturalists in Southwest Asia kept goats and sheep.
- **Plant domestication**, the growing of crops that people planted, raised, and harvested, probably began after animal domestication. Sauer believed that people first used vegetative planting, growing crops using parts of the stems or roots of existing plants. Later they began to plant seeds.

Eventually, people in these separate agricultural hearths began to trade with each other, thus creating an exchange of both crops and innovations.

| MAJOR HEARTHS OF CROP AGRICULTURE | | | |
|---|---|---|---|
| **Time Period** | **Location** | **Crops** | **Early Diffusion Pattern** |
| **10,000 to 12,000 Years Ago** | Southwest Asia (Fertile Crescent) | • Barley<br>• Wheat<br>• Lentils<br>• Olives<br>• Oats<br>• Rye | • North Africa<br>• Southern Europe<br>• Central Asia |
| **10,000 Years Ago** | Southeast Asia | • Mango<br>• Taro<br>• Coconut | • Southeastern Asia |
| **9,500 Years Ago** | East Asia | • Rice<br>• Soybean<br>• Walnut | • North Central Asia<br>• Korean peninsula |
| **7,000 Years Ago** | Sub-Saharan Africa | • Yams<br>• Sorghum<br>• Cowpeas<br>• Coffee<br>• African rice | • Western Africa<br>• North Africa |
| **5,500 Years Ago** | Mesoamerica | • Squash<br>• Peppers<br>• Maize (corn)<br>• Potato<br>• Sweet potato<br>• Cassava | • North America<br>• South America |

## Diffusion of the First Agricultural Revolution

The major hearths of agriculture led to the first urban centers. These first settlements grew into the first civilizations, large societies with cities and powerful states. Civilization brought increased trade, larger empires, and conquest. As societies grew wealthier, people had time to specialize in their work and even develop new occupations and technologies. This led to the advent of the full-time metalworker, artist, soldier, weaver, and other specialized jobs.

Over thousands of years, agriculture spread widely and led to increased trade among cultures. The diffusion paths in the ancient world were somewhat expansive given the transportation technology of the time. For example, the great empire based in Rome that reached its peak around 200 C.E. carried on extensive trade in wheat and other agricultural products from present-day England to Africa and southwest Asia. On the Silk Roads, the routes connecting Rome with China, people traded silk, rice, and other goods.

One of the most dramatic shifts in agriculture came after the voyage of Christopher Columbus in 1492. The **Columbian Exchange** was the global movement of plants and animals between Afro-Eurasia and the Americas. Europeans brought hundreds of plants and animals west across the Atlantic Ocean to the Americas and took hundreds of plants and animals back east. Crops such as coffee (originally from eastern Africa) and bananas (originally from New Guinea) continue to thrive today in the tropical climates of the Americas. Temperate climate crops such as potatoes (originally from northwest South America) and maize (originally from southern Mexico) continue to thrive today in Europe, Asia, and Africa, as well as in the Americas.

### THE FIRST AGRICULTURAL HEARTHS

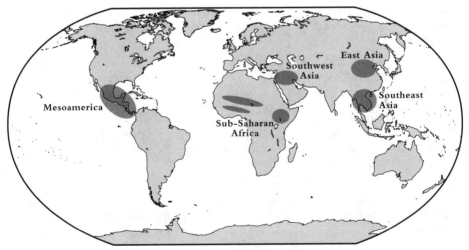

# Physical Geography and Agriculture

Physical geography features, such as climate, soil types, and landforms, influence how people farm in a region. As agriculture and technology have progressed and advanced throughout history, so too have attempts by humans to alter the natural environment. Irrigation, terrace farming, deforestation, desertification, and the drainage of wetlands have occurred as farmers try to increase production to feed an ever-growing human population.

Wherever crops grow and animals live, they need water. Even cattle herders in the Sahel, a dry region on the southern edge of the Sahara, must have access to water. Nutrient levels in soils have influenced the type of agriculture that takes place in a particular area. For example, cotton needs nutrient-rich soil while sorghum can grow in nutrient-poor soils, in places such as tropical rainforests. Climatic differences influenced by latitude and physical geography can have a dramatic impact on what crops can be grown.

Landforms can also greatly influence the types of agricultural activity in a specific place. The flat land found in large, expansive valleys provides excellent landscapes for agriculture. In contrast, mountains, ridges, and hills limit agricultural activity and often require more human inputs in order to make the land more useful for agricultural production.

## Humans Altering the Landscape for Agriculture

Ever since the first humans began to farm, they altered the landscape to their advantage. Things that people today consider natural—building earthworks, redirecting streams, or removing natural obstacles—were at one time innovations. Far from natural, these undertakings were fresh, creative solutions to challenges faced by the earliest agriculturalists.

### Terracing

One of the earliest human alterations of the landscape was **terrace farming**, in which farmers build a series of steps into the side of a hill. This creates flat surfaces, which have several benefits over steeply graded hillsides:

- Planting, tending, and harvesting crops is physically easier for farmers.
- The land collects rainfall rather than allowing it to run down a sloped hillside. The water helps sustain crops.
- The reduction in water running down the hillside reduces soil erosion.

However, if terraces are not carefully maintained, a heavy rainfall can cause disastrous and deadly mudslides.

Terrace farming has long been used throughout the world. In East Asia, terrace farming is often used to grow rice. In northern Africa, people often grow fruit and olive trees on terraced land. In South America, potatoes and maize (corn) are the main crops.

## Managing Water

**Irrigation** is the process of diverting water from its natural course or location to aid in the production of crops. Humans have used irrigation to increase food production and increase their standard of living for thousands of years. The earliest forms of irrigation probably involved people simply carrying containers of water from a river or lake to pour onto plants. But by about 6,000 B.C.E., civilizations in Mesopotamia and Egypt used organized strategies (digging canals and creating earthworks) to manage their water resources.

Following these humble beginnings, irrigation technologies became more concentrated and more effective. In the 19th and 20th centuries, the successful use of large-scale irrigation contributed greatly to feeding the rapidly growing population of the world.

However, creating irrigation systems can damage the local environment. When misused, irrigation can cause several problems:

- It can disrupt the natural drainage of water and reduce the normal regeneration of soils caused by natural flooding.
- It can result in the salinization—increasing the salt content—of soil, which can result in decreases in crop yield and soil fertility.
- It can pump so much groundwater to the surface that it causes land subsidence—the collapse of land resulting from the removal of underground water that supports the surface land.

Two regions of the United States use irrigation extensively. One is California, particularly the Central and Imperial Valleys. The other is a region roughly from Nebraska to northern Texas that uses an underground water supply called the Ogallala Aquifer.

People have also drained wetlands to provide more farmable land. In most cases, this recovered land is rich in nutrients. Increased farmland increases a region's **carrying capacity**, which is the number of crops or people that an area can support. However, a major drawback to the draining of wetlands is the reduction of biodiversity in both plants and animals. In addition, wetlands often act as natural filters that protect and promote surface water and groundwater quality.

## Clearing Trees and Other Vegetation

**Deforestation**, the removal of large tracts of forest, has occurred throughout human history. Northern and central Europe were once heavily forested. Now, the region is mostly farmland and urban areas. Today, deforestation occurs mostly in Southeast Asia, parts of Africa, and, most famously, in the rainforests of South America.

Cutting down trees can result in local problems, such as soil erosion, decrease in rainfall, and **desertification** (the transition of land from fertile to desert). In addition, it can cause devastating global environmental damage.

In particular, the rainforests absorb so much carbon dioxide that shrinking them leads to an increase in atmospheric carbon dioxide, which contributes to worldwide climate change.

**Slash-and-burn agriculture**, in which all vegetation in an area of forest is cut down and burned in place, is likely one of the earliest agricultural practices. The ash provides some soil nutrients, and the land can be farmed for a few years before the soil becomes depleted and the plot is abandoned. The plot then returns to a natural, if somewhat altered state, while the farmers move on to burn and plant in a new space. Because slash-and-burn agriculture requires people to move regularly, it is also known as shifting cultivation. On a small scale, this system is beneficial to humans, and the environment recovers quickly. However, slash-and-burn agriculture on a large scale might seriously damage the environment.

Rather than use fire, farmers usually remove vegetation by cutting it down, pulling it out, or killing it with herbicides. On the Great Plains and prairies of the United States, farmers removed the tall prairie grasses in order to plant wheat and other grains. These new crops lacked the extensive root systems of prairie grass. Without the anchor of strong roots, and with a lack of rain and some wind, the valuable topsoil can simply blow away. The worst period of this occurred in the 1930s, and is known as the Dust Bowl. This era of massive soil erosion was one of the worst ecological disasters in U.S. history.

### Recent Trends

In the modern era, **commercial agriculture**, in which farmers focus on raising one specific crop to sell for profit, has increasingly replaced **subsistence farming**, in which farmers focus on raising food they need to live. Increasing numbers of farming operations evolved from small enterprises owned by a single family into large-scale, capital-intensive businesses. This shift put more stress on the alteration of the environment than ever before.

## Impact of the Second Agricultural Revolution

The **Second Agricultural Revolution**, which accompanied the Industrial Revolution that began in Great Britain in the 18th century, involved the mechanization of agricultural production, advances in transportation, development of large-scale irrigation, and changes to consumption patterns of agricultural goods. Innovations such as the steel plough and mechanized harvesting greatly increased food production.

### The Effects of Technology

Advances in food production technology in the mid-19th century through the early half of the 20th century led to better diets, longer life spans, and an increase in population. As population increased, so too did the pool for workers in industry. Since most of these industrial jobs existed in cities and new factory towns, mass migration to urban areas began to unfold. Urbanization, a process that is continuing today, changed the cultural landscape and population distributions throughout the world.

## Land Usage and Farming Advances

Paralleling changes in technology were changes in the law. The **Enclosure Acts** were a series of laws enacted by the British government that enabled landowners to purchase and enclose land for their own use that had previously been common land used by peasant farmers. Similar enclosure movements occurred throughout Europe. Farms became larger, production became more efficient, producers raised crops to sell for profit rather than simply for their own consumption, and people were forced off the land, which created a workforce for the growing factories.

However, the enclosures were not popular with everyone. People who lost their traditional way of life suffered greatly.

Several advancements in sowing (planting) and reaping (harvesting), storage, irrigation, and transportation were made in agriculture throughout the 19th century. Some of these are listed in the chart below.

| EARLY ADVANCES IN MODERN AGRICULTURE | | |
|---|---|---|
| **Advancement** | **Date** | **Effect** |
| **Iron/Steel Plough** | 1819 | • Reduced human labor<br>• Could break through harder soils<br>• Increased amount of crops grown per acre<br>• Increased size of farms |
| **Mechanized Seed Drilling** | 18th century | • Planted and covered each seed quickly<br>• Resulted in increased yield per acre |
| **McCormick Reaper/ Harvester** | 1831 | • Increased harvest<br>• Reduced human labor<br>• Reduced amount of crops that perished in the field before harvest |
| **Grain Elevator** | 1849 | • Increased storage space and food supply<br>• Protected harvested food from animals and the elements |
| **Barbed Wire** | 1870s | • Provided inexpensive fencing to keep livestock in grazing areas |
| **Mixed Nitrogen and Nitric Acid Fertilizer** | 1903 | • Increased crop yields per acre |

## Agricultural Changes and Shifting Demographics

The Second Agricultural Revolution resulted in fewer, larger, and much more productive farms, caused a decrease in the number of farm owners and an even greater drop-off in the need for agricultural laborers. By the late 19th century, an increased number of displaced farm laborers led to farmers and other rural residents migrating to urban centers in Europe and the United States. The 1920 U.S. Census showed for the first time in the country's history that more people lived in urban areas than in rural areas. Only 30 percent of the labor force worked in agriculture, less than half what it was in 1840.

# The Third Agricultural Revolution

Starting in the mid-20th century, science, research, and technology generated a Third Agricultural Revolution. It involved the development and dissemination of better and more efficient farming equipment and practices, particularly in the area of vastly improved varieties of grain.

## The Green Revolution

The advances in plant biology that began in the mid-20th century are known as the **Green Revolution**, the development of higher-yielding, disease-resistant, faster-growing varieties of grains. The biggest advances were in growing rice, corn, and wheat. The Green Revolution allowed more farmers to double crop (grow more than one crop in a year) and increased use of fertilizer and pesticides in developing countries in Asia and the Americas. Countries such as India developed large-scale irrigation projects in order to make the most efficient use of their water resources.

INCREASE IN GRAIN PRODUCTION BY REGION

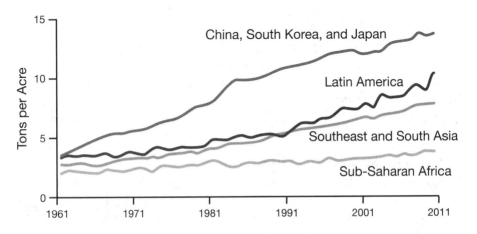

Source: "World Development Report 2013: Jobs," World Bank, 2013.

**Hybrids** Seed hybridization is the process of breeding together two plants that have desirable characteristics. For hundreds of years, humans have been creating plant hybrids from local varieties available to them. However, the Green Revolution scientists focused their attention on grains. Further, living in an increasingly globalized world, they had a much wider range of plants from which to crossbreed than did local farmers.

One example of hybridization is that in the 1960s scientists created a new strain of rice. They used the long-grain Indonesian rice and the denser-grain Taiwan dwarf rice to produce a rice grain that was both longer and denser. The hybridization of these two strains of rice was introduced to rice-growing countries in East and Southeast Asia.

The chief architect of the Green Revolution was Norman Borlaug, a microbiologist born in Iowa and educated at the University of Minnesota. His research was successful in turning Mexico from a wheat-importing country to one that was self-sufficient and even had a wheat surplus. This transfer of agricultural technology during the 1930s from the United States to Mexico would serve as a model for the Green Revolution that would occur after the Second World War. This period of advancements in seed hybridization, chemical fertilizers, and mechanization was the beginning of the Third Agricultural Revolution.

**GMOs** Hybridization differs from the production of a genetically modified organism (GMO), a process by which humans use engineering techniques to change the DNA of a seed. These techniques were first used in the 1970s. GMO crops started becoming widely used in the 1990s. Today, most corn, soybeans, and cotton grown in the United States are GMO varieties. They have been developed to increase yield, or to resist diseases or the chemicals used to kill weeds or pests. While GMOs seem to offer benefits, many people remain cautious about their use, arguing that potential problems have not been adequately studied.

**Machinery** In addition to using hybrids, chemical fertilizers, and pesticides, proponents of the Green Revolution encouraged the transfer of mechanical technology, as well. Machinery such as tractors, tillers, broadcast seeders, and grain carts were introduced to the beneficiaries of the Green Revolution in the developing world. The introduction of these agricultural technologies assisted in production and challenged traditional labor-intensive farming practices that had been in place for thousands of years.

## Positive Impacts of the Green Revolution

During the Green Revolution, global food production increased dramatically. The introduction of new seed technology, mechanization, pesticides, chemical (human-made) fertilizers, and irrigation led to increased yields. More food led to reduced hunger, lower death rates, and a growing population in many parts of the developing world.

## Higher Yields

Increased food production in the developing world was believed to have prevented a devastating famine in the early 1960s. By the mid-1950s, crop yields had increased without cultivating more land. The increased yields have kept up with global population growth, but experts debate whether agricultural production increases or population increases will be faster in the future.

The Green Revolution was most successful in Latin America, South Asia, East Asia, and Southeast Asia. Similar to what occurred in Mexico, India went from being an importer of wheat to harvesting a surplus of wheat within a few decades after the end of World War II. India's increased wheat output curbed hunger in the country.

The result was higher yields on relatively the same plots of land. Despite rapid population growth in these regions during the mid- to late 20th century, the increased crop output helped to stave off hunger and famine. By the second decade of the 21st century, The World Bank estimated that 80 percent of the developing world's population had an adequate diet. The UN Food and Agriculture Organization (FAO) in Rome, Italy, reported the following yield increases from 1960 to 2000:

- wheat: 208%
- corn: 157%
- rice: 109%
- potatoes: 78%

## Money for Research and Business

The Green Revolution helped to create high rates of investment in both the public and private sectors. Using grant money from the government, universities in the United States and other developed countries undertook the basic research on seed hybridization, fertilizers, and pesticides that were the basis for the Green Revolution. This research was then used by for-profit corporations to create and market the products that farmers used. So, while the Green Revolution benefited hungry people in poor regions, it also financially benefited universities and corporations in more prosperous regions.

## Food Prices

Higher yields and increased production led to falling real (adjusted for inflation) food prices. The supply of certain crops, mainly wheat, corn, and rice, became abundant through the mid- to late 20th century and, as a result, led to lower prices. More food at affordable prices helped to ease the economic stress of hunger and famine on governments and economic systems in the developing world. However, starting in 2005, global food prices began rising. This might explain some of the political turmoil in the Middle East and North Africa.

## Negative Consequences of the Green Revolution

Like all large and rapid changes, the Green Revolution had some negative consequences. Some of these were environmental damage, lack of sustained investment, and a disregard for local needs.

Much of the success of the Green Revolution hinged on human-manufactured products such as hybrid seeds, chemical fertilizers, pesticides, and fossil-fueled equipment. While crop yields increased, they often did so at the expense of the natural environment. Critics of the Green Revolution argued that it was not a sustainable system.

Increased yields and the application of human-made fertilizers put a strain on the land. This intensive use of land (double cropping) coupled with more aggressive irrigation led to soil erosion.

In addition, intense land use and irrigation drained the land of its natural nutrients, which had to be supplemented with more human-made fertilizers. This made farmers more dependent on more artificial products. The introduction of these chemicals to the environment resulted in potentially hazardous runoff into streams, rivers, and lakes, which posed serious consequences to the local ecosystems, habitats, and communities. Hazards included polluted drinking water, species extinction, and health issues for the population.

The transfer of technology from the developed countries to the developing countries included machinery such as tractors, tillers, and harvesters. These new technologies required vast amounts of fossil-based fuels. These petroleum-fueled machines increased air, water, and sound pollution. Therefore, in order for the Green Revolution to succeed, it needed mechanization to keep up with crop production, thus resulting in further environmental stress.

## The Green Revolution's Impact on Gender Roles

Many countries in the developing world that participated in the Green Revolution had traditional economies. In a traditional economy, subsistence farming is the cornerstone of economic activity. Even though much of the farming labor is performed by women, men usually dominate societies based on a traditional economy socially, politically, and economically.

When the Green Revolution and its technologies were introduced to these countries, it was the men who usually benefited and who were given decision-making powers. Men operated machinery and were educated on newer methods of farming. Women were often excluded from learning the new methods. This further marginalized the role of women within many societies.

## Economic Changes

Initial successes of the Green Revolution were a mixture of private and public investments. The transfer of farming technology heavily relied on private investment by corporations and public support by governments. As research and production increased, so too did the cost of production. Machinery, seeds, fertilizers, and pesticides became more expensive and the cost was passed on to farmers in the developing world and the organizations that helped to support these farmers. As profit margins decreased, many corporations began to curtail further investments in the Green Revolution. Without a clear financial incentive, their motivation waned.

In addition, the labor markets of less developed countries began to change. As with the Second Agricultural Revolution, the Green Revolution allowed— or pushed—people from rural areas to move to urban areas in search of industrial and service sector jobs. The available and relatively cheap labor also attracted many multinational corporations who moved manufacturing facilities to countries like Vietnam, China, and India.

Demographers predict that migration from rural to urban in the developing world will continue. In the future, the percentage of people living in cities will dwarf the rural population.

## The Green Revolution's Poor Success in Africa

Unlike Latin America and Asia, Africa saw few successes from the Green Revolution. Reasons the Green Revolution failed throughout the continent of Africa are both environmental and cultural:

- Africa has a greater diversity of climate and soils than other places. Hence, developing the right fertilizers proved to be very expensive.
- Africa has many regions with harsh environmental conditions. Insects, plants, and viral strains proved to be extremely challenging to the Green Revolution technologies and researchers.
- Africa is so large, and so lacking of sufficient transportation infrastructure, that the costs of investment in research and development and transportation were very high.
- Africa's staple crops such as sorghum, millet, cassava, yams, cowpeas, and peanuts were not always included in research seed hybridization programs.

During the period known as the Green Revolution, the world's population more than doubled. Most of this growth was in poor countries on the periphery of the global economy. From the mid-20th century to the 21st century, the continent with the highest population growth rate was Africa. Since that was the region where the Green Revolution had the least impact, hunger remained a greater problem there than elsewhere. Today, nearly 30 percent of Africa's population has been affected by food insecurity.

In response to the ongoing food problems in Africa, private foundations and governments are working together. They hope to develop a new Green Revolution there, using updated technology.

An old saying among historians is that the first law of human history is that a person must eat. Geographers focus on how the need to eat has shaped where people live and how they govern their societies.

## Higher Density Settlements

Before humans developed agriculture, they had existed as hunters and gatherers for tens of thousands of years. They lived in small, mobile groups—maybe 30 to 50 people who could move easily in search of food. Larger groups would surpass the carrying capacity of their respective regions. People survived by living in low density regions.

The development of agriculture allowed people to live in permanent, higher-density communities. These communities were usually along rivers, which provided a source of water. But rivers such as the Nile had another benefit. They flooded regularly, which spread nutrients across the land that contributed to soil fertility. Since this made agriculture more productive, farmers could support denser settlements, and it freed more people to specialize in tasks other than growing food. People could dedicate themselves to building structures, providing protection (military), and innovating new ideas and products.

## Centralization of Political Power

Increased job specialization began to reshape the spatial distribution of political power. Traditional hunting and gathering societies were usually tight-knit communities in which people shared responsibilities. This meant political power was decentralized. But as the roles in societies became more diverse and specialized, and as the population increased, divisions among social class became sharper and people desired new forms of governments. As a result, political power became more centralized.

| KEY TERMS | | |
|---|---|---|
| agriculture | terrace farming | Second Agricultural Revolution |
| commercial agriculture | irrigation | |
| subsistence agriculture | carrying capacity | Enclosure Acts |
| plant domestication | slash-and-burn | barbed wire |
| animal domestication | swidden | Third Agricultural Revolution |
| First Agricultural Revolution | deforestation | |
| | desertification | Green Revolution |
| | commercial agriculture | GMOs |

**Question 1 refers to the following photograph.**

1. Which concept is demonstrated in the picture above?

    (A) the results of the enclosure movement

    (B) the impact of the Green Revolution

    (C) the significance of carrying capacity

    (D) the use of terrace farming

    (E) the results of deforestation

2. The domestication of plants and animals occurred in the

    (A) First Agricultural Revolution

    (B) Green Revolution

    (C) Second Agricultural Revolution

    (D) Columbian Exchange

    (E) Industrial Revolution

3. As a result of the Columbian Exchange, which crop was transferred to Europe from the Americas and later spread through the world?

    (A) coffee

    (B) maize (corn)

    (C) rice

    (D) olives

    (E) wheat

**4.** A farmer who converts forested land and marshland into cropland has
(A) created an agricultural hearth
(B) fulfilled the promise of the Green Revolution
(C) increased the land's carrying capacity
(D) shown the advantages of the Columbian Exchange
(E) increased the yield of the crops on her land

**Question 5 refers to the following photograph.**

**5.** This image represents the changes brought about by the
(A) Columbian Exchange
(B) hearths of agriculture
(C) Industrial Revolution
(D) Enclosure Acts
(E) Green Revolution

**6.** Deforestation has resulted in
(A) more farmland in some places but more desertification in others
(B) more farmland in some places and less desertification in others
(C) less farmland in some places but more desertification in others
(D) less farmland in some places and less desertification in others
(E) no noticeable change in the amount of farmland or desertification

7. Southwest Asia, Southeast Asia, East Asia, Mesoamerica, and the Sub-Saharan regions were all
   (A) leaders in starting the Columbian Exchange
   (B) sites where the Second Agricultural Revolution began
   (C) areas noted for widespread terracing
   (D) hearths of plant domestication
   (E) regions where the Third Agricultural Revolution failed

8. The Green Revolution involved all of the following EXCEPT
   (A) an increased use of scientific research in agriculture
   (B) an increased use of fertilizer
   (C) a decreased reliance on humans for agricultural labor
   (D) a decreased use of pesticides
   (E) the development of higher-yielding seeds

## FREE-RESPONSE QUESTION

1. From 1960 to 2000, the Green Revolution introduced substantial changes in agriculture, especially in the developing countries.
   A. Identify and describe TWO positive consequences of the Green Revolution.
   B. Identify and describe TWO negative consequences of the Green Revolution.

**THINK AS A GEOGRAPHER:** USE SCALE TO ANALYZE FAIR TRADE

The concept of scale is useful in analyzing how the principles of fair trade work out in practice. The underlying principle of fair trade is to insure that the people who produce products are fairly compensated for their work. The main principles of fair trade include: fair pricing, poverty alleviation, mutual benefit (seller-producer), gender equity, safe working conditions, and environmental responsibility.

At the global scale, fair trade works when consumers in core countries desire fair trade products from the periphery countries of the world. The concept can be also be applied at the neighborhood or family scale.

*Apply the concept of scale to the principle of fair trade in each question.*

| FAIR TRADE IMPORTS TO THE UNITED STATES, 1998–2015 | | | | |
|---|---|---|---|---|
| Year | Coffee | Tea | Cocoa | Sugar |
| 1998 | 76,059 | no data | no data | no data |
| 2000 | 4,249,534 | no data | no data | no data |
| 2005 | 44,585,323 | 490,645 | 1,036,696 | 271,680 |
| 2010 | 105,251,476 | 1,483,666 | 4,392,674 | 18,146,124 |
| 2015 | 163,630,275 | 2,347,699 | 38,492,988 | 38,173,065 |
| Total, 1998 to 2015 | 1,359,418,892 | 16,002,044 | 129,087,925 | 151,248,397 |

Source: *Fair Trade USA 2015 Almanac. Quantities measured in pounds or other units.*

1. At the household scale, how does a family that grows food in a garden for their own consumption demonstrate some but not all of the principles of fair trade?

2. At the community scale, how does a farmer's market demonstrate the principles of fair trade?

3. At the global scale, how does the data suggest that the idea of fair trade is becoming more widespread?

4. How does the practice of fair trade affect each of the following groups: producers in periphery countries, multinational companies, and consumers in highly developed countries?

# Agricultural Regions

*Without agriculture it is not possible to have a city, stock market, banks, university, church or army. Agriculture is the foundation of civilization and any stable economy.*

—Allan Savory, biologist and farmer, Zimbabwe

**Essential Question:** Why does agriculture vary so greatly around the world?

Two driving forces have always shaped agriculture. One is physical geography. Climate and landforms determine what crops can be grown and what animals can be raised in each region of the world. For example, coffee grows well only in low latitudes. And in North America, blueberries do well in Michigan, Washington, and Oregon—places just east of large bodies of water that also have periods of cold weather.

The other force is economics, the workings of supply and demand that influence the competing use of the land. Whether consumers want to purchase peaches or plums influences what farmers will decide to grow.

## Climate and Agriculture

Plant and animal production are directly linked to the climate in which they exist. Despite human intervention, climate, soil types, and levels of precipitation still govern what types of crops will be grown and what types of animals will be raised.

### Climate Conditions and Agricultural Production

Climate always has and will continue to play a major role in determining what types of agriculture will take place throughout the world. Most of the earth's land surface supports some type of agricultural activity. The few exceptions are in the high latitudes—around the north and south poles—and the high altitudes—the tops of mountains.

The following chart summarizes the types of agriculture most commonly found in each type of climate region. American geographer Derwent Whittlesey identified these eleven main agricultural regions in 1936.

## AGRICULTURAL REGIONS

| Agricultural Practice | Climate | Locations |
|---|---|---|
| Pastoral Nomadism | Drylands | • Southwest, Central, and East Asia<br>• North Africa |
| Shifting Cultivation | Tropical | • Latin America<br>• Sub-Saharan Africa<br>• Southeast Asia |
| Plantation | Tropical/Sub-Tropical | • Latin America<br>• Sub-Saharan Africa<br>• South and Southeast Asia |
| Mixed Crop/ Livestock | Cold and Warm Mid-Latitude | • Midwestern United States and Canada<br>• Central Europe |
| Grain | Cold Mid-Latitude | • North Central United States<br>• South Central Canada<br>• Eastern Europe |
| Commercial Gardening | Warm Mid-Latitude | • Southeastern United States<br>• Southeastern Australia |
| Dairy | Cold and Warm Mid-Latitude | • Northeastern United States<br>• Southeastern Canada<br>• Northwestern Europe |
| Mediterranean | Warm Mid-Latitude | • Southern coast of Europe<br>• Northern coast of Africa<br>• Pacific coast of the United States<br>• Southern tip of Africa<br>• Chile |
| Livestock Ranching | Drylands | • Western North America<br>• Southeastern South America<br>• Central Asia<br>• Southern Africa |
| Intensive Subsistence | Warm Mid-Latitude | • South, Southeast, and East Asia<br>• Near large populations |
| None | Polar | • Arctic<br>• Antarctica |

Climate influences what agricultural activities will take place. For example, animal herding takes place in drier climates such as the western United States, North Africa, and Southwest Asia. However, animal herding can vary greatly depending on economic factors. In **pastoral nomadism**, a form of **subsistence agriculture** practiced in the developing world, people travel from place to place with their herds of domesticated animals. In contrast, in **ranching**, a form of commercial agriculture found in the developed world, livestock graze over large areas while the owners remain in the same place.

However, technology can overcome climate. In the chilly climates of Iceland and Greenland, farmers can grow crops in greenhouses. The tomato market, once dominated by sunny states such as Florida and California, now includes the products of large Canadian indoor growing facilities.

Cultural preferences also shape economic activity. Consider food preferences. The climate of southwest Asia is fine for raising hogs. However, in a region dominated by Muslims and Jews, most people have religious objections to eating or raising hogs, so farmers choose to raise other animals.

## Agricultural Regions Associated with Bioclimatic Zones

Crops and livestock thrive best in specific types of bioclimates. So, each bioclimatic zone is home to different types of agriculture.

**Pastoral Nomadism** As previously stated, pastoral nomadism is practiced in arid and semi-arid climates throughout the world. Nomads rely on the animals for survival. Animals such as cattle, camels, reindeer, goats, yaks, sheep, and horses provide meat and sometimes milk for food and hides for clothing and shelter. Pastoral nomads move their herds to different pastures within their territory and often trade meat for crops with nearby subsistence crop farmers. Nomads in different regions rely upon different animals, depending on their culture and the climate in which they live:

- in south central Asia and east Africa: cattle, because they adapt to the hot climate
- in desert regions of the Middle East: camels, because they can survive without water for long periods
- in northern Siberia: reindeer, because they can thrive in cold weather

**Shifting Cultivation** Subsistence agriculture in which farmers, usually in tropical climate regions, move from one field to another is called **shifting cultivation**. It is also known as slash-and-burn agriculture and as swidden agriculture because farmers sometimes clear the land by burning vegetation, a process that enriches nutrient-poor soil by adding nitrogen to it. On the cleared land, they plant and harvest crops until the soil becomes less fertile. Then, the people move to another area of dense, wild vegetation and repeat the process.

Unlike crop rotation, in which farmers change which crops are grown within a field, shifting cultivation involves using entirely new fields.

Farmers using shifting cultivation grow crops such as rice in South East Asia, maize (corn) in South America, and millet and sorghum in sub-Sahara Africa. Most families grow food for their own consumption, so one field will yield a variety of crops. Ownership of the land usually belongs to the community or village as a whole.

**Plantation Agriculture** One of the legacies of colonialism was the replacement of subsistence farming with commercial agriculture in many less developed regions. A **plantation** is a large commercial farm that specializes in one crop, usually found in the low latitudes (tropics), and in hot, humid climates with substantial precipitation. Plantations are typically labor intensive and often exploit the cheap labor available in nearby villages and towns. In order to reduce the cost of transporting bulky crops, some of the processing occurs near the plantation. The valuable portion of the crop is then transported to global markets. Common plantation crops include coffee, cocoa, rubber, sugarcane, bananas, tobacco, tea, coconuts, and cotton.

**Mixed Crop/Livestock Farming** Mixed crop and livestock farming is an integrated system common in developed regions, such as the Midwestern United States, northern Europe, and Canada, but it has also diffused to many parts of the developing world. On these farms, the majority of the crops raised are fed directly to livestock. The livestock is fattened on these grains for eventual slaughter, or the grains are fed to dairy cows. The animals' manure is in turn used to help fertilize the crops. The owners of the land and livestock may be different people, but what is important is the interrelationship among them. The most common grains used for these purposes in the United States are corn and soybeans. Each can be used for animal feed, processed into oil, or used to make other products.

**Grain Farming** In regions too dry for mixed crop agriculture, farmers often raise wheat. Consumed mostly by people, wheat is produced in the prairies and plains. China, India, and Russia are the world's top wheat producers, with the United States fourth. The type of wheat grown reflects the climate:

- **Spring wheat** is planted in early spring and harvested in early autumn. It is grown in a colder region that includes North Dakota, South Dakota, Montana, and the prairie provinces of Canada.

- **Winter wheat** is planted in the fall and harvested in early summer. It is grown in a warmer region that includes Kansas, Oklahoma, and Colorado.

**Commercial Gardening** In the United States, commercial gardening and fruit farming, known as **market gardening**, is found mostly in California and the Southeast in order to take advantage of long growing seasons. This type of farming is also referred to as **truck farming** because the products were traditionally driven to urban markets and sold. However, today most of the products are sold to companies for canning or freezing. Fruits and vegetables grown in the United States that are the result of truck farming include lettuce, broccoli, apples, oranges, and tomatoes.

**Dairy Farming** Traditionally, dairies and creameries were local farms and businesses supplying dairy products to customers in a small geographic area. This pattern still exists in many less developed regions of the world.

However, during the latter part of the twentieth century, improvements in refrigeration and transportation expanded the **milk shed**, the geographic distance that milk is delivered. Large corporate dairy operations replaced smaller family-owned farms, which has resulted in a decrease in the number of farms but an increase in dairy production. Most commercial dairy farms are located in the United States, Canada, Europe, and other highly developed countries near urban centers and transportation corridors.

In a few countries demand for dairy products increased faster than the pressure for consolidation. So, in Argentina and Brazil, as the economy developed and average incomes increased, the number of dairy farms also went up.

**Mediterranean Agriculture** Mediterranean agriculture is practiced in regions with hot-dry summers, mild winters, narrow valleys, and often some type of irrigation system. Some of these regions are southern Europe, northern Africa, southwestern Africa, southwestern Asia, southwestern Australia, California, and central Chile. Common crops grown in Mediterranean agriculture include figs, dates, olives, and grapes. Herders in these regions often practice **transhumance**, the seasonal herding of animals from higher elevations in the summer to lower elevations and valleys in the winter. Because the regions have rugged terrain, goats and sheep are the principal livestock.

**Livestock Ranching** Livestock ranching is a commercial grazing of animals confined to a specific area. Similar to pastoral nomadism, livestock ranching is found in areas that are too dry for growing crops in large quantities. Ranching is a prevalent agricultural activity in the western United States; the pampas of Argentina, southern Brazil, and Uruguay; parts of Spain and Portugal; China; and central Australia.

## Economic Forces that Influence Agriculture

Among the many factors that influence the decisions farmers make about how to farm are the relative costs of land, labor, and capital. Because of these different costs, farmers balance the use of these resources differently. If land is plentiful and costs little, they use it extensively. If land is scarce or expensive, they use it intensely.

**Extensive Land Use** Agriculture that uses fewer inputs of capital and paid labor relative to the amount of space being used is **extensive farming**. It includes practices such as shifting cultivation, nomadic herding, and ranching.

**Intensive Land Use** Agriculture that involves greater inputs of capital and paid labor relative to the space being used is **intensive farming**. Intensive practices are used in various regions and conditions:

- Paddy rice farming in south, southeast, and east Asia is very labor intensive. However, the nature of the fields, often on terraces, can make using machinery difficult.
- Market gardening in California, Texas, and Florida, and near large cities is sometimes capital intensive, but it is nearly always labor intensive. Many vegetable and fruit farms use large numbers of migrant workers to tend and harvest crops. These workers are traditionally paid low wages.
- The largest scale of intensive agriculture occurs on plantations in low latitudes.

One technique to maximize output on a small amount of land is **double cropping**, the planting and harvesting on the same parcel of land twice per year. Another technique, **intercropping**, also known as multicropping, is when farmers grow two or more crops simultaneously on the same field. For example, a farmer might plant a legume crop alongside a cereal crop in order to add nitrogen to the soil and guard against soil erosion.

Extensive and intensive farming methods can be used for either subsistence or commercial purpose. The following chart shows how these methods and purposes can mix.

| PURPOSES OF AGRICULTURE | | |
|---|---|---|
| **Land Use Methods** | **Commercial** | **Subsistence** |
| **Intensive** | • *Location:* usually near urban centers or transportation hubs<br>• *Examples:* truck farming and dairy farming<br>• *Inputs:* large amounts of labor and machinery, often on large amounts of land | • *Location:* usually near densely populated areas with access to local markets<br>• *Examples:* farmers who grow wide variety of crops such as corn, cassava, millet, or yams and raise some livestock<br>• *Inputs:* often labor-intensive production on small plots |
| **Extensive** | • *Location:* usually near transportation centers with access to processing centers<br>• *Examples:* livestock ranching; some grain farming<br>• *Inputs:* minimal amount of labor and machinery on a large expanse of land | • *Location:* usually in sparsely populated areas with access to local markets<br>• *Examples:* pastoral nomadism and shifting cultivation<br>• *Inputs:* minimal amount of machinery, but sometimes labor-intensive work on a large plot of land that might be owned communally |

**Increasing Intensity** Regions of the world that traditionally relied on extensive agricultural techniques are under pressure from local increases in demand, regional population growth, and global competition to use land more intensely. These demographic and economic forces place more stress on the land because they push farmers to use land continually, rather than letting lie fallow and recover. Those who rely on shifting cultivation find it more difficult to practice these methods as global demand for tropical cash crops such as coffee, tea, and cacao compete for more land use. The timber industry has also put an economic strain on shifting cultivation. For subsistence farmers, the competition for space to grow timber, rubber, or products that are not eaten, coupled with increasing population, have resulted in food security issues, most noticeably on the continent of Africa.

**The Beef Industry** Some agricultural products combine extensive and intensive phases. Raising cattle in Wyoming is an example of extensive farming. The cattle roam and feed on grass in large ranches that average nearly six square miles in size. As the cattle reach maturity, the intensive phase begins. Farmers transport the cattle to feedlots, known as concentrated animal feeding operations (CAFOs) in northern Colorado. The density of animals is high, and the cattle are fed corn and water in order to fatten them up before being processed into meat for the market.

The global expansion of fast-food operations along with increased demand for meat has led to larger ranching operations not only in the United States but in South America as well. In the United States, the competition for space, animal size, and raising time have led to the creation of **feed lots**, which are confined spaces in which cattle and hogs have limited movement. Because of their reduced movement, animals gain weight faster and require less room.

The economic structure of livestock raising has changed in the past few decades. The increased demand for beef, poultry, and pork has created factory farms and processing centers. Cattle are less likely to graze on large expanses of land, but instead are raised in feedlots or CAFOs. The animals can grow bigger in a shorter period of time. This new practice maximizes the use of space and prepares the animal for slaughter quickly, thus maximizing profit.

## Commercial Agriculture and Agribusiness

**Agribusiness** is the integration of various steps of production in the food-processing industry. It not only includes large-scale commercial agriculture, but also the steps of processing and production, transportation, marketing, retail, and research and development. Given the enormity of this system, agribusiness operations are performed by transnational corporations. These large-scale operations are commercial, highly mechanized, and much of the raising of crops and animals involve chemicals and biotechnology. The following chart compares farming at the scale of a homeowner and an agribusiness.

| VEGETABLE FARMING ON TWO SCALES | | |
|---|---|---|
| **Activity** | **Homeowner Scale** | **Agribusiness Scale** |
| **Growing Food** | Raising vegetables in a backyard garden | Owning farms of thousands of acres that are worked by large staffs of employees |
| **Processing Food** | Eating fresh, home-grown vegetables for dinner and preserving vegetables for future use | Canning and freezing products in factories that are often located near the fields |
| **Selling Food** | Selling vegetables at a local market | Selling to wholesale distributors who sell to supermarkets and restaurants |
| **Financing the Food Industry** | Giving some vegetables to a neighbor in exchange for using some of their land for a garden | Borrowing money from banks and selling stock to raise money for operating expenses |
| **Researching Food Options** | Growing different varieties of tomatoes to see which grow best | Investing in research and development of new seeds, fertilizers, and pesticides |

# Impact of Large-Scale Farms

Globalization has accelerated the growth of agribusiness during the latter half of the 20th century. Competition in agricultural products and services has encouraged large-scale farming operations, thus eliminating many small-scale operations. Even "family-owned and operated farms" are corporations far larger than the farms of the past.

This system of resources, producer transportation, communication, information, and consumers is referred to as a **supply chain**, or a commodity chain. Often these supply-chain businesses are owned by one corporation. Vertical integration is when a company owns several smaller businesses involved in different steps in developing a product. A vertically integrated agribusiness might include one company that contracts with farmers to raise the crop, a trucking firm that transports the crop, a factory that processes it, and a wholesaler that distributes it to stores. This gives the company control over most of the product development process.

### Large-Scale Replacing Small-Scale Farms

Large-scale farming usually practices **monoculture**, which is the raising of a single cash crop on large plots of land. Family farmers in developed countries and subsistence farmers in developing countries cannot compete with large-scale farming operations because large-scale farming produces food at a cheaper per unit cost. Many projects funded by the World Bank have encouraged agribusiness ventures in the developing world, often at the expense of subsistence farmers. As a consequence of globalization and the Green Revolution, many subsistence farmers have lost available land and now work for agribusiness enterprises. A **suitcase farm** is one in which no one lives on the farm and the harvesting and planting is performed by farmers who live nearby or by migratory labor. These are common in the Midwest and Great Plains in the United States.

## Commodity Chains and Consumption

The transformation of agriculture into a large-scale agribusiness entity has resulted in a complex system of connecting producers and consumers at a global scale. This complex and enormous system enables someone who lives in a small American town to consume bananas from Ecuador, coffee from Brazil, chocolate from Switzerland, and apples from Honduras. This transformation may be attributed to advancements in biotechnology, mechanization, transportation, and food preservation.

A **commodity chain** is a process used by corporations to gather resources and transform them into goods and then transport them to consumers. The visual below illustrates a simplified commodity chain for corn.

### Commodity Chain for Corn

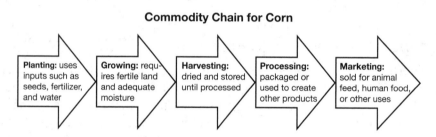

| Planting: uses inputs such as seeds, fertilizer, and water | Growing: requires fertile land and adequate moisture | Harvesting: dried and stored until processed | Processing: packaged or used to create other products | Marketing: sold for animal feed, human food, or other uses |

Because of improvements in agricultural technology, advances in transportation, and an increasingly globalized economy, farmers can raise crops and animals far from their final market, and consumers can still purchase the final products at low prices. Corn has numerous uses, such as livestock feed, sweetener, or fuel, and the commodity chain for each use would be more specialized and complex than the one shown.

## Technological Improvements

In 1962, one farmer fed an average of 26 people. By the early 21st century, one farmer fed an average of 155 people. This improvement is attributed to technological advancements in transportation, fertilizers, and harvesting equipment and a deeper understanding of the science of plants and animals. Advances in refrigeration created **cool chains**, which are transportation networks that keep food cool throughout a trip. Fruits and vegetables from the tropics could be delivered fresh to the temperate climates of North America and Europe at relatively low prices for consumers.

Intensive use of fertilizers, herbicides, and pesticides over large lots of land has increased production. This mass production of agricultural products has accounted for higher crop yields. Whether it is wheat fields in Kansas or banana plantations in Ecuador, large-scale agriculture would not be possible without these advancements in technology.

However, the combination of more intense land use, increased application of chemicals, and reduced amount of time for land to recover has led to environmental damage. The loss of wetlands and large tracts of rainforest cleared to increase farmable land have led to the loss of biodiversity and water resources. Petroleum-based fertilizers, pesticides, and herbicides have caused soil, water, and air pollution, and threatened ecosystems.

# Regional Interdependence

The globalization of agriculture has created more interdependence, or connections among the regions of the world. Developed countries such as the United States and ones in Europe rely on producers in Mexico, Chile, and elsewhere in warm climates or the Southern Hemisphere to provide them with fresh fruits and vegetables year-round.

### Food on a Global Scale

Food production and consumption are part of a complex global supply chain. For example, nearly half of U.S.-grown soybeans are exported. Major purchasers of U.S. agricultural products include China, Mexico, and Europe.

Low-latitude countries with tropical climates produce products such as coffee, tea, bananas, pineapples, and cocoa that cannot be grown in mid-latitude countries. But the mid-latitudes include developed countries in Europe and North America that provide a large market for these products. These tropical foods are examples of **luxury crops**, ones not essential to human survival but that have a high profit margin. For example, the cocoa bean (fruit of the cacao) is too bitter to be consumed in its raw form. It is highly processed in several stages beginning in the country where it is harvested and ending in a developed country, where it is commonly processed into chocolate.

The globalized commodity chain provides wealthy consumers with wide choices. However, it can lead to problems in developing countries:

- Farmers who are producing crops might not be able to afford to consume what they produce.
- By focusing on crops for export, the supply of locally grown food decreases, which drives up the cost for local consumers. A farmer in Honduras who grows chili peppers for the global market is not growing corn, beans, or other crops dominant in the diet.
- Finally, production might not be sustainable. Farmers might choose to follow practices that erode the soil or cause chemical pollution that harms the long-term use of the land.

## Political Systems, Infrastructure, and Trade

The efficient exchange of food around the world depends on effective political systems, strong infrastructure, and supportive trade policies. These conditions have evolved over time to make agricultural trade vital in most countries.

### Colonialism and Neocolonialism

Many connections that exist between Europe and the developing world were established through colonization. Although there are very few colonies in the world today, the economic relationship between developed countries and developing countries resembles certain aspects of colonialism. **Neocolonialism**, the use of economic, political, and social pressures to control former colonies, can be one way to describe the current state of global food distribution.

For example, while the extraction and processing of cocoa is expensive, the profit margin in selling chocolate is very high. Most of the revenue generated from chocolate remains with the transnational corporation based in the wealthy country while very little revenue finds its way back to the cocoa growers.

### Fair Trade

In recent years, many consumers have become more aware of the disparity between high incomes of those in developed countries who manage trade and the low incomes of the producers in the developing world. One result of this awareness is the **fair trade movement**, an effort to promote higher incomes for producers and for more sustainable farming practices. Fair trade agreements between retailers and producers have been reached for several crops grown in the developing world, including cotton and coffee. While these agreements often increase the prices for consumers slightly, they provide a bigger share of revenue to producers and growers in the developing world.

### Government Subsidies and Infrastructure

Governments in the developed world often provide **subsidies**, or public support, to farmers to ensure that consumers have a dependable, low-cost supply of food. The subsidies are designed to achieve three goals:

- to protect national security by insuring a dependable food supply
- to help farmers by increasing agricultural exports
- to help consumers by reducing food costs

Many agricultural products, such as grain or meat, are bulky to transport. Hence, one of the key components in determining the cost of the consumer products made from them is **infrastructure** (roads, bridges, tunnels, ports, electrical grids, sewers, telecommunications, and so on) that serves the country where they are produced. The U.S. government subsidizes the exports of corn, soybeans, and other agricultural products from the Midwest by spending money to make the Mississippi River navigable for barge traffic. Because water transportation is so inexpensive compared to land travel, these products enter the global food supply chain with a lower price than they would without the government support. Because of these subsidies, consumers in Mexico City can purchase corn more cheaply from the United States than from parts or rural Mexico.

Most infrastructure improvements in developing countries connect resources to ports so goods can be exported. Often, other infrastructure in the country is lacking. As the map of the west African country Ghana shows, the major rail lines in the country connect the interior, where resources are located, to the ports where they can be exported to the developed world.

## TRANSPORTATION ROUTES IN GHANA

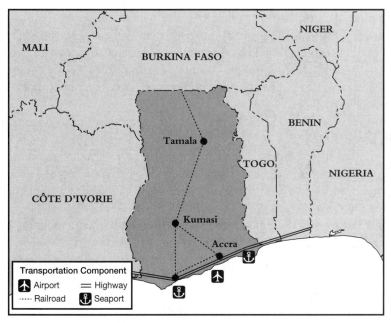

## GEOGRAPHIC PERSPECTIVES: DIFFUSION OF CROPS

A modern diet is rich in food from around the world. Geographers have traced the diffusion of these crops from their hearths and the networks created through trade.

### Crops and Locations
Florida oranges, Irish potatoes, Colombian coffee, Swiss chocolate, and Italian tomato sauces are closely associated with specific geographic locations. But each of these items originated in hearths distant from where they are produced today. Similarly, black pepper from India, cinnamon from Sri Lanka, and nutmeg from the Moluccas are among the many non-native luxuries that diffused to the European mainland. The goal of reducing the friction of distance between Europe and these

faraway lands in order to improve the variety of peoples' diets was a significant factor in the diffusion of crops from one location to another.

**Rate of Adoption**

But people are creatures of habit, so it can take centuries for the new crops to be accepted by another culture. For example, when Europeans brought tomatoes from the Americas back to Europe, they became popular in Italy—but only for ornamental purposes. Initially believed to be poisonous, tomatoes did not find their way into conventional Italian cuisine until the 19th century.

**Impact of Land and Climate**

Successful diffusion depends on more than what people want. Crops are notoriously fickle with respect to the conditions in which they grow best. A slight change in soil conditions, mean temperature, growing season, moisture, and latitudinal position can severely hinder the production of a crop.

For instance, natural latex, extracted from rubber trees originating in South America, was first introduced to France in the 18th century. Today, over 90 percent of its production is concentrated in Southeast Asian countries such as Thailand, Indonesia, and Malaysia. This primarily has to do with the availability of abundant cheap labor in those regions, as opposed to the Americas. However, this has occurred only because both regions' distances from the equator and relative climates are very similar.

| KEY TERMS | | |
|---|---|---|
| pastoral nomadism | subsistence agriculture | commodity chain |
| ranching | Mediterranean agriculture | monoculture |
| shifting cultivation | | suitcase farm |
| plantation | dairy | cool chains |
| market gardening | extensive farming | luxury crops |
| truck farming | intensive farming | neocolonialism |
| milk shed | double-cropping | fair trade movement |
| winter wheat | intercropping | subsidy |
| spring wheat | feed lots | infrastructure |
| transhumance | agribusiness | |
| | supply chain | |

## MULTIPLE-CHOICE QUESTIONS

1. Which was one result of the development of cool chains?
   (A) They eliminated the need for air transport of agricultural products.
   (B) They decreased the use of high-speed rail for transporting food.
   (C) They increased the distance that fresh fruits and vegetables could travel.
   (D) They were a result of advances in agricultural productivity.
   (E) They caused the development of large ships for transporting meat products.

2. What agricultural practice is employed by people who move from place to place with their cattle?
   (A) dairying
   (B) intensive subsistence
   (C) ranching
   (D) shifting cultivation
   (E) pastoral nomadism

**Question 3 refers to the following image.**

3. What farming practice does the above image show?
   (A) shifting cultivation
   (B) intercropping
   (C) market gardening
   (D) double cropping
   (E) plantation agriculture

**4.** Which describes a change in agriculture that shows the clearest impact of development of agribusiness?

(A) The small-scale farming sector has grown stronger.

(B) The number of farmers involved in sustainable agriculture has increased dramatically.

(C) The use of organic farming methods has increased greatly.

(D) The networks for production and distribution have become more efficient.

(E) The emphasis on local trade has increased significantly.

**5.** Slash-and-burn agriculture is often used by farmers who live in areas that have

(A) soil that lacks sufficient amounts of nitrogen to grow food crops quickly

(B) a climate of extremes, one that includes very hot summers and very cold winters

(C) a shortage of rain throughout the year, such as an arid or desert region

(D) very high elevations, such as in mountain ranges in South America and South Asia

(E) a combination of climate and physical features that result in crops growing very slowly

**6.** The building of the Erie Canal in the 1820s to connect New York City with the Midwest was paid for by the state of New York. It is an example of

(A) agribusiness

(B) vertical integration

(C) a subsidy

(D) a supply chain

(E) an economy of scale

7. Which statement best explains why a large number of agricultural products are imported into the United States from Chile?

(A) Inexpensive labor in Chile reduces the cost of production.

(B) The growing season in Chile allows U.S. consumers to have fresh fruits and vegetables in the winter.

(C) Subsides in the United States make agricultural products less expensive.

(D) Improvements in agricultural technologies have increased Chile's output.

(E) The number of U.S. farmers has declined so significantly that the country cannot produce enough food for consumers.

8. Which statement explains why pastoral nomads move from place to place with their cattle?

(A) They have been contracted to raise these animals for a multinational corporation.

(B) It has proven to be an effective method of subsistence agriculture in the semi-arid region in which they live.

(C) Recent improvements in refrigeration and transportation have greatly expanded how far milk can be delivered.

(D) It allows the owners of the livestock to stay in one place while the cattle graze over a large area.

(E) Green Revolution technologies have made this practice possible since the mid-20th century.

## FREE-RESPONSE QUESTION

1. Pastoral nomadism and livestock ranching are two types of agriculture involving animals.

A. Identify a region of the world where livestock ranching is common and another region of the world where pastoral nomadism is common.

B. Identify the climate type associated with these activities and explain why it is.

C. Identify and describe TWO differences between the way pastoral nomadism and livestock ranching are practiced.

At the scale of a country, Mexico is a vitally important region for the food that people in the United States eat. Around 45 percent of the vegetables imported by the United States come from Mexico. But at the scale of states in Mexico, the distribution of food is not even, nor are the exports consistent throughout the year. Mexico exports twice as much in the six months from December through May as it does in the other six months of the year.

Use the map to help answer the questions below it.

EXPORTS OF FRUITS AND VEGETABLES FROM
MEXICAN STATES

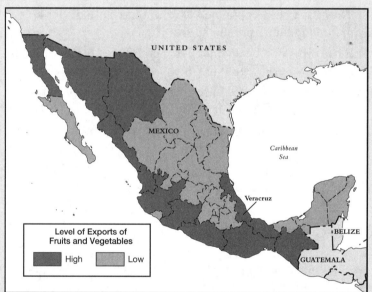

1. Suggest one or more possible reasons to explain why Mexican exports have the seasonal pattern they do.

2. What might explain the spatial pattern in Mexican exports?

3. The state of Veracruz has a climate similar to part of the east coast of India. Why does Veracruz export more fruits and vegetables to the United States than do similar regions in India?

**14**

# Rural Land Use Patterns

*To most people, this is just dirt. To a farmer, it is potential.*
—Anonymous

**Essential Question:** How do farmers and others who live in rural areas decide how to use land?

The distribution of people in rural areas, and the distribution of agricultural production, indicates a great deal about how people in rural areas live. Using the agricultural landscape as his canvas, Johann von Thünen produced one of the most significant models ever created to illustrate the relationship among markets, production, and distance. Because it became the foundation of many economic location models, von Thünen's work illuminates many areas of geography.

## The Cultural Landscape of Rural Settlements

The rural landscape reflects both the economic activities and the cultural attributes of the people who live in an area. Landscape features such as place names, road signs, churches, and the layout of villages often provide evidence of the origins, languages, and religious beliefs of generations of inhabitants. Several factors affect rural settlement patterns. In addition to personal preferences, politics, religion, and the physical landscape can all play a role.

### Clustered and Dispersed Rural Settlement Patterns

Throughout European history, rural residents commonly lived in **clustered settlements**, groups of homes located near each other in a hamlet or village. Clustered settlements fostered a strong sense of community and were convenient for sharing services, such as schools and churches. However, farmers spent part of each day walking to and from their fields, and watching over crops and animals was difficult.

In contrast to Europeans, North American farmers usually created **dispersed settlements**, a pattern in which farmers lived in homes spread throughout the countryside. In Canada and the United States, the governments promoted westward expansion by giving farmers land (in the United States, usually 160 acres) if they agreed to reside on it for several years. As a result, agricultural villages were extremely rare in this region.

### Establishing Property Boundaries

In England, fields often had irregular shapes that reflected the location of physical features and traditional patterns of use. Plot boundaries were described using the **metes and bounds** system. Metes were used for short distances and often referred to features of specific points, such as "from the oak tree, 100 yards north, to the corner of the barn." Bounds cover larger areas, and were based on larger features, such as streams or roads.

The English colonists in America also used metes and bounds. However, beginning in 1785, the United States switched to a system based on surveying rather than landscape features. The government organized land into **townships**, areas six miles long and six miles wide. Each square mile, or **section**, consisted of 640 acres, and it could be divided into smaller lots, such as half sections or quarter sections. The Public Land Survey System created rectangular plots of consistent size.

Two groups of Christians created their own distinctive patterns in order to emphasize their sense of community:

- Hutterites in Canada and the northern United States clustered all homes together in one rectangle, often with a large dining hall in the center where people shared meals. Barns were located in a separate part of the colony.

- Mennonites created street villages. Each family had a house and a barn, but all were along a single street. The land surrounding the region of homes and barns was divided into three areas, with each family working a thin strip of land in each area.

French settlers in North America emphasized the value of access to a river for water and trade. So that many farmers could have some river frontage, they developed the **French long-lot system**, in which farms were long thin sections of land that ran perpendicular to a river. The best examples of the this system in North America occur in Quebec and Louisiana.

## Von Thünen's Land Use Model Zones

In 1826, Johann von Thünen, a farm owner in Germany, created an economic model that suggested a pattern for the types of products that farmers would produce at different positions relative to the market where they sold their goods. He assumed that farming was an economic activity, that farmers were in business to make a profit, that there was one market where farmers in the surrounding lands sold their products, and that the market was situated in the center of a plain that is **isotropic**, which means flat and featureless.

Von Thünen believed that decisions regarding what to produce were based largely upon transportation costs and that these costs were proportional to the distance from the market. The cost of land was another factor that influenced decisions regarding agricultural products, and there was a distance decay pattern between the cost of land and the distance from the market. His model showed similar distance decay patterns existed between intensity of land use and distance from market, as well as between perishability of the product and distance from market.

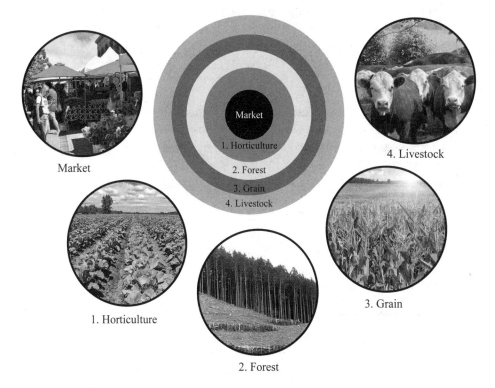

Market

4. Livestock

3. Grain

1. Horticulture

2. Forest

Market
1. Horticulture
2. Forest
3. Grain
4. Livestock

### *Description and Explanation of the Model*

In the zone closest to the market, von Thünen suggested that **horticulture**, a type of agriculture that includes **market gardening/truck farming**, and dairying would occur. Horticulture produces perishable items, and farmers need to get them to market quickly. In the days before trucks and refrigeration, this was particularly important. Growing highly perishable crops, such as tomatoes and strawberries, and dairy farming are considered to be intensive forms of agriculture.

Von Thünen's second zone included forests. Wood was an extremely important resource in 1826, both as building material and as a source of fuel. Von Thünen thought that wood products would be close to the market because they were not only important, but heavy and hence difficult to transport.

Farther from the market, in the third ring, were crops such as wheat and corn. Though valuable, they did not perish as quickly as vegetables and milk and were not as difficult to transport as wood.

The final ring was used for grazing of livestock such as beef cattle. They could be farther from the market because they could walk when it was time to transport them.

The extensive nature of grain and livestock farming meant that the farms were larger than those located in the inner ring of the model. While there is more farmland available in the larger outer rings, that was not necessarily the reason for these crops locating here. Grain and livestock farmers could find adequate space in the innermost ring if they were willing to pay enough to acquire the land.

### Land Value

The value of land was influenced by its relationship to the market. Because the land in the inner ring was closest to the market, it was more valuable. Therefore, most farmers could not afford large amounts of it. Consequently, only farmers who used the land intensely and could make a profit from a small amount of land could be successful in the inner ring.

Land farther from the market was less valuable. Because grain and livestock are less perishable than the crops in the inner ring, the farmers could locate in the area of cheaper land farther from the market and still transport the product to market successfully. Though meat is perishable, and this was a significant concern in 1826, spoilage could be avoided if the animals were walked to market and were slaughtered there.

### The Bid Rent Curve

In the case of von Thünen's model, a **bid rent curve**, also known as a bid price curve, can be used to indicate the starting position for each land use relative to the market, as well as where each land use would end. Each line on the graph reflects the farmers' willingness to pay for land at various distances from the market. Notice that each type of farmer is willing to pay more closer to the market than farther away. However, how much more varies with the types of activities. In a free market economy, the farmer willing to pay the most at each location will occupy the land. It is where the uppermost line on the graph intersects with the next uppermost line that represents the start and/or end of a zone.

For example, where the strawberry line intersects the forest line indicates the end of where strawberries will be grown and the beginning of where forests will be found. Where the forest line intersects the wheat line indicates where the forest zone ends and the wheat zone begins.

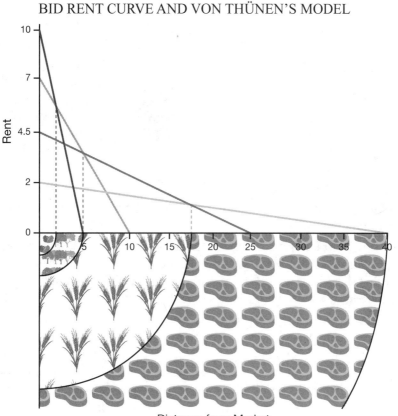

BID RENT CURVE AND VON THÜNEN'S MODEL

Distance from Market

## Applying Von Thünen's Model

Von Thünen's model has been valuable in many ways. It has had application far beyond the topic of agriculture. His recognition of the spatial pattern in how farmers made decisions about using resources was the first economic location model. It provided the basis for the industrial location models of Alfred Weber and others who followed.

In addition, even though Von Thünen created his model nearly two centuries ago, it continues to apply today. Like all models, it needs to be adapted to actual conditions and changes in technology.

**Non-Isotropic Plains** Von Thünen's model assumed that land was an isotropic plain—but real land includes rivers, mountains, and other physical features that make it non-isotropic. Von Thünen considered how various landscape situations would alter the shape of each land use ring. For example, if a river flowed through the plain, making transportation easier and cheaper along the river, then the zones would stretch out along the river. In addition, some areas have better climates or soil conditions for certain crops. These areas have a **comparative advantage**, or naturally occurring beneficial conditions

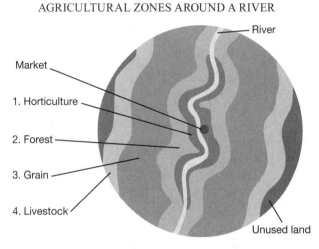

AGRICULTURAL ZONES AROUND A RIVER

River
Market
1. Horticulture
2. Forest
3. Grain
4. Livestock
Unused land

that would prompt farmers to plant crops different from those predicted by von Thünen's model.

**Multiple Markets** Von Thünen assumed that a farmer had one primary market, but they often have secondary markets as well. A dairy farmer might primarily sell milk to a local dairy. But the farmer might also make and sell some cheese, which does not spoil as quickly as milk, in a distant market.

**Changes in Transportation** The development of trains, cars, planes, and storage techniques such as refrigeration has allowed food to be transported much longer distances without spoiling than in 1826. As a result, the rings in the model are wider than originally. For example, rapidly perishable goods such as strawberries and milk can be produced much farther away from the market than in Von Thünen's time. But relative locations remain the same. They are still produced closer to the market than are grains and livestock.

The cut flower market demonstrates the impact of transportation on the application of von Thünen's model. Since cut flowers perish quickly and thus have to arrive at the market quickly, they are similar to horticulture and dairy products that the model predicts will be produced nearby and trucked to market. However, many flowers sold in New York City were grown in the Caribbean and flown to market. While air travel costs from the Caribbean are far higher than truck transport from the outskirts of New York, other costs of flower production are much less. Land, labor, and energy costs are so much lower in the Caribbean than they are in the outskirts of New York that they outweigh the extra transportation costs. Hence, producers can grow flowers for New York more profitably in the Caribbean than in nearby states.

**Other Changes in Technology** Changes in technology have modified demand for products. Since 1826, wood has been mostly replaced by oil, natural gas, and electricity as a fuel for heating homes, so forests are rarely located near communities today. Now, forested land at a city's edge is probably highly valued as a **greenbelt**, an area of recreational parks or other undeveloped land, rather than a source of fuel.

**Special Circumstances** No model accounts for every variation that occurs in practice. For example, von Thünen's model does not fit some areas of specialty farming, such as citrus farming in Florida, or the variety of crops grown in the Central Valley of California. Nor does it explain the decisions by developers who purchase land close to a city and use it for less intensive agricultural use than they could. They usually want to invest as little money as possible into the farmland while they decide when the time is right to build homes, retail space, or commercial structures on it.

Despite these issues in applying the **von Thünen model**, it remains important. When adjusted for real circumstances, it can still guide geographers as they study the relative value of land and transportation costs.

# Modification of Natural Ecosystems

The development of agriculture significantly modified the natural landscape. Subsistence farming brought some change, but large-scale commercial agriculture brought far more.

### Side Effects of Modern Food Production

Modern farming methods have made healthy diets possible for billions of people. However, each change to the natural ecosystem to increase food production has come with costs:

- Farmers have replaced forests with fields. These developed fields are unlikely to ever return to forest. In order to farm these fields year after year, farmers constantly replace nutrients with chemical fertilizers that can pollute rivers and lakes.

- Farmers have grazed animals in areas too arid to support crop production. Herders must be careful to prevent overgrazing or a somewhat productive area can undergo desertification and be unable to produce food.

- Farmers have used irrigation to make some arid areas productive for crops. Irrigation of land near the Nile River and in many parts of the western United States has led to conflicts between farmers and others who need water in these dry areas.

- Farmers have drained lands too wet for agricultural practices. The loss of wetlands can damage the ecosystem and lead to greater flooding.

- Farmers have terraced hilly or mountainous areas in order to produce flat areas for easier and more productive agriculture. Altering the natural flow of water and soil changes the conditions in which wild animals live.

### Protecting Natural Ecosystems

To counter the damaging effects of destroying the natural landscape and the various flora and fauna that inhabit it, people are finding ways to preserve or restore ecosystems. At a global scale, people around the world in the 1980s joined a "Save the Rainforest" movement that supported farming and logging practices that did not damage the Brazilian rainforest. At a regional scale, in the tar sands of Alberta, scientists are attempting to return the disturbed landscape from open pit mining to its natural state. At a local scale, many communities have created natural habitats in their parks for plants and animals.

# Agricultural Innovations

Agricultural scientists are constantly doing research to increase yields to feed the growing population, improve foods' nutritional value, and increase the profitability of farming. While agricultural innovations often accomplish at least one of these three goals, people disagree over their other affects. As noted in Chapter 12, the Green Revolution was both successful and controversial. Similarly, other innovations often raise concerns.

### Genetically Modified Organisms

A more recent controversial innovation has been the use of **genetically modified organisms** (GMOs), which are plants or animals that scientists in a laboratory modified by extracting genes of one species and inserting them into the DNA of another species. Compared to traditional foods, GMOs can be more nutritious, more resistant to weather and pest-related damage, and more long-lasting before they spoil. The majority of scientists have found them safe for humans. However, only a few countries such as the United States, Brazil, and Argentina have large GMO production. Many countries, particularly in Europe, have restricted the use of GMOs. Some concerns about GMOs include:

- GMO seeds are too expensive for poor farmers to use, in part because they are often sterile, so new seeds must be purchased each year.
- GMO seeds that are resistant to pests and herbicides might lead to the development of super pests or super weeds.
- GMOs might have potential long-term risks to consumers, such as organ problems or reduced immunity to diseases, that no one yet recognizes.

### Organic Foods

The demand for organically grown food is increasing in the United States. Many consumers believe that food produced without the use of pesticides, synthetic fertilizers or other unnatural processes is healthier for them and for the environment. Since organic farming tends to be more labor-intensive than other forms of agriculture, it creates more jobs but the food produced is more expensive.

Organic agriculture has possible drawbacks. One potential environmental cost resulting from organic farming is that it might require more land in order to produce the same quantity of food. This could result in deforestation or destruction of wetlands and the corresponding loss of flora and fauna from these ecosystems. Also, some organic production of such commodities as milk, cereal, and pork produce more greenhouse gases than conventional farming techniques. And while organic farming regulations prohibit the use of synthetic pesticides, they do allow farmers to use naturally occurring chemicals that can be very harmful to humans and other life forms.

### Aquaculture

With population growth increasing the demand for food, and supplies of fish in the ocean and some lakes being depleted by overfishing, people have turned to **aquaculture**, the practice of raising and harvesting fish and other forms of food that live in water. People in China and Southeast Asia have practiced aquaculture for thousands of years, but it is newer in the rest of the world. Aquaculture has dramatically increased the availability of fish protein to many people. Often referred to as the **Blue Revolution**, the practice is now the fastest growing form of food production on the planet and responsible for approximately 50 percent of the world's seafood.

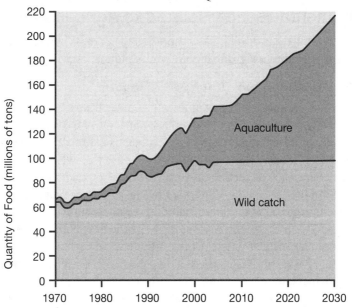

THE GROWTH OF AQUACULTURE

Source: futuretimeline.net

As with other forms of food production, there are environmental concerns related to the practice. Critics of open-pen systems, in which a cage or net is moored to the seafloor and the farm fish are able, to some extent, to interact with the wild surroundings, point out these problems:

- High fish density in enclosures means diseases and parasites thrive and spread easily.
- Parasites and diseases can easily spread from fish in the enclosures to the nearby wild stock.
- Chemicals and antibiotics used to counter parasites and diseases can damage the ecosystem around the enclosures.
- Fish can escape pens and may breed or compete with native stocks of fish.
- Excess feed and the concentration of fish waste can produce dangerously high levels of organic matter in the ocean.

There are also social concerns regarding aquaculture. The installation of fish farms can challenge traditional fishing and lead to conflicts between the two groups of fishers, disrupting the local way of life. Another concern is that owners of the aquaculture operations may unethically exploit both the local labor as well as the local environment. Some people are concerned that fish from fish farms contain high levels of pesticides that could harm humans.

# Environmental Issues Related to Agriculture

Modern agriculture has dramatically modified the natural landscape. Some of these changes constitute significant environmental damage.

### Agricultural Chemicals and Fossil Fuels

Much of the environmental impact of farming comes from the use of chemicals. Farmers have long used fertilizers to replace nutrients in the soil. Traditionally, the fertilizer was human or animal waste. When used properly, these products both provided the soil with nutrients and disposed of wastes. While some farmers still use waste as fertilizer, most rely more on chemical fertilizers. If too much is applied, the excess contaminates nearby water supplies, producing significant environmental damage, including algal blooms.

A second group of potentially harmful chemicals includes ones designed to kill unwanted insects or plants. Both pesticides and herbicides destroy parts of the natural ecosystem. When used or disposed of incorrectly, they can cause significant damage to other life forms, including humans.

A third group of powerful chemicals are those given to livestock, such as antibiotics to prevent disease and hormones to promote growth. Many consumers fear the consequences of consuming meat from these animals.

Lastly, modern farming machines that run on fossil fuel, such as combines and tractors, result in air pollution from the exhaust, depletion of fossil fuel reserves, and leaks or spills of various petroleum products that can contaminate soil and water.

## Depletion of Water Supplies

Farming can also damage the environment by misusing water. Worldwide, approximately 70 percent of all accessible fresh water is used for agriculture. Some of this water is wasted through inefficient irrigation. Farmers sometimes apply more water than their crops need, operate irrigation pipes that leak, or try to grow crops in arid places. Poor irrigation can cause several problems:

- Excessive irrigation can increase the level of salts in the soil, a process known as salinization. This reduces the ability of plants to grow.
- Irrigation can reduce the amount of underground water in aquifers. India, Pakistan, and other countries that adopted the crops of the Green Revolution have suffered from this problem.
- Irrigation can reduce the amount of surface water in rivers and lakes. In central Asia, the Aral Sea has shrunk by more than 60 percent over the past five decades, as the photos below indicate.

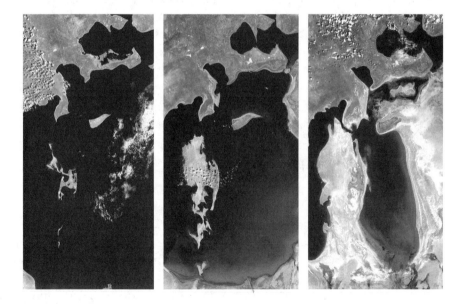

## Loss of Biodiversity

Changes in agriculture often reduce biodiversity. As improved varieties of crops are developed, farmers often abandon older varieties. In addition, many farmers are growing fewer varieties of crops than ever before. Specializing in one crop, which is known as **monocropping**, or **monoculture**, then reduces the diversity of the insects, animals, and other organisms that depend on other varieties of plants. To keep abandoned varieties of plants from disappearing forever, scientists save seeds in international and national seed banks.

## Soil Degradation and Erosion

The image of grazing animals seems to suggest very low impact on the natural landscape. In a large open area, the animals will simply wander from area to area seeking better grass and giving the grazed areas time to recover. In restricted areas, farmers move their herds between enclosures to allow for the recovery of the grasslands.

However, if the density of animals is greater than the grasslands can support, then in their search for food, the animals will **overgraze**, damage the grasslands to the extent that the vegetation will not refresh itself even after the animals leave. Overgrazing most often occurs when farmers or herders have too many animals, they control too little land, or climatic conditions worsen and there is less pasture available than usual. With the right combination of overgrazing and environmental circumstances, catastrophic levels of soil erosion become a real danger. The Sahel region of Africa, a continent-wide belt of land on the southern edge of the Sahara Desert, is an excellent example of where this pressure is occurring.

Overgrazing is increasingly occurring in **pastoral nomadism/migratory husbandry** situations as the amount of land available to the herders and their families has shrunk in recent decades. Since there is less land available for the migratory herders, they have to remain longer in fewer locations, significantly increasing the risk of overgrazing. Several changes have decreased the availability of pasture land, each of which makes overgrazing more likely:

- Governments have become much more protective of their borders, which makes it much more difficult for some herders to follow their traditional migratory routes that often crossed international borders.
- Some former pasture land is now being irrigated and used for growing crops and housing permanent residents.
- Other areas of former pasture land are now being used for mining and petroleum operations.

Once overgrazing occurs, the grasses will not recover as quickly, if at all, and this leaves the exposed soil much more susceptible to erosion.

The practices mentioned above can all lead to soil degradation and soil erosion. When farmers drain the soil of nutrients from practices such as overuse, lack of crop rotation, or failure to replace nutrients, the soil loses its ability to support plant growth. Once this happens, the soil can be much more easily eroded by wind or water. Overgrazing and over tilling, or plowing, can also result in soils susceptible to erosion by wind and water.

## Animal Waste

The raising of animals for food today generally includes the use of feedlots. On these lots, thousands of animals might be contained in a very limited amount of land, consuming high-quality feed for several months before they are slaughtered. The large amount of waste they produce can include gases such as ammonia, methane, and hydrogen sulfide that can pollute the air, and liquid wastes that can pollute the water supply. Feedlots must be well-managed to avoid causing significant environmental damage. Many scientists are concerned about the concentration of waste in small areas.

### Sustainability and Agriculture

Farmers today face many challenges to operate in ways that are sustainable in the long term. Maintaining soil fertility without degrading the soil is possible, but it takes careful planning. Sustainable grazing and tilling practices help to minimize soil erosion. Managing chemical levels and sedimentation in bodies of water, conserving water, employing renewable energy resources, and preserving biodiversity are all part of an environmentally sustainable perspective. Farmers have to constantly analyze their decisions in order to strike a balance between immediate profitability and long-term sustainability.

# Changes in Food Production and Consumption

The broad trends in agriculture over the past century have been toward larger farms, more corporate ownership, more intensive use of machinery and chemicals, and higher output. However, smaller trends are also evident, such as the increase in organic farming discussed previously.

### Fair Trade and Local Food

Some consumers support the **fair trade** movement, which is designed to get more money into the hands of the small farmers in poor countries who actually raise the crops, rather than supporting large transnational corporations that manage trade in these products. The most widely sold fair-trade products are coffee, tea, bananas, and chocolate.

Another trend among some consumers is to "eat local"—seeking out food produced nearby. Advocates, sometimes called "locavores," point out that this both supports local farmers and reduces the use of fossil fuel used to transport products. Farmers markets, where consumers can purchase fruits, vegetables, and other food items directly from farmers, have become more popular in the past three decades. Many farmers who cater to local consumers produce specialty crops such as herbs, mushrooms, and free-range chickens that are provided in small quantities but sold at relatively high prices.

### Location of Food Production Facilities

Traditionally, companies located food processing facilities in rural areas or small towns. By locating facilities close to where the harvest occurs, companies could work with very fresh products—and benefit from the lower labor and land costs in rural areas. However, improvements in roads, truck efficiencies, and storage techniques have prompted many companies to close older, smaller facilities and open new, larger, more efficient ones. These new facilities have allowed them to take advantage of **economies of scale**. This change has shifted jobs from rural to urban locations.

The importance of transportation and storage techniques is clear in the lobster industry. Worldwide demand for fresh live lobster is so high that lobster processors now use very expensive air freight to ship millions of pounds of live lobster from the east coast of Canada to destinations in Europe and Asia.

## Gender Roles in the Food System

In most cultures throughout history, males and females have had distinct roles in producing and preparing food. However, some of these roles have changed as technology has changed.

**Food Production** Women have played a major role in agriculture since people first started farming. Today, they make up about 40 percent of the world's agricultural labor force. In regions where subsistence farming remains common, the figure is 70 percent:

- In many areas of the developing world, men migrate to urban areas in search of employment, while women stay at home and work their farms along with their children. In operations where farms sell their farm products at local market, women are often the sellers.
- Where farming has modernized and machines have been introduced, women have become less involved with the field work.
- In large-scale agribusinesses, women have taken on newer roles. Besides raising crops and tending animals, and processing products, they work in management, sales, distribution, and research.

**Food Preparation** How people prepare food has changed as people changed where they live and work. As people moved from rural areas to urban areas, they grew less of the food they consumed and purchased more of it. And as more women worked outside of the home, they had less time to prepare food.

One result of these changes has been that women spend less time preparing food than did women in previous generations. People purchase more convenience foods than previously, from cake mixes to entire meals that simply need to be heated. The demand for these foods has grown so much that food companies are committing significant research money to developing visually appealing, tasty, healthy food products. In addition, in the regions of the world with greater gender equality, men have become more involved in food preparation, particularly in households where both partners are working.

A second result is that people eat in restaurants more than ever before. In 2015 for the first time in history, Americans spent more money eating out than they spent on groceries.

Washington, Oregon, and California line the west coast of the United States. Despite their location on the edge of the country, they have become the center of organic farming in the United States.

**Chemical and Organic Farming**

The production of food by means of modern chemical farming—utilizing synthetic fertilizers, pesticides, herbicides, and fungicides—is largely extensive in nature. It is lucrative over vast areas of land.

In contrast, organic farming—which is more expensive—has proven to be more profitable through further intensification. While organic agricultural sales have boomed over the past decade, both the number of farms and total acreage of land have declined, where the individual farms have become more productive.

While the organic food industry has grown, its market share remains under five percent. Furthermore, while non-organic modern agriculture produces food for the masses and is often sold globally, organic food has been largely seized upon by local-food movements.

**The Distribution of the Organic Food Market**

As is the case with virtually all industries, the location of organic food consumption can be best explained through the spatial analysis of socioeconomic factors, and the concentration of these locations is predictably uneven. Farmers markets and supermarkets offering organic foods are largely found in the more affluent regions. Almost half of all organic food is sold and consumed within 100 miles of its production. Moreover, most consumption takes place around urban areas, where the market demand is greatest, such as Portland, San Francisco, and Seattle.

| KEY TERMS | | |
|---|---|---|
| clustered settlements | market gardening/truck farming | Blue Revolution |
| dispersed settlements | bid rent curve/bid price curve | monoculture/ monocropping |
| metes and bounds | comparative advantage | biodiversity |
| township | greenbelt | overgrazing |
| section | genetically modified organisms (GMO) | fair trade |
| French long-lot system | organic food | pastoral nomadism / migratory husbandry |
| von Thünen Model | aquaculture | economies of scale |
| isotropic | | |
| horticulture | | |

## MULTIPLE-CHOICE QUESTIONS

1. Which aspect of von Thünen's Model has changed as a result of developments in transporation?

   (A) The market is no longer at the center.

   (B) The width of the rings has increased.

   (C) The width of the rings has decreased.

   (D) The rings now stretch along rivers.

   (E) The model now includes a ring for transportation.

**Question 2 refers to the image below.**

BID PRICE CURVE

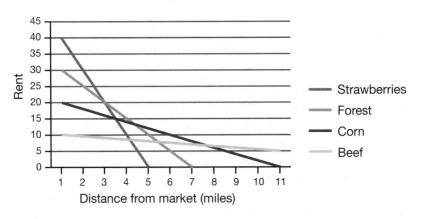

2. Based upon the bid price curve above, in which zone should corn be grown?

   (A) 1 mile to 11 miles

   (B) 3.5 miles to 4.5 miles

   (C) 4.5 miles to 7.6 miles

   (D) 7.6 miles to 11 miles

   (E) 4.5 miles to 11 miles

**3.** In which group of countries are GMOs used the most widely in agriculture?

(A) United States, Brazil, and Argentina

(B) France, Germany, and the Netherlands

(C) Kenya, Tanzania, and Ethiopia

(D) India and Bangladesh

(E) Australia and New Zealand

**Question 4 refers to the image below.**

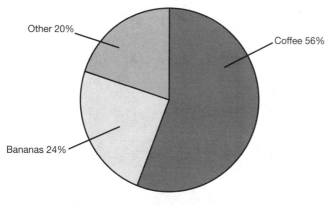

Source: Center for Global Development.

**4.** The graph above shows the increasing sales over a period of time for what category of agricultural products?

(A) greenhouse-grown crops

(B) fair trade crops

(C) GMO crops

(D) Green Revolution crops

(E) hydroponically grown crops

**5.** In which state or province is the long-lot land division most common?

(A) Montana

(B) Quebec

(C) Texas

(D) Iowa

(E) British Columbia

**6.** Which lists products in the order in which they will be produced, starting closest to the market, according to von Thünen's Model?

(A) grain, forest, beef cattle, dairy cattle

(B) tomatoes, grain, forest, beef cattle

(C) dairy cattle, beef cattle, forest

(D) dairy cattle, forest, grain, beef cattle

(E) forest, tomatoes, beef cattle, dairy cattle

**7.** Which issue is an important concern in both aquaculture and feed lots?

(A) animal waste

(B) spread of diseases to nearby wild animals

(C) cost of feed

(D) pesticide contamination

(E) foul odors

**Question 8 refers to the image below.**

**8.** Which best explains the growing popularity of the type of agricultural system shown above?

(A) It reduces the use of fossil fuels in transporting food.

(B) It reduces the price of food to the lowest possible level.

(C) It provides the maximum variety of food throughout the year.

(D) It provides the large quantity of food the world's population needs.

(E) It creates a global system of food production and exchange.

1. Von Thünen's agricultural land use model is one of the principal economic models within the field of human geography.

   A. Identify and explain what happens to the intensity of agricultural land use as the distance from the market increases.

   B. Explain why it made sense in 1826 for von Thünen to suggest forests be positioned in the second ring from the market.

   C. Explain why von Thünen thought dairy cattle would be raised close to the market while beef cattle would be raised far from the market.

   D. Explain how von Thünen's model suggests why flowers sold in New York are grown in the Caribbean or Central America.

---

**THINK AS A GEOGRAPHER:** ANALYZING RURAL NETWORKS

Since the mid-1800s, railroads have connected rural communities with markets—food processors, grocery stores, etc.—in large urban areas. Use the map of Illinois railroads to answer the questions below.

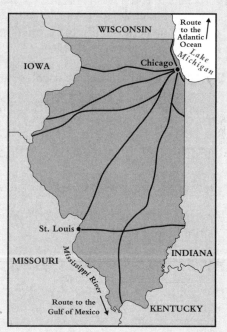

1. Describe the pattern of Illinois railroads shown on the map.

2. What does the map indicate about interaction between rural and urban areas?

3. What features on the edges of Illinois have influenced the state's interaction with the rest of the world?

4. Explain how rural and urban areas contribute to the growth and prosperity of each other.

# UNIT 5: Review

## WRITE AS A GEOGRAPHER: USE RELEVANT INFORMATION

One problem students face when answering a free-response question is to decide what information actually supports claims that answer the question. Students should leave out all other information that is not clearly, directly related to the question. For example, a free-response question might ask about how farmers in Mexico make decisions about what crops to grow.

*Which of the following statements are relevant to answering this question? For ones that are not, explain why they are not.*

1. Most of southern Mexico has a warm, moist climate that supports growing many fruits and vegetables.

2. Brazil has areas of heavy rainfall that are excellent for growing sugar and rice.

3. Improvements in the ports in New Orleans and on the Florida coast reduced the cost of importing goods.

4. Concerns about the long-term effects of soil erosion and fertilizer run-off have persuaded some farmers to consider changing the crops they grow.

5. Von Thünen's model can be used to study decisions by farmers.

6. The primary language spoken throughout Mexico is Spanish.

## REFLECT ON THE CHAPTER ESSENTIAL QUESTIONS

*Write a one- to three-paragraph answer to each question.*

1. How has the development of agriculture affected the spatial distribution of people?

2. Why does agriculture vary so greatly around the world?

3. How do farmers and others who live in rural areas decide how to use land?

# UNIT 6: Industrialization and Economic Development

## Unit Overview

The hearth of the Industrial Revolution was Great Britain in the 18th century. As people learned to use water power and coal energy to manufacture goods, they saw large increases in agricultural productivity, population, and wealth. Industrialization has diffused throughout the world, reshaping all aspects of life.

### Measures of Development

Since the start of the Industrial Revolution, people have developed statistical measures to describe changes in society. Some measure the total output of each country, the distribution of income, rates of childbirth, the number of people who can read, or rates of literacy, and the different opportunities available to males and females. Scholars such as W. W. Rostow and Immanuel Wallerstein used this information to create models or theories of spatial patterns of economic and social development in countries around the world.

### Variations in Development

The diffusion of industrialization generally increased trade and interdependence, which improved the standard of living for most people. But as jobs moved from one place to another place, some people lost their jobs and an international division of labor emerged. One cost was to the environment. In response to the depletion of natural resources, pollution, and the results of climate change, some people have advocated an evolved model that stresses sustainable development.

---

### Enduring Understandings

**VI.** *Industrialization and Economic Development*

- **A.** The Industrial Revolution, as it diffused from its hearth, facilitated improvements in standards of living.
- **B.** Measures of development are used to understand patterns of social and economic differences at a variety of scales.
- **C.** Development is a process that varies across space and time.
- **D.** Sustainable development is a strategy to address resource depletion and environmental degradation.

**Source:** *CollegeBoard AP®. Human Geography Course Description. 2015.*

---

# 15

# Industrialization and Economic Structure

*The political and economic consequences of the Renaissance had helped to spread European domination worldwide. . . . [T]he forces of industrialization helped to complete that process of world domination by dividing the world between the advanced industrialized nations (originally Europe and North America) and the underdeveloped, non-industrialized nations.*

—Richard T. LeGates and Frederic Stout, eds. *The City Reader,* 2000

**Essential Question:** How did the diffusion of industrialism affect people around the world?

## The Growth and Diffusion of Industrialization

The **Industrial Revolution** was a set of changes in technology that dramatically increased manufacturing productivity. It reshaped how people worked and behaved, where they lived, and how they related to each other spatially.

### Diffusion of the Industrial Revolution

The start of the Industrial Revolution in the mid-1700s was like tossing a rock in a pond. It caused a large initial splash in England and then the ripples spread outwards. On a large scale, the first continents and countries affected were near England: France and the Netherlands. By the mid-1800s, industrialization had spread east to Germany and west to the United States. By the early 1900s, it had reached all of Europe, Japan, and parts of China and South America. Today, most of the world is industrialized.

On a smaller scale, within countries, the first factories were usually built near sources of power, such as rivers or coal deposits, and near transportation routes. With the development of electrical power and the construction of new roads, canals, and harbors, later factories were added in more diverse locations.

As the Industrial Revolution progressed, improvements in farm machinery and farming techniques, along with the enclosure movement, increased agricultural productivity. Machine power replaced human and animal power. Hence, many people in rural areas were no longer needed for their labor.

These displaced farm workers moved to towns and cities, causing an explosion in urban populations everywhere industrialization occurred. As urban residents, they promoted the growth of industries in two crucial ways:

- As workers, they toiled in factories, running the machines that made textiles, steel, and other products.
- As consumers, they provided a market for the expanding quantities of food and manufactured goods.

## Growth of Population and Cities

As the number of industries in factory cities increased and rural-urban migration continued, cities grew rapidly. London grew from one million people in 1800 to six million in 1900. Old systems for handling human waste, burying the dead, and cleaning up horse manure were overwhelmed. Since people burned wood and coal to heat their homes and run factories, air pollution increased to harmful, even deadly, levels. In some weeks, smog got so bad that it doubled the normal rate of death. Over time, people supported stronger government action to build sewers, regulate cemeteries, and so on, to protect public health.

Public health measures became increasingly important as cities became even more dense by expanding vertically. The development of elevators, stronger and more affordable steel, and techniques to construct stronger foundations combined to allow for taller buildings.

Cities also expanded horizontally. Improvements in intra-urban transportation, such as trains, cars, and trucks, allowed cities to spread out farther from the downtown core. People could live farther from their workplace and still commute to work easily. And food could be transported from the countryside into cities to feed a growing population.

## Colonialism, Imperialism, and the Industrial Revolution

The Industrial Revolution built on the earlier rise of **imperialism**, a policy of extending a country's political and economic power. As countries such as Great Britain and France industrialized, they recognized the value of controlling trading posts and colonies around the world. Colonies provided several resources and other contributions to the economy:

- raw materials such as sugar, cotton, foodstuffs, lumber, and minerals for use in mills and factories
- labor to extract raw materials
- markets where manufacturers could sell finished products
- ports where trading ships could stop to get resupplied
- profits to use for investing in new factories, canals, and railroads

By the early 1900s, several other European countries and the United States also had far-flung possessions. The development of imperialism made wealthy countries even wealthier, leading to a great divide between the advanced, industrialized states and the underdeveloped, nonindustrialized states.

### Fordism and Post-Fordism

In the 19th century, production increased with the shift from a system of cottage industry, in which people would weave cloth and make products in their homes, to a system of large factories with machines powered by water or coal. But each product was often made individually. Early in the 20th century, Henry Ford took another big step in advancing productivity by developing the **assembly line**, in which an item moved from worker to worker, with each worker performing the same task repeatedly. The use of assembly lines allowed companies to produce more standardized products more rapidly and with less-skilled workers than ever before.

This system of mass production, known as **Fordism**, soon became standard practice across industries. Capitalists copied his methods—as did communists. Ford became a cult hero in Russia because it was through economic efficiency that Russian workers realized they might become productive enough to achieve the goals of communism. As consumers, people appreciated that the cost of goods plummeted. However, as workers, people resented how dull and repetitive the assembly line made work.

Fordism quickly changed manufacturing. One issue was the lack of variety. Every product was identical to every other product. Since not every consumer wanted a black car identical to their neighbor's black car, companies gradually modified the assembly line process to produce more varied products. These changes added time and cost to the process.

In recent years, with the use of computers and increased automation, every product coming off the assembly line can be different. In modern factories, the **substitution principle**, in which businesses seek to maximize profit by substituting one factor of production for another, has been applied to a significant percentage of the labor force. Through mechanization, also known as automation, companies have replaced workers with machines. For example, U.S. industrial output doubled between 1984 and 2015—but industrial employment declined by one-third.

Although expensive to install, the machines often save a company money over the long term. They can work 24 hours a day without breaks or vacations, and they produce consistent, high-quality work. The workers who don't lose their jobs are often trained to do more than one job, so they can rotate among a few different workstations during a day. These changes in the production process constitute the basis of the **post-Fordism** system.

## Economic Sectors

Some economists analyze a country's workforce by dividing it into three sectors according to how closely people work with natural resources. The following chart shows these three sectors for United States history.

| THE THREE ECONOMIC SECTORS IN THE UNITED STATES | | | |
| --- | --- | --- | --- |
| Sector | Task | Examples | Economic Role |
| Primary | Extracting natural resources | • Farming<br>• Mining<br>• Fishing<br>• Forestry | Dominated the economy until the Civil War |
| Secondary | Processing natural resources | • Manufacturing<br>• Building | Significant labor growth 1840s to 1960s |
| Tertiary | Providing services rather than working with natural resources | • Marketing<br>• Banking<br>• Design | Most people in the U.S. labor force today |

The composition of a country's economy changes over time. When the United States was formed, nearly everyone farmed or did other work in the **primary sector**. Today, in the United States and other developed countries, the primary sector usually employs less than 5 percent of the labor force. In a least-developed country, the figure is over 70 percent.

LABOR FORCE BY SECTOR IN TWO COUNTRIES

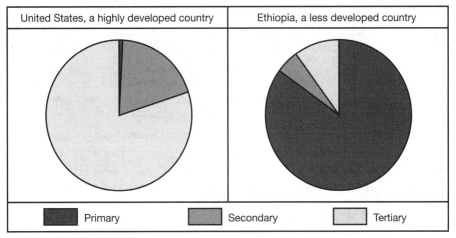

The **tertiary sector** is also known as the service sector because it consists of providing services to people and businesses. It includes people involved in retail sales, automotive repair, plumbing, the restaurant industries, and accounting. In developed countries, where manufacturing is on the decline, the tertiary sector is expanding and dominating the labor force.

### Refining the Tertiary Sector

In recent decades, the tertiary sector has gotten so large that economists have begun to divide it into smaller segments:

- The **quaternary sector** is the knowledge-based sector that includes research and development, business consulting, financial services, education, public administration, and software development.
- The **quinary sector** consists of the highest levels of decision-making and includes the top officials in various levels of government and business. A decision made by a country's president or senior advisors or by corporate executives can affect millions of people.

### Changing Employment Sectors and Economic Development

As countries industrialized, the primary sector shrank and the secondary sector grew. As part of this shift, countries became wealthier because wages in the secondary sector were higher than those in the primary sector.

In addition to higher wages, the secondary sector jobs also had a greater **multiplier effect**, a term for the potential of a job to produce additional jobs. For example, when a tire manufacturer expanded a plant and created 100 new jobs in a community, the new workers would have more money to spend on food, clothes, movies, and other items from nearby businesses. These businesses would prosper and sometimes add more staff.

However, the multiplier effect also works in reverse. In recent decades, the shrinkage of the secondary sector workforce in the United States and other developed countries has caused many other businesses to suffer as well. In addition, the opening of a new store can have a negative effect on other stores in the region. A large retail store opening in a community might employ hundreds of people—but smaller stores nearby might close or lay off employees.

Governments in developed countries often attempt to replace manufacturing jobs lost because of deindustrialization and automation with new quaternary jobs. Both types of jobs pay higher-than-average wages and both can generate additional jobs. Cities such as Denver, Pittsburgh, and Austin are using quaternary jobs to drive their rapidly growing economies. With research and high-tech jobs flowing into the cities, other sectors of the economy are benefiting, especially entertainment, tourism, and education. This quaternary sector growth also boosts the secondary sector because it requires construction and improved infrastructure. One challenge of shifting from manufacturing to quaternary jobs is that many of the displaced workers do not possess the skills required for the new jobs.

# Theories on Industrial Location

Geographers have developed many models explaining the geographic distribution of economic activities. By focusing on the key factors in a process, a model is useful for making predictions about how a change in one factor affects the entire process. In 1909, the German economist Alfred Weber developed an influential theory, known as the **least cost theory**, to explain the key decisions made by businesses about where to locate factories.

Least cost theory attempts to predict the location of a manufacturing site relative to the location of the resources needed to produce the product and where the final product will be sold (market). Weber's theory focused on three key variables: transportation, labor, and agglomeration.

## *The Importance of Weight*

One major factor in the cost of obtaining raw materials and shipping finished products is weight. The heavier an item, the higher the cost of transporting it. Copper ore is very heavy, but most of the ore is waste that is discarded in the refining process. Hence, transporting copper ore is expensive, but transporting refined copper is not. This is known as a **bulk-reducing industry**, a **weight-losing industry**, a **raw material-oriented industry**, or a **raw material-dependent industry**. In bulk-reducing industries, companies try to locate processing plants near the source of raw materials.

Products that are heaviest when finished are in a **bulk-gaining industry** or **weight-gaining industry**, a **market-oriented industry**, or a **market-dependent industry**. Consider soft drinks. The heaviest component of the product is water. Since water is widely available, companies try to add it as close to the market as possible, rather than pay to ship the weight of the water. For example, soft drinks are often sold to restaurants as thick syrup, and then water is added at the restaurant. In bulk-gaining industries, companies try to locate factories near the market.

## *The Importance of Energy*

The history of manufacturing demonstrates the importance of a source of power. The type of power influenced where factories were established:

- Water power was not mobile, so early mills and factories were located on streams and rivers.
- Coal could be transported, so companies had wider options about where to locate factories. However, coal is bulky and expensive to transport. It was so important to early manufacturing that industrial plants, even iron mills that relied on a bulky raw material such as iron ore, were still located near coalfields.
- With the development of electricity in the late 19th century, power became even more mobile. It could move through wires. Hence the location of energy sources became less important.

The aluminum industry is one type of industry that is still an **energy-oriented** or **energy-dependent industry**. Even though the aluminum industry requires raw materials such as minerals, the energy demands are so high that factories are built in close proximity to major sources of abundant, cheap power. China and Canada are major producers of aluminum, but Iceland's production is on the rise because it has abundant and cheap geothermal energy.

## Weber's Least Cost Model

Rather than simply studying each industry to see how companies located factories, Weber developed a general theory. He argued that factory owners balance three factors in deciding where to open a factory: transport costs (getting raw materials to a factory and getting finished products to the market), labor costs (the wages and salaries of employees), and **agglomeration economies** (the spatial grouping of businesses in order to share costs, as when several factories share the cost of building an access road to connect with a public highway). According to Weber's model, companies should minimize transport and labor cost and maximize agglomeration economies.

**The Locational Triangle** One way to show Weber's model is to use a **locational triangle**. In this situation, the market for a good is at one location and the resources needed to make the good are obtained at two other locations. These three points make up the points of a triangle.

As Weber realized, transportation costs are important to manufacturers. So whether a raw material loses weight during processing influences where a factory should be. If neither raw material used in production loses weight during processing, then the company gets no advantage from locating the factory near either location. The manufacturing could take place at the location of the market.

If only one raw material loses weight when processed, then the company can save money by moving production close to the location for that raw material. It does not need to pay the cost of shipping the full weight of the material when only part of it is needed.

In most cases, both raw materials lose weight as they are processed. When this happens, then the manufacturing site (D) will be somewhere between the locations of the two raw materials (A and B). The intermediate location will be closer to the one that loses the greater percentage of its weight. The finished product would then be shipped directly from the processing facility (D) to the market (M).

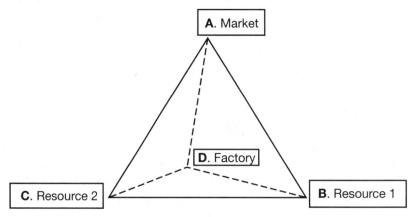

Sometimes the cost savings from either cheaper labor or from agglomeration economies could be greater than the savings derived from locating at the cheapest spot relative to transport costs. In these cases, Weber recognized that business owners should choose to locate where the cheaper labor or benefits from the agglomeration economies existed.

**Applying Weber's Theory** Models are simplified versions of a complex process. But they are very useful for making predictions, understanding how changes in one factor affect changes in other decisions. Applying a model usefully requires recognizing how it differs from reality.

| COMPARING WEBER'S THEORY AND REALITY | | |
|---|---|---|
| **Issue** | **Weber's Assumption** | **Real Conditions** |
| **Uniformity of Area** | The area considered is an **isotropic plain**, which means that human and physical geographic features are uniform throughout the entire area. | Isotropic plains rarely exist. Mountains, densely populated urban areas, and other features can alter the transport costs. |
| **Labor** | Sufficient labor is available in fixed locations and it is immobile. | Labor is relatively mobile. Automation reduces the need for labor. |
| **Raw Materials** | Raw materials are found only in certain fixed locations. | Raw materials are often available in many locations. The substitution principal may allow for alternative inputs. |
| **Number of Products and Markets** | There is one product produced, and it is for a single market in a fixed location. | Products are sold in more than one location. Globalization may result in numerous markets. |
| **Transportation Costs** | Transportation costs are directly related to the distance of travel and to the weight of the items. | Cost per mile mile may decrease as the distance increases. Space-time compression can reduce the overall cost of transportation. |
| **Influences on Location** | Economic factors dominate the decision about where to locate a factory. | Emotional factors, such as tradition, a desire to have the factory close to where the owner lives, or the existence of existing facilities can influence where a factory is opened. |
| **Significance of Costs** | Owners want to minimize costs. | Maximizing revenues and having predictable future costs is sometimes more important than minimizing costs. |

**Additional Models** Other geographers have used different assumptions than Weber did. For example, Weber emphasized minimizing costs while August

Losch argued that higher expenses for transportation, labor, or raw materials were justifiable if they resulted in higher profits.

Another model is Harold Hotelling's linear city model which explains the behavior of two competing shops. The classic example is that if two food vendors want to locate their carts on a beach, they should locate next to each other in order to split the market and maximize revenue and market share.

**Other Considerations and Factors** One refinement to Weber's theory, and to most theories, is that not all industries make decisions the same way. For example, the cost of raw materials is more influential for a steel plant than it is for a factory making high-end clothing. It is useful to think of a hierarchy of locational factors as shown in the chart below—the most important factors used to pick a general region or state and secondary factors used to narrow down the location to a particular county. Finally, another group of factors may be used to determine the exact site of the factory.

| FACTORS IN LOCATING A MANUFACTURING FACILITY | | |
|---|---|---|
| Scale | Example | Factors |
| Large | Region or state, such as northeastern United States | • Closeness to the market<br>• Closeness to raw materials<br>• Availability of adequate labor supply<br>• Quality of transportation network<br>• Adequate supply of power |
| Medium | City or neighborhood | • Level of taxes and subsidies<br>• Location of highways and on/off ramps<br>• Location of railway lines<br>• Availability of a skilled work force<br>• Quality of municipal police, fire, and other services<br>• Quality of education and recreational facilities for employees and their children |
| Small | Specific property | • Large and flat piece of land<br>• Adequate municipal water and sewer lines<br>• Highways and public transit routes |

Weber's model discussed labor but in a very simple way. It did not differentiate among different types of labor. But some industries require people with very specific skills. High-tech companies want people trained in the computer or engineering fields. Consequently, they often locate close to major training institutions, such as colleges or universities. These industries are known as **labor-oriented industries** or **labor-dependent industries**.

While geographers debate how to refine models such as Weber's and recognize the value of different assumptions, they recognize the value of models. They provide the most useful way to recognize patterns in making decisions. Most importantly, they help people make predictions. Weber's model and other models inspired by it remain valuable tools for understanding the spatial distribution of factories, offices, and all types of business that employ workers.

### Other Locational Issues

Weber's theory also addressed other issues. Because cars are considered a "bulk-gaining product," car assembly plants have traditionally been located close to where the greatest numbers of customers live. This remains true in the United States: most car assembly plants are located in the eastern third of the country. Older plants are centered in northern states—Michigan and Ohio. Newer plants, often owned by foreign car companies, are located farther south. These states are attractive to companies because they offer lower costs because of weaker labor unions, generous state incentives, and a growing population of consumers.

**Significance of Other Factories** In some cases, the location decision for a factory is dependent upon the location of other factories, a condition referred to as **locational interdependence**. Being near similar factories allows the businesses to make use of the same services, such as transportation firms or accounting firms that might specialize in servicing their industry. It also allows firms to keep an eye on their competition and to occasionally hire away talented young employees trained by someone else.

In addition, the finished product from one factory could be an input at another factory. In this case, it is somewhat of a market-dependent situation. For example, an auto assembly plant is the market for the output from an auto parts factory. Consequently, the location of the parts factory is very dependent upon the location of the assembly plants.

Auto assembly plants make use of **just-in-time delivery**, a system in which the inputs needed in the assembly process arrive at the assembly plant very close to when they are needed. Using this system reduces expensive storage costs and avoids tying up money in inventory—but at the risk of running short. It works only if a factory has confidence in its suppliers, its communications and transportation systems, and its ability to predict its need accurately. Suppliers also need to consider transportation costs and the time it takes to get their parts to the assembly plant.

**Significance of Government** Government policies can often influence location decisions. Many governments offer a variety of incentives to get companies to locate their factories in specific areas:

- At the international level, trade agreements such as NAFTA or the European Union can change the rules of how business is conducted and thereby change locational factors.
- At the national or regional level, governments hope to attract industries to encourage economic growth. Many businesses prefer to do business in the United States rather than in Russia because U.S. procedures are more predictable and transparent.
- At the local scale, communities commonly provide incentives such as tax breaks and low-interest loans to attract companies.

## Tertiary and Quaternary Considerations

For face-to-face retail businesses or services, such as a grocery store or a physical therapy center, being conveniently located close to a large customer base or market is crucial. However, if the retail business is virtual, then proximity to the customers is not especially important as long as there is an efficient and affordable delivery system available. Bookstores were once mostly small, intimate, neighborhood businesses. Most of these went out of business as they were replaced by outlets of large bookstore chains. Then many of these chain stores went out of business, replaced by online sellers.

**Flexible Locations** If the service is an informational type of service, such as a call center, there is far greater flexibility in locational requirements. An office can be set up anyplace with good communication systems. All the business needs to be successful is a group of trained people who can speak the language of their customers, computers, and good phone and Internet links.

Over the past two decades, hundreds of call centers serving U.S. customers have set up in rural areas of the United States, Canada, India, and the Philippines to take advantage of high unemployment and low wages. Towns and cities trying to generate economic development opportunities often recruit these types of businesses, since the locational demands are minimal. However, because of these minimal demands, these businesses are **footloose**, meaning they can pack up and leave for a new location quickly and easily.

**Prestige and Location** Sometimes companies have different locational needs for different parts of the business. A corporation might want its main office for its top executives to have a high profile to signal its power. So the company might choose a location on the upper floors of a large building in the downtown of a city. Such a location also allows the executives to easily interact with executives from other nearby business institutions. These types of spaces, known as **front offices**, are very expensive, and therefore businesses do not want to occupy more space than necessary.

A corporation might decide that the rest of its employees do not need to be in high-profile locations. They could be located in much cheaper office spaces, known as **back offices**. Since the back office workers are able to communicate with their customers and the head office through the computer and phone systems, they can be located anywhere these technologies are available.

Some companies move their back offices to other countries, a process known as **offshoring**. Companies will locate services in other countries if the costs of doing business are lower and worth the risk of moving some operations overseas. Many software and manufacturing companies in the United States and Europe locate facilities in India and China to take advantage of the highly skilled but lower-cost labor.

**Outsourcing** In order to lower costs or just focus on their core business, many companies outsource a variety of business functions. **Outsourcing** is contracting work out to noncompany employees or other companies. The contracting company might be less expensive because it specializes in the work and does it more efficiently or because it hires workers for lower wages or benefits. Companies often outsource work on their taxes and payroll.

Sometimes companies will both offshore and outsource. An excellent example is how Boeing developed and built a new airplane, the 787 Dreamliner. The planes were designed by Boeing in Seattle, the nose section was outsourced to a company in Kansas, wing tips were made in South Korea by Korean Air, wings were assembled by Boeing in Canada, and final assembly was done by Boeing outside of Seattle. The final product demonstrated outsourcing, offshoring, globalization, and the international division of labor.

| EMPLOYMENT CHANGES FOR U.S. MULTINATIONAL COMPANIES | | |
|---|---|---|
| Industry | Change in Number of U.S.-Based Employees, 1999 to 2008 | Change in Foreign-Based Employees of U.S.-Based Corporations, 1999 to 2008 |
| Manufacturing | -1,938,000 | +243,000 |
| Nonmanufacturing | +35,000 | +2,115,000 |
| All Industries | -1,903,000 | +2,358,000 |

**Source:** Adapted from David Altig, "Is Offshoring Behind U.S. Employment's Current Problems?" Data from Bureau of Economic Analysis.

**GEOGRAPHIC PERSPECTIVES:** NEIGHBORHOODS FOR NEW CLASSES

Prior to the Industrial Revolution that began in the mid-18th century, most people in European societies were poor farmers who lived in rural communities. A few were wealthy nobles who lived on estates or in the centers of cities. With industrialization, the number of people who belonged to neither of these classes expanded dramatically.

## Middle Class

Many of the jobs that expanded, such as factory managers, business owners, and professionals, made people wealthier than farmers but not as wealthy as nobles. Hence the people in these expanding categories became known as the middle class. They lived and worked mostly in urban areas, but in widely scattered locations. Some could afford to live in the center of the city. Others lived in new areas built on the outskirts of an urban area. And some lived above their shops, wherever they were located. The spatial distribution of the middle class made building a sense of unity in the new class difficult.

## Working Class

The other type of job that greatly expanded in numbers was working in factories. People doing these jobs became known as the working class. They found housing in urban neighborhoods outside the central business districts. The spatial dimensions of their lives—toiling together in large groups in factories and living near each other in distinctive neighborhoods—created strong social bonds among them. These bonds led them to form labor unions, which gave them power to push for higher wages and better working conditions.

| KEY TERMS | | |
|---|---|---|
| Industrial Revolution | agglomeration economies | energy-oriented or energy-dependent industry |
| imperialism | isotropic plain | labor-oriented or labor-dependent industries |
| assembly line | least cost theory | |
| Fordism | locational triangle | locational interdependence |
| substitution principle | bulk-reducing industry or weight-losing industry or raw material-oriented or raw material-dependent industry | just-in-time delivery |
| post-Fordism | | footloose |
| primary sector | | front offices |
| secondary sector | | back offices |
| tertiary sector | bulk-gaining industry or weight-gaining industry or market-oriented or market-dependent industry | offshoring |
| quaternary sector | | outsourcing |
| quinary sector | | |
| multiplier effect | | |

**Question 1 refers to the photo below.**

1. This image represents the concept of

   (A) an agglomeration economy

   (B) outsourcing

   (C) the primary sector

   (D) just-in-time delivery

   (E) the substitution principle

2. The shift of manufacturing within the United States to the South can be explained by all of the following traits of the South EXCEPT

   (A) lower wages

   (B) increased population

   (C) more government regulations

   (D) more land available for development

   (E) greater accessibility to numerous highways

**3.** Which is the best example of a footloose activity?

(A) a steel mill

(B) an auto assembly plant

(C) a university

(D) a real estate office

(E) an aluminum smelter

**Question 4 refers to the following diagram.**

### IMPACT OF AUTO ASSEMBLY JOBS

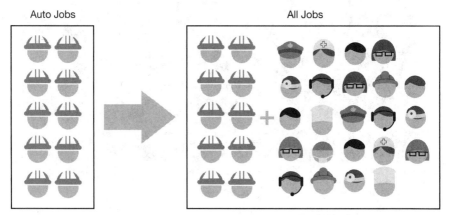

Source: Adapted from kcworkforce.com, based on data from EMSI and WANTED Analytics.

**4.** The diagram shows the concept of the

(A) add-on effect

(B) multiplier effect

(C) primary sector

(D) secondary sector

(E) substitution principle

**5.** Which person is more likely to work in a front office than a back office?

(A) a customer-service representative who handles phone calls

(B) the chief executive for a large corporation

(C) an assembly worker in the auto industry

(D) an accountant who handles a company's payroll

(E) a writer who works on marketing materials

**6.** Silicon Valley in Northern California is famous as the home to many businesses that produce high-tech products or serve high-tech companies. This demonstrates the principle of

(A) outsourcing

(B) post-Fordism

(C) market dependence

(D) back office processing

(E) agglomeration economies

**7.** Fishing, farming, forestry, and mining are considered part of which economic sector?

(A) primary

(B) secondary

(C) tertiary

(D) quaternary

(E) quinary

**Question 8 refers to the following diagram.**

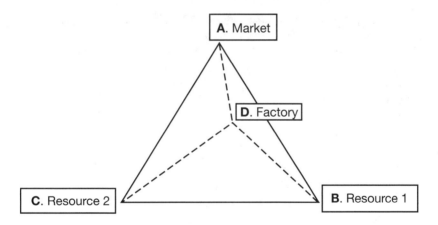

**8.** Which reason explains why, according to Weberian analysis, an automobile assembly plant is most likely to be located at an intermediate location approximately at D?

(A) Automobiles are a weight-gain industry made of multiple parts.

(B) Cars are expensive to import because of high tariffs.

(C) The weight-loss element of cars requires a location near a resource.

(D) Environmental regulations require cars to be assembled near cities.

(E) Labor costs are usually lower in high population areas.

1. Some segments of the U.S. technology industry heavily use offshoring for tasks such as programming and technology support.

   A. What does *offshoring* mean?

   B. Explain the relationship between the front office and the back office that exists in technology businesses that use offshoring.

   C. Give and explain three reasons why India might be a preferred destination for U.S. technology industry offshoring.

---

**THINK AS A GEOGRAPHER:** INDUSTRIAL GROWTH AT DIFFERENT SCALES

One way to understand the process of industrialization at different scales is to analyze the opening or closing of a factory. At the local, national, and global scales, starting up a new factory or shutting down an existing one will have economic, social, political, and environmental effects. The chart below lists some of these.

Make a list of the additional effects at the local, national, and global scales for the closing or opening of an aircraft factory.

| IMPACT OF AN AIRCRAFT FACTORY | | |
|---|---|---|
| **Event** | **Effect** | **Additional Effects** |
| **Aircraft Factory Closes** | Local: The amount of empty space in the community's industrial area increases. | 1. Local |
| | National: The federal government funds a program to retrain unemployed workers. | 2. National |
| | Global: The supply of aircraft decreases, which causes airplane prices to increase. | 3. Global |
| **Aircraft Factory Opens** | Local: The unemployment rate decreases and total income in the community increases. | 4. Local |
| | National: Total federal tax revenue increases. | 5. National |
| | Global: The supply of aircraft increases, which causes airplane prices to decrease. | 6. Global |

# 16

# Economic Interdependence

*Globalization, the increasing integration and interdependence of domestic and overseas markets, has three sides: the good side, the bad side, and the ugly side.*

—Panos Mourdoukoutas, "The Good, the Bad, and the Ugly Side of Globalization," *Forbes*, 2011

**Essential Question:** How has growing economic interdependence changed spatial relationships among people in the world?

Few, if any, places in the world are independent any longer. Vast improvements in transportation and communications over the past few decades have linked people throughout the world. The political, cultural, and economic processes of each region are linked with those of other regions, resulting in a degree of global interdependence not seen before. But, as Panos Mourdoukoutas indicated, not everyone has been pleased with the results.

## Trade and Interdependence

The Internet and worldwide TV coverage have increased what people can easily know about the resources and products available for trade in other regions. This, combined with improved transportation, has caused international trade to increase significantly.

### Complementarity and Comparative Advantage

Trade occurs when one party desires a good or service that it does not have or cannot produce as efficiently as someone else can, and another party has the desired good or service and is willing to part with it. Trade sometimes occurs through **barter**, a system of exchange in which no money changes hands. This is most common between individuals. In the movie *To Kill a Mockingbird*, the main character, a lawyer, provides legal services to a poor farmer in exchange for bags of food. However, trade usually occurs with an exchange of money or credit.

Parties tend to trade goods or services in which each has a comparative advantage in producing. For example, climate and soil give farmers in Florida an advantage over farmers in Maine in growing oranges. But Maine farmers have an advantage in growing potatoes.

Trade between parties is even more attractive when **complementarity** exists—when both parties have goods or services that the other party desires. Sometimes complementarity does not exist, and the trade is heavily weighted in one direction. For example, the United States wants far more products made in China than China wants products made in the United States. This can create tension. In particular, the country with the trade deficit might see the relationship as favoring the other side.

### International Trade and Trading Blocs

Globalization has resulted in increased international trade. Larger and faster ships, improvements to major canals such as the Panama and Suez Canals, new port facilities capable of handling larger ships, and increases in air cargo all made the transport of goods faster and less expensive. In the United States, trade increased from 5 percent of the total economy in 1960 to 13 percent in 2015. In China, over this period, it went from 4 percent to 22 percent.

Because of the increasing importance of trade, countries have strengthened their relationships with their most important trading partners. This has resulted in the formation of **trading blocs**, groups of countries that agree to a common set of trade rules. One of these is the North American Free Trade Agreement (NAFTA) between Canada, the United States, and Mexico, which took effect in 1994.

These agreements encourage and ease trade restrictions. The creation of the European Union (EU) has also allowed for the easy movement of goods among the member states. Members of these supranational organizations have much greater access to each other's markets. Not only can goods move more easily between the member countries, but people, services, and capital can also usually move more easily among the member states than they could prior to the agreements.

### Manufacturing in NICs

One aspect of globalization has been that companies have moved industrial production from highly developed countries to developing countries. The speed of phone and Internet communications means that decision makers of transnational corporations can easily maintain contact with the management of new processing plants in the developing world. The ease of transportation results in frequent travel between the head offices and the factories in the **newly industrialized countries (NICs)**. The manufactured goods can also be easily shipped to markets in developed countries and the rest of the world.

### Consumption Patterns

As countries become more prosperous, citizens consume goods and services increasingly rapidly. Many of the consumers in these countries have a high level of disposable income and, consequently, purchase a great deal. Most residents of developing countries do not have the same level of disposable income and thus purchase only necessities. One of the wealthiest countries on Earth, the United States, consumes about one-fifth of all resources, although it includes only about one-twentieth of all people. Maps and charts of consumption, such as the one below, show the overwhelming significance of the developed world.

While the spatial pattern of consumption is strongly skewed towards the developed world, the environmental impact of the consumption is spread more broadly. Many natural resources used to manufacture goods are extracted and processed in the developing world and then consumed in the developed world. Consequently, problems with mining and manufacturing plague poor countries, but problems with use are more often found in wealthy countries.

Not only do citizens of developed countries consume many more resources on a daily basis than do citizens of developing countries, they also live considerably longer. As a result, over a person's lifetime, the imbalance in resource use is even larger than it seems at first glance. For example, at current rates of consumption, in its lifetime a baby born in the United States will consume more than 200 times the energy resources as will a baby born in Bangladesh.

### ENERGY CONSUMPTION AROUND THE WORLD

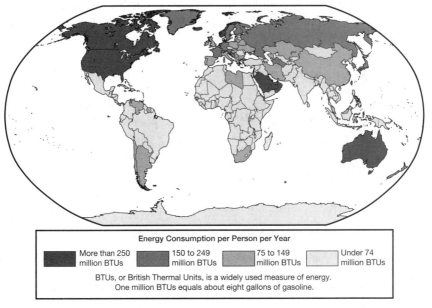

**Energy Consumption per Person per Year**

More than 250 million BTUs · 150 to 249 million BTUs · 75 to 149 million BTUs · Under 74 million BTUs

BTUs, or British Thermal Units, is a widely used measure of energy. One million BTUs equals about eight gallons of gasoline.

**Source:** World Bank, 2013.

## *The Impact of Global Financial Crises*

Increased interdependency links the economies of countries, for both better and worse. Growth in one country can result in new economic opportunities in other countries. For example, as China has gotten wealthier, it has purchased more grains and meat from U.S. farmers.

But an economic downturn in one country can lead to economic challenges elsewhere. When the price of oil dropped in mid-2014, consumers everywhere enjoyed lower gas prices, and manufacturers could produce goods at lower costs. However, economies in all oil-producing regions suffered. The effects were far-reaching and often acutely damaging:

- Oil companies lost revenue. For example, Royal Dutch Shell, based in the Netherlands, saw its earnings fall 80 percent from 2014 ($19 billion) to 2015 ($3.84 billion).
- Worldwide, about 250,000 workers lost their jobs. These included people in the field extracting oil but also workers for tanker firms or in ports around the world who were no longer needed by their companies.
- Governments in oil-dependent countries, such as Venezuela, lost tax revenue, forcing them to lay off public employees and reduce public services.
- Coal companies that could not compete with lower-cost oil reduced production, leading them to lay off workers.
- Energy industry investors saw significant losses as well. Share prices of energy companies plummeted alongside oil prices. In the second half of 2014, the 24 energy producers in the Fortune 500 lost a staggering $263 billion in market value.

# The Changing Global Economy

Over the past several decades, automation has reduced the need for labor in manufacturing industries. At the same time, the spatial distribution of manufacturing is shifting. At the global scale, many companies have moved manufacturing plants from highly developed countries such as the United States to less-developed countries such as Indonesia and Vietnam. At the regional scale, factories in the United States have moved from the Northeast and Midwest to the Southeast and Southwest.

## Outsourcing and Economic Restructuring

As part of globalization, **transnational corporations**, companies that operate in more than one country, have shifted manufacturing jobs away from the highly developed countries to the less-developed countries in order to increase profits. Corporations desire to pay lower wages—and a recognition that firms they compete with will also be attempting to pay lower wages—is an important factor. As a result, there is constant downward pressure on wages. Workers always face the possibility of losing their jobs to automation or to lower-wage workers in another country.

While workers may suffer from lower wages, consumers can benefit. When companies produce goods at lower cost, some of the savings might be passed along to consumers in the form of lower prices.

# MANUFACTURING COSTS IN SELECTED COUNTRIES

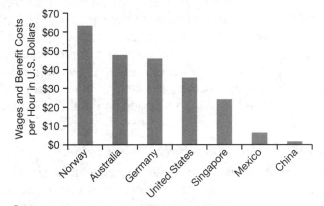

**Source:** Adapted from businessinsider.com. Data from 2012.

Companies may also save money by taking advantage of weaker laws protecting worker safety and the environment in newly industrializing countries, and they may receive government incentives such as tax breaks to relocate there. However, transportation costs are likely to increase because the main markets for manufactured products usually remain in wealthier countries. Globalization has created a **new international division of labor**, a system of employment in the various economic sectors spread throughout the world:

- Core countries such as the United States and Germany have rapidly increasing quaternary sectors that emphasize research and development.

- Middle income countries such as China, Mexico, and Indonesia usually manufacture goods that are developed in the highly developed countries.

- The least developed countries have large primary sectors and may export minerals and resources used in the production process.

Weak laws also affect non-industrial sectors. The Cayman Islands in the Caribbean Sea made itself a global center for the investment industry through its low taxes and lax regulation of this business. Other countries profit greatly through trade in cocaine, heroin, or other illegal drugs.

## Transnationals and Export Processing Zones

Many governments in the developing world offer incentives to attract manufacturing jobs. One common technique used in over 100 countries is the creation of **export processing zones** (EPZs). These are physical spaces within a country where special regulations benefit foreign-controlled businesses. These zones are known by different names in different countries: **maquiladoras** in Mexico, free zones in Dominican Republic, and special economic zones in China. They are often situated near international airports, seaports, or land borders from where the products can be exported easily.

One incentive that countries use in EPZs is tax breaks. Transnationals typically do not pay taxes on the machinery and raw materials they import into an EPZ as long as these items are used to make products for export. This regulation protects existing businesses that cater to the local market. For example, if a resident entrepreneur employs 20 people producing T-shirts to sell locally, the new T-shirt factory in the EPZ will not drive the resident owner out of business with cheaper products. The country hopes that existing jobs in the locally owned factory will remain in addition to the jobs added in the foreign-owned factory.

### Ethics and Societal Changes Related to EPZs

People disagree about whether EPZs are ethical. Critics charge that the transnationals are taking advantage of the workers and paying them a fraction of what they would pay workers in their home countries. Proponents of EPZs believe that the wages are reasonable for the region and thousands of people, mainly women, have access to paid employment at better wages than would otherwise be available to them. In addition, low wages keep the cost of items manufactured low, which allows lower-income people to purchase them.

EPZs and the employment of women in general can make significant changes on the status of women in their society. As women earn wages, they become less dependent upon men. As a result, women find that their concerns are more likely to be heard by their partners and governments. In addition, birth rates decline as more women gain employment.

# The Postindustrial Landscape

As the types of economic activities that exist in a region evolve, so does the economic landscape. Many wealthier countries now have a **postindustrial** economy, one that no longer employs large numbers of people in factories. Most people are providing services and processing information. The shift from an industrial to a postindustrial economy changes the landscape of a country.

### The Fate of Brownfields

The stereotyped image of a postindustrial landscape is one of deteriorating buildings surrounded by weeds and marked by broken or boarded-up windows and rusting metal. These sites of abandoned factories are known as **brownfields**. Because of the rusting metal, the region of the United States hit hardest by deindustrialization, the Northeast and lands around the Great Lakes, is often called the **Rust Belt**. In reality, old buildings are usually torn down, so brownfields are often empty.

However, if the factory building remains structurally solid, an entrepreneur might renovate it for a new use and keep enough of its exterior so that people know the building's history. People have converted old factories into apartments, restaurants, recreational facilities, and artisan boutiques. In central

Iowa, Grinnell College now has many of its offices in a building that once manufactured gloves.

If the factories have been torn down and the land cleaned of debris and pollution, the land might be converted to new uses such as a park, a housing development, or a shopping mall. If no memorial indicates the former use of the land, newcomers to the area might not realize the site was used for a factory.

In most communities that have experienced factory closures, the affected landscape includes far more than the former industrial site. Unless the community successfully replaced the lost manufacturing jobs, much of the community may show signs of decline. Because many people will have moved away from the area seeking employment and many of those who have stayed remain unemployed or have much lower-paying jobs, there are often many abandoned stores and homes. And as tax revenues shrink, public buildings and parks might also show signs of neglect.

## Corporate Parks and Campuses

It is not just the existence, removal, or repurposing of old factories that typifies a postindustrial landscape. New jobs that are created also help to shape the postindustrial landscape. As a result of this growth, office buildings and other commercial spaces are more likely to be evident on the landscape. Increasingly, these office buildings congregate in **corporate parks** or **business parks**.

| COMPARING CORPORATE AND INDUSTRIAL PARKS | | |
| --- | --- | --- |
| **Attribute** | **Corporate Parks** | **Industrial Parks** |
| **Size of Tract** | Large | Large |
| **Location** | Edges of communities where land is inexpensive and near residential areas | Edges of communities where land is inexpensive and near residential areas |
| **Buildings** | Low-rise office buildings | Large factories or warehouses |
| **Roads** | Designed for cars: small and can be curvy | Designed for trucks: wide and straight |
| **Grounds** | Park-like: spacious lawns, sidewalks, walking trails, sitting areas | Very functional |

Some very large corporations create their own corporate parks where they are the only tenant. Samsung has its headquarters, known as Samsung Digital City, in a park 13 miles south of Seoul, South Korea. The campus covers an area about equal to 40 city blocks. About 35,000 people work there, and it includes 135 buildings, of which four are large office towers. Other facilities include research laboratories, gymnasiums, swimming pools, medical offices, a heliport, daycare facilities, and housing for guests and visiting employees.

## Technopoles

Just as agglomeration economies can encourage the spatial grouping of manufacturing plants, the same principles can apply to technology companies. A **technopole** is a hub for information-based industry and high-tech manufacturing. It allows for benefits such as the possible sharing of certain services and attracting highly skilled workers to the area. Often these technopoles are located near universities well known for their computer, mathematics, engineering, science, and entrepreneurial business faculties:

- Silicon Valley, with the University of California, Berkeley, and Stanford University campuses nearby, is perhaps the most famous technopole.
- Harvard University and the Massachusetts Institute of Technology have acted as a catalyst for the development of the Route 128 high technology corridor near Boston.
- The Research Triangle in North Carolina developed because of three major research universities: Duke University, North Carolina State University, and the University of North Carolina, Chapel Hill.
- A smaller-scale technopole, the Technology Triangle near the University of Waterloo and the University of Guelph in Ontario, Canada, is a very important economic stimulus to much of southern Ontario.

**Economic Growth** Because of the economic stimulus associated with the technopoles, they can be called **growth poles** or **growth centers**. The concentration of high-value economic development in the growth pole attracts even more economic development. Once the process starts, the cumulative causation effect means it tends to feed upon itself. Each time new businesses are attracted to the growth pole, the "magnet" becomes even stronger and attracts still more businesses.

**Desired Side-Effects** Economic planners promoting a growth pole policy hope that it will have **spin-off benefits**, positive outcomes in addition to the main outcome. Spin-offs can help communities far beyond the growth pole itself. For example, farmers a hundred miles away from the pole should have expanded markets in which to sell their produce, resulting in increased sales and profits.

**Unwanted Side-Effects** The possible downsides of growth poles are the **backwash effects**. One of these is the loss of the highly educated young people from distant communities as they migrate to the growth pole for employment. As a result, the distant communities might suffer depopulation, loss of tax revenue, and the closure of various services. These changes can be detrimental for a community. This is an ongoing issue in many countries. In China, the impressive growth in prosperity for people in large urban areas in the eastern part of the country has pulled in people from rural areas in the west. One backwash effect of this has been that the rural western areas sometimes face a shortage of working age people and people to take care of elderly family members.

## Government Development Initiatives

Because of the desire for economic development, governments at all levels provide various incentives to encourage the expansion of existing economic activities or the creation of new ones. Depending upon the nature of the economic development and what level of government is supporting the development, the type of incentive may vary. In most cases, the government providing the incentives insists that the company receiving the incentive must achieve certain targets such as providing a certain number of full-time jobs. The common incentives used to stimulate economic development are described in the table below.

| GOVERNMENT EFFORTS TO PROMOTE ECONOMIC GROWTH | |
|---|---|
| **Type of Incentive** | **What Businesses Receive** |
| **Tax Breaks** | • A tax holiday (a temporary exemption from some taxes)<br>• A tax break for money invested in research and development |
| **Loans** | • Forgivable loans<br>• Money to borrow at below-normal interest rates |
| **Direct Assistance** | • The use of land or buildings free of charge<br>• Infrastructure such as roads and sewers paid for by government<br>• A subsidy for each full-time job created |
| **Changes in Regulations** | • Legislation that weakens unions<br>• Legislation that reduces environmental rules |

Throughout most of U.S. history, government efforts to promote economic growth have been controversial. In the nineteenth century, the debate over the proper role of government reflected strong regional differences. Compared to the states in the South, states in New England and the Midwest supported more active government:

- At a national scale, New England and the Midwest supported high tariffs to fund government construction of roads, canals, and harbors, and to subsidize construction of railroads.
- At the local scale, citizens of New England and the Midwest supported higher taxes to pay for local transportation projects and, most importantly, public schools.

The distribution of income draws the attention of many scholars—economists, historians, sociologists, and others. Geographers focus on how wealth and income are distributed through space.

### Africa and South America

While some African states have growing economies, average incomes remain low compared with most developed countries. South America has had uneven economic growth in the past two decades, often not enough to match its population growth.

### Asia

The largest income gains in recent decades have been in Asia. South Korea, Hong Kong, and Singapore have transformed themselves from lands of grinding poverty to lands of relative comfort in less than a century. However, the really big increases in the size of the middle class have occurred in two enormous countries: China and India.

### North America and Europe

North America and Europe have been relatively prosperous over the past century. However, middle-class incomes have stagnated in recent decades. As a result, income inequality, particularly in the United States, has increased.

### GDP BY CONTINENT, 2016

| Continent | GDP (in trillions of U.S. dollars) |
|---|---|
| ■ Asia | $24.3 |
| ■ North America | $21.7 |
| ■ Europe | $19.1 |
| ■ S. America | $3.6 |
| ■ Africa | $2.2 |
| ■ Oceania | $1.4 |

| KEY TERMS | | |
|---|---|---|
| barter | new international division of labor | corporate park or business park |
| complementarity | | |
| trading blocs | Export Processing Zone (EPZ) | technopoles |
| newly industrialized countries | maquiladoras | growth poles or growth centers |
| transnational corporations | postindustrial | spin-off benefits |
| | brownfields | backwash effects |
| | Rust Belt | |

**Question 1 refers to the chart below.**

EMPLOYMENT IN SELECTED EXPORT PROCESSING ZONES

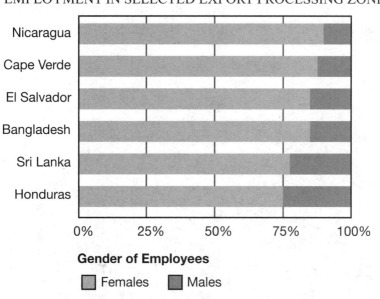

Source: International Labor Organization, 2007.

1. Which statement about the employment of men and women in EPZs is most clearly supported by the graph above?

   (A) Unemployment is probably an acute issue for men in these countries.

   (B) Women make up the vast majority of each country's secondary sector employees.

   (C) Men generally prefer to work in quaternary sector positions than in the positions found in these EPZs.

   (D) The governments of these countries will be more likely to listen to the concerns of the women.

   (E) Resource consumption by women working in EPZs will surpass that of men in these countries, causing great social change.

**2.** Silicon Valley is an example of a technopole because it

(A) takes its name from the material used to make microchips

(B) demonstrates the concept of agglomeration economies

(C) is a center for developing new ideas that generate growth

(D) has attracted new universities to locate in the region

(E) reuses brownfield sites that were once industrial factories

**Question 3 refers to the map below.**

**3.** Which statement best describes the darker shaded region in the above map?

(A) Growing prosperity in this region over the past several decades has had a spin-off effect on nearby regions.

(B) Industries in the region have a comparative advantage over ones in the South and Southwest regions in recent years.

(C) Brownfields are one sign of the economic recovery occurring in the region.

(D) The region is known as the Rust Belt because of the many closed factories in it.

(E) The region has always had a shortage of jobs in the secondary sector.

**4.** The EPZs found in Mexico are known as

(A) free zones

(B) special economic zones

(C) urban enterprise zones

(D) maquiladoras

(E) backwash regions

**5.** Which feature is typical of a postindustrial landscape?

(A) a corporate research park

(B) a modern dairy farm

(C) an offshore natural gas well

(D) an aluminum smelter

(E) a large manufacturing area near an urban core

**6.** Which is most responsible for deindustrialization in highly developed countries?

(A) easy capital financing available in developing countries

(B) low wages in developing countries

(C) labor shortages in developed countries

(D) the lack of strong unions in developed countries

(E) the shortage of raw materials in developed countries

**7.** The main benefit for countries that host Export Processing Zones is that these zones

(A) create thousands of relatively high-paying jobs for their citizens

(B) increase availability of manufactured products for their citizens

(C) attract thousands of foreign workers, which results in millions of extra dollars in tax revenue

(D) increase opportunities for the citizens to work for American companies and to learn English

(E) provide an efficient way to increase imports from the United States

**Question 8 refers to the photo below.**

8. Which phrase best describes what is shown in the photo?

   (A) an industrial landscape

   (B) an urban brownfield

   (C) an export processing zone (EPZ)

   (D) a transnational corporation

   (E) a maquiladora

### FREE-RESPONSE QUESTION

1. Changes in the spatial distribution of industrialization cause several changes in the landscape. Define each of the following terms and explain how they reflect economic changes to the landscape.

   A. brownfields

   B. corporate parks

   C. technopoles

Geographers study patterns of interaction among people who live in different places. One of these interactions is trade in goods and services. Many less-developed countries hope that trade will provide them an opportunity to create jobs and improve the lives of their citizens. The experience of the United States in economic development might provide a model for some countries to follow.

Use the graph showing average tariffs (taxes on imports) in the United States to answer the questions about the role of trade in economic development.

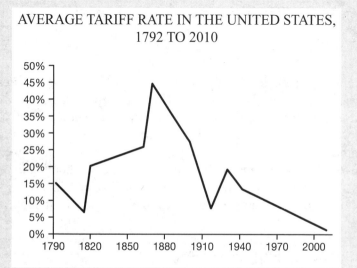

AVERAGE TARIFF RATE IN THE UNITED STATES, 1792 TO 2010

1. Describe the general level of tariff rates between 1792 and 1860.

2. How did tariff rates between 1860 and 1900 compare to earlier and later tariff rates?

3. What has been the trend in tariff rates since 1942?

4. How might some developing countries today use the experience of the United States to justify either high tariffs or low tariffs?

# 17

# Measures of Development

*A nation's growth depends, among other factors, on whether and how it educates and integrates its talent.*

—World Economic Forum, "Gender Parity." 2016

**Essential Question:** What does development mean, how can it be measured, and how can it be encouraged?

The opening quotation highlights a key issue in making progress: using the talents of all members of society. Until the past century, many countries have restricted the opportunities of minority ethnic groups and women to help develop society. Development includes both economic advances, such as creating new jobs and improving incomes for people, and other cultural changes, such as improving health care and providing schooling for everyone. Having measurable data regarding the level of development allows people to make comparisons to evaluate the success of development attempts in various regions.

## Measures of Development

Measurements of economic development focus on types of jobs, income, and economic output. In order to make the numbers from different countries comparable, the income and output figures are usually converted to U.S. dollars and stated as a certain amount of money **per capita**, which means "per person." Three common measures describe the total output of the country (each with slightly different technical meanings):

- **gross national product (GNP)** per capita
- **gross domestic product (GDP)** per capita
- **gross national income (GNI)** per capita

Other common measures used to measure wealth are sectoral (job) structure of the labor force, consumption per capita, income distribution, and energy use per capita.

Measures of social or human development indicate the quality of life that people experience in a country and the level of equity that exists. The most common measures cover variables such as birth rate, death rate, fertility rate, infant mortality rate, child mortality rate, life expectancy, literacy rate, caloric intake, gender inequality, school enrollment rate, and access to health care.

## Terms of Development

Development is a continuum that reflects the relative wealth and development of countries. People use various sets of terms to categorize countries on this continuum. The table below summarizes some of these sets.

| COMPARING NAMES FOR LEVELS OF DEVELOPMENT | | | |
|---|---|---|---|
| **System** | **Low End** | **Middle Range** | **High End** |
| **Economic Level** (based on GDP) | Low Income | Middle Income | High Income |
| **Economic Development** (focuses on economics) | Less Economically Developed Country (LEDC) | Emerging or Developing Economies | More Economically Developed Country (MEDC) |
| **Level of Industrialization** (based on amount of industry) | Non-Industrialized | Newly Industrialized Country (NIC) | Post Industrial Economy |
| **Human Development Index** (combines economic and social factors) | Low HDI | Medium HDI | High and Very High HDI |
| **World Systems Theory** (developed by Immanuel Wallerstein) | Periphery Country | Semiperiphery Country | Core Country |
| **Stages of Economic Growth** (developed by W. W. Rostow) | Stages 1+2 | Stage 3 | Stages 4+5 |

Please note that the stages used by Rostow in his analysis of economic growth are not the same as the stages in the Demographic Transition Model.

Since most wealthy countries are in North America and Europe, and most poor countries are in South America, sub-Saharan Africa, and southern Asia, some people divide the world into a more developed "North" and a less developed "South." The imaginary line separating the two regions is sometimes called the Brandt Line, named for Willy Brandt, a German politician interested in development. Australia and New Zealand are considered part of the North economically, even though they are geographically located far south.

## Measuring Economic Development

One way to measure economic development is by the sectoral distribution of the workforce. The least developed countries in the world have higher percentages of their labor force in the primary sector, while more developed countries have higher percentages in the tertiary sector.

A second way to measure economic development is by comparing either the annual incomes of people or the total accumulated wealth of people who live in various locations. This can be complicated by three problems:

- Countries have different currencies. This problem can be solved by converting all amounts to one currency, such as the U.S. dollar.
- The value of a currency changes over time. This problem can be solved by converting all amounts to their amount in a specific year.
- Prices vary from country to country. In 2016, the same collection of goods that cost $1,000 in the United States cost $590 in the Czech Republic, but $1,620 in Switzerland. This problem can be solved by converting amounts to their **purchasing power parity (PPP)**, which is based on what an amount of money will buy.

## Income Equality

The **Gini coefficient**, sometimes called the Gini index, measures the distribution of income within a population. The values range between 0 and 1. A 0 would mean everyone's income was the same. The higher the number, the higher the degree of income inequality. In general, developing countries have the highest income inequality. Highly developed countries, such as those in Western Europe, tend to have lower income inequality.

GINI COEFFICIENT BY COUNTRY

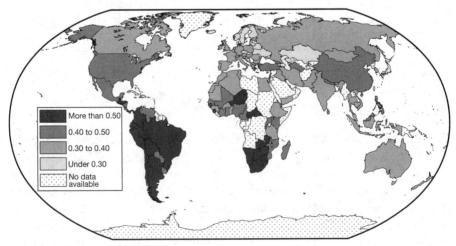

## Measuring Social Development

Noneconomic statistics that reflect a country's development status typically focus on the conditions in which people live. Life expectancy measures the number of years a person is anticipated to live. Since life expectancy is usually calculated from the time of birth, high infant and child mortality rates greatly affect it. A low life expectancy suggests that people in a society do not have adequate nutrition and health care, which indicates a low level of development.

Before the 19th century, people who survived to adulthood often lived until they were 50 or more years old. But because so many people died as infants or children, life expectancy in most of the world was under 40 years.

As a result of the dramatic declines in infant mortality over the past two centuries, and particularly in the past 50 years, life expectancy has increased substantially. In 2015, nearly 70 percent of the world's countries had a life expectancy above 70 years and 15 percent had a life expectancy of more than 80 years. However, there are still countries such as Angola, where more than one in ten babies dies before reaching a first birthday, and the life expectancy at birth is only 56 years.

Besides access to health care, access to education promotes a healthy population. Geographers use the literacy rate (the percent of population that can read and write usually at an 8th grade level) as another social measure. Literacy rates above 99 percent are common in highly developed countries, and according to UNESCO, more than 90 percent of the world population in 2015 was literate. This still leaves more than 730 million people who are not literate. Most are female, and most live in less developed countries.

## The Gender Gap

Differences in the privileges afforded to males and females in a culture are referred to as the **gender gap**. These differences might appear in educational opportunities, or in employment, wages, voting rights, health care, political empowerment, property rights, the ability to drive a car, inheritance rights, or the right to make contraception decisions. The size of the gender gap varies tremendously among countries based upon different aspects of society. Over the past decade, the gap in education and health care has been reduced. The gap in political empowerment and economic participation remains significant.

## Gender Inequality Index (GII)

One way to summarize the different opportunities open to males and females in a society is through the **Gender Inequality Index (GII)**, a composite index for measurement of gender disparity. The GII considers the reproductive health, empowerment, and labor market participation of women to determine a country's composite score. Maternal mortality rates and adolescent fertility rates are used as indicators of reproductive health. The indicators of empowerment are the share of government seats held by each sex and the proportion of adult females and males with at least some secondary education.

The labor market participation aspect of the index is indicated by the labor force participation rate of female and male populations aged 15 years and older.

The composite score is a measure of the percentage of potential human development lost due to gender inequality. For example, Guatemala has a composite score of 0.533 compared to Sweden's score of 0.055. This means that there is a 53.3 percent loss in potential human development due to gender inequality in Guatemala compared to only 5.5 percent in Sweden.

### The Human Development Index (HDI)

In 1990, a group of researchers led by Pakistani economist Mahbub ul Haq released an alternative measure of development, one that considers more than just income. The **Human Development Index (HDI)** combines one economic measure (GNI per capita) with several social measures, such as life expectancy and the average education level:

- The rankings of countries by HDI and income are often similar. Norway ranks 1st in HDI and 6th in income. The United States ranks 11th in HDI and 8th in income.

- Countries that invest heavily in education and medical care rank higher in HDI than in income. Ireland ranks 6th in HDI but only 22nd in income. Cuba ranks 67 in HDI but only 114th in income.

- Some countries that are rich in oil or other natural resources rank higher in income than in HDI. Qatar ranks first in the world in income, but only 32nd in HDI.

# Analyzing Spatial Patterns of Development

Regardless of the variables considered to classify the levels of development, certain spatial patterns emerge. North America, Europe, Australia, and Japan are more developed than most of Africa and parts of Asia and South America.

### Rostow's Stages of Economic Growth

In 1960, American economist Walt W. Rostow developed a **modernization model**, one that focuses on the shift from traditional to modern forms of society, called the **Stages of Economic Growth Model**. He assumed that all countries wanted to modernize, and that all would, though at different speeds. He saw economic development as a linear progression in which countries moved from one stage to the next until they reached the fifth and final stage—high mass consumption.

Like the Demographic Transition Model (DTM), the Stages of Economic Growth model is a generalization based upon how the United States and western Europe evolved, and both identify distinct stages. However, the DTM is a population model and Rostow's model is economic, so they differ fundamentally.

Rostow suggested that different ingredients and levels of investment were required to allow countries to move from one stage to the next. The model suggests a recipe for development: do this, then this, and eventually a country will become developed. There are key characteristics associated with each stage as outlined in the following chart.

| ROSTOW'S STAGES OF ECONOMIC GROWTH | | |
|---|---|---|
| **Stage** | **Characteristics** | **Examples** |
| **1. Traditional Society** | • Depends upon primary sector activities (farming, fishing, hunting) for subsistence<br>• Uses limited technology<br>• Carries out local or regional trading<br>• Enjoys limited socio-economic mobility | • English colonies in North America in the 17th century<br>• Medieval Europe<br>• No entire country is at this stage today |
| **2. Pre-Condition for Take-Off** | • Improves infrastructure (roads, electrical grid, water systems, etc.)<br>• Improves farming techniques and shifts toward commercial agriculture<br>• Exports agricultural and raw materials (international trade)<br>• Diffuses technology more widely<br>• Starts individual socio-economic mobility | • United States in the early 19th century<br>• Nigeria today<br>• Afghanistan today |
| **3. Take-Off** | • Open to major technological innovations<br>• Starts industrialization and primary sector begins to shrink<br>• Spreads entrepreneurial mentality<br>• Begins to urbanize<br>• Initiates self-sustaining growth | • United States, mid-19th century<br>• Japan, late 19th century<br>• Bangladesh today |
| **4. Drive to Maturity** | • Creates new industries while strengthening existing ones<br>• Improves energy, transportation, and communication systems<br>• Sees economic growth greater than population growth<br>• Invests in social infrastructure (schools, hospitals, etc.) | • United States, late 19th century<br>• Germany, early 20th century<br>• Brazil today |
| **5. High Mass Consumption** | • Spends money on nonessential goods (consumerism)<br>• Purchases of high order goods become common<br>• Desires to create an egalitarian society<br>• Supports a strong tertiary sector | • United States, early 1920s to present<br>• Japan, mid-1950s to present |

## Criticisms of Rostow's Model

Some of the criticisms of Rostow's model include:

- The model was based on American and European examples, so it did not fit countries of nonwestern cultures or noncapitalist countries.
- The model encouraged the exploitation of less developed countries (LDCs), and some LDCs could get trapped in a state of dependency with highly developed countries.
- The model suggested linear change, always in the direction of progress. However, LDCs often need the assistance, money, and technology of developed countries in order to develop. And in some cases, countries might regress in economic development.
- The model suggested all countries have the potential to develop, but there are significant differences among countries, such as the physical size, population, natural resources, relative location, political systems, and climate, which could affect their ability to develop.
- The model assumed that everyone could eventually lead a life of high mass consumption, but failed to consider sustainable development or the carrying capacity of the earth.
- The model failed to recognize that most of the countries that reached the stage of high mass consumption did so by exploiting the resources of lesser developed countries. Countries that were still developing would have difficulty finding other countries to exploit.

Despite these criticisms, the Stages of Economic Growth model continues to provide one way to view the changes countries have been going through over the past two centuries. Part of its value was that it prompted others to think about economic and social change in a global context, and it challenged them to provide their own framework.

### Wallerstein's World System Theory

In the 1970s, historian Immanuel Wallerstein proposed an alternative view to Rostow's on economic development, which he called the **World Systems Theory**. It is a **dependency model**, meaning that countries do not exist in isolation but are part of an intertwined world system in which all countries are dependent on each other. Because the World Systems Theory includes both political and economic elements, it is sometimes viewed as a political theory and sometimes as an economic theory.

Wallerstein divided countries into three types: core, semiperiphery, and periphery. As a result, his theory is sometimes referred to as the **Core-Periphery model**. The traits of each type of country are identified in the following chart.

| WALLERSTEIN'S WORLD SYSTEMS THEORY | | |
|---|---|---|
| **Category** | **Characteristics** | **Examples** |
| **Core** | • Includes the economically advantaged area of the world and the center of world businesses and finances; headquarters of most large multinational companies are located in core countries<br>• Focuses on higher skill, capital-intensive production<br>• Promotes capital accumulation<br>• Dominates periphery and semiperiphery economically and politically, and by paying low wages and exploiting weak environmental laws<br>• Benefits greatly from international trade | • United States<br>• United Kingdom<br>• Japan<br>• Australia<br>• Germany |
| **Semi-periphery** | • Includes the middle-income countries<br>• Sometimes known as the emerging economies<br>• Provides the core with manufactured goods and services that the core once provided for itself, but no longer does | • India<br>• Mexico<br>• South Africa<br>• Brazil<br>• China |
| **Periphery** | • Includes the least-developed countries<br>• Has a high percentage of jobs in low-skill, labor-intensive production and extraction of raw materials<br>• Provides the core and semiperiphery with inexpensive raw materials, labor, and agricultural production<br>• Receives jobs but few profits from manufacturing<br>• Often have weak laws protecting workers and the environment | • Afghanistan<br>• Zimbabwe<br>• Peru<br>• Kenya |

**Core Dominance** The core countries achieved their initial dominance through the industrial production of goods, which led to political control through colonization. As countries successfully won their political independence, the style of colonialism nearly vanished.

But core countries continued to maintain their supremacy by controlling the production of goods in countries in the semiperiphery and periphery. This new form of control, which relied on economic and cultural influence rather than political power, was called neocolonialism.

Private corporations worked closely with governments under both colonialism and neocolonialism. Large multinational companies, which are often headquartered in core countries, have had significant influence over the economies of periphery and semiperiphery countries.

**Changing Categories** Unlike Rostow's model, Wallerstein's model does not suggest that all countries can reach the highest level of development, nor does it explain how countries can improve their position. In contrast, it indicates that as a result of the nature of dependency, the world system will always include a combination of types of countries. But countries can change categories:

- In 1750, the British colonies in North America were part of the periphery. But by 1870, at least one former colony—which had become the United States—was part of the core.

- In 1900, Argentina was a core country. By 2000, it had become part of the semiperiphery.

- In the past few decades, the BRICS countries—Brazil, Russia, India, China, and South Africa—have challenged the dominance of the core countries. With new virtual and just-in-time business models transforming the world economy, predicting the change in economic power among countries is challenging.

## THE WORLD SYSTEM

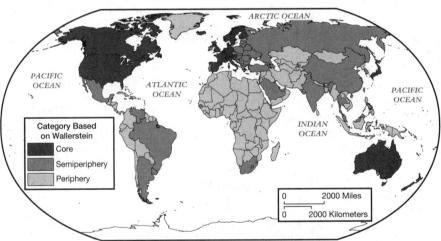

**Labor Trends** Wallerstein's model provides a framework for analyzing where sectors of workers in new international division of labor live and work:

- Peripheral countries are often where primary sector workers engaged in the extraction of raw materials are located.

- Semiperipheral countries are often home to many workers in the secondary sector (such as factory workers) and in the tertiary sector (such as call center staff).

- Core countries include most quinary and quaternary sector workers, such as the senior managers and research staffs of transnational companies.

**Systems Theory at the Country Scale** While Wallerstein built his model for a global scale, geographers apply the concepts of core, semiperiphery, and periphery to smaller scales, such as a country. In the United States, the core would be the major cities, such as New York and Chicago. The semiperiphery would be the manufacturing belt in the Midwest and parts of the South. The periphery would be the rural areas of the Great Plains and the West.

**Criticisms of World Systems Theory** The World Systems Theory has its detractors. Criticisms of Wallerstein's model include the following:

- It downplays the role of culture. For example, it focuses heavily on U.S. economic influence (investments and purchases of raw materials), but it pays little attention to the pervasive influence of U.S. culture (movies, music, and television).

- It is somewhat outdated. It was based on industrial production, but many countries are postindustrial. Core economies have transformed into high-tech, high-skilled tertiary economies.

- It is of limited practical use. It suggests that countries can change their status, but it does not explain how.

- It fails to recognize the role of nongovernmental organizations. It discusses countries, but not the role of influential UN agencies or private nonprofit charitable groups such as the ones in the chart below.

| TEN LEADING NGOS | | |
|---|---|---|
| **Name** | **Headquarters** | **Mission** |
| **Brac** | Bangladesh | Promote economic development |
| **Medicins Sans Frontieres** (Doctors without Borders) | Switzerland | Provide health care and respond to emergencies |
| **Skoll Foundation** | United States | Promote economic development |
| **Danish Refugee Council** | Denmark | Protect human rights |
| **Ashoka** | United States | Promote economic development |
| **Mercy Corps** | United States | Distribute humanitarian aid |
| **Oxfam** | United Kingdom | Overcome global poverty |
| **Handicap International** | United States | Support for people with disabilities |
| **Landesa** | United States | Promote rural development |
| **Acumen** | United States | Promote economic development |

**Source:** Adapted from NGO Advisor, "Top 20 NGOs in the World.," ngoadvisor.net.

# The UN Millennium Development Goals

In 2000, the UN identified the most challenging barriers to development, as well as eight key development goals. The result of this process was the UN Millennium Declaration, the keystone of a movement to concentrate on improving the lives of those living in countries with the lowest standards of human development. These goals, known as the Millennium Development Goals (MDGs), were created to assist in overcoming the barriers. The goals had 21 very specific targets and a series of measurable indicators for each target that would allow for evaluating the success of the program.

According to the Millennium Development Goals Report of 2015, the global efforts to achieve the goals produced the most successful anti-poverty program in history. By focusing very specific and globally accepted goals, countries cooperated to lift nearly one billion people out of extreme poverty, reduce hunger, and increase the number of girls attending school. Some details on these successes are provided in the chart below.

| UN MILLENNIUM DEVELOPMENT GOALS AND PROGRESS | |
|---|---|
| **Goal** | **Example of Progress** |
| 1. Eradicate extreme poverty and hunger | The number of people in extreme poverty fell from 1.7 billion to 0.8 billion. |
| 2. Achieve universal primary education | The number of children not in school fell from 100 million in 2000 to 57 million in 2015. |
| 3. Promote gender equality and empower women | Gender disparity in education was eliminated in developing regions overall. |
| 4. Reduce child mortality | The global mortality rate for children under the age of five dropped from 90 per 1,000 to 43 per 1,000 between 1990 and 2015. |
| 5. Improve maternal health | Maternal mortality was reduced by 45 percent since 1945. |
| 6. Combat HIV/AIDS, malaria, and other diseases | The number of projected new HIV cases was cut by 1.4 million between 2000 and 2013. |
| 7. Ensure environmental sustainability | Ozone-depleting chemicals have been almost totally eliminated since 1990. |
| 8. Develop a global partnership for development | Developed countries increased their development assistance by 66 percent, up to $135.2 billion since 2000. |

Despite the success in meeting the MDGs, many challenges remained. In 2016, the UN launched the 2030 Agenda for Sustainable Development. It established a new set of goals in order to tackle problems facing countries as they develop.

# Sustainable Development

In the list above, Goal 7 calls for "environmental sustainability." **Sustainable development** is any economic development that serves the current needs of people without making it harder for people in the future to live well. Concern for sustainable development is a modern problem. With mass consumption and increased population density, people place greater burdens on the environment.

### Resource Depletion

Development is not sustainable when people overuse resources. For example, if farmers grow crops in ways that cause extensive soil erosion, land that is fertile today will not be in the future, and food supplies will decrease. To protect the soil, many farmers have changed how they plow and plant.

### Environmental Degradation

Sustainable development also includes reducing air and water pollution, reducing waste through recycling and composting, and fighting climate change. Shifts in climate patterns can cause dramatic problems for people:

- If climates get warmer, diseases once confined to areas around the equator could spread and devastate new areas.
- If ocean levels rise, people along coasts could be forced to move or spend huge sums to hold back the water.
- If storms and droughts become more extreme, people with the fewest resources to move or to protect themselves will be at greatest risk.

### Ecotourism

One effort to promote sustainable development is **ecotourism**, tourism that attempts to protect local ecosystems and to educate visitors about them. For example, tourists who visit selected sites in Costa Rica's Cloud Forest, Botswana's wildlife habitats, and Australia's coral reefs might be charged a fee to fund maintenance of these special areas and to create sustainable jobs.

# Economic Development and Gender Equity

The status of females correlates to the level of development of a country. In general, higher status for females goes along with higher overall development.

### World Gender Equity Statistics

The Gender Inequality Index (GII) uses indicators such as reproductive health, empowerment, and the labor market participation of women to measure the percentage of potential human development lost due to gender inequality in different nations. GII scores can be very telling from a development point of view. For example, Switzerland, with a GII of 0.028 is highly developed, while Niger, with a GII of 0.713, is among the least developed countries in the world.

As an increasing number of females gain employment outside the home or the agricultural sector, the economy of a country improves. The link between the level of equity in maternal health and empowerment and the level of development is not as obvious, but nonetheless it exists. The better maternal health care that women experience, the more capable they are of contributing to the economy; and the more educated they are, the greater contribution they can make.

The chart below shows the countries with the highest and lowest GII scores. The spatial distribution is clear. Gender equality is most advanced in Europe, and least advanced in West Africa and Southwest Asia.

| GENDER INEQUALITY AND DEVELOPMENT, 2015 | | | |
|---|---|---|---|
| **Highest Equality Countries** | | **Highest Inequality Countries** | |
| *Country* | *GII* | *Country* | *GII* |
| **Slovenia** | 0.016 | **Cote d'Ivoire** | 0.679 |
| **Switzerland** | 0.028 | **Afghanistan** | 0.693 |
| **Germany** | 0.041 | **Chad** | 0.706 |
| **Denmark** | 0.048 | **Niger** | 0.713 |
| **Austria** | 0.053 | **Yemen** | 0.744 |

**Source:** UN Development Report.

## More Jobs and Low Pay for Women

The third Millennium Development Goal dealt specifically with gender equality and empowering women. Several programs enacted by governments and international non-profit agencies, known as **non-governmental organizations** (NGOs), helped women find jobs outside the home. As a result, employment opportunities for women have increased sharply in recent decades.

One reason for the expanded employment opportunities for women has been the efforts of transnational corporations. As these businesses have opened more factories in developing countries, they often employed women because they were available and because they would work for lower wages. Because of very low birth rates in countries such as Japan and Singapore, there would be severe labor shortages if women were not accepted as an integral part of the labor force.

Increased educational opportunities for females during the past two decades also prepared more women to work outside their homes. Globally, more than 250 million additional women joined the paid workforce between 2006 and 2015. Many of the women who previously had low-paying jobs began earning significantly more in manufacturing jobs.

Despite these significant increases in the number of women working and the wages of women, globally there remains a large wage gap between men and women, even when they are doing comparable work. In the United States, if a man and a woman do the same type of job, a man would typically make a salary that is 17.5 percent higher than a woman.

Another trend reflecting employment discrimination toward women is that women rarely obtain upper-level jobs in companies, particularly in developing countries. The situation has been improving in recent years in developed countries, but the glass ceiling remains.

## Microloans and Opportunities for Women

In recent years nongovernmental organizations (NGOs) such as the Grameen Bank, based in Bangladesh, have initiated **microcredit** or **microfinance** programs. These programs provide small loans to start or expand a business to entrepreneurs who would not normally qualify for credit from traditional sources. These loans have been particularly active in South Asia and South America. The vast majority of the entrepreneurs taking advantage of microcredit loans are women, many of whom are quite poor. While the idea of lending money to very poor people is unusual, the repayment rate is unusually high—more that 98 percent.

The success of microcredit programs has resulted in several changes to societies where the loans are available. The increased financial clout of women has given them more influence in their homes and communities. And as working women have more voice in child-bearing decisions, more money to pay for contraceptives, less time to raise children, and less need for additional children, birth rates have decreased. Women's increased wealth also allows for the children to be better nourished, which has helped to reduce child mortality.

---

**GEOGRAPHIC PERSPECTIVES:** ARGENTINA AND KOREA

The economic fortunes of Argentina and South Korea have been influenced by their physical locations as well as their roles within global trading networks. Argentina is situated along the Atlantic Coast of South America, so trade with the East Coast of the United States is convenient. Korea is between China and Japan, two large markets.

**Conditions in the Early 20th Century**

A century ago, Argentina was wealthy and Korea was poor. Argentina's income per worker made it one of the top ten economies in the world. Its industrial growth created significant pull factors, and migrants poured in from Europe, particularly Italy. Korea was a heavily agricultural country, and its income per worker ranked it toward the bottom quarter of all countries.

## Conditions Today

Currently, about 60 percent of the workers in each country are employed in the service sector. Beyond that, the economies differ greatly.

Argentina, like many countries in Latin America over the past half century, suffered periods of massive inflation, military dictatorships, and heavy foreign debt. These combined to severely limit overall economic growth. Today, Argentina is a semiperipheral state that relies heavily on agricultural exports such as beef, fruit, and grains.

In contrast, Korea, along with much of East Asia, has been one of the success stories of modern economic development. Through a combination of intense education, heavy government subsidies, tough trade restrictions, and strong corporations, Korea focused on making products it could export. The plan worked: today, Korea is a high-tech industrialized economy. Exports—mostly manufactured goods—account for nearly half of its GDP. Its levels of health, wealth, and education rank it as a core state, with about 2 percent of its population involved in primary activities and about 40 percent in secondary activities.

| KEY TERMS | | |
|---|---|---|
| per capita | gender gap | dependency model |
| gross national product (GNP) per capita | Gender Inequality Index (GII) | Core-Periphery model |
| gross domestic product (GDP) per capita | Human Development Index (HDI) | core |
| | | periphery |
| gross national income (GNI) per capita | W. W. Rostow | semiperiphery |
| | Stages of Economic Growth model | sustainable development |
| purchasing power parity (PPP) | modernization model | NGOs |
| Gini coefficient or Gini index | Immanuel Wallerstein | microcredit or microfinance |
| | World Systems Theory | |

## MULTIPLE-CHOICE QUESTIONS

**Question 1 refers to the following graph.**

### GLOBAL GENDER GAP PERFORMANCE

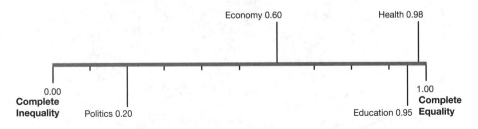

Source: Based on data from the World Economic Forum, "The Global Gender Gap Report 2015."

1. The two categories that have the largest degree of gender inequality are in the areas of
   (A) economy and education
   (B) health and education
   (C) economy and politics
   (D) education and politics
   (E) health and politics

2. Based upon Wallerstein's World Systems Theory, which of the following countries best fits the description of a peripheral country?
   (A) Brazil
   (B) Mali
   (C) Japan
   (D) Germany
   (E) China

3. Which question would most likely be studied using the Gini Index?
   (A) whether a country is moving closer to gender equality
   (B) whether religious traditions influence educational achievements
   (C) whether climate influences the infant mortality rate
   (D) whether push or pull factors are more influential on migration
   (E) whether the income distribution influences economic growth

**Question 4 refers to the map below.**

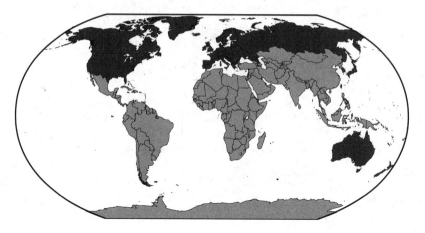

4. Which is the best description of the countries shown on the map in the darker shade?

   (A) semiperipheral countries

   (B) developing countries

   (C) core countries

   (D) least developed countries

   (E) periphery countries

5. Modernization models of economic development suggest that

   (A) there will always be a combination of more developed countries and less developed countries

   (B) industries will always try to locate to enable them to take advantage of agglomeration economies

   (C) geographic factors, such as the availability of natural resources, determine how a country develops

   (D) it is possible for all countries to reach a high level of economic development

   (E) governments should not provide stimulus for economic development

6. Which statement best demonstrates why purchasing power parity is useful in comparing income and wealth in various countries?

   (A) The euro is worth about $1.05.

   (B) A pair of blue jeans that cost $27 in Pakistan cost $40 in Laos.

   (C) Inflation is 2 percent higher in Indonesia than it is in Peru.

   (D) Unemployment is 2 percent higher in Israel than it is in Japan.

   (E) Germany's national debt is twice as high as Panama's.

7. All are stages of Rostow's Stages of Economic Growth model **except**

    (A) pre-condition for take-off

    (B) drive to maturity

    (C) high mass consumption

    (D) late expanding

    (E) traditional society

**Question 8 refers to the graph below.**

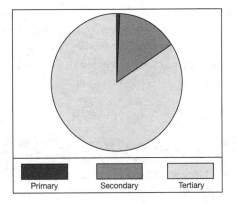

8. The country shown in the pie graph is probably a

    (A) developed country

    (B) less developed country

    (C) emerging economy

    (D) semiperipheral country

    (E) developing country

## FREE-RESPONSE QUESTION

1. Two models of economic development are Wallerstein's World Systems and Rostow's Stages of Economic Growth.

    A. What does each model suggest about the possibility of all countries achieving a high level of development?

    B. Explain how colonialism helps explain the historical and political aspects of Wallerstein's model, while neocolonialism helps explain its contemporary economic development aspects.

    C. In the past 20 years, development has affected gender equality. Discuss a positive impact of development for women and a challenge that women still face relative to gender equality.

The Human Development Index illustrates the level of development of countries using both economic and social measures. Immanuel Wallerstein asserted that the inter-regional interaction between economically developed (**core**) countries and economically developing (periphery) countries was dynamic and was the primary influence on the global economy. Wallerstein believed the core countries had more disposable income to invest in new technologies and higher skilled labor, while peripheral countries provided more low-skill, labor-intensive labor.

Critics of Wallerstein's World Systems Theory argue that core countries develop political policies that essentially create a relationship between the core and periphery that locks peripheral countries into being dependent on the core countries. Some argue this dependency is neocolonialism in the late 20th and early 21st century.

Use the data in the chart to answer the questions below it.

| HDI DATA FOR SELECTED COUNTRIES, 2015 | | | |
| --- | --- | --- | --- |
| Country | Life Expectancy at Birth | Expected Years of Schooling at Birth | Income per Capita |
| Japan | 83.5 | 15.3 | $36,927 |
| United States | 79.1 | 16.5 | $52,946 |
| Brazil | 74.5 | 15.2 | $15,175 |
| Bangladesh | 71.6 | 10.0 | $3,191 |
| India | 68.0 | 11.7 | $5,497 |
| Haiti | 62.8 | 8.7 | $1,668 |
| Nigeria | 52.8 | 9.0 | $5,341 |

**Source:** United Nations Development Programme, Human Development Reports.

1. Using the data above, which countries demonstrate characteristics more closely aligned to being a part of the global economic core?

2. Identify one of the countries in the chart above that would be considered in the global economic periphery.

3. Explain what the country that is in the periphery could do to become more economically developed.

4. Explain where Brazil fits into Wallerstein's World Systems Theory. Identify evidence from the data that supports this view of Brazil.

# UNIT 6: Review

## WRITE AS A GEOGRAPHER: GIVE FULL EXPLANATIONS

Answers to free-response questions can be very basic—or they can be fully explained for additional credit on an exam. Consider the question, Why did Chicago develop where it did? The basic answer is that Chicago grew into a major city because it was located where two water transportation networks come together—the Great Lakes and the Mississippi River system. This is correct but basic. A fuller explanation would include claims that explain the context and the details to give significance to these basic facts. It would explain:

- the importance of water travel in the 1800s
- the wealth of food—wheat, corn, beef, and pork—produced in the Midwest
- the increasing demand in the East and Europe for food as industrial cities grew
- the increasing demand in the Midwest for manufactured goods produced in the East

*For each question, write a basic answer in one or two sentences. Then list three additional points that would provide a fuller explanation.*

1. Explain why purchasing power parity is a more useful refinement of gross national income.

2. Which criticisms of Rostow's Stages of Economic Growth model could also be made against Wallerstein's World Systems Theory?

3. What are the costs and benefits of sustainable growth?

## REFLECT ON THE CHAPTER ESSENTIAL QUESTIONS

*Write a one- to three-paragraph answer to each question.*

1. How did the diffusion of industrialism affect people around the world?

2. How has growing economic interdependence changed spatial relationships among people in the world?

3. What does development mean, how can it be measured, and how can it be encouraged?

# UNIT 7: Cities and Urban Land Use

## Unit Overview

Cities and the suburbs around them are constantly changing—in how they are laid out, how they work, and how large they are. One of the most basic questions geographers study is why people move into or out of various parts of urban areas.

### Models of Urban Areas

Geographers create models to show the distribution and size of cities. They identify patterns that help explain why cities grow to various sizes and how people in different cities are connected to each other. Other models help geographers analyze how cities are organized and develop. Cities generally have zones for commerce, housing, and other functions.

### Urban Landscapes and Urban Challenges

People express their attitudes and values through the landscapes they build and how they organize social spaces. The choices people make, such as how closely to live next to other people and where to build an airport or how much to plan for the future, all reflect what they consider important.

Large concentrations of people can produce both great opportunities for progress and great challenges. Some challenges result from decline, such as the movement of industry out of cities. Others result from sustainability, such as how to keep air and water clean.

---

### Enduring Understandings

**VII.**  Cities and Urban Land Use

  **A.** The form, function, and size of urban settlements are constantly changing.

  **B.** Models help to understand the distribution and size of cities.

  **C.** Models of internal city structure and urban development provide a framework for urban analysis.

  **D.** Built landscapes and social space reflect the attitudes and values of a population.

  **E.** Urban areas face economic, social, political, cultural, and environmental challenges.

**Source:** *CollegeBoard AP®. Human Geography Course Description. 2015.*

---

**18**

# Urban Location Theory and Interaction

*Cities are extremely local and intimate places...*
*At the same time they are the product of complex*
*interactions with other places near and far away.*
—David Lanegran, *The Introductory Reader in Human Geography*

**Essential Question:** In what ways do geographers study and understand the growth and importance of cities?

The permanently inhabited portion of the earth's surface—what the classical Greeks called the **ecumene**—is a bewildering variety of types of communities with a range of population densities. To analyze complex situations, geographers create a model, a set of assumptions that reflect the world but simplify it enough so they can study it. The model for the ecumene includes:

- **Urban** areas (cities) with high concentrations of people.
- **Suburbs** that are primarily residential areas near cities.
- **Rural** areas (farms and villages) with low concentrations of people.

## Factors Driving Urbanization and Suburbanization

A **settlement** is a place with a permanent human population. The first agricultural settlements appeared around 12,000 years ago. Before that, people survived by hunting and gathering, so they lived in temporary or movable shelters. The first permanent settlements were small enough that the inhabitants could all farm and subsist on the surrounding fields. Over time, in several places around the world, small agricultural settlements began to develop characteristics that made them the first true urban settlements, or cities. These characteristics included:

- the presence of an agricultural surplus
- the rise of social stratification and a leadership class or urban elite
- the beginning of job specialization

A surplus of food became available as irrigation, farming, and domestication of animals and plants developed. These changes enabled increasing numbers of people to live in the same location. A ruling class emerged to control the products that were accumulating and the people living in the community. Because not everyone was needed to produce food, some people could specialize in making things, such as tools, weapons, and art. Others specialized as accountants or religious leaders—the first members of a service sector.

## Urbanization

The process of developing towns and cities is known as **urbanization**, an ongoing process that does not end once a city is formed. Urbanization also involves the causes of and effects on existing cities that are growing ever larger. Describing a region as urbanized indicates that cities are present there. A common statistic associated with regions, countries, and even continents is **percent urban**, an indicator of the proportion of the population that lives in cities and towns as compared to those that live in rural areas.

Urbanization is one of the most important phenomena of the 19th and 20th centuries, and geographers continue to study its development through the 21st century. Today more than 50 percent of the world's population lives in cities, and demographers estimate that by the year 2030, 60 percent will live in cities. Most of those people will be in the less developed countries (LDCs) of the world's periphery and semiperiphery. While urbanization can be positive for both individuals and societies, the challenges can be overwhelming if cities are not prepared to grow or urbanization occurs too rapidly.

## Suburbanization

A suburb is a largely residential area adjacent to an urban area. **Suburbanization** involves the process of people moving, usually from cities, to residential areas on the outskirts of cities. There they form communities that are connected to the city for jobs and services. However, they are often less densely populated and less ethnically diverse than cities.

### Causes of Suburbanization

Several causes contributed to the growing suburbanization in North America after World War II. Among these were economic expansion, greater purchasing power for many families, the growth of a car-centered lifestyle, and the government's construction of a vast system of new highways, which allowed workers to commute from their city jobs to suburban homes. In the United States, the Federal Housing Administration provided mortgage loans for families to move to the suburbs, which were newly zoned for single-family housing.

Racial tensions provided another impetus toward suburban growth. As African Americans came to the North in search of jobs and better education, many white Americans moved to the suburbs in what became known as "white flight." Government investment in continued suburban growth, along with a lack of investment in inner cities, hastened both urban decline and suburban growth. Industries and jobs left the cities, and residents followed them. In addition, highways were sometimes built in locations that uprooted or divided existing urban communities.

### Shifting Trends

The process of suburbanization is one effect of urban growth. In the developed world, especially in North America, it has been the most prominent change in urban areas since the middle of the 20th century. In 1960, the U.S. population was roughly equally divided: about 60 million people lived in each of the three types of areas: urban, suburban, and rural. Since then, the rural population has dipped slightly and the urban population has increased a little. Just over half of Americans now describe where they live as suburban.

Suburbanization has affected rural areas by increasing population density, building homes and businesses on former farmlands, and adding new residents from urban backgrounds to communities. However, suburbanization itself is currently changing in North America, as some suburbanites return to live in the city in a process called **reurbanization**, while others move farther out into rural areas and work remotely, in a process known as **exurbanization**. When an established town near a very large city grows into a city independent of the larger one, it is called a **satellite city**.

POPULATION CHANGE IN NEW YORK CITY AND ITS SUBURBS

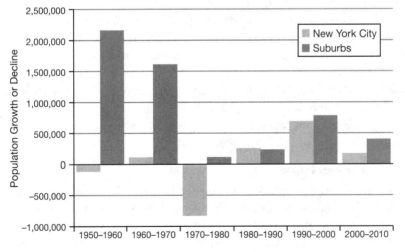

Source: Adapted from Wendell Cox, "The Accelerating Suburbanization of New York." New Geography, 2011.

The graph of city and suburban growth in New York illustrates the massive growth of suburbs after World War II as well as the later process of reurbanization.

# Influence of Site and Situation on Cities

The most prosperous of the earliest agricultural settlements grew into urban centers shortly after the Neolithic Revolution, about 10,000 B.C.E., as human groups began to grow crops and domesticate animals. The most successful of these settlements became the world's first **city-states**.

## Early City-States

City-states consisted of an urban center (the city) and its surrounding territory and agricultural villages. A city-state had its own political system and functioned independently from other city-states. The population in the surrounding villages and territory received services and protection from the urban center. Because of the wealth of these communities, they were often raided by other groups. As a result, defense was a primary consideration, and military leaders evolved into political rulers, known as kings.

Early city-states emerged in several locations around the globe in **urban hearths**, areas generally associated with river valleys in which seasonal floods and fertile soils aided the production of an agricultural surplus. These urban hearths included:

- the Tigris-Euphrates Valley (Mesopotamia) in modern Iraq
- the Nile River Valley and Nile Delta in modern Egypt
- the Indus River Valley in modern Pakistan
- the Huang-He floodplain in modern China

Urban centers also emerged in Mesoamerica (in modern Mexico) and in the Andean region of South America.

City-states eventually coalesced to form early states and empires. The ancient Babylonian Empire grew from the original city-state of Babylon. Examples of city-states through history include those of Classical Greece (Athens, Sparta, Corinth), those of the Middle Ages in Europe, and Venice and Italian city-states during the Renaissance. Monaco, a city-state located entirely within the boundaries of Italy, has endured to modern times. Vatican City and Singapore are also modern city-states, though they did not evolve from previous agricultural settlements.

## Centers for Services

As cities grew, more people developed specialized skills other than producing food. This changed the relationship between cities and the areas around them. City residents depended on farmers for food. In return, people in cities focused on supplying services for their inhabitants and the inhabitants of surrounding regions.

Early cities often specialized in particular services. Some emerged as administrative centers from which the elite ruled. Others, often associated with important shrines, became religious centers. Defensive strongholds, university towns, and centers of specialized production (located at resource sites) also emerged.

# Defining Cities

Most definitions of city describe a place in which there is a relative concentration of people. Cities are places where people come together to build a nucleated, or clustered, settlement.

## Legal Definition of a City

The easiest way to define a city is legally. A city is the territory inside officially recognized boundaries. This definition is useful for determining the precise population, for taxing residents, and for establishing and enforcing governing rules. Most large cities today, as defined legally, share boundaries with adjacent cities, yet those boundaries are visible only on a map. On the ground, a person leaving one city might have no idea they were entering a new (legal) city.

## Metropolitan Areas

A collection of adjacent cities across which population density is high and continuous is a **metropolitan area**, sometimes called a **metro area**. Most large cities in the world today are really metro areas of a series of legally defined cities, but they are referred to using only the name of the largest city. For example, the metro area of Denver, Colorado, consists of the cities of Denver, Aurora, Lakewood, Englewood, Greenwood Village, and other neighboring, legally defined cities.

In the United States the term **metropolitan statistical area** (MSA) is another way to define a city. An MSA consists of a city of at least 50,000 people, the county in which it is located, and adjacent counties that have a high degree of social and economic integration or connection with the urban core. Similarly, **micropolitan statistical areas** are cities of more than 10,000 inhabitants (but less than 50,000), the county in which they are located, and surrounding counties with a high degree of integration. Note that this designation is really one in which a city is defined as a **nodal region**, or focal point in a matrix of connections.

An urban area can also be described by its morphology, or physical characteristics, such as the buildings, streets, public places, and homes:

- The built-up area is where the landscape has a high concentration of people and things constructed by people.
- The places where built-up areas begin to give way to open spaces and underdeveloped areas are the outskirts of the city.
- This end of the continuously built-up area can be considered an urban border, whether or not it coincides with a legally defined city boundary.

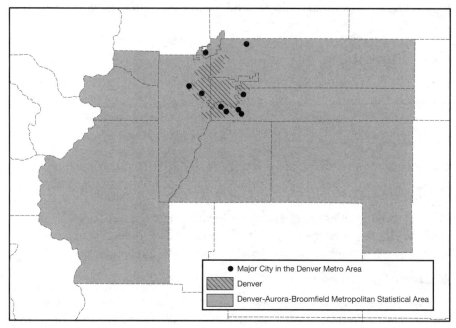

## Population Characteristics

A third way to define cities relies on social characteristics to distinguish urban areas. **Social heterogeneity** is particularly high in cities, meaning that the population of cities, as compared to other areas, contains a great variety of people. Diversity in cultural interests, sexual orientations, languages spoken, professional pursuits, and other characteristics are present in cities to a much larger degree than in small towns or rural areas.

One reason cities are diverse is because they are centers of immigration. In addition, because of the higher population density and the relative anonymity of cities, urban residents are generally more accustomed to diversity. The large size of the population of a city means that it is easier for individuals with less common cultures, interests, or ways of life to find others who share them.

# Transportation

Cities have grown in number and size as improvements in transportation have. Trains, buses, and cars have enabled people to move farther from the center of the city, but still visit or work in the city. Hence, the urban area expands. That change illustrates how **time-space compression**, in the form of transportation improvements, has led to urban growth. The development of the internet—to transport ideas rather than people—has allowed more and more people to work from home, which has further increased the distance people can live from the center of a city.

## Borchert's Model

Geographer John Borchert developed **Borchert's Model** to describe urban growth based on transportation technology. Each new form of technology produced a new system that changed how people moved themselves and goods in and between urban areas. He divided urban history into four periods, which he called epochs. Each epoch had profound effects on the form (shape), size, density, and spatial arrangement of cities. The epochs are shown in the table below.

| BORCHERT'S MODEL OF URBAN GROWTH | | |
|---|---|---|
| **Epoch** | **Time Period** | **Conditions and Effects** |
| **Sail-Wagon** | 1790–1830 | • Water ports became very important.<br>• Poor road conditions made long-distance travel between cities difficult. |
| **Iron Horse** | 1830–1870 | • Steam engines powered boats, which promoted the growth of river cities.<br>• Regional rail networks connected cities.<br>• Rail lines connected resources and industrial sites. |
| **Steel Rail** | 1870–1920 | • Transcontinental railways emerged.<br>• Cities emerged along rail lines in the interior of continents. |
| **Auto-Air-Amenity** | 1920–1970 | • Cars allowed cities to spread out.<br>• Airport hubs emerged.<br>• Cities became far more interconnected. |

While Borchert's model ended in 1970, it could be expanded. Since 1970, some cities have encouraged mass transit (rail lines), biking (separate bike lanes on roads and new bike paths), and walking (car-free areas in cities).

## Infrastructure

Changes in infrastructure within cities themselves also had important effects on the urban structure. The earliest urban centers were **pedestrian cities**, ones shaped by the distances people could walk. A horse-and-buggy era allowed for city size to increase as people could move farther from the center and its concentration of services and jobs. Streetcar systems encouraged the movement of the population even farther from the center of a city, and growth became concentrated along the lines of these small urban rail systems. **Streetcar suburbs**, communities that grew up along rail lines, emerged, often creating a pinwheel shaped city.

The advent of the automobile had profound effects on the growth of cities. Using cars and the highways built to facilitate their movement, the population of cities was able to spread out over ever-increasing distances from the urban core. The lower density suburbs that emerged around original cities developed as separate legal cities but functioned as part of the metropolitan area focused on the central, or original, city. Transportation methods thus had profound effects on the growth and shape of cities.

## Distribution and Interaction of Cities

Cities today range in size from just a few thousand people to ones such as Karachi, Pakistan that are over 20 million. Often a city exists in an **urban system**—an interdependent set of cities within a region. Models have emerged to help explain the distribution and interaction of these urban systems.

### Gravity Model

The **gravity model** states that places that are larger and closer together will have a greater interaction than places that are smaller and farther away from each other. This model can be used to predict the flow of workers, shoppers, vacationers, mail, migrants, and nearly any other flow between cities. It holds that there are greater flows to bigger cities and greater flows between nearer cities.

Interactions between cities are complicated by factors beyond size and distance, however. Cities such as Orlando, Florida, and Las Vegas, Nevada, are tourist destinations that attract far more visitors than their size and their distance from other cities alone could predict. Similarly, religious sites such as Jerusalem and Mecca, government centers such as Washington, D.C., and various cultural destinations distort effects predicted by the gravity model. However, the basic theory applies to most places.

### Rank-Size Rule

The **rank-size rule** describes one way in which the sizes of cities within a region may develop. It states that the nth largest city in any region will be 1/n the size of the largest city. That is, that the rank of a city within an urban system will predict the size of the city. For example, the third largest city in a system that exhibits the rank-size distribution would be approximately one-third the size of the largest city.

Geographers consider rank-size distributions to be characteristic of well-developed regions or countries. Such distributions are also more common in federal governments that typically share power with other levels of government. A rank-size distribution includes cities of all sizes in the system. This implies that there are cities with a wide variety of services available within the system, from very high order services in the largest cities to lower order ones in the smaller cities. As a general rule, geographers consider rank-size distribution to be one indicator of an urban system that can efficiently provide needed services to its population. Countries that demonstrate the rank-size rule include the United States, Canada, Australia, and India.

### Primate Cities

If the largest city in an urban system is more than twice as large as the next largest city, the largest city is said to have primacy, or be a **primate city**. A primate city is usually a social, political, or economic hub for the system, and it offers wider services than do the many smaller cities. Because services are more centralized, it is more typical of less developed countries and regions. In addition, countries that follow a unitary form of government or extremely strong central government often follow a primate city model.

The United Kingdom exhibits urban primacy. London is by far the largest city in the country. However, the relatively small size of the country, its unitary government, and its well-developed transportation infrastructure all reduce the need for a number of medium-sized cities and mid-level services. In the United Kingdom, people can get to London for services relatively easily. Northern Scotland is less than a two-hour flight from London.

Mexico illustrates a different model for a country with a primate city. Mexico City provides many services that are not as easily available to portions of the population. Across large portions of northern Mexico, people would have to travel great distances to receive even mid-level services due to the lack of medium-sized cities. Of course, population density is thin in these regions as well, illustrating that a simple knowledge of rank-size distribution or urban primacy is not enough to completely understand an urban system.

| TWO PRIMATE CITIES: LONDON AND MEXICO CITY | | |
|---|---|---|
| **Trait** | **United Kingdom** | **Mexico** |
| **Largest Urban Area** | London: 14.0 million | Mexico City: 21.2 million |
| **Second Largest Urban Area** | Manchester: 2.6 million | Guadalajara: 4.3 million |
| **Distance from Primate City to Farthest Edge of Country** | 675 miles | 1,750 miles |
| **Transportation Network** (buses, trains, planes) | Excellent | Poor |
| **Population Density** | 660 people/sq. mi. | 148 people/sq. mi. |

## Central Place Theory

Proposed by German geographer Walter Christaller in 1933, **central place theory** was developed to explain the distribution of cities of different sizes across a region. Christaller defined a **central place** as a location where people go to receive goods and services. It might be a tiny community, such as a hamlet, with only a convenience store, a post office, and a religious center. Or it might be a slightly larger village, or town, or small city with more stores and services. Or the central place might be a major city, where one can get direct air flights to other major cities, or obtain a heart transplant. In Christaller's model, each level, or size, of settlement would be evenly distributed across space.

## The Shape of Market Areas

A **market area** surrounds each central place, for which it provides goods and services and from which it draws population. Christaller chose to depict these market areas as **hexagonal hinterlands** because this shape was a compromise between a square (in which people living in the corners would be farther from the central place) and a circle (in which there would be overlapping areas of service). Nesting hexagons allowed for central places of different sizes to distribute themselves in a clean pattern across the region.

CHRISTALLER'S CENTRAL PLACE THEORY

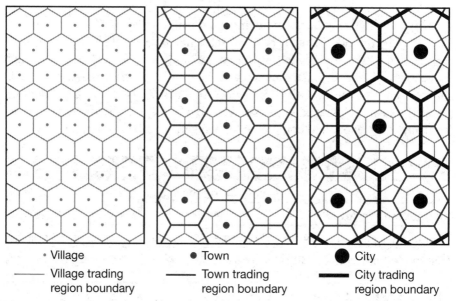

- Village
——— Village trading
region boundary

● Town
——— Town trading
region boundary

● City
——— City trading
region boundary

## Threshold and Range

What determines which services will be available in any central place? How far apart should central areas of the same population size be located? Central place theory uses the concepts of threshold and range to answer these questions.

**Threshold** is the size of population necessary for any particular service to exist and remain profitable. Services with a very low threshold, such as a convenience store or a gas station, are present even in very small central places. Restaurants, hospitals, high schools, and department stores have higher thresholds, so they require a larger population within the market area to survive economically. Only in the largest market areas can services appear that depend on the support of huge populations: stock market exchanges, major sports teams, symphony orchestras, and elite research centers. As cities grow in size, the number and variety of their services increase with the population.

**Range** is the distance people will travel to obtain specific goods or services. People will travel very far for high-order services such as wedding rings and heart transplants, but they are less likely to be willing to travel very far for basic services such as fast food or toothpaste. This helps explain why fast food restaurants can be found in nearly any town but a shop dealing in diamond jewelry would be found only in larger cities.

# Megacities

**Megacities** are the world's largest cities and typically have more than ten million people. These urban giants often exert an influence that is felt regionally and sometimes worldwide. This influence is due to the size of their populations but in other cases their influence is derived as much from their political, economic, and cultural power.

### Urbanization in the Developing World

Megacities were once found only at the centers of large empires or the most powerful countries. However, that pattern has changed. In the past century, a combination of high birth rates and rural-to-urban migration in less developed countries has made megacities more common in these countries than in the developed world. Of the 30 largest metropolitan areas in the world in 2015, about half were in semiperiphery or periphery countries:

- three were in Africa: Cairo, Lagos, Kinshasa
- five were in South Asia: Mumbai, Delhi, Kolkata, Dhaka, Karachi
- five were in South America: Sao Paulo, Buenos Aires, Rio de Janeiro, Lima, and Bogota

Megacities in relatively poor countries face the same challenges as megacities in wealthy countries, but without as many resources to respond. Social problems between ethnic groups, joblessness, lack of infrastructure, inadequate housing, and environmental problems, such as Mexico City's severe air pollution, are common in these megacities.

### World Cities

Cities such as New York, London, Tokyo, and Paris are **world cities**, or **global cities**, ones that exert influence far beyond their national boundaries. All are currently media hubs and financial centers with influential stock exchanges, banks, and corporate headquarters. Many are the headquarters of international organizations. For example, New York is home to the United Nations.

Some geographers also include cities that are powerful in a particular region as world cities. These include Dubai in the Middle East, Singapore in Southeast Asia, Shanghai in East Asia, and Sydney in the South Pacific.

## Megalopolis

The term **megalopolis** goes back to the early 1900s and describes a chain of connected cities. It became more common after 1961, when French geographer Jean Gottman used it to describe the continuously developed string of cities from Boston through New York and Philadelphia all the way to Baltimore and Washington, D.C. The "Bos-Wash Corridor" now includes nearly 50 million residents.

These cities had grown until they formed a single **conurbation**; they had essentially merged into a single, uninterrupted urban area. The cities crossed state boundaries and exceeded the definition of a metropolitan area, which is focused on a single, urban center. Gottman noted that, although legally the major cities remained separate, they and their suburbs had become a single region that had taken on some characteristics of a single, massive city.

Since that time, with urban growth occurring across the planet, other cities have combined into megalopolises. The corridor in California from San Diego through Los Angeles to San Francisco is a single, growing metropolitan corridor on the West Coast of the United States. Tokyo-Yokohama is a megalopolis in Japan.

---

**GEOGRAPHIC PERSPECTIVES:** THE PLANNED CITY OF BRASÍLIA

Built from the ground up in just four years, Brasília became Brazil's new capital city in 1960. The country's former capital, Rio de Janeiro, was more densely populated and more developed than the rest of Brazil, and located in the southeastern corner of the country. The Brazilian government sought to relieve the population pressure around Rio, and promote further development in its interior by locating its capital there. Brasília is an example of a forward-thrust capital, a seat of government built or relocated in a spot to promote development in a region of a country.

**A New Plan**

Brasília's contemporary architectural plan was reminiscent of the City Beautiful Movement, which highlighted grand monuments and attempted to promote a more cohesive society. The designers discarded the radiating streets and plazas, as well as other references to Brazil's traditional cultural landscape associated with its colonial past.

**Brasília Today**

While Brasília boasts impressive civic buildings and massive open spaces, critics say it lacks a sense of place because it has too few streets where people can walk and too few public spaces for people to congregate.

Brasília's utopian ideal physically embodied the country's developmental ambitions, as its original design was in the shape of an airplane. Initially designed to house half a million people, it has swelled to over 2.5 million, boosted by substantial internal migration. However, the originally designed central city mostly houses the rich and politically connected. Most of Brasília's residents live in satellite cities—reminiscent of Brazil's cultural urban past. Plazas and streets in these areas bustle with people and energy, while Brasília's core remains unfriendly for pedestrians. Brasília's story illustrates that while planned cities are nationally—and even globally—ambitious in design, their long-term layouts often revert back to the patterns people find comfortable.

## Cities Similar to Brasília

Brasília is just one of many examples of a city built to express a single, unified vision of how space in a city should be organized. In the 1700s, Russia's tsar, Peter the Great, replaced a small fort in the northwest of his empire with a new city, Saint Petersburg, that he hoped would increase trade between Russia and western Europe. In the 1940s, the United States wanted an isolated location in which to develop atomic weapons. It bought up land around the sparsely settled community of Los Alamos, New Mexico, and created an entirely new town.

| KEY TERMS | | |
|---|---|---|
| ecumene | metropolitan statistical area (MSA) | rank-size rule |
| urban | | primate city |
| rural | micropolitan statistical area | central place theory |
| suburb | | central place |
| settlement | nodal region | market area |
| urbanization | social heterogeneity | hexagonal hinterlands |
| percent urban | time-space compression | threshold |
| suburbanization | | range |
| reurbanization | Borchert's model | megacities |
| exurbinization | pedestrian cities | megalopolis |
| satellite city | streetcar suburbs | conurbation |
| city-states | urban system | world cities |
| urban hearths | gravity model | global cities |
| metropolitan area | | |
| metro area | | |

**Question 1 refers to the chart below.**

| BORCHERT'S MODEL OF URBAN GROWTH | | |
|---|---|---|
| **Epoch** | **Time Period** | **Conditions and effects** |
| **Sail-Wagon** | 1790–1830 | • Water ports became very important. <br> • Poor road conditions made long-distance travel between cities difficult. |
| **Iron Horse** | 1830–1870 | • Steam engines powered boats, which promoted the growth of river cities. <br> • Regional rail networks connected cities. <br> • Rail lines connected resources and industrial sites. |
| **Steel Rail** | 1870–1920 | • Transcontinental rail emerged. <br> • Cities emerged along rail lines in the interior of continents. |
| **Auto-Air-Amenity** | 1920–1970 | • Automobiles allowed great expansion of city size. <br> • Airport hubs expanded. <br> • Cities became far more interconnected. |

1. Which generalization does the chart above support?

   (A) Each new form of transportation technology slowed urban growth by leading to suburbanization, reurbanization, and exurbanization.

   (B) The United States government played a strong role in promoting new forms of transportation technology that spurred urban growth.

   (C) Each new form of transportation technology spurred urban growth by allowing more people to live and work in the central city.

   (D) Each new form of transportation technology spurred urban growth by producing a new system for moving people and goods.

   (E) Some new forms of transportation technology spurred urban growth and others slowed it down.

**2.** What is the meaning of "percent urban"?

(A) the population of people living in a city

(B) the ratio of people living in cities compared to rural areas

(C) the percent of people who work in cities

(D) the amount of land devoted to buildings versus green areas

(E) the number of cities in a given area

**3.** Monaco is an example of a modern city-state because it

(A) is a city and surrounding territory with its own independent government

(B) has survived for centuries in an important and ancient urban hearth

(C) has historical connections to the Italian city-states of the Renaissance

(D) is located entirely within the boundaries of the independent nation of Italy

(E) is a self-governing city that has never fully gained independence from Italy

**4.** Which statement most accurately describes the urban hearths where the first city-states developed?

(A) any urban center and its surrounding territory and fertile agricultural lands

(B) a location that was a service center, producing tools, dwellings, and weapons

(C) a river valley where floods and fertile soil aided production of an agricultural surplus

(D) a location where a city-state has endured to the present, such as Monaco and Vatican City

(E) a city-state in the Tigris-Euphrates Valley, Mesoamerica, or the Andes of South America

**5.** Which term most accurately describes a city with a population of approximately 60,500 in 2016 that was strongly integrated with its adjacent counties, socially and economically?

(A) metropolitan area

(B) metropolitan statistical area

(C) micropolitan statistical area

(D) primate city

(E) suburban area

**Question 6 refers to the following chart.**

| LARGEST CITIES IN OHIO | | |
|---|---|---|
| City | Population | Population (rounded) |
| Columbus | 787,033 | 800,000 |
| Cleveland | 396,815 | 400,000 |
| Cincinnati | 296,943 | 300,000 |
| Toledo | 287,208 | 300,000 |
| Akron | 199,110 | 200,000 |
| Dayton | 141,527 | 100,000 |
| Parma | 81,601 | 100,000 |
| Canton | 73,007 | 100,000 |

6. Which concept is most clearly demonstrated by the population information shown in the chart?

   (A) primate city
   (B) rank-size rule
   (C) central place theory
   (D) forward thrust capital
   (E) unitary state

7. Which feature would most distort the predictions of the gravity model of flow and interaction among urban areas?

   (A) St. Peter's Cathedral in New York City
   (B) the Mississippi River shore in St. Louis
   (C) Lake Michigan in Chicago
   (D) the state capital in Raleigh, North Carolina
   (E) Disney World in Orlando, Florida

8. Which best describes a typical megacity of the periphery?

   (A) an urban area facing numerous challenges, as rapid growth brings many social problems
   (B) a megalopolis that exerts international influence and power far beyond its boundaries
   (C) a world city with economic and cultural dominance over a wide area
   (D) a city with a concentration of global corporations and media hubs
   (E) a vast slum where housing, food, and services are hard to obtain

## MAJOR URBAN AREAS IN IOWA

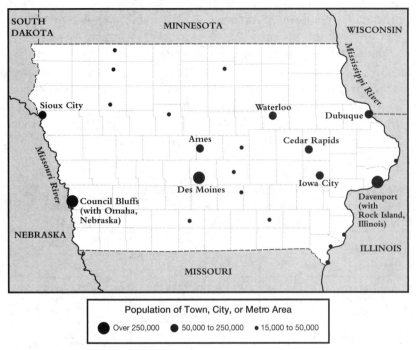

**Population of Town, City, or Metro Area**
● Over 250,000   ● 50,000 to 250,000   • 15,000 to 50,000

**1.** The distribution of villages, towns, and cities follows certain patterns that enable geographers to create models that predict the relative size of communities.

A. Explain the idea of central place theory and how the theory is shown by this map of Iowa.

B. Explain the terms *market area* and *central place* and how they further help people to understand the map and the real-life conditions in Iowa.

C. Explain the terms *threshold* and *range* and what they add to the understanding of the map. In your answer, explain why certain kinds of businesses might be located in some cities but not in others.

Comparing similar places, regions, or trends is one way to highlight significant elements in phenomena. For example, comparing the size of the largest cities on earth suggests patterns in urban developments. Over the past 12,000 years, the size of the largest cities in the world has generally increased. The first cities to reach a population of 100,000 were probably in Iraq around 2000 B.C.E. By the beginning of the Common Era, several cities were approaching or had passed 1,000,000. Sometime in the late 1800s, London probably exceeded 5 million residents. Today, nearly 30 urban areas, which include several neighboring cities, have more than 10,000,000 residents each.

| WORLD'S LARGEST METROPOLITAN STATISTICAL AREAS (MSA) | | |
|---|---|---|
| City | Entire MSA | Main City Alone |
| Tokyo, Japan | 37,833,000 | 8,968,000 |
| Delhi, India | 24,953,000 | 11,008,000 |
| Shanghai, China | 22,991,000 | 17,836,000 |
| Mexico City, Mexico | 20,843,000 | 8,873,000 |
| Sao Paulo, Brazil | 20,831,000 | 11,822,000 |
| Mumbai, India | 20,741,000 | 12,478,000 |
| Osaka, Japan | 20,123,000 | 8,860,000 |
| Beijing, China | 19,520,000 | 11,716,000 |
| New York, United States | 18,591,000 | 8,337,000 |
| Cairo, Egypt | 18,419,000 | 6,760,000 |

1. Based on the data for these ten MSAs, which region of the world has the most megacities?

2. How many of these cities are on seacoasts? (Use a map to check their location if necessary.) Explain why this might be significant.

3. Estimate the typical ratio between the relationship in size between the entire MSAs and the main cities alone. What factors of political or physical geography might explain the variations in ratios?

# 19

# Urban Land Use Models

*Like a piece of architecture, the city is a construction in space,*
*but one of vast scale.*

—Kevin Lynch, *The Image of the City*, 1960

**Essential Question:** How do geographers describe and analyze the structure and functions of cities?

Cities are enormously important and complex. Since the first cities emerged in human civilization, they have been centers of economic, political, and cultural power. They have been places of innovation. And they are growing faster today than ever before in history, a trend projected to continue.

Cities, as concentrations of humans and the human-created built environment, are a core component of human geography. They play a key role in the study of population, cultures, politics, economics, and even agriculture.

## Urban Models

Like most other models, the urban models used by geographers are based on observations of real places. Though models vary, all share certain characteristics:

- They classify and categorize land use in urban areas.
- They describe how various urban land uses are segregated spatially.
- They offer explanations for the location of different urban land uses.

### Urban Zones

One principle underlying all urban models is **functional zonation**, the idea that portions of an urban area—regions, or zones, within the city—have specific and distinct purposes. The various zones fit together like a puzzle to create the entirety of the city. However, unlike a puzzle, the pieces of a city are not clearly delineated, and geographers have tried to identify and classify them with models. The resulting urban models provide geographers with a framework to describe, understand, and analyze cities.

### The Central Business District

A vital part of any urban model is the **central business district**, or CBD, which is the commercial heart of a city. Often located near the physical center of a city, or the crossroads where the city was founded, the CBD is the focus of transportation and services. Just as the concept of bid rent explains agricultural land use, it helps explain land use in central business districts. The value of land in CBDs is often too high for uses other than commerce.

Competition for the limited space available in the CBD gives it certain identifiable characteristics:

- In some countries, including the United States and Canada, the CBD has skyscrapers and "underground cities" that might include facilities for parking, shopping, and rapid transit.

- In Europe, many CBDs are located in the historic heart of the city where buildings are lower but services are still concentrated.

- Because the cost of land is high in CBDs, manufacturing activities are rarely in them.

- Residential portions of CBDs are usually high-density housing, such as high-rise apartment buildings. The costs are too high and the space too limited for low-density housing.

The central business district of Chicago, Illinois

## Models of North American Cities

The first three models described in the following text are the "classic models" that were based on the city of Chicago. Located on prairie at the southern end of Lake Michigan, Chicago expanded to the north, west, and south without physical interruptions. This made the city a good place to examine urban structure without the complications caused by irregular topography.

## Concentric Zones

The **concentric zone model** describes a city as a series of rings that surrounds a central business district. The first ring surrounding the CBD is a **zone of transition** that includes industrial uses mixed with poorer quality housing. Manufacturing there can take advantage of proximity to the city-center workers and affordable land. Housing in this zone often consists of older, subdivided homes that result in high density. This model is also known as the **Burgess Model**, after sociologist E. W. Burgess who proposed it in the 1920s.

Burgess described three additional rings, all residential. As distance from the CBD increased, he noted a zone of working-class housing, followed by a ring of higher quality housing, and finally a zone of larger homes and lots in suburban areas on the edge of the city. With greater distance from the CBD, land became more plentiful and affordable, residences became larger and of higher quality, and population densities decreased. The suburbs of the 1920s were much closer to the CBD than are the suburbs of today.

## Sectors

In the 1930s, economist Homer Hoyt developed a different way of looking at cities—the **sector model**. While Burgess had seen rings of land use growing outward from CBD, Hoyt described how different types of land use and housing were all located near the CBD early in a city's history. Each grew outward as the city expanded, creating wedges, or sectors of land use, rather than rings.

**Hoyt's Model** describes sectors of land use for low-, medium-, and high-income housing. The model also notes a sector for transportation extending from the edge to the center of the city. This sector would contain rail, canal, and other major transport networks within it. The transportation sector would also favor an adjacent zone of manufacturing. The model places the sectors for the low-income, lower-quality housing next to these industrial and transportation zones, and it places high-income residences extending in a wedge away from these zones along wide tree-lined boulevards or on higher ground.

## Multiple Nuclei

Geographers **Chauncy Harris** and **Edward Ullman** developed the **multiple-nuclei model** by studying changes in cities in the 1940s. This model suggested that functional zonation occurred around multiple centers, or nodes. The characteristics of each node either attracted or repelled certain types of activities. The result was a city that consisted of a patchwork of land uses, each with its own center, or nucleus.

In the multiple-nuclei model, the CBD and related functions continued to exist but were joined by smaller business districts that emerged in the suburbs. A zone of industry could be in a variety of locations, including the traditional CBD or port, or it could move to new outlying locations near an airport or other

## URBAN LAND USE MODELS

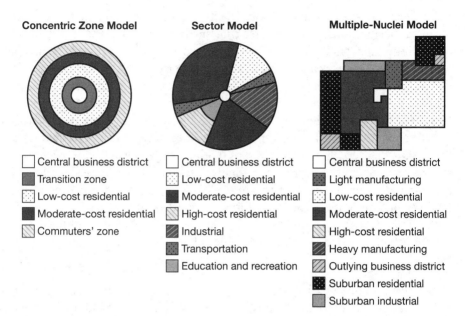

**Concentric Zone Model**

- ☐ Central business district
- ■ Transition zone
- ▨ Low-cost residential
- ■ Moderate-cost residential
- ▨ Commuters' zone

**Sector Model**

- ☐ Central business district
- ▨ Low-cost residential
- ■ Moderate-cost residential
- ▨ High-cost residential
- ▨ Industrial
- ▨ Transportation
- ▨ Education and recreation

**Multiple-Nuclei Model**

- ☐ Central business district
- ■ Light manufacturing
- ▨ Low-cost residential
- ■ Moderate-cost residential
- ▨ High-cost residential
- ▨ Heavy manufacturing
- ▨ Outlying business district
- ▨ Suburban residential
- ▨ Suburban industrial

transportation junction. This industrial zone would attract related industries and an area of higher density housing. A university or a business park might attract nearby restaurants, theaters, and other amenities. As a result, people might create a district of student housing or high-quality homes nearby.

The **peripheral model**, a variant of the multiple-nuclei model, describes suburban neighborhoods surrounding an inner city and served by nodes of commercial activity along a ring road or beltway. This model's name derives from the role of the service nodes with their related suburbs that develop on the periphery of the original city.

### Galactic Cities

Beginning in the 1950s, suburban growth in the United States skyrocketed as governments built highways that improved transportation in and out of cities and subsidized the purchase of houses. These developments and a close study of Detroit prompted Chauncy Harris to create the **galactic city model**, describing the spread of U.S. cities outward from the CBD to the suburbs, leaving a declining inner city. As suburbs grew, some of the functions of the CBD began to appear in them. At key locations along transportation routes, mini-downtowns of hotels, malls, restaurants, and office complexes emerged. Modern geographers have dubbed these nodes **edge cities**.

Edge cities are nodes of economic activity that have developed in the periphery of large cities. They usually have tall office buildings, a concentration of retail shops, relatively few residences, and are located at the junction of major transportation routes.

# World-Regional Models

Geographers have also developed models to describe cities outside of North America. Rings, sectors, and multiple-nuclei can be found in these models, along with some additional elements. But the models share the same basic characteristic of North American models, that of functional zonation.

## Latin American Cities

The **Griffen-Ford Model** is often used to describe Latin American cities. It places a two-part CBD at the center of the city: a traditional market center adjacent to a modern high-rise center. The most desirable housing in the city is located there, adjacent to the developed center of the city. This high-quality housing extends outward from the urban core, accompanied by a commercial **spine** of development. Theaters, restaurants, parks, and other amenities are also located along this spine, or corridor, which ends in a growing secondary center. In the model, this secondary center is identified as a **mall**.

In contrast to the concentric zone model in North America, as distance increases from the center of Latin American cities, the quality of housing decreases. Public transportation, the urban water supply, and access to electricity all decrease away from the center, sometimes disappearing altogether. The outer ring of the city, the **periférico,** is characterized by poverty, lack of infrastructure, and areas of poorly built housing known as **shantytowns**. Often, the residents of shantytowns are recent migrants to the city. The model notes the possible presence of an industrial node and, closer to the commercial spine, middle-class neighborhoods.

Many Latin American cities also contain **favelas**, or **barrios**, which are neighborhoods where extreme poverty, homelessness, and lawlessness are common. Most favelas are in **disamenity zones**, areas not connected to city services and under the control of drug lords and gangs. Disamenity zones are often in physically unsafe locations, such as on ravines or on steep, unstable mountain slopes.

Favelas in southeastern Brazil

## European Cities

Many of today's cities in Europe are descendants of medieval and pre-industrial cities. City walls, which had been built for protection before the wide use of gunpowder weapons, restrained growth. These cities grew very slowly for centuries, with little planning. The result is a dense mix of commercial and residential land use with narrow, winding streets. Distinct land-use zones are hard to find in the core areas of these cities. Later urban renovations cut through areas to produce elegant, wide boulevards with high-quality housing and shops.

Central business districts in Europe differ in important ways from those in North America. Attempting to preserve the historic character of their urban cores, city leaders have limited new construction and restricted the height of buildings. Often, former palace grounds have been transformed into large urban parks. European CBDs also have many more residents living in relatively low-rise apartment buildings. As a result of the larger population living downtown, commercial uses go beyond those in North America by including many more small businesses such as vegetable markets, bakeries, and butcher shops.

In contrast to North America, European suburbs are likely to have a higher percentage of taller buildings. Most are apartment buildings, so population densities are higher in Europe's suburbs than in North America's. International immigration creates ethnic diversity in the suburbs, and this diversity often reflects the colonial heritage of the country. For example, suburban London includes a large number of South Asians and their descendants, and suburban Paris includes many people of North African heritage.

| TALL BUILDINGS IN THE UNITED STATES AND EUROPE | | | | |
|---|---|---|---|---|
| City Population | Height of Tallest Building (in feet) | | Height of Tenth Tallest Building (in feet) | |
| | United States | Europe | United States | Europe |
| 2 million to 3 million | Chicago: 1,451 | Paris: 689 | Chicago: 850 | Paris: 574 |
| 3 million to 4 million | Los Angeles: 1,018 | Madrid: 817 | Los Angeles: 699 | Madrid: 377 |
| 8 million to 9 million | New York: 1,776 | London: 1,016 | New York: 952 | London: 590 |

## African Cities

Large cities were rare in most of Africa until the 19th century, when Europeans colonized the continent. But in recent decades, urban areas in Africa have grown rapidly. New cities have been built next to or on top of existing ones. These new cities can include several identifiable regions:

- The **traditional CBD**, which existed before European colonization, has small shops clustered along narrow, twisting streets. It includes the formal economy: permanent stores that hire workers with full-time jobs at set wages and that comply with local regulations.
- The **colonial CBD** has broad, straight avenues and large homes, parks, and administrative centers.
- The **informal economy zone** thrives with curbside, car-side, and stall-based businesses that often hire people temporarily and do not follow all regulations. This zone also includes **periodic markets**, where small-scale merchants congregate weekly or yearly, to sell their goods.
- A zone of mining and manufacturing also exists in many cities.
- Residential zones are often based on ethnicity. These mirror the multi-ethnic makeup of African countries.
- The periphery of cities often consists of **informal settlements**, densely populated areas built without coordinated planning and without sufficient public services for electricity, water, and sewage.

The growth of informal settlements often results from the rapid influx of migrants into cities who simply reside wherever they can find space, creating **squatter settlements**. One of the largest squatter settlements in the world is Kibera, on the western edge of Nairobi, Kenya. As do Latin American favelas, these communities face problems with drugs, crime, and disease.

### Middle Eastern and Islamic Cities

Cities shaped by the spread of Islam are common in the Middle East, North Africa, parts of Spain and East Africa, and a few locations in Southeast Asia. The dominant feature of these cities is a central mosque that includes one or more tall and highly visible minarets. The principal **mosque** in the center of an Islamic city is usually surrounded by a complex of structures to serve the public, such as schools for children and soup kitchens for the poor. As cities grew, additional mosques were added in outlying neighborhoods.

Many Islamic cities were built with a defensive **citadel**, a fort designed to protect the city, with its related palace and barracks for soldiers. Walls with gates and towers were typical in earlier times and they, or their remnants, still survive in many modern Islamic cities. Major roads run from the gates to the center, and along these roads are traditional outdoor markets or covered bazaars, called **suqs**. These markets often exhibit spatial differentiation with more expensive shops and luxury items

found near the center of town and bulkier, less valuable materials for sale near the wall and gates.

Residential neighborhoods often reflect the differences in ethnicity, tribe, or branch of Islam. The organization and architecture found in these neighborhoods often have three features:

- Streets and alleys are often twisting, and dead-end streets are common.
- Homes have central courtyards rather than yards in front or back.
- Windows are small and located above eye level.

The above features create shady areas, which suggests they might be cultural adaptations to the sun and heat of the Middle East. They also create privacy, which suggests that they express an important value within Islam.

### Southeast Asian Cities

The **McGee Model** describes the land use in many of the larger cities in Southeast Asia. The focus of the modern city is often a former colonial port zone. This export-oriented zone shares commercial uses similar to the CBD in North American cities. Additionally, these cities might include a government zone. If the city is a national or regional capital, it might have a commercial zone dominated by foreign merchants and ambassadors. A belt of market gardening surrounds and supplies the typical Southeast Asian city.

Cities of Southeast Asia have a history of Chinese immigration and commercial interest that dates back a few centuries. As a result of this immigration, many cities include a secondary commercial zone dominated by Chinese businesses. As the importance of industry in Southeast Asia has risen in the last few decades, industrial parks and regions of manufacturing have emerged on the peripheries of some cities.

## Local Regulations on Land Use

People want to use land in ways that can conflict. For example, most homeowners want a place that is quiet at night so they can sleep. However, a factory owner might want to continue production, which can be noisy, around the clock. To balance competing desires, cities and counties use **zoning ordinances**, regulations that define how property in specific geographic regions can be used. The three general zoning categories are residential (where people live), commercial (where people sell goods and services), and industrial (where people make things).

Municipal governments use zoning ordinances as a tool of **urban planning**, a process of promoting growth and controlling change in land use. Zoning laws can result in very clear land-use segregation. However, not all cities have zoning ordinances, and many include some unzoned areas.

## Residential Zones

Those areas of a city devoted to where people live rather than to commercial or industrial functions are **residential zones**. Ordinances for these zones often set limits on the density and size of houses in specific zones. For this reason, some residential neighborhoods contain only large homes on spacious lots, while other zones are composed of smaller homes on small lots, and still others contain apartment buildings.

Zoning can create various types of neighborhoods that appeal to people with various housing needs and lifestyles. However, it can also be used to prevent socioeconomic diversity or ethnic diversity in a neighborhood.

In North America, residential areas surrounding the CBD are known as the inner city. This residential zone has the highest population density and is dominated by apartment buildings and townhomes. As one moves farther from the inner city, population density declines along with the type and density of housing units. This variation is known as the **residential density gradient**.

Suburbs are often characterized by single-family detached houses. More than half of all Americans now live in suburbs. Many suburbs are noticeably homogenous in terms of housing size and style. However, in recent years, homeowners have been tearing down existing homes and building new ones that are much larger. These new homes, known as McMansions, do not always conform to the style of other homes in the neighborhood.

## Changes in Urban and Suburban Areas

Neighborhoods undergo transformations over time as existing residents move out and new ones move in. Through a process known as **filtering**, houses pass from one social group to another. This usually occurs as the wealthiest residents move to new homes and people with less wealth move into the homes they leave. This creates a ripple effect down the social scale. The filter process might include the changing use of a house. For example, a home built for a single family might be subdivided for use by two or more families or replaced with apartments.

Filtering can become most noticeable when a neighborhood that is an ethnic enclave changes from one group to another. The term **invasion and succession** refers to the process by which one social or ethic group gradually replaces another through filtering.

The rise of **gated communities** is another example of change in suburbs and occasionally in cities. These neighborhoods are planned in order to control access and aesthetics within the community. They are fenced (or even walled) in with a limited number of streets going in and out. Security guards and cameras are sometimes found at the entrances. The landscaping, housing styles, and other visual elements of the community are strictly regulated.

Another change involves the availability of businesses. Suburban residents have always been able to finds shops for food and necessities in their neighborhoods. Recent decades have seen marked growth in the size and number of stores:

- Strip malls and shopping malls have become common.
- **Big-box retail** stores have been successful.
- Offices and business services have moved to the suburbs.

All of these changes are part of the **suburbanization of business**, the movement of commerce out of cities to suburbs where rents are cheaper and commutes for employees are shorter. As a result, many cities have faced declines in job opportunities, consumer choices, and services.

### Residential Land Use Outside North America

Outside of the United States and Canada, the residential density gradient does not usually run from higher to lower the farther one goes from the CBD. Instead, population density tends to increase in the suburbs even though land is more plentiful. In Europe, as explained earlier, the centers of cities contain many historic structures, and population densities are fairly low. The suburbs on the edges of the central cities contain multistory apartment complexes and have very high population densities.

In Latin America the peripheral areas of cities may contain suburbs typical of the United States, with single-family houses and low densities, and also suburbs similar to Europe with high-rise apartments. In addition, very densely settled squatter settlements, or favelas, are where the poorest residents live. Gated communities are increasingly common in Latin America as the region develops. Because of their popularity with wealthy urban elites, these security-minded neighborhoods are emerging in residential areas in all regions of the world today.

# Political Organization of Cities

A city is also a political entity. The term **municipal** refers to the local government, or the services provided by the government, of a city or town. For example, a mayor and city council make up the core of the municipal government, and a local water supply is the municipal water supply. **Municipality** refers to a local entity that is all under the same jurisdiction. In essence, a municipality is one way of referring to the political and legal aspect of a city.

### Annexation and Incorporation

As cities have grown in the past two centuries, they have expanded in physical extent, pushing their boundaries farther from the original core. When these settled areas move beyond the legal boundaries of the city, the inhabitants may be left without political representation or services from the city. The process of adding land to a city's legally defined territory is known as **annexation**. Annexation generally requires a vote by residents in the affected areas.

Sometimes, residents living beyond the legal boundaries of the city do not desire to become part of the central city. In such cases, residents may choose the option of **incorporation**, the act of legally joining together to form a new city. One reason is that the newly created municipality is smaller and political representation is more "local" than if the residents had opted for annexation. Of course, many such peripheral municipalities are cities only in terms of legal and political considerations. They may lack a real CBD and continue to function as **bedroom communities**, or commuter suburbs, within the larger metro area.

## Patterns of Municipal Government

Over time, and due to population growth, urban expansion, and incorporation, metropolitan areas become a jigsaw of interlocking municipalities. Each of these has its own local government with the responsibility to provide local services. Coordination of regional issues, such as the development of roads and other infrastructure, can be difficult.

One solution to the problem of this legal fragmentation is the **consolidation** of city and county governments. When this occurs, certain elements of government are handled jointly, across numerous separate municipalities, while other elements of local government continue to be handled by individual municipalities.

Additionally, many cities have created **special districts** that attempt to solve a specific need, such as for public transportation, over a larger region. For example, Colorado has created a regional transportation district, or authority, that includes Denver and surrounding areas to facilitate mass transit for the multiple communities in the region.

Some populated regions do not fall within the legal boundary of any city or municipality. These are known as **unincorporated areas**. Usually a nearby municipality provides their services and administration, through some higher division of civil government such as a county, borough, parish, or province. Over time, these areas may consider annexation by an existing city or incorporation as their own city.

## Population Data in Urban Areas

The Constitution requires that the federal government conduct a nationwide census every ten years for the purpose of establishing Congressional districts. But the data collected in this census, as well as in smaller data-gathering projects, also provide a picture of where people live, their incomes, family sizes, and other details. That information is valuable to researchers and businesses trying to identify goods and services that people desire.

U.S. census data is available at many scales. Urban areas in many countries are divided into **census tracts**, contiguous geographic regions that function as the building blocks of a census. In the United States a census tract typically consists of between 4,000 and 12,000 people. Each tract is subdivided into block groups, and each block group is further subdivided into blocks. A **census block** in a densely populated urban area may be very small, consisting of a single block bounded by four streets. In suburban and rural areas, because of their lower population densities, a census block typically covers a larger area.

| GEOGRAPHIC CATEGORIES IN THE CENSUS | | | |
|---|---|---|---|
| Category | 2010 Census | Increase over the 2000 Census | Average Number of People in the 2010 Census |
| Population | 308,745,538 | 9.7% | ----- |
| Census Tracts | 73,057 | 11.8% | 4,226 people/tract |
| Block Groups | 217,740 | 4.3% | 1,418 people/group |
| Blocks | 11,078,297 | 35.0% | 28 people/block |

Source: Bureau of the Census.

City governments also collect qualitative data. This type of data comes from surveys and field studies conducted in the urban area. Questions and study topics gather information about how individuals and communities feel about urban growth, zoning changes, local government, crime rates, and anything else that may affect the lives of people living in the city. These qualitative and quantitative data can be used in **social area analysis** in order to gain an overall understanding of the lives and characteristics of people living within urban areas.

**GEOGRAPHIC PERSPECTIVES:** WHERE THE WEALTHY CHOOSE TO LIVE

One basic geographic decision that every person makes is where to live. Since they have more money than others, wealthy people have more options. The choices they make reflect what people in that culture value. In turn, these choices shape the spatial distribution of public services.

**Different Places, Different Choices**
In Europe and Canada, wealthy people have traditionally chosen to concentrate in central cities. They have always valued having a short commute to their place of work, as well as easy access to concerts, plays, museums, and other forms of entertainment.

In contrast, in the United States, wealthy citizens have been more likely to choose to live in suburbs. The attractions of spacious homes, large yards, and clean air have outweighed the longer commute to work. Smart growth approaches have transformed large swaths of sprawled suburbia into lively, walkable, and wealthy neighborhoods.

## The Impact of Choices

The distribution of wealth, by area, affects the distribution of political power. The strong core of wealthy residents in central cities in Europe and Canada has created political pressure on governments to provide excellent public transit and other public services to these areas. In U.S. cities, without as many wealthy people, the pressure for those services has been less—but pressure to provide suburban rail lines and freeways has been greater.

Geographers study how changes in work and public policy affect choices about where people live. As more people work at home, they worry less about a long commute to an office. And as more people fly for work, living near an airport becomes a bigger benefit. For these reasons, more wealthy people in Europe and Canada are moving to the suburbs.

At the same time, stricter pollution regulations have cleaned up the air and water in central cities, making them more desirable places to live. Since families are smaller today, the desire for a large house and yard is less important than it once was. For these reasons, more wealthy people in the United States are moving downtown, and these areas are increasing their political power.

| KEY TERMS | | |
|---|---|---|
| functional zonation | shantytowns | urban planning |
| central business district (CBD) | favelas | filtering |
| | barrios | invasion and succession |
| concentric zone model | disamenity zones | gated communities |
| zone of transition | traditional CBD | big-box retail |
| Burgess Model | colonial CBD | suburbanization of business |
| sector model | informal economy zone | |
| Hoyt's model | periodic markets | municipal |
| Chauncy Harris | informal settlements | municipality |
| Edward Ullman | squatter settlements | annexation |
| multiple-nuclei model | mosque | incorporation |
| peripheral model | citadel | bedroom communities |
| galactic city model | suqs | urban planning |
| edge cities | McGee Model | consolidation |
| Griffen-Ford Model | residential zones | special districts |
| spine | residential density gradient | unincorporated areas |
| mall | | census tracts |
| periférico | zoning ordinances | census block |
| | | social area analysis |

**Question 1 refers to the photograph below.**

1. Which phrase best describes the urban central business district (CBD) shown in the photograph?

   (A) a European CBD that mixes low-rise historic buildings with new skyscrapers

   (B) a Latin American CBD that mixes traditional markets with modern high-rises

   (C) a European suburban CBD with high-rise residential buildings and high population

   (D) an African colonial CBD with broad avenues, large homes, and administrative centers

   (E) a North American CBD near the city's center, offering commercial space, parking, and transportation

**2.** Which best provides a general explanation of functional zonation?

(A) Urban areas pass laws to define how property in specific areas can be used in order to separate commercial and residential spaces.

(B) A city is made up of a series of rings that surrounds the central business district, each having a different function.

(C) Different portions of an urban area have specific and separate purposes, which fit together to create the entirety of the city.

(D) In cities around the world, residential areas are based on ethnicity, and cities are thus divided into ethnic enclaves.

(E) An urban area's inner city has its highest population density, and population density declines in areas farther from the city.

**3.** Which urban model would best describe a city that includes edge cities along its beltways?

(A) galactic city

(B) concentric zone

(C) multiple-nuclei

(D) sector

(E) Griffen-Ford

**4.** Houses with small, high windows and no front yards, situated on dead-end streets, are common in Islamic cities. These characteristics might reflect the Islamic emphasis on

(A) the need for safety

(B) the high crime rate

(C) the value of privacy

(D) the power of the government

(E) the lack of development

**5.** Why do many African cities contain multiple commercial districts?

(A) Colonial central business districts emerged separately from the traditional commercial centers.

(B) Africans were traditionally not allowed to use the central business districts used by Europeans.

(C) African governments promoted multiple central business districts through urban planning.

(D) One central business district is not enough to serve Africa's fast-growing urban population.

(E) Locations of Africa's business districts were poorly chosen, requiring multiple downtowns.

**Question 6 refers to the photograph below.**

6. What feature of many large Latin American cities is illustrated by Mexico City's Paseo de la Reforma, a wide avenue lined with trees, tall office buildings, and mansions?

(A) the disamenity zone

(B) the periférico

(C) the favelas

(D) the commercial spine

(E) the zone in transition

7. Which best explains why European central business districts have largely resisted the construction of skyscrapers and the resulting impressive skylines that typify American cities?

(A) Competition for valuable commercial space is not as keen in European cities as it is in the United States.

(B) European culture prefers lower buildings and has negative attitudes toward commercialism and skyscrapers.

(C) The centers of European cities contain many historically significant buildings that leaders choose to preserve.

(D) The European Union regulates the height of buildings and has forbidden tall buildings because of safety concerns.

(E) European cities tend to have stronger mass transit systems, so people do not need to be as concentrated in CBDs.

**8.** What concept describes the process of when a wealthy family sells its house to a less-wealthy family of a different ethnic group, who then divides the house into two units?

(A) functional zonation

(B) filtering

(C) zoning

(D) urban planning

(E) density gradient

## FREE-RESPONSE QUESTION

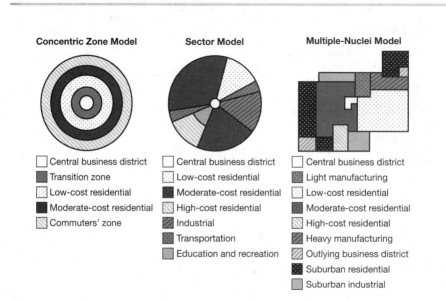

**Concentric Zone Model**

- ☐ Central business district
- ■ Transition zone
- ▦ Low-cost residential
- ■ Moderate-cost residential
- ▨ Commuters' zone

**Sector Model**

- ☐ Central business district
- ▦ Low-cost residential
- ■ Moderate-cost residential
- ▨ High-cost residential
- ▨ Industrial
- ▦ Transportation
- ▨ Education and recreation

**Multiple-Nuclei Model**

- ☐ Central business district
- ▦ Light manufacturing
- ▦ Low-cost residential
- ■ Moderate-cost residential
- ▨ High-cost residential
- ▨ Heavy manufacturing
- ▨ Outlying business district
- ▦ Suburban residential
- ▦ Suburban industrial

**1.** The diagrams show three early models of urban development and land use in North America.

A. Identify and explain two similarities that North American models share in how they describe land use.

B. Choose one of the models and discuss in detail the rationale for a specific land use location.

C. Contrast these models with one pattern of urban development and land use on a continent other than North America and account for the differences.

Geographers compare data describing different regions or communities as a way to highlight what makes each place distinctive. Large cities feature diverse populations, including a variety of ethnicities, religions, income levels, forms of entertainment, and health services.

Use the information in this chart to compare life in Philadelphia, Minneapolis, and Orlando and to help you answer the questions below.

| COMPARING LIFE IN THREE CITIES | | | |
|---|---|---|---|
| **Statistic** | **Philadelphia** | **Minneapolis** | **Orlando** |
| **Population: City** | 1,517,550 | 382,618 | 185,951 |
| **Popluation: Metropolitan Statistical Region** (MSR) | 6,188,463 | 3,615,902 | 1,644,561 |
| **Median Household Income** (Entire MSR) | $47,528 | $54,304 | $41,871 |
| **Murder Rate per 100,000 Population** (City Only) | 15.9 | 7.7 | 5.8 |
| **Median Age** (City Only) | 34.2 | 31.2 | 32.9 |

1. What are the advantages and disadvantages of living in a large metropolitan area?

2. In which of the major urban areas listed above would you prefer to live? Use the data from the chart to support your answer.

**20**

# Urban Challenges

*Whenever and wherever societies have flourished and prospered rather than stagnated and decayed, creative and workable cities have been at the core of the phenomenon . . . . Decaying cities, declining economies, and mounting social troubles travel together. The combination is not coincidental.*
—Jane Jacobs, *The Death and Life of Great American Cities,* 1961

**Essential Question:** What are the challenges facing cities around the world, and how are cities responding to these challenges?

Cities are nodes, places characterized by numerous interconnections and complexity. This can make them leading centers for innovation, cultural diversity, and art. They are often engines of economic growth and centers of political power. But the dense concentration of people combined with the interconnections and complexity can make solving problems difficult. Cities can be places of poverty, violence, and environmental decay.

The world is more urbanized than ever, and experts expect the percentage of people living in cities to continue to grow. Consequently, understanding and helping solve urban challenges will continue to be an important part of the work of geographers.

## Economic Problems in Cities

The root of many of the challenges faced by urban areas is economic. The role of cities in more developed countries has changed rapidly as they have shifted from centers of industry to centers of services. Conversely, in less developed countries, cities have experienced problems that accompany rapid industrialization and crushing numbers of new migrants.

And while people with great wealth concentrate in cities, so do people with little wealth. Urban poverty exists throughout the world, from **inner cities**, the regions just outside the central business districts in North American cities, to  densely settled peripheral suburbs in Europe, to the squatter settlements and favelas of less developed countries. According to a United Nations report, about one-sixth of the world's population lives in urban poverty, and most of these are in developing countries.

## Overcoming Poverty

Some people refer to the higher concentration of poor residents as the **underclass**, people who face social hardships that contribute to their poverty. Where poverty is persistent, people sometimes develop a **culture of poverty**, a way of living that reflects a lack of income and accumulated wealth:

- The shortage of inexpensive housing may force a person to spend a high percentage of his or her income on rent or may result in homelessness.
- The distribution of political power might result in students in poor neighborhoods attending inadequately funded schools.
- Poor individuals often live far from places with concentrations of entry-level jobs.
- People have difficulty getting credit in any form: credit cards for everyday purchases, a mortgage to buy a house, and loans to start a business.

These problems can be particularly difficult to address in less developed countries, where the general level of wealth is low.

## Urban Decay

Industry once thrived in central cities of developed countries. Yet newer technologies have decreased the need for workers, undercutting the economic strength of many cities. In addition, manufacturing moved to the suburbs, where land was cheaper, and to other countries, where labor was less expensive.

As manufacturing moved away, cities were left with unemployed residents and abandoned factories. **Brownfields** are visual reminders on the landscape of how the centers of cities have changed over time. A typical brownfield consists of dilapidated buildings and polluted or contaminated soils. These are expensive to remove or repair and often remain in cities, devaluing neighboring properties for many years.

Housing has also suffered from decay in central cities. **Filtering** is the change in the use of a house from a single-family home to rented units in a multifamily dwelling and eventually to an abandoned building. At the scale of a single house, a wealthy family might have built a large home decades ago, during a prosperous era. The family might have moved to suburbs to become absentee landlords of less wealthy residents. As the house grew older, it might have been further subdivided into apartments, as the building deteriorated and attracted poorer and poorer residents.

At the neighborhood scale, filtering can be made worse by **redlining**, the process by which banks refuse loans to those who want to purchase and improve properties in certain urban areas. The banks might consider investments in some areas too risky. The term originated as banks sometimes identified these no-loan areas by red lines on maps. Redlining reinforces the downward spiral of struggling neighborhoods. Laws now restrict redlining so that it is not based on racial discrimination.

### Redevelopment

The process of **urban redevelopment** involves renovating a site within a city by removing the existing landscape and rebuilding from the ground up. The process of urban redevelopment usually begins when a local government declares that an area it wishes to develop is "blighted." **Eminent domain** laws allow the government to seize land for public use after paying owners the market value for their property. Cities often use these laws to enable them to build new roads or schools, but they can also sell the land to private businesses or groups to build hotels, hospitals, or other developments.

While redevelopment initiatives sometimes replace brownfields or low-quality housing with successful enterprises, critics point out that these efforts can cause problems. They can force poor people to leave their homes and communities. Redevelopment can break up and eliminate historic neighborhoods. Private developers are also sometimes given tax-break incentives to purchase and build. By reducing tax revenues on these projects, the city shifts the tax burden to other taxpayers.

## Social and Cultural Problems in Cities

Cities are diverse, heterogeneous places. Their ethnic and cultural diversity enriches the community through a variety of groups of people, restaurants, stores, architecture, and art. But this same diversity can promote division. Incomes range from the super rich to the middle class to the poor and homeless in cities. What is a problem for one group may not be for another, and the solutions to any problem will have impacts on other issues. Cities must cope with the intersecting problems of multiple groups.

### Housing

In developing countries, poor residents construct housing from whatever materials are available. Bricks and cement blocks are more durable, but sheets of tin and plastic are also used. Because of a lack of enforcement of housing codes, living in these buildings is dangerous. In 2013, 74 people died when an apartment building collapsed in Mumbra, India.

Housing for poor residents in the inner cities in the developed world is characterized by at least three problems. It is of poor quality, insufficient availability, and significant unaffordability. Much of the housing is older and has not been maintained. The physical conditions of the buildings need updates to be safe and comfortable. Properly maintaining and repairing plumbing, electrical systems, roofing, stairwells, and heating systems are often unaffordable to inner city residents. Landlords often delay making expensive repairs. Therefore, over time, the overall quality of the housing suffers. This process is often visible in the transitional areas of cities as well as in ethnic enclaves, since both have a high percentage of renters.

As land values rise in inner cities along the growing edge of the central business district, urban residents are pushed out by rising rents. **Gentrification** (explained in greater detail on page 343), the process of wealthier residents moving into a neighborhood and making it unaffordable for existing residents, usually improves the housing quality. But as property values increase, older residents on fixed incomes and lower-income residents can no longer afford to pay taxes on their homes or rents for their apartments. Unable to afford housing in the suburbs or in the central business district, residents often crowd into the housing that is available and affordable.

Even finding housing in the inner city can be a challenge. Homes and buildings might be dilapidated and uninhabitable. Owners sometimes demolish buildings to make way for new structures. This interrupts the filtering process, which can create housing for poor residents. Investors might conclude that they cannot make a profit building affordable housing, and so little is built. Infrastructure developments such as freeways, rail lines, and transit hubs—all of which benefit suburban and wealthy central business district residents— compete for space in the inner city.

## Government Support for Housing

Governments have responded to the shortage of low-income housing in various ways. The federal government provides financial subsidies to help low-income residents with the cost of housing. New York City, Denver, and some other cities have rent control policies that keep some affordable units available when a neighborhood gentrifies. However, critics point out that these policies reduce incentives for investors to build new housing.

One reason for the shortage of affordable housing in urban neighborhoods is that the cost of building and managing it can be greater than the profits a business can make from it. So governments and charitable groups, in both the United States and other countries, often step in to provide assistance, either by building and operating housing or by providing subsidies for others to do so.

These public housing developments—sometimes called "projects"—were first built in areas of the inner city where other structures had been torn down. Many provided decent housing and a solid sense of community. However, many cities built high-rise apartment buildings, which concentrated poverty in a small area within the city. These buildings experienced problems common in other urban neighborhoods where the poor were concentrated, such as drugs, high crime rates, and poor maintenance.

In some cities, another approach called **scattered site** was employed to alleviate the problems of public housing. In this approach, public housing was dispersed throughout areas of the city. Children thus had access to better local schools and amenities available in wealthier neighborhoods.

The scattered-site approach has faced opposition from the "not-in-my-backyard" (NIMBY) response. People fear that adding public housing near them will reduce property values and create problems for local schools.

## Homelessness

The extreme end of housing problems is **homelessness**, the condition of not having a permanent place to live. While some homeless people find temporary shelter with friends or relatives, others live on the streets. In the United States, the homeless were once primarily single men, but the problem expanded in the late 20th century to include more women and children. Government, religious groups, and nonprofit organizations responded by building shelters, advocating for public funding to support housing, and helping the homeless learn new skills. In cities without strong public transit systems, homeless people have difficulty traveling to where jobs and services are available.

SERVICES FOR HOMELESS PEOPLE IN MEMPHIS

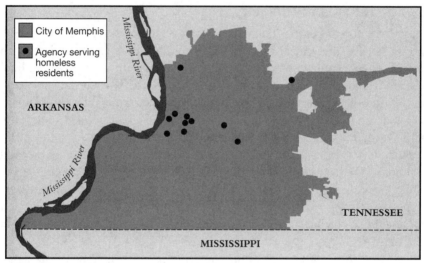

## Services

Much like housing, shops and other services struggle to survive in some urban neighborhoods. If the patrons are poor, prices for services must be low to maintain a customer base. The result is very tight margins with little money available for shop owners to spend on maintenance or improvement of their facilities. The decay that afflicts housing thus spreads across the service sector. Public services such as parks and swimming pools might be rare in urban neighborhoods with low tax bases. Private businesses, such as doctors and dentists, are often scarce in poor neighborhoods. They are particularly scarce in poor, heavily urbanized countries. In Bangladesh, the number of doctors per capita is about one-fifth the number in the United States.

## Food Deserts

Access to food stores in urban neighborhoods can be a particular problem. Fresh, healthy food may be far less available than fast food. Grocery stores and supermarkets tend to favor suburban locations, where residents are wealthier and parking lots can be expansive. Additionally, less healthful fast food options are less expensive than fresh food is, so poor families may have little choice beyond fast foods. These urban zones that lack food stores are known as **food deserts**, and they contribute to health problems for poorer urban residents.

An urban food desert can be defined as an area where residents have limited or no access to healthy food because of inadequate transportation. One striking example of a food desert is a neighborhood in Raleigh, North Carolina. Even though the neighborhood is an upscale area that includes a popular stretch of eateries known as Restaurant Row, one particular home for low-income elderly people has no grocery store within walking distance.

### Gender, Race, and Ethnicity

Women are more numerous than men in large, central cities in North America. One reason for this disparity is the high number of households headed by females. These women and their children who live with them are more likely to be poor than men. Hence they concentrate in areas where housing is the least expensive, even if these areas often have higher crime rates. Problems for women and children may be compounded by the lack of good schools, parks and playgrounds, and available day care options.

**Racial segregation** in housing occurs when people live in separate neighborhoods based on their ethnicity or race. Segregation often occurs involuntarily. In particular, throughout U.S. history, many communities had neighborhoods where African Americans could live and neighborhoods where they could not. Such segregation was enforced through custom, violence, and real estate practices.

One of these practices was **blockbusting**, in which people of one ethnic group, usually middle-class whites, would be frightened into selling their homes at low prices when they heard that a family of another group, usually African American or Hispanic, was moving into the neighborhood. Investors would profit by buying houses at low prices and reselling them for more money. Real estate agents would profit from a flurry of transactions.

Segregated neighborhoods can sometimes become **ghettos**, areas of poverty occupied by a minority group as a result of discrimination. Ghetto residents often feel trapped because of social or political factors or lack of economic opportunities.

Segregated housing can also result when people voluntarily choose to live near people of their own race or ethnicity for social reasons. Immigrants have created ethnic enclaves, also know as **urban colonies**, where new residents can be close to religious institutions, stores that sell familiar goods, and friends and relatives who speak their language. Hence, cities across the United States include neighborhoods with names such as Chinatown, Little Italy, and Greektown. More recently, ethnic enclaves have been composed of Serbian,

Ethiopian, Filipino, Somalian, and Hmong immigrants. Over time, as the immigrants acculturate, the enclave might disappear.

## Gentrification

Gentrification often occurs when old, inner-city housing is purchased at low prices and renovated by investors or by new residents with higher incomes. Often these neighborhoods are near the central business district and its many theaters, restaurants, and museums and available public transportation. The newcomers are often a combination of two groups. One is young urban professionals ("yuppies") with high-paying jobs. The other is older couples whose children have moved out ("empty nesters").

While gentrification brings investment to communities, it often creates problems for existing residents. If investments drive up rents and property taxes, longtime but less wealthy residents cannot afford to remain in the neighborhood. They often have to move. The graph below shows how property values increased in the Mission District neighborhood in San Francisco.

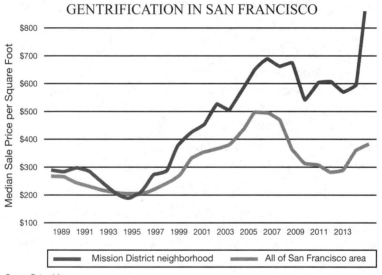

GENTRIFICATION IN SAN FRANCISCO

Source: Dataquick.

## A Study in Gentrification

In the 1970s, Chicago's Wicker Park was a diverse working-class neighborhood of immigrants from Eastern Europe and Latin America. Developers began to renovate old buildings and either resold the buildings at high prices or recruited artists and young people to fill them and give Wicker Park a "trendy" identity. As real estate values skyrocketed, many of the older residents had to leave. Eventually, many of the artists had to relocate as well, to other less expensive neighborhoods. By the early 2000s, gentrification had transformed Wicker Park from an ethnic neighborhood into an expensive area.

### Gated Communities

Walled or fenced neighborhoods with limited access and entry points are called **gated communities**. They represent a redesign of urban living with an attempt to recapture features more commonly found outside urban areas: safety, quiet, and homogeneity.

Gated communities are growing in cities all around the world. Some have referred to them as *citadels,* after historic castles and forts built to ensure safety inside the walls amid lawlessness and crime outside. The growth of gated communities can reinforce separation in terms of not just economics but also social status, ethnicity, and even political views.

## Political Issues in Cities

Running cities is complex. As a result of this complexity, municipal governments face many challenges. Populations are concentrated there, and so are their needs and problems. Local governments need to provide services for sometimes enormous populations. Governments must build and take care of infrastructure, maintain order, and mediate competing interests for the benefit of the population as a whole.

### Public Transportation

The dense population of cities, combined with the high number of suburban residents who commute to central cities for jobs each day, places great demands on the transportation system. The use of large numbers of individual automobiles creates problems:

- air pollution, which is both a local and a global concern
- congested roads that result in people moving slowly
- the use of valuable real estate for parking areas

One solution to moving people around an urban area is **public transportation**: buses, subways, light rail, and trains operated by a government agency. Some cities in the United States, such as New York City, Washington, D.C., and San Francisco, are known for the success of their mass transit systems. However, few cities have extensive systems, and in most of the country, ridership is low. Fares rarely cover operating costs, but when fares increase, passenger numbers decline. The poor, who need public transportation the most, are often not able to get where they need to go using the system.

In contrast, governments in other countries have placed a higher priority on building, maintaining, and promoting the use of public transportation. A much higher percentage of the population of cities in Europe, Latin America, and parts of Asia relies on public transportation. Of the ten most used urban train systems in the world, only one, New York City, is in the United States. Of the top 50, only two, New York City and Washington, D.C., are in the United States.

## Other Infrastructure

Transportation systems are among the most noticeable elements of the infrastructure of a large city. Other elements include the following:

- Transportation features, such as roads, bridges, parking lots, and signs
- Buildings, such as police stations, courthouses, and fire stations
- Distribution systems for water, gas, and electricity
- Collection systems for sewage and garbage
- Open spaces, such as public parks and town squares
- Entertainment venues, such as museums, theaters, and sports facilities

Building, repairing, and replacing infrastructure is costly and, in a busy urban setting, disruptive to people trying to move about. Not surprisingly, the infrastructure of cities around the world is often old and deteriorating.

Disposing of garbage is a particular problem because of garbage's potential health hazards. While wealthy cities in developed countries produce more total waste than poorer cities, it is poorer cities that suffer the most from streets with piles of garbage, animals eating food waste, and fires to burn rubbish.

Deciding who pays for elements of infrastructure, where they should be built, and what economic and social benefits they offer are usually hotly debated issues. Using public resources to build sports stadiums is particularly controversial, and the results are difficult to predict. In Denver, building a baseball stadium for the Colorado Rockies served as an anchor for economic development that helped revitalize a dilapidated area. In Atlanta, building a stadium displaced African American neighborhoods and provided limited economic benefits to the community.

## Informal Economy

The **informal economy** is the portion of the economy that is not taxed, regulated, or managed by the government. In the slums and squatter settlements of cities in the less developed world, the informal economy is important, effective, and vibrant. The majority of the population may be part of it. Where governments have been ineffective at promoting the growth of businesses, individuals have taken on that role. Some economists estimate that nearly 50 percent of people in Latin America work in the informal economy.

**Shadow Economy** In more developed countries, the informal economy operates as a **shadow economy**. Local governments are concerned not just because of their lost tax revenue but also because these shadow enterprises are not regulated for the safety of either workers or consumers. In addition, they undercut businesses that do operate openly and follow regulations. Many businesses such as food carts, parade vendors, and street markets eventually come into the legal economy. The shadow economy is probably about 10 percent of the U.S. economy.

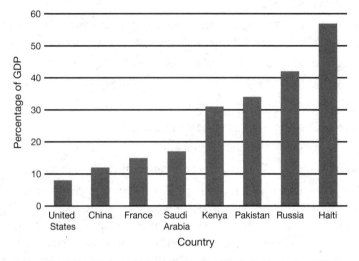

ESTIMATED SIZE OF SHADOW ECONOMICS

Source: Schneider, Friedrich, Andreas Buehn, and Claudio E. Montenegro (2010). "New Estimates for the Shadow Economies all over the World," *International Economic Journal*, 24:4, 443-461.

**Crime** Criminal activity is concentrated in urban areas. In large, crowded cities, people can be more anonymous and are more likely to be temporary residents; both of these traits make people less concerned about community reprisals. Increased police presence, organized neighborhood watch groups, revived downtown nightlife, and improved street lighting all represent attempts at reducing urban crime.

**Terrorism** Cities are also more likely than rural areas to be targets of terrorism. The symbolic value and newsworthiness of cities make them attractive targets. Their dense population makes inflicting great damage easier. Finally, as centers of toleration and diversity, they can anger those who reject these values.

# Environmental Problems in Cities

Cities have environmental impacts in at least two important ways. The actual city structure itself—the buildings and streets—are human modifications of the natural environment. And the concentration of so many people in one location can dramatically affect the landscape. Simply by living, a person places stress on nature, and in cities that stress is greatly magnified.

## Environmental Effects of Cities

The physical landscape of an urban area affects the natural environment in many ways:

- **Urban canyons**, streets lined with tall buildings, can channel and intensify wind. These tall buildings also prevent natural sunlight from reaching the ground.

- Soils are compacted and replaced with surfaces impermeable to water, such as buildings, streets, and parking lots. As a result, rainwater runs off instead of soaking into the ground, which can cause flooding.
- The concentration of buildings in the core of a city creates an **urban heat island**, a portion of a city warmer than surrounding regions. The diagram of Paris below shows that the central city is relatively warm. In contrast, the Seine River, which has no buildings, is relatively cool.

### PARIS AS A HEAT ISLAND

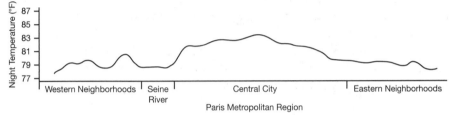

Source: Data is from the summer of 2003, nasa.gov.

## Cities and Wildlife

Wildlife is also affected by urban areas. Cities destroy animal and plant habitats, redirect or replace natural hydrologic (water) systems such as rivers and lakes, and break up ecosystems. The interruption of continuous ecosystems makes it difficult, if not impossible, for animal species to survive. When animals do survive, they often are in conflict with humans:

- Native animals such as deer, coyotes, skunks, alligators, bears, cougars, monkeys, and leopards cause problems where cities have invaded or abutted their natural territories.
- **Urban wildlife** such as rats, raccoons, and pigeons can thrive in cities, but they can spread diseases and be a nuisance to people.
- Feral (wild) populations of cats, dogs, snakes, and other former pets that have escaped their human owners or been abandoned can be dangerous or upset the ecological balance.

## Pollution

Increased environmental degradation is associated with rising urbanism. Industrial and human waste, concentrated in cities and sometimes untreated, pollutes rivers, coasts, and aquifers. The rise of industry pollutes the air in cities in less developed countries, and rising wealth increases the number of cars and their emissions. Poorer inhabitants in these cities burn charcoal, wood, and kerosene, all of which pollute the air. The health of city dwellers is negatively affected by all these contaminants in both the water and the air.

In developed countries, automobile pollution problems can be acute. The huge number of commuters to central business districts and surrounding edge cities creates problems beyond congestion. During **rush hour**, the commuting periods in early morning and in late afternoon or early evening when many people travel to and from work, idling cars on roads increase and concentrate air pollutants in the city. The result is smog, a plague in large cities such as Los Angeles, Beijing, Delhi, and Mexico City.

Many cities have physical geography factors such as mountains or climatic conditions that intensify or trap pollution. For example, Mexico City is surrounded by mountains, and during temperature inversions (when a layer of hot air sits above cool air), smog can be trapped and concentrated close to the ground for days with negative effects on the health of the city's inhabitants. According to the World Health Organization, air pollution results in three million deaths a year. One-third of those are in China, where coal is widely used both in industry and to heat homes.

### Urban Sprawl

Before automobiles became popular, cities tended to grow vertically through taller buildings as population expanded. Since the mid-20th century, cities and everything that goes with them—such as roads and commercial developments— have expanded horizontally across the landscape. This rapid spread of development outward from the inner city is called **urban sprawl**. In the United States, sprawl is most common in fast-growing areas in the Southeast and West.

Urban areas experience sprawl for several reasons. The availability of automobiles, the creation of interstate and other high-speed highways, and the presence of inexpensive land outside the urban area all contribute to urban sprawl. Developers purchase land beyond the periphery of the city's built-up area in a process called **leapfrogging**. Neighborhoods built there may be farther from the central business district in actual distance, but the presence of highways makes them relatively close in time.

# Sustainability and the Future

Maintaining the **sustainability**, or long-term viability, of cities has become a discussion for city planners, developers, and citizens. New development concepts are shaping the debate about city landscapes around the world.

### Greenbelts and Smart Growth

To combat urban sprawl, policymakers and planners have tried to limit sprawl by restricting the activities of developers. In Europe, **greenbelts**, areas of undeveloped land around an urban area, have been created. The photo on the following page shows a greenbelt outside Feltham, England.

A similar phenomenon in the United States is known as **smart growth**, a set of policies to preserve farmland and other open, undeveloped spaces near a city. Under the principles of smart growth, cities are allowed to annex land only in areas specifically designated by laws. New Jersey, Rhode Island, Washington, Tennessee, and Oregon have all enacted smart growth policies.

## New Urbanism

A movement in urban planning emerged in the 1990s called **new urbanism**. Its goals included reducing sprawl, increasing affordable housing, and creating vibrant, livable neighborhoods—largely walkable, **mixed-use neighborhoods**. That is, unlike the clear separation between residential and commercial uses created by zoning in most cities, these neighborhoods would have a mix of homes and businesses. Homes would include a variety of sizes and price ranges in order to create a socially diverse community. New urbanism faced two large obstacles:

- The existing system of zoning: the system had created segregated areas by land use and thus contributed to sprawl.
- Public opinion: some people who were accustomed to traditional land-use patterns in cities were not convinced that the new urbanism was an improvement.

However, in communities that changed their zoning laws and where people changed their attitudes toward mixed-use neighborhoods, new urbanism took hold.

## Urban Infill

The opposite of leapfrog development and sprawl is **urban infill**, the process of building up underused lands within a city. Cities have areas of vacant or undeveloped land of varying sizes. These may be remnants of previous industrial activity, old airports, closed military bases, closed hospitals, zones with difficult terrain, or remnants of orchards or farms surrounded by later development. Infill is the process of building up these areas for urban uses rather than expanding the edge of the city.

The community of Civita, California, is an example of both urban infill and new urbanism. This master-planned community was built on the site of a former quarry located in the Mission Valley section of San Diego. Today, Civita includes a mix of housing types, parks and community centers, and commercial zones. It is well connected by public transit. The community also promotes sustainability by using sustainable building materials, solar panels, electric vehicle charging stations, and energy management tools for residents and businesses.

## Exurbanism

While cities are the destination for most of the world's migrants, the counter-flow of urban residents leaving cities is known as **counter-urbanization** or **deurbanization**. Many of these migrants are relocating to **exurbs**, the prosperous residential districts beyond the suburbs. Contributing to exurbanism is the ability of people to work remotely via technology. This removes their need to commute. Other factors include relative affordability and cultural preferences.

While many people move into the city to be near cultural amenities, exurbanites are attracted to different features, such as mountains, streams, or other elements of the physical landscape. Some people prefer the calm of a smaller, more isolated community to the vibrancy of a larger, more interconnected city.

## Other Changes

Cities adapt to their growing and evolving populations. For example, the creation of pedestrian zones where street fairs, festivals, and public events can be held help make inner cities both safer and more desirable destinations. The creation of bike lanes and an increase in bike usage reduces traffic congestion and parking needs while encouraging a healthful lifestyle. In addition, increasing the number of running paths, community gardens, and dog parks further promotes the health and well-being of residents. Many cities are actively developing relationships with local farmers, which benefits both urban and rural citizens through the spread of farmers' markets and the promotion of a more sustainable local economy.

**GEOGRAPHIC PERSPECTIVES:** URBAN LIFE IN 2050

A century ago, approximately 10 percent of the world's population lived in cities. By 2008, the world passed a milestone: more than half the populace was urban. While urbanization and suburbanization continue to expand in more developed countries (North America and Europe), the pace remains slow and steady.

## American Cities

In the United States, as millennials have formed families, they have relocated out of central cities into enclaves inspired by new urbanist designs. These "urban burbs" offer walkable streets, local markets, public transit, and less expensive accommodations than CBDs. In the future, self-driving cars and other new technology could reduce the friction of distance. If so, edge cities and exurbs will likely expand.

Immigration will likely continue, making the population more diverse. Voluntary segregation will likely continue, and the number of ethnic neighborhoods will flourish.

## Megacities in Asia and Africa

The megacities of the less developed countries of Asia and Africa will likely get even larger. The economic, social, and educational opportunities these cities offer will continue to pull in migration from rural areas. However, if growth exceeds carrying capacity, the standard of living will deteriorate. In addition, the increasingly dense concentration of people will increase the impacts of deadly epidemics, natural disasters, environmental changes, immense pollution, criminal networks, terrorist activity, and civic unrest.

These megacities are already home to more than one billion squatters, and many people breathe unhealthy air and lack access to safe drinking water. Without dramatic economic and political changes, these problems seem likely to worsen. However, efforts to address these problems have had some success, which suggests that megacities may become more liveable in the future.

| KEY TERMS | | |
|---|---|---|
| inner cities | gated communities | urban sprawl |
| underclass | homelessness | leapfrogging |
| culture of poverty | food deserts | sustainability |
| brownfields | racial segregation | greenbelts |
| filtering | blockbusting | smart growth |
| urban redlining | public transportation | new urbanism |
| redevelopment | informal economy | mixed-use |
| eminent domain | shadow economy | neighborhoods |
| gentrification | urban canyons | urban infill |
| scattered site | urban heat island | counter-urbanization |
| ghettos | urban wildlife | deurbanization |
| urban colonies | rush hour | exurbs |

**Question 1 refers to the table below.**

| USE OF PUBLIC TRANSPORTATION | | | |
|---|---|---|---|
| City | Metropolitan Area Population | Daily Bus Commuters | Daily Subway Commuters |
| Seoul | 25,000,000 | 4,500,000 | 5,600,000 |
| New York | 20,000,000 | 2,500,000 | 3,800,000 |
| Chicago | 9,500,000 | 1,000,000 | 750,000 |
| Berlin | 5,000,000 | 1,000,000 | 1,000,000 |

1. Which generalization comparing the use of urban transportation systems in four cities does the table support?

   (A) People in no country have placed much importance on urban public transportation.

   (B) Europeans and Asians have placed about the same importance on urban public transportation as have people in the United States.

   (C) People in the United States have placed more importance on urban public transportation than have Europeans and Asians.

   (D) European and Asian urban transportation systems serve a higher proportion of residents than do systems in the United States

   (E) European and Asian urban transportation systems meet the needs of residents, but systems in the United States fail to do so.

2. Based on current and historical conditions, which would be most likely to help alleviate the problem of food deserts?

   (A) encouraging food trucks that are part of the informal economy to serve food deserts

   (B) encouraging gentrification and building upscale housing in poor neighborhoods

   (C) establishing new farmers' markets in the suburban and exurban communities

   (D) opening upscale food stores in neighborhoods that have already gentrified

   (E) opening supermarkets in inner city neighborhoods that have poor public transportation

**3.** Which has been a partially effective response to the problems of public housing?

(A) gentrification, because it creates a safer and more diverse community

(B) scattered-site housing, because it places families in safer areas with better schools

(C) redlining, because it limits bad housing investments in the inner city

(D) eminent domain, because it allows government to gain vast urban lands to develop

(E) blockbusting, because it makes affordable housing more available

**Question 4 refers to the table below.**

| ESTIMATED SIZE OF SHADOW ECONOMIES | |
|---|---|
| **Country** | **Percentage of GDP** |
| **Canada** | 15% |
| **Greece** | 26% |
| **Egypt** | 34% |

**Source:** Schneider, Friedrich, Andreas Buehn, and Claudio E. Montenegro, (2010) 'New Estimates for the Shadow Economies all over the World', *International Economic Journal*, 24: 4, 443-461.

**4.** Based on the table, Egypt would be much more likely than Canada or Greece to have

(A) government control over sectors of the shadow economy

(B) cost-free infrastructure, such as water and sewer systems

(C) strong promotion and regulation of emerging small businesses

(D) taxation on food carts, parade vendors, and street markets

(E) black market sales and paid labor not being reported

5. Which activity most directly uses racial prejudice to perpetuate segregation in housing?

(A) gentrification by young professionals and suburbanites moving into the inner city

(B) leapfrogging over suburbs by developers to expand communities far from the inner city

(C) blockbusting by realtors who want to promote movement to the suburbs

(D) scattered-site housing by city governments to keep the poor in the city

(E) ideas of new urbanism applied by developers who are creating mixed-use neighborhoods

6. The revival of downtown nightlife and an increase in street lighting are methods used by city governments primarily to

(A) deter criminal activity

(B) generate tax revenue during evening hours

(C) decrease traffic congestion during the day

(D) promote new urbanism

(E) reduce the effects of exurbanization

7. Which common urban characteristic contributes most directly to the environmental problem of flooding?

(A) urban canyons created by streets lined with tall buildings

(B) skyscrapers that keep sunlight from reaching the ground

(C) the radiation of heat from buildings and rooftops

(D) hard surfaces such as streets, sidewalks, and parking lots

(E) the increased concentration of pollutants in the air

8. A diverse, walkable, mixed-use neighborhood would most directly be a core goal of

(A) restrictive zoning

(B) gentrification

(C) exurbanism

(D) new urbanism

(E) counter-urbanization

1. The Brookings Institution, a research organization based in Washington, D.C., issued a report that stated, "Urban areas face daunting economic challenges that have increased in scope in recent years. At the same time, cities provide exciting opportunities for growth and revitalization. The interplay of these challenges and opportunities creates important tasks for policymakers and researchers."

   A. Describe ONE economic problem of urban areas today that the quotation could be referring to, and explain its possible cause or causes.

   B. Describe and explain TWO social or political problems created by the economic issue you chose.

   C. Explain ONE of the "exciting opportunities for growth and revitalization" of urban areas referred to in the quotation, and explain how it might help solve the problems you described.

The size, shape, and number of municipalities in counties vary widely in the United States. By studying these variables, geographers can understand how space affects the way people relate to each other and to their government.

| | COOK COUNTY, ILLINOIS | MARION COUNTY, INDIANA |
|---|---|---|
| **Area, in Square Miles** | 1,635 | 403 |
| **Number of Municipalities** | 135 | 1 |
| **Major City** | Chicago | Indianapolis |
| **Population** | 5,238,000 | 939,000 |
| **North-South Distance** | c. 48 miles | c. 20 miles |
| **East-West Distance** | c. 32 miles | c. 20 miles |

1. Explain how the different physical shapes of the counties might affect how each county government works.

2. Describe the borders within each county and what that suggests about the role of county government.

3. How might the difference in population explain the differences in the number of municipalities?

4. How does the number of communities in each county affect how the government operates?

# UNIT 7: Review

## WRITE AS A GEOGRAPHER: ORGANIZE IDEAS

Well-written paragraphs usually begin with a topic sentence stating the paragraph's primary claim. The other sentences then provide support for this idea, such as examples, explanations, or applications of a concept.

*Below are sets of points that could be used in a paragraph in response to a question about sustainability. For each set, write a topic sentence for a paragraph that includes them.*

1. **Set A**
   - a city begins a public service to help residents compost
   - a state provides incentives for consumers to use less electricity
   - a national organization runs public service ads about reducing pollution
   - countries of the world sign an agreement to combat climate change

2. **Set B**
   - early 1800s: John James Audubon's paintings of birds remind people of nature's beauty
   - late 1800s: John Muir helps establish the first national parks, places for people to appreciate the outdoors
   - 1962: Rachel Carson publishes *Silent Spring,* alerting people to the dangers of pesticides
   - late 1900s: Wendell Berry's poems and essays support efforts of a growing environmental movement

3. **Set C**
   - United States: commuting by bike increased by 62 percent between 2000 and 2013
   - Brazil: rainforest loss in 2014 was one-sixth the rate in 2004
   - Germany: production of solar energy increased from 1 percent of all energy production in 2009 to nearly 7 percent in 2015
   - Zimbabwe: farmers adopt new methods to reduce overgrazing
   - China: efforts to reduce air pollution have begun to show success

## REFLECT ON THE CHAPTER ESSENTIAL QUESTIONS

*Write a one- to three-paragraph answer to each question.*

1. In what ways do geographers study and understand the growth and importance of cities?

2. How do geographers describe and analyze the structure of cities?

3. What are the challenges facing cities around the world, and how are cities responding to these challenges?

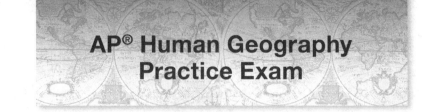
## MULTIPLE-CHOICE ITEMS

***Questions 1 and 2 refer to the map below.***

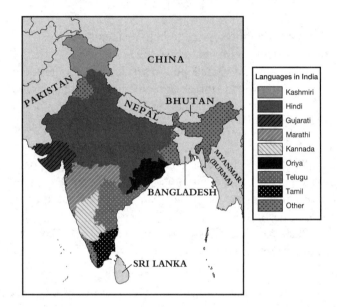

1. Which subfield of human geography is illustrated in the map above?

   (A) population

   (B) culture

   (C) economics

   (D) urban areas

   (E) politics

2. Which argument does this map most clearly support?

   (A) All languages in India are part of the Indo-European family.

   (B) All Indians grow up multilingual.

   (C) A lingua franca would be useful in India.

   (D) Each caste in India has its own language.

   (E) India's languages have shaped its diverse climate.

**Questions 3 and 4 refer to the photo below.**

3. This aerial photograph is useful to geographers because it shows
   (A) a defined boundary
   (B) spatial association
   (C) relative location
   (D) random distribution
   (E) spatial data

4. Which geographic concept is best illustrated by the photo above?
   (A) mental map
   (B) gravity model
   (C) urban hearths
   (D) cultural landscape
   (E) sense of place

5. The purpose of the locational triangle in Weber's model was to show where
   (A) different kinds of neighborhoods would be located in a city
   (B) various types of agriculture would be located
   (C) industries would decide to locate a factory
   (D) cities of various sizes would be located in a state or country
   (E) culture hearths were most likely to be located

**Question 6 refers to the map below.**

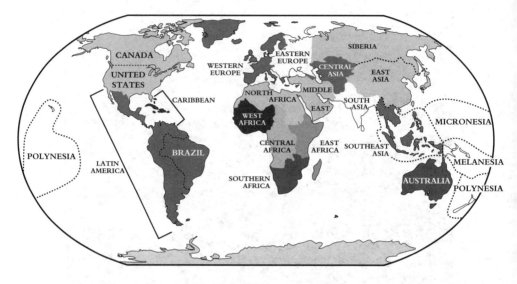

6. Why is regionalization sometimes a challenge for geographers?

(A) The boundaries of many world regions can be defined in several different ways, producing overlapping areas.

(B) Geographers do not all agree that the concept of region is an appropriate way to look at the world.

(C) Large areas of the world are unpopulated or only sparsely populated and therefore do not fit well in any type of region.

(D) Distortion on map projections makes the accurate portrayal of world regions difficult.

(E) The process of how people create regions has not been studied in depth.

7. Which invention or development most directly affected where von Thünen's Model predicted dairy farms would be located?

(A) GMOs

(B) aquaculture

(C) the Green Revolution

(D) agribusiness

(E) refrigeration

8. After the fall of Soviet communism in 1991, which regions had the greatest proliferation of newly independent states?

   (A) North America and South America

   (B) North Africa and Sub-Saharan Africa

   (C) Europe and Central Asia

   (D) South Asia and East Asia

   (E) Oceania

9. In 2014, Russia invaded and annexed a region of Ukraine that had earlier been part of Russia and where many people spoke Russian as their primary language. This suggests that the annexation was an example of

   (A) ethnic separatism

   (B) terrorism

   (C) horizontal integration

   (D) subnationalism

   (E) irredentism

10. The grain elevator, McCormick reaper, and iron/steel plough were advancements made during the

    (A) First Agricultural Revolution

    (B) Columbian Exchange

    (C) Green Revolution

    (D) Second Agricultural Revolution

    (E) Third Agricultural Revolution

11. Which category of modernization or economic development includes Brazil, India, and Mexico?

    (A) core

    (B) semiperiphery

    (C) periphery

    (D) postindustrial

    (E) mass consumption

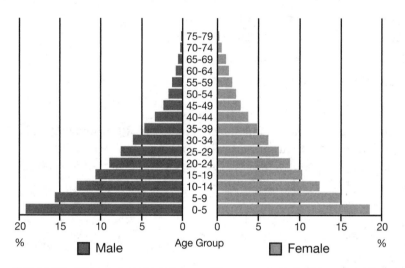

Source: Population Analysis for Policies and Programmes. Paris: International Union for the Scientific Study of Population.

12. Which type of population pyramid is pictured above?

    (A) expansive

    (B) urbanizing

    (C) stationary

    (D) declining

    (E) inverted

13. The above population pyramid is typical of countries

    (A) from the 1800s, but not today

    (B) in Europe and North America

    (C) in less developed regions

    (D) with a stable population size

    (E) with a shrinking population

**14.** Prior to the 19th century, the total fertility rate was much higher than today, but population growth was low primarily because

(A) religion had greater influence on societies in the past

(B) the Industrial Revolution had shortened life expectancy

(C) infant mortality rates were higher in the past

(D) crude birth rates were comparatively low

(E) government programs discouraged large families

**15.** Dependency models of economic development suggest that

(A) the world will always include a combination of well-developed countries and poorly developed countries

(B) industries will always try to locate in spots where they can take advantage of agglomeration economies

(C) centrally planned economies will always develop more successfully than capitalist economies

(D) the gap between wealthy and poor countries should get smaller over time

(E) government efforts to encourage economic development rarely work

**16.** Which is a major positive impact that migrants have on their country of origin?

(A) Migrants often return to open businesses and employ workers.

(B) Migrants regularly send remittances to their family.

(C) Migrants do not use social welfare benefits in their country of origin.

(D) Migrants who commit crimes are sent abroad to save the cost of prison.

(E) Migrants bring over family members, easing the tax burden of their country.

RELOCATION OF PEOPLE AFTER HURRICANE KATRINA

**Number of People Relocated from New Orleans**

More than 50,000

10,000 to 50,000

Fewer than 10,000

New Orleans

17. Which is the most accurate term to describe the people who were forced to move away from New Orleans after Hurricane Katrina struck in 2005?

(A) refugees

(B) asylum seekers

(C) forced migrants

(D) chain migrants

(E) internally displaced persons

18. The movement of people out of New Orleans after Hurricane Katrina demonstrates the concept of

(A) distance decay

(B) outsourcing

(C) random distribution

(D) reverse hierarchical diffusion

(E) time-space compression

19. What effect does emigration usually have on the demographics of the country of origin?

   (A) Average age increases because most people who migrate are older.

   (B) Demographics skew towards males, as women leave to work abroad.

   (C) Population gets less urban as people own larger areas of land.

   (D) Population skews to young and old residents as working-age people migrate.

   (E) Demographics change little, as immigrants replace the emigrants.

20. The nation-state first became a widely desired form of political entity in

   (A) the Mediterranean world of classical Greece and Rome

   (B) the Middle East during the Crusades

   (C) Europe in the 17th century

   (D) Africa and Asia during eras of colonization

   (E) Europe after World War II

21. Which of the following is NOT part of vertical integration in agriculture?

   (A) traditional family farms

   (B) rail lines

   (C) supermarkets

   (D) marketing/advertising

   (E) processing centers

22. Clearly defined gender roles are most closely associated with

   (A) popular culture

   (B) folk culture

   (C) global culture

   (D) multiculturalism

   (E) acculturation

**23.** How are filtering and gentrification related?

(A) They both lead to similar changes in the average income in a neighborhood.

(B) They both occur more in rural areas than in urban areas.

(C) After years of filtering, a neighborhood might be ready for gentrification.

(D) Gentrification is one step in the filtering process.

(E) Filtering and gentrification are the same thing.

**Question 24 refers to the photo below.**

**24.** The above sign, which is in both Welsh and English, represents the effort by the people of Wales

(A) to guard against the development of a creole language

(B) to develop a lingua franca in the country

(C) to resist forces that could make their traditional language disappear

(D) to replace their traditional language with English

(E) to use two languages that are not closely related

**25.** Why is French often considered a lingua franca, while other languages that are spoken by far more people are not?

(A) French is an easier language to learn than are most other languages.

(B) French is widely used in many of France's former colonies around the world.

(C) People in Europe and the Americas never learned non-European languages such as Arabic and Mandarin.

(D) French is used around the world by artists and musicians, so it is widely known in the international community.

(E) French never merged with other languages to create vast numbers of creole speakers.

**26.** Genetically modified organisms have resulted in all of the following characteristics EXCEPT

(A) herbicide-resistant crops

(B) pest-resistant crops

(C) sterile seeds

(D) less expensive seeds

(E) more nutritious food

**27.** Which type of boundary exists between the United States and Canada for most of the distance from Minnesota to Washington?

(A) geometric

(B) militarized

(C) natural

(D) physical

(E) district

**28.** A map showing where Mormons live in the United States would indicate

(A) the difference between an ethnic and a universal religion

(B) the similarity between the distributions of Mormons and Baptists

(C) the pattern of hierarchical diffusion within Utah

(D) the process of filtering in Utah

(E) the effect of distance-decay from a concentration in Utah

**29.** Which factor is strongest in promoting exurbanism?

(A) Subsidies for mass transit have made commuting to central city offices less expensive.

(B) Increases in land prices have made living on the edges of metropolitan areas more costly.

(C) Improvements in communications technology have made working from home easier.

(D) Decreases in family size have made living in central cities more affordable.

(E) Reductions in air pollution have made living in central cities more pleasant.

**30.** Which best explains why the Spanish language diffused widely in Latin America?

(A) Indigenous people had long tried to develop a lingua franca.

(B) Indigenous people found it easier to learn than other languages.

(C) Spanish was the first Indo-European language in the Americas.

(D) Spanish was part of the spread of Spanish control over the region.

(E) Spanish developed out of a creole language.

## Question 31 refers to the chart below.

| THE CULTURE OF GREECE | |
|---|---|
| **Category** | **Data** |
| **Population** | 10,773,253 |
| **Ethnicity** | • Greek 93%<br>• Other 7% |
| **Language** | • Greek 99%<br>• Other 1% |
| **Religion** | • Greek Orthodox 98%<br>• Other 2% |

**Source:** World Factbook.

**31.** Based on the data in the chart, what phrase best describes Greece?

(A) a nation but not a state

(B) a state but not a nation

(C) a nation-state

(D) a multinational state

(E) an autonomous region within an empire

**32.** In the 1990s, the southeast European country of Yugoslavia became

(A) a united country through the centripetal force of opposition to Soviet control

(B) an independent country and member of NATO

(C) two independent countries through the Velvet Divorce

(D) several autonomous, self-governing regions within one country

(E) balkanized into several countries as a result of centrifugal forces

**33.** Which would cause an increase in carrying capacity?

(A) Immigration causes an increase in ethnic enclaves in a region.

(B) Farmers use new techniques to increase the wheat production per acre.

(C) People begin delaying marriage, so the total fertility rate decreases.

(D) The number of people moving to cities to take secondary sector jobs increases.

(E) Improved health care increases the percentage of elderly people in a population.

**34.** Why does the U.S. Constitution require reapportionment every decade?

(A) to adjust the number of Congressional representatives to reflect changes in state populations

(B) to redraw Congressional district lines to reflect changing political views

(C) to change the lines for Congressional districts so that voters can elect new leaders

(D) to allow for Congress to expand to reflect a growing population

(E) to guarantee a balance in representation between the major political parties

**35.** The process of dividing voters who share values among several districts so that they cannot elect a representative who reflects their views is known as

(A) packing

(B) stacking

(C) cracking

(D) hijacking

(E) kidnapping

36. Which describes Uruguay's state morphology type?

    (A) compact

    (B) elongated

    (C) prorupted

    (D) perforated

    (E) fragmented

37. The clearest example of relocation diffusion is the spread of

    (A) an ethnic religion to a new place

    (B) a religion after a king adopts that faith

    (C) the ideas of a religion through books and letters

    (D) a religion by merchants along a trade route

    (E) a religion by missionaries who move somewhere temporarily

38. The Gulf Cooperation Council, an association of six states on the Persian Gulf that attempts to coordinate trade policies, is an example of

    (A) globalization

    (B) a nation-state

    (C) irredentism

    (D) economic supranationalism

    (E) subnationalism

**39.** One advantage a large multinational corporation has over a small business is that it can

(A) react slowly to market changes

(B) benefit from the economies of scale

(C) provide more personalized service

(D) do business in only one currency

(E) resist the pressures of globalization

**40.** Which often happens to an industrial site after the factory on it closes?

(A) In old industrial areas, it often becomes a brownfield site.

(B) In EPZs, it is almost always reclaimed as a recreational site.

(C) In the Great Lakes region, it usually attracts new industry.

(D) In the South and West of the United States, it usually remains vacant.

(E) In most poor countries, it often becomes an office park.

**41.** Which is the most likely explantion for why Southeast Asia has a higher population density than Southern Africa?

(A) Southeast Asia has been settled by humans for a longer time.

(B) Southeast Asia has poorer soil so it became more urbanized.

(C) Southeast Asia lost fewer people to European diseases.

(D) Southeast Asia has better conditions for agriculture.

(E) Southeast Asia has a higher total fertility rate.

**42.** The enclosure movement in Europe did all of the following EXCEPT

(A) provide more land for small farmers

(B) reshape the landscape

(C) promote agrarian capitalism

(D) improve agricultural efficiency

(E) increase average farm size

**43.** According to the gravity model, the greatest interaction would be between two cities that are

(A) 100 miles apart and have populations of 200,000 each

(B) 100 miles apart and have populations of 1,000,000 each

(C) 100 miles apart and have populations of 2,000,000 each

(D) 500 miles apart and have populations of 200,000 each

(E) 500 miles apart and have populations of 2,000,000 each

**44.** The photo illustrates what type of landscape modification?

  (A) cutting and burning of forests

  (B) terracing

  (C) draining of wetlands

  (D) destruction of grasslands

  (E) river diversion

**45.** All of the following were positive consequences of the Green Revolution EXCEPT

  (A) increased crop yields

  (B) increased use of traditional farming methods

  (C) reduced hunger and famine

  (D) reduced crop losses from diseases

  (E) reduced dependency on food imports

**46.** For the past five thousand years, the Nile River Valley has had the greatest concentration of population in Egypt because of the region's

  (A) alpine climate

  (B) famous tourist attractions

  (C) extensive in-migration from neighboring arid areas

  (D) many sacred sites

  (E) high quality agricultural land

**47.** Traditionally, North American cities have been more likely than European cities to have a higher percentage of

(A) historic buildings in the central business district

(B) wealthy people living near the central business district

(C) tall buildings in the central business district

(D) residents living in high-density suburbs

(E) workers who use public transportation to go to work

**48.** Which is most likely to decrease as a neighborhood becomes gentrified?

(A) property tax rates

(B) enrollment in private high schools

(C) number of older buildings

(D) average household income

(E) variety of cultural opportunities

**49.** Which economic change would affect subsistence farmers the LEAST?

(A) increased demand for beef in urban areas

(B) increased land for local agriculture

(C) increased global demand for cash crops

(D) increased land for plantation crops

(E) increased global population growth

**50.** A traditional community is characterized by all of the following values EXCEPT

(A) an emphasis on following existing patterns of behavior

(B) a focus on a strong community

(C) an emphasis on expressing individuality

(D) well-defined gender roles

(E) a pattern of families living close to their relatives

51. What agricultural concept is demonstrated by the photo above of fields of a crop called rapeseed being grown in China?

    (A) a green belt

    (B) monoculture

    (C) a supply chain

    (D) vertical integration

    (E) desertification

52. The type of farming shown in the photo above is

    (A) commerical agriculture

    (B) intensive subsistence

    (C) slash-and-burn

    (D) double cropping

    (E) shifting cultivation

**53.** A U.S. government agency, the Army Corps of Engineers, regularly dredges the Mississippi River so that large vessels can transport grain and livestock at low cost. This is an example of

(A) providing public assistance to farmers

(B) helping the freshwater fishing industry

(C) promoting the fair trade movement

(D) encouraging the market for luxury products

(E) maintaining access for importing agricultural products

**54.** Why is a tree the most common symbol for displaying world languages?

(A) Major branches of a tree are connected to each other, but each smaller branch continues to grow just as languages are connected but evolving.

(B) Like a tree, human language began in one place and has spread over time without changing very much.

(C) Just as people prune a tree to remove dead branches periodically, the tree of language needs to be pruned of dead languages over time.

(D) A tree is rooted in one place in the physical landscape, just as each language is rooted in one place in the cultural landscape.

(E) The branches of a tree continue to evolve away from each other, just as languages each tend to evolve to be more unlike each other.

**55.** Which occupation is the best example of a quaternary sector job?

(A) grain farmer in the Midwest

(B) waiter in an urban restaurant

(C) computer programmer for a large corporation

(D) assembly line worker in a car plant

(E) sales clerk in a computer shop

**Question 56 refers to the table below.**

| ORGANIC FOOD SALES IN THE UNITED STATES | |
|---|---|
| **Year** | **Total Sales (in billions of dollars)** |
| **2004** | 11 |
| **2005** | 13 |
| **2006** | 15 |
| **2007** | 17 |
| **2008** | 19 |
| **2009** | 21 |
| **2010** | 22 |
| **2011** | 24 |
| **2012** | 26 |
| **2013** | 29 |

Source: farmxchange.org.

56. If the trend shown in the graph continues, the most likely consequence is an increase in
    (A) the development of super pests
    (B) the number of jobs in the agricultural sector
    (C) the amount of topsoil lost to erosion
    (D) the total quantity of food
    (E) the use of chemical pesticides

57. Two of the first industries affected by the Industrial Revolution were
    (A) textiles and iron
    (B) rail locomotives and automobiles
    (C) mining and shipping
    (D) newspapers and telephones
    (E) pharmaceuticals and computers

**Question 58 refers to the photo below.**

**58.** The system of aquaculture pictured above often leads to all of the following EXCEPT

(A) the reduction in parasites that live on fish

(B) the spread of diseases to wild fish stock

(C) the use of antibiotics that damage ecosystems

(D) the escape of fish that can breed with native stocks of fish

(E) the increased availability of fish protein

**59.** The concept of a mental map is most similar to the concept of

(A) a landscape interpretation

(B) a map projection

(C) a vernacular region

(D) human ecology

(E) spatial analysis

**Questions 60 and 61 refer to the graphs below.**

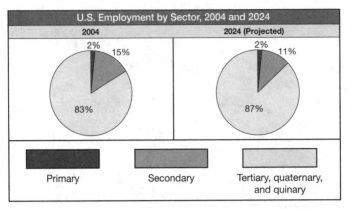

Source: U.S. Bureau of Labor Statistics.

**60.** Which projected change in the percentage of workers in each employment sector concerns economic analysts the most?

(A) the stability in the primary sector even though natural resources are becoming increasingly scarce

(B) the decline in the secondary sector because these jobs pay high wages and help create other jobs

(C) the decline in the secondary sector because this points to the increased use of human labor

(D) the growth in the tertiary, quaternary, and quinary sector because they indicate a decrease in productivity

(E) the growth in the tertiary, quaternary, and quinary sectors because these jobs pay low wages

**61.** In contrast to the projections for the future, between 1916 and 2016 the percentage of workers

(A) in the primary sector significantly decreased

(B) in the secondary sector steadily increased

(C) in the tertiary sector constantly decreased

(D) in the primary and secondary sectors remained constant

(E) in the secondary and tertiary sectors changed in the same direction

**62.** The best example of a job in the quinary sector of the economy is

   (A) chef at a top-rated restaurant

   (B) short-order cook at a diner

   (C) maintenance engineer at a tire plant

   (D) athletic trainer for a professional sports team

   (E) minister of finance in a national government

**63.** How do geographers use cartographic scale?

   (A) to indicate the relationship between size on the map and in reality

   (B) to increase the amount of land that can be shown on a map

   (C) to simplify the amount of detail which will be presented on the map

   (D) to reduce the amount of distortion caused by a particular projection

   (E) to show how maps can be used in different ways

**64.** Why was the North Atlantic Treaty Organization founded in 1949?

   (A) to establish an economic alliance in Europe

   (B) to encourage free trade in North America

   (C) to stabilize petroleum production and prices

   (D) to promote human rights and peace

   (E) to counter the threat of Soviet expansion

**65.** Which is the most common result of the global, interconnected nature of today's economy?

   (A) Disparities in consumption patterns between the developed and developing worlds are becoming very small.

   (B) Financial crises that arise in one region of the world can now be isolated to that region.

   (C) Developments in one part of the world affect workers and investors worldwide.

   (D) Transnational corporations have moved many primary and secondary sector jobs from developing countries to developed countries.

   (E) Brownfields and other signs of a postindustrial landscape have become less common in highly developed countries.

66. Which is NOT a result associated with the proliferation of trading blocs in many regions of the world?

    (A) Consumers have benefitted from an increase in global trade.

    (B) Industrial workers in the developed world have had their wages increase.

    (C) Countries that are trading partners have strengthened their relationships.

    (D) Manufacturing companies have reduced their production costs.

    (E) Banks have been able to move capital among member states more easily.

67. Which statement about median ages in countries is most accurate?

    (A) Africa has a higher median age than does Europe.

    (B) The warmer a country is, the higher its median ages.

    (C) Countries with low median ages usually have more gender inequality.

    (D) Highly developed countries tend to have low median ages.

    (E) Countries with a high median age often have a low level of development.

68. Which accurately explains a difference between the HDI composite index and GDP as measures of development?

    (A) HDI is always reported as a per capita measure but GDP rarely is.

    (B) HDI includes life expectancy and educational variables, while GDP focuses on only economic development.

    (C) HDI does not include indicators of health, but GDP does.

    (D) HDI is used more for analyzing less developed countries, while GDP is used mostly for more developed countries.

    (E) HDI shows Latin America is more developed than Europe, while GDP shows the opposite.

## Question 69 refers to the map below.

GINI COEFFICIENT BY COUNTRY

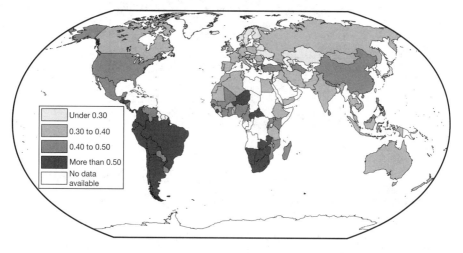

Under 0.30
0.30 to 0.40
0.40 to 0.50
More than 0.50
No data available

**69.** Based on the data in the map above, which region generally has the greatest degree of income inequality?

(A) Western Europe

(B) North Africa

(C) East Asia

(D) Australia

(E) South America

**70.** According to Ravenstein's laws of migration, which statement explains why men are more likely than women to migrate internationally?

(A) Men are more likely than women to migrate for political reasons, so they often have to leave their country.

(B) Men are better educated than women, so they are more likely to be able to learn the new language of a country they move to.

(C) Men are more likely to find work in the destination country, so women are more reluctant to migrate.

(D) Women have greater job opportunities in their local communities than men do, so they are less likely to migrate a long distance.

(E) Women stay in school longer than men do, so they can find better jobs without migrating than males can.

| SENEGAL'S MOST POPULOUS CITIES | |
|---|---|
| **City** | **Population (estimated)** |
| **Dakar** | 2,476,000 |
| **Pikine** | 874,000 |
| **Touba** | 529,000 |
| **Thiès Nones** | 252,000 |
| **Saint-Louis** | 176,000 |

71. The information in the table shows that Dakar can be classified as a
    (A) city-state
    (B) megacity
    (C) world city
    (D) primate city
    (E) nodal region

72. According to the rank-size rule, the population of Touba should be
    (A) one-half the size of Dakar
    (B) one-half the population of Pikine
    (C) one-third the size of Dakar
    (D) twice the size of Thiès Nones
    (E) the size of Thiès Nones and Saint-Louis combined

73. Which best represents the concept of a megacity?
    (A) Melbourne, Australia, is one of the largest cities by land area outside the United States.
    (B) Taipei, Taiwan, is one of the most densely populated cities in the world.
    (C) Jakarta, Indonesia, has a population of 32 million.
    (D) Luanda is the largest city in Angola.
    (E) Islamabad is the capital of Pakistan.

**Question 74 refers to the diagram below.**

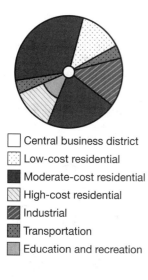

☐ Central business district
▨ Low-cost residential
■ Moderate-cost residential
▨ High-cost residential
▨ Industrial
▨ Transportation
▨ Education and recreation

74. The diagram shows an example of a

(A) concentric zone model

(B) peripheral model

(C) multiple nuclei model

(D) Griffin-Ford model

(E) sector model

75. What effect does low ridership have on public transportation systems in U.S. cities?

(A) Low ridership leads to lower fares to attract more riders.

(B) Low ridership leads to increased routes in order to find more riders.

(C) Low ridership leads to higher fares to cover costs, which lowers ridership further.

(D) Low ridership has no effect, as governments recognize the importance of the systems.

(E) Low ridership leads poorer residents to buy more cars, leading to higher rates of pollution and congestion.

**1.** The Sami people live in the area shown in this map, which is known as Sápmi. Their forebears have lived in and near this region for thousands of years. There are three specific groups of Sami who speak dialects of the same language. In spite of linguistic differences, the three groups consider themselves unified, both culturally and historically. Although they have created their own national anthem and flag for their territory, there is no formal movement for independence.

A. Define each of the following terms and explain how well each of the terms applies to the people who live in Sápmi:
- state
- nation
- nation-state

B. Identify another group of people whose territory stretches across three countries and explain a challenge this group faces.

**2.** Agriculture has changed dramatically over time, starting with the First Agricultural Revolution.

  A. Discuss the type of agriculture typical of the First Agricultural Revolution.

  B. Identify two ancient agricultural hearths and a crop that orginated in each one.

  C. Using the concept of globalization, explain two impacts of the Columbian Exchange on agriculture.

**3.** In addition to basic information about age and sex composition, population pyramids can also provide evidence regarding the level of economic development of a country.

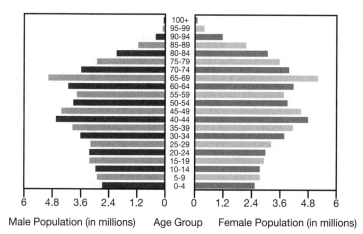

Male Population (in millions)    Age Group    Female Population (in millions)

  A. Using the population pyramid and your knowledge of the demographic transition model, identify the stage of the country shown and name one country that would have a similar pyramid.

  B. Identify the level of development of the country represented and explain two economic characteristics of the country.

  C. Identify and explain a major challenge that the country will face in the future.

# Index

*Note: Page numbers followed by an "f" refer to figures.*

Crops
  diffusion of, 221–222
  fair trade, 208, 220, 239
  genetically modified, 200, 234
  local, 239
  luxury, 219
  organic, 234–235, 241
Crude birth rate (CBR), 55, 65
Crude death rate (CDR), 65
Cultivation, shifting, 211–212
  *See also* Agriculture; Farming
Cultural border, 95
Cultural boundary, 157
Cultural complex, 91, 92*f*
Cultural diffusion, 90, 93, 98–99,
  105
Cultural ecology, 9
Cultural landscape
  built environment and, 10–11
  changes in, 94, 94*f*
  definition of, 93
  examples of, 94
  language and, 111–112
  religion and, 126–128
  of rural settlements, 227–228
Cultural practices, 184
Cultural regions, 90, 93
Cultural trait, 91
Culture hearth, 92, 93, 121
Culture of poverty, 338
Culture realm, 95, 95*f*
Culture(s)
  definition of, 91
  diffusion of, 90, 93, 98–99, 105
  geography of gender and, 97–98
  globalization and changes in,
    95–96
  interaction of, 90, 99–100
  language and, 119
  territoriality and, 155
  ways children learn, 92

Cut flower market, von Thünen's
  Model of Land Use and, 232

# D

Dairy farming, 213
Darwin, Charles, 153
Data
  geospatial, 26–27
  grouping and interpretation of,
    16
  quantitative and qualitative, 27
  scale of the, 18
  spatial, 10
  U.S. census, 161, 329–330
Decolonization, 143
Defined boundary, 157
Definitional boundary dispute, 157
Deforestation, 196–197
Delimited boundary, 157
Demarcated boundary, 157
Democratization, 182
Demographic Balancing Equation,
  65
Demographic Transition Model
  migration patterns and, 75–76,
    82
  policy implications of stages
    in, 65
  population pyramids and, 63–64
  stages in, 61, 62–64, 62*f*
Density, 8
  *See also* Population density
Dependency model, 286
Dependency ratio (DR), 48–49
Dependent population, 48
Desertification, 196
Deurbanization, 350
Developing world
  civil wars in, 143–144
  megacities in, 311, 351

Development
    measures of, 247
    measures of social, 280–281,
        283
    terms of, 281
    *See also* Economic development
Devolution
    definition of, 178
    forces leading to, 178–181
    fragmentation of states and,
        181–182
Dialect, 108–109
Diffusion, cultural, 90, 93, 98–99,
    105
Disamenity zone, 323
Dispersed settlement, 227
Displaced person, 79–80
Distance, 1, 7
    connection and, 8
    friction of, 8
    perception of, 11–12
    time and, 7
Distance-decay, 8, 8*f,* 77
Domestication, plant and animal,
    193
Dot distribution map, 20, 20*f*
Double cropping, 214
Dust Bowl, 197

# E

Earnings. *See* Wages
Echo, in population pyramid, 46
Economic development
    as centripetal force, 184
    gender equity and, 291–293
    government initiatives for, 273
    measures of
        comparison of wealth or
            income, 282
        output, 280

sectoral distribution of
    workforce, 282
models of spatial patterns of
    Stages of Economic Growth
        Model, 284–286
    World Systems Theory,
        286–289, 288*f*
sustainable, 291
Economic issues
    devolution and, 179–180
    territoriality and, 156
Economic sectors, 250–252
Economy
    informal, 345
    shadow, 345, 346*f*
Economy of scale, 176
Ecosystems, 233–234
Ecumene, 301
Edge city, 322
Elections, free, in Eastern Europe,
    145
Electoral districts, 42
Electorate, 160
Emigrant, definition of, 65
Eminent domain law, 339
Enclave, ethnic (urban colony), 80,
    94–95, 342–343
Enclosure Acts, 198
Energy
    global consumption of, 267*f*
    importance of, in industrial
        location, 253
Energy-oriented industry, 253
English, as lingua franca, 110
Environment
    agriculture's impact on, 233,
        236–239
    built, 10–11
    cities and, 346–348
    migration and, 75

population distribution and
density and, 42
supranationalism and, 178
sustainable development and,
291
Environmental determinism, 9
Epidemiological Transition Model,
66–67
EPZ. *See* Export Processing Zone
(EPZ)
Equator, 5
Eratosthenes, 4
*Essay on the Principles of
Population, An* (Malthus), 67
ETA. *See* Euskadi Ta Askatasuna
Ethiopia, composition of labor
force, by economic sector, 251*f*
Ethnic cleansing, in Yugoslavia,
146
Ethnic enclave (urban colony), 80,
94–95, 342–343
Ethnic island, 129
Ethnic religion, 124
Ethnic separatism, devolution and,
179
Ethnicity
impact of, on spaces, 129
population distribution and,
43–44, 43*f*
religion, nationality and,
120–121
U.S. regional patterns of, 121
European cities, 324
European Union (EU)
economic supranationalism and,
176
map of, 177*f*
members, mission, headquarters
of, 175
Euskadi Ta Askatasuna (ETA), 179

Exclusive Economic Zone (EEZ),
160
Expansion diffusion, 98–99
Expansive population pyramid, 63,
63*f*
Export Processing Zone (EPZ),
269–270
Extensive farming, 214–216
Exurb, 350
Exurbanization, 303

# F

Factory, scale analysis of opening/
closing of, 264
Fair trade crops, 208, 220, 239
Fair trade movement, 220, 239
Family planning, total fertility rate
and, 56–57
Farming
dairy, 213
grain, 213
on homeowner *vs.* agribusiness
scale, 217
mixed crop/livestock, 212–213
subsistence, 192, 197
terrace, 195
*See also* Agribusiness;
Agriculture
Fast food, diffusion of, 99
Favela, 323
Federal system of governance,
163–165, 164*f*
Feed lot, 216, 238–239
Fertility, reasons for changes in,
55–59
Fertilizers, 236
Field observation, 10
Fieldwork, 27
Filtering, 327, 338

Islam
    beliefs of, 123
    cultural landscape of, 128
    diffusion of, 124, 125
    hearth of, 121
    territoriality and, 155, 156*f*
    *See also* Muslim immigrants
Islamic cities, 325–326
Isogloss, 108
Isoline (isometric) map, 20, 20*f*
Isotropic plain, 229
Italy
    19th-century independent states
        of, 141*f*
    boundaries and unification of,
        162
Ivory Coast, population doubling
    time of, 66

# J

Japan
    as nation-state, 138
    population pyramid of, 64, 64*f*
    restriction of immigration in, 82
Jenner, Edward, 61
Judaism, 123, 124, 128
Just-in-time delivery, 257

# K

Kashmir
    boundary dispute over, 152
    devolution and, 178–179
Korea, 293–294
Korean Peninsula, boundary of, 159
Kurdistan region, 140, 140*f*

# L

Labor, new international division
    of, 269
Labor force. *See* Workforce

Labor-oriented industry, 257
Lakota, culture of, 91
Landscape
    human alteration of, for
        agriculture, 195–197
    and origin and meaning of term,
        10
    postindustrial, 270–273
    urban, 300, 350–351
    *See also* Cultural landscape
Landscape analysis, 10–11
Land use
    extensive and intensive,
        214–216
    for organic food, 241
    regulations on urban/suburban,
        326–328
    von Thünen's model of, 23,
        229–233, 231*f*
Language
    cultural landscape and, 111–112
    culture and, 119
    diffusion of, 107, 109–110
    official, 112
Language family, 107
Language tree, 107, 107*f*
Large region, 25
Latex, natural, 222
Latin, 108
Latin American cities/suburbs, 323,
    323*f,* 328
Latin words, 108
Latitude, 5
Law of the Sea, United Nations
    Convention of the, 160
League of Nations, 175
Leapfrogging, 348
Least cost theory, 252, 253,
    254–255
*Lebensraum,* 154

# N

Nagorno-Karabakh, 180–181
Nation
    definition of, 138
    multistate, 140
    *vs.* state and nation-state, 139*f*
    stateless, 139–140
Nationalism, definition of, 141, 184
Nationality, religion, ethnicity and, 120–121
Nation-state(s)
    examples of, 138
    *vs.* nation and state, 139*f*
    rise of concept of, 140–141
Nativism, 100
NATO. *See* North Atlantic Treaty Organization (NATO)
Natural boundary, 157
Natural increase rate (NIR), 65
Natural resources, devolution and, 179–180
Navajo, loss of language of, 106
Neocolonialism, 143, 220
    *See also* Colonialism
Neolithic Agricultural Revolution
    *See* First Agricultural Revolution
Neolocalism, 122
Neo-Malthusian, 67
Netherlands, agricultural population density of, 41
Network(s)
    analysis of rural, 245
    definition of, 174
Newly industrialized country (NIC), 266
New urbanism, 349
New York City, population change in suburbs and, 303*f*

NIC. *See* Newly industrialized country (NIC)
Niger
    dependency ratio of, *vs.* United States, 48–49
    population pyramid of, 45, 45*f*, 63, 63*f*
Nodal (functional) region, 24, 93
Nomadism, pastoral, 211, 238
Nongovernmental organizations (NGOs), 289, 292, 293
Non-isotropic plains, 232
Nonspatial model, 22
North American Free Trade Agreement (NAFTA), 175, 177, 258, 266
North Atlantic Treaty Organization (NATO)
    formation and growth of, 146*f*
    members, mission, headquarters of, 175
    supranationalism and, 177–178
Northern Ireland, 163
Nutrition, life expectancy and, 60

# O

Observation. *See* Field observation
*Odyssey* (Homer), 3
Office building, 271
Official language, 112
Offshoring, 259
Oil, impact of lower prices of, 268
Omran, Abdel, 66
Operational boundary dispute, 158
Organic foods, 234–235, 241
Organic Theory, 153–154
Organization of the Petroleum Exporting Countries (OPEC), 177
Outsourcing, 259

Overgrazing, 238
Overpopulation
 as concern of Neo-Malthusians,
  67
 population distribution and
  density and, 42

# P

Pakistan, Kashmir boundary dispute
 and, 152
Pastoral nomadism, 211, 238
Pedestrian city, 307
Penicillin, 61
Per capita, 280
Percent urban, 302
Perceptual (vernacular) region, 24,
 93
Periférico, 323
Periodic market, 325
Peripheral model, 322
Pesticide, 236
Peters projection, 21, 22*f*
Photography, aerial, 10
Physical geography
 agriculture and, 195
 definition of, 3
 *See also* Landscape
Physiological population density, 40
Pidgin language, 110
Pilgrimage, 125
Place, 6–7
Place names, political power and
 changes in, 173
Plain
 isotropic, 229
 non-isotropic, 232
Plantation, 212
Plantation agriculture, 212
Plant domestication, 193
Political identity, 184

Political map
 evolution of contemporary,
  140–142
 geopolitical forces influencing
  today's, 143–146
 old *vs.* modern, 136
Political power
 changes in place names and,
  173
 distribution of, at different
  scales, 167
 overview of, 136
 theories of, 153–155
Pollution, urban, 347–348
Polytheistic religion, 123
Popular culture, 96–97
Population, dependent, 48
Population composition, 43–44
Population density
 application of, at many scales,
  53
 arithmetic, 39, 39*f,* 40
 of Australia, 18*f*
 definition of, 8, 36
 food production and, 204
 physiological, 40
 processes and factors in, 41–43
 time and, 41
 *See also* Residential density
  gradient
Population distribution
 definition of, 36
 human factors influencing, 38
 overview of, 35
 patterns of, 9
 physical factors influencing, 37
 processes and factors in, 41–43
 scale of analysis and, 38–39
 of world, 37*f*

Population growth
    arithmetic, 65
    doubling time of, 65–66
    exponential, 65
    impact of China's gender
        imbalance on, 58f
    during Industrial Revolution,
        249
    of world since 1760, 54, 54f
Population growth and decline
    changes in fertility and, 55–59
    Demographic Balancing
        Equation and, 65
    Demographic Transition Model
        and, 61–64
    Epidemiological Transition
        Model and, 66–67
    life expectancy and, 59–61
    natural increase rate (NIR) and,
        65
    overview of, 35
    prediction of, 72
    See also Total fertility rate(s)
        (TFRs)
Population pyramid
    anomalies in, 47
    Demographic Transition Model
        and, 63–64
    dependency ratio (DR) and, 48
    expansive, 63, 63f
    patterns in, 45
    stationary, 64, 64f
    structure of, 44
Porcelain, diffusion of, 99
Possibilism, 9
Post-Fordism, 250
Postindustrial landscape, 270–273
Potential workforce, 48
Poverty, urban, 337–338
Power. See Political power

PPP. See Purchasing power parity
    (PPP)
Primate city, 309
Prime meridian, 5
Processes, 17
Projection, 21, 22f
Pro-natalist policy, 59
Proximity, 7
Ptolemy, 4
Ptolemy's map of world, 4f
Public housing, 340
Public Land Survey System, 228
Public sanitation, life expectancy
    and, 60–61
Public transportation, 344
Pull factor, 73
    See also Migration, push and
        pull factors influencing
Purchasing power parity (PPP), 282
Push factor, 73
    See also Migration, push and
        pull factors influencing

## Q

Qualitative data, 27
Quantitative data, 27
Quebec, 139, 181, 182–183

## R

Racial segregation, 342
Railroad network, analysis of, 245
Ranching
    as extensive farming, 215–216
    definition of, 211, 214
    overgrazing and, 238
    See also Mixed crop/livestock
        farming
Random distribution, 9
Range, in central place theory, 311

Rust Belt, 270
Rwanda, 143

# S

Salt Lake City, relative location of, 6*f*
Samsung headquarters, 271
San Francisco Mission District, land prices in, 343*f*
Satellite city, 303
Satellite state, 144
Saudi Arabia, religion, territoriality and, 155
Sauer, Carl, 5, 193
Saying (adage), 108
Scale
    cartographic, 17–18
    definition of, 17
    geographic, 18
Scale analysis
    of distribution of political power, 167
    of distribution of religious elements, 134
    of distribution of Spanish speakers, 113–114
    of factory openings and closings, 264
    of fair trade, 208
    of industrial growth, 264
    population distribution and, 38–39
Scale of the data, 18
Scattered site, 340
Second Agricultural Revolution, 192, 197–199
Section (land), 228
Sector (Hoyt's) model, 321, 322*f*
Sectors. *See* Economic sectors

Seed hybridization, 200
Segregation, racial, 342
Sense of place, 7
Separatism, ethnic, devolution and, 179
Sequent occupance, 129
Services, in inner city, 341
Service (tertiary) sector, 251–252
Settlement(s)
    abandoned, 6
    definition of, 301
    early, 301–302
    informal, 325
    squatter, 325
    *See also* Rural settlements
Seven Years' War, 142
Sewer systems, life expectancy and, 60–61
Sex. *See* Gender; Gender roles
Shadow economy, 345, 346*f*
Shantytowns, 323
Sharia, 121
Shatterbelt, 162
Shelter, folk culture and, 92–93
Shia Muslims, territoriality and, 155, 156*f*
Shifting cultivation, 211–212
Shinto, 128
Sinhalese, 163
Site, 6
Situation, 6
Slang, 110
Slash-and-burn agriculture, 197
Slavery
    creole languages and, 111
    modern, 79
Slave trade, Atlantic, 79
Smaller region, 26
Smallpox, 61
Smart growth, 348–349

World Island, 154, 155*f*
World regions, 24–26, 25*f,* 26*f*
World Systems Theory, 286–289, 288*f*
Write As a Geographer
 comprehend the prompt, 34
 giving full explanations, 299
 organizing ideas, 357
 plan the answer, 89
 use examples, 190
 use relevant information, 246
 write in complete thoughts, 135

# X

Xenophobia, 82

# Y

Yugoslavia, 146

# Z

Zelinsky, Wilbur, 75–76, 82, 93
Zone
 disamenity, 323
 informal economy, 325
 of transition, 321
 residential, 327
 urban, 319–320
Zoning ordinance, 326

# Credits

Cover: Thinkstock
Page xiii: Thinkstock
Page xix: Patrick Forde/Cartoonstock
Page 4: Franceso di Antonio del
  Chierco
Page 14: Thinkstock
Page 68: Thinkstock
Page 83: PATTIE
Page 94: Thinkstock
Page 111: Thinkstock
Page 127: Thinkstock
Page 128: Thinkstock
Page 132: Thinkstock
Page 134: (top left) Jorge Royan,
  (bottom left) Thinkstock, (right)
  Thinkstock
Page 159: Friar's Balsam
Page 169: Central Intelligence
  Agency
Page 180: Andrijko Z
Page 205: Thinkstock
Page 206: Thinkstock
Page 212: Thinkstock
Page 216: Thinkstock
Page 223: USDA
Page 228: Shutterstock
Page 229: (market) iStock, (1, 2, 3,
  and 4) Thinkstock
Page 231: Contentra
Page 237: USGS
Page 244: iStock
Page 261: Thinkstock
Page 278: LHOON
Page 320: Thinkstock
Page 323: Thinkstock
Page 325: Dreamstime

Page 332: Thinkstock
Page 334: Mariordo (Mario Roberto
  Duràn Ortiz)
Page 349: Thinkstock
Page 359: Thinkstock
Page 366: Thinkstock
Page 372: Thinkstock
Page 374: Thinkstock
Page 377: Thinkstock